AF880349

Economic Integration Across the
Taiwan Strait

Economic Integration Across the Taiwan Strait

Global Perspectives

Edited by

Peter C.Y. Chow

City University of New York, USA

Edward Elgar

Cheltenham, UK • Northampton, MA, USA

© Peter C.Y. Chow 2013

All rights reserved. No part of this publication may be reproduced, stored in a retrieval system or transmitted in any form or by any means, electronic, mechanical or photocopying, recording, or otherwise without the prior permission of the publisher.

Published by
Edward Elgar Publishing Limited
The Lypiatts
15 Lansdown Road
Cheltenham
Glos GL50 2JA
UK

Edward Elgar Publishing, Inc.
William Pratt House
9 Dewey Court
Northampton
Massachusetts 01060
USA

A catalogue record for this book
is available from the British Library

Library of Congress Control Number: 2012946679

MIX
Paper from
responsible sources
FSC
www.fsc.org
FSC® C018575

ISBN 978 0 85793 972 2

Typeset by Servis Filmsetting Ltd, Stockport, Cheshire
Printed and bound by MPG Books Group, UK

Contents

Contributors

Richard C.K. Burdekin, Claremont McKenna College, USA

Chih-Ping Chen, National Kaohsiung First University of Science and Technology, Taiwan

Tain-Jy Chen, National Taiwan University, Taiwan

Wan-Jiun Paul Chiou, Central Michigan University, USA

Peter C.Y. Chow, The City College and the Graduate Center, City University of New York, USA

Ming-chin Monique Chu, SOAS, University of London, UK

Kai-Wen Hsieh, National Kaohsiung Marine University, Taiwan

Chun-Pin Hsu, York College of the City University of New York, USA

Chin-Wen Huang, Western Connecticut State University, USA

Ying-Hua Ku, Chung Hwa Institution for Economic Research, Taiwan

Hong-Jen Abraham Lin, Brooklyn College of the City University of New York, USA

Winston T. Lin, State University of New York at Buffalo, USA

Yijing Shen, Claremont McKenna College, USA

Yun-Wing Sung, Chinese University of Hong Kong, Hong Kong

Hsin-hui I.H. Whited, Colorado State University–Pueblo, USA

Monica Yang, Adelphi University, USA

Preface

The economies in East Asia are far from homogeneous in terms of levels of economic development, degrees of industrialization, and extent of cultural assimilation. Generally speaking, East Asian economies are much more divergent than were the original ten members of European Union (EU-10) before the enlargement of the economic union into its current form. Hence, the proliferation of regional trading arrangements in East Asia since the 1990s grouped many diverse economies together. But never before has any pair of rival regimes with overlapping claims of sovereignty experienced economic integration as closely as Taiwan and China. Obviously, the developments are interesting not just for the two economies of the Taiwan Strait but also for other countries inside and outside the region.

De facto economic integration through the trade-investment nexus in East Asia has been moving much faster since the 1980s than de jure integration through institutional establishment. If Hong Kong is grouped with China, Taiwan's trade dependency on China's markets accounts for nearly 40 percent of its total exports, and outward foreign direct investment has been increasing steadily, with more than 60 percent of capital outflows destined for China. Industrial clusters in the Yangtze River Delta, the Pearl River Delta, and other parts of China were created through foreign invested enterprises, many of them from Taiwan, and have accounted for a substantial percentage of China's total exports to the world. In regional and global perspectives, those industrial clusters have become part of the global production network, especially in the information and computer technology sectors. The significance of economic integration between Taiwan and China, its resultant industrial clusters in coastal China, and its role in the global supply chain go far beyond the conventional cost–benefit analysis of foreign direct investment in host and home countries. The process bears important policy implications for the economic and security interests of many involved nations.

The signing of the Economic Cooperation Framework Agreement (ECFA) between Taiwan and China in June 2010 may evolve into de jure economic integration in the near future. ECFA is a framework and precedes any eventual free trade agreement (FTA). If China and Taiwan should engage in a formal FTA in the context of the Greater

China Economic Zone, the economic and political implications would be far more significant than any bilateral trade pacts signed by any East Asia countries. Given the two different socio-political systems across the Taiwan Strait, the extent to which economic integration would affect the economic development in Taiwan is of great concern, not just for the people of Taiwan but also for all who cherish the universal values of freedom and democracy. Will the signing of the ECFA be the end of the beginning of multiple FTAs or the beginning of the end for any trade pacts for Taiwan? To what extent will Taiwan be immune from being marginalized in East Asian economic integration? Various scenarios are currently being debated by scholars from all political spectrums, but few of them can bring in hard evidence or convincing theses on these controversial issues.

This book is a collection of wisdom acquired from scholars in various fields through their long and dedicated research. The authors use their expertise to tackle economic integration in various sectors and to assess the eventual impacts on the overall economy. Their in-depth analyses on each subject offer important lessons for those who are interested in the outcome of economic integration. Though some ongoing developments cannot yet be identified by existing empirical data, the trend of their future prospects is thoroughly analysed. The profound knowledge and research experiences will enable readers to understand the plausible consequences of further economic integration in general and future developments across the Taiwan Strait in particular.

I am deeply indebted to all these contributors for their enthusiastic support of this book project and for their dedication to their scholastic research. Each one of them has contributed greatly to the subject they are most familiar with, and in this book, each one of them presents the best research output to further the current state of knowledge. Next, I would like to thank Edward Elgar Publishing, and especially its Executive Director Alan Sturmer, for their strong interest in this book even at the very early stages of proposal. Finally, I would like to thank all members of my family for their support of my endeavors and their tolerance of my negligence of family obligations while working on this book.

Peter C.Y. Chow
June 16, 2012

Abbreviations

APEC	Asian Pacific Economic Community
ARATS	Association for Relations Across the Taiwan Strait
ASEAN	Association of Southeast Asian Nations
ASMC	Advanced Semiconductor Manufacturing Corporation
BC	Box–Cox
BT	Box–Tidwell
BTO	build to order
CBMAs	cross-border mergers and acquisitions
CD	Cobb–Douglas
CEA	Chinese Economic Area
CEPA	Closer Economic Partnership Arrangement
CGE	computable general equilibrium
CMOS	complementary metal oxide semiconductor
COO	chief operating officer
CPU	central processing unit
CSEC	Cross-Straits Economic Cooperation committee
CSIA	China Semiconductor Industry Association
CT	communications technology
CTO	chief technology officer
DEA	Data Envelopment Analysis
DI	direct investment
DPP	Democratic Progressive Party
DSM	Dispute Settlement Mechanism
ECCPC	Economic and Cultural Co-operation and Promotion Council
ECFA	Economic Cooperation Framework Agreement
EDA	Electronic Design Automation
EFTA	European Free Trade Association
EG	economic growth
EHP	Early Harvest Program
ETDZ	economic and technological development zone
FDI	foreign direct investment
FIE	foreign-invested enterprise
FPGA	field programmable gate array

FTA	free trade agreement
GATT	General Agreement on Tariffs and Trade
GPN	global production network
HB	home bias
HS	Harmonized System
IBM	International Business Machines Corporation
IC	integrated circuit
ICT	information and communication technologies
IDM	integrated device manufacturer
IT	information technology
IP	intellectual property
IPO	Initial Public Offering
IPR	Intellectual Property Rights
IVS	Individual Visit Scheme
LDCs	less developed countries
M&As	mergers and acquisitions
MFN	Most Favored Nation
MNC	multinational corporation
MNE	multinational enterprise
MOEA	Ministry of Economic Affairs
MOU	Memorandum of Understanding
MPW	Multi-Project Wafer
MSCI	Morgan Stanley Capital International
MSR	maximum Sharpe ratio
MVP	minimum-variance portfolio
NICs	newly industrialized countries
NOR	Not-OR
ODM	original design manufacturer
OEM	original equipment manufacturer
OFDI	outward foreign direct investment
OLS	ordinary least squares
PC	personal computer
PCB	printed circuit board
P/E	price/earnings
PG	productivity growth
PLA	People's Liberation Army
PRC	People's Republic of China
PRD	Pearl River Delta
PTA	preferential trade agreement
QPL	Qualified Product List
RTA	Regional Trading Agreement
SAR	Special Administrative Region

SEF	Straits Exchange Foundation
SEMATECH	International Semiconductor Manufacturing Technology
SEMI	Semiconductor Equipment and Materials International
SEZ	special economic zone
SIA	Semiconductor Industry Association
SIM	Shanghai Institute of Metallurgy
SITC	Standard International Trade Classification
SOC	system-on-a-chip
SS	short sales
SST	Silicon Storage Technology, Inc.
TDR	Taiwan Depository Receipts
TEEMA	Taiwan Electrical and Electronic Manufacturers' Association
TFP	total factor productivity
TFT-LED	thin film transistor liquid crystal display
TPP	Trans-Pacific Partnership Agreement
TVE	township and village enterprise
VAT	value added tax
VEU	validated end-user
VMI	vendor managed inventory
WSMC	Worldwide Semiconductor Manufacturing Corporation
WTO	World Trade Organization

Introduction

Peter C.Y. Chow

Since the mid-1980s, East Asia's dynamism has been characterized by a significant trade-investment nexus with active de facto economic integration within the region (Ozeki, 2008) and active participation in the global production network (Chow, 2012a). After the 1997–98 Asian financial crisis, the de facto economic integration led to the proliferation of regional trading arrangements and the emergence of trade blocs (Kawai and Wignaraja, 2009). In particular, the de facto economic integration between the two politically competitive regimes of China and Taiwan has stimulated much literature on trade and the political economy. China, rising as a powerhouse in the global economy, has inevitably affected its neighbors. But because Beijing's claims of sovereignty overlap those of Taipei, China's rise has had strong repercussions in the economic development and democratization of Taiwan.

On the one hand, Taiwan, having experienced an economic miracle between 1960 and 2000, as measured by an annual economic growth rate averaging about 7 percent, faces a strong challenge of industrial restructuring in its pursuit of globalization. China, as the second largest economy in terms of total GDP, is a market that none of its neighboring countries, including Taiwan, can ignore. On the other hand, the trade-investment nexus and the de facto economic integration across the Taiwan Strait, though it has reduced the political tensions between the two rival regimes, has made Taiwan's trade dependency vulnerable to China. China's leaders for generations have been claiming Taiwan as a renegade province, despite the fact that Taiwan has been a de facto independent country since before the establishment of the People's Republic in 1949.

Deepening economic integration between China and Taiwan, though it has substantially reduced the mutual distrust between the Communists in China and the Nationalists in Taiwan, has not led to mutual recognition of each other's existence in the international community.[1] Several scenarios can be speculated about the developments from de facto to de jure economic integration between the two economies across the Taiwan Strait, because any form of 'de jure' economic integration must be 'a political establishment,' as William Wallace (1982) argued decades ago. Essentially, mutual recognition among the signatories is the fundamental principle that underlies any trade pact. Despite the fact that both China and Taiwan are members of the WTO, many of the trade pacts signed by Beijing and Taipei after the Nationalist Party (Kuomintang) came back to power under the leadership of President Ma Ying-jeou in May 2008, notably the Economic Cooperation Framework Agreement (ECFA), are still not registered under the WTO trade framework.[2] Whether the signing of the ECFA in June 2010 will lead to what the Ma administration has claimed will be determined by future developments.

This book is a collection of the wisdom of a group of scholars from the US, Europe, Taiwan, and Hong Kong who are experts on various subjects in economic integration across the Taiwan Strait and, to a greater extent, the emerging 'Greater Chinese Economic Zone.' Aside from political considerations for autonomous political sovereignty, this book addresses the extent to which an integrated economy between China and Taiwan will affect various sectors of the economy such as the high-tech industry, banking, the financial markets, and industrial clusters. It then analyses those developments in the greater context of regional economic integration in East Asia.

In Chapter 1, Richard C.K. Burdekin, Yijing Shen, and Hsin-hui I.H. Whited address the historical perspective on the economic interactions and present some empirical evidence of the ongoing economic integration. Cross-Strait economic ties have developed rapidly since Taiwan's government announced a policy of non-interference with indirect exports to the mainland in 1985. China quickly adopted new measures to attract Taiwanese investment, including the setting-up of two special economic zones in Fujian province in May 1989 that offered special tax privileges for Taiwan-invested enterprises. Despite the disallowance of direct trade links, China became Taiwan's second largest export market by 1993 and has been its top export market since 2002. Taiwan's overall positive trade balance in recent years has, in fact, been very much dependent upon its surpluses with China. Officially-reported figures continue to understate the importance of the Cross-Strait economies ties, however, by failing to fully account for re-exporting from Taiwan to China via Hong Kong and also by ignoring substantial Taiwanese investment via holding companies in tax-exempt areas like the British Virgin Islands and the Cayman Islands. In this chapter, the authors detail the evolving economic ties between China and Taiwan and provide an up-to-date picture of the trade and investment flows between the two economies.

Moreover, macroeconomic interdependence between China and Taiwan is assessed in terms of an array of output, price, money, stock market, and interest-rate measures for each economy. This enables the authors to determine the extent to which the trade and investment nexus has been reflected in measurable economic symbiosis. The transmission of money supply movements across the Taiwan Straits is perhaps the most striking feature of the econometric analysis and is evident in both the Ganger-causality testing and the co-integration analysis. Such interdependence suggests possible gains from monetary policy coordination. Whereas recent initiatives have led to a valuable easing of the impediments to trade and investment flows between China and Taiwan, this has not so far extended to any formal cooperation in the monetary policy arena. The chapter's empirical findings suggest that, even if actual monetary union between China and Taiwan remains out of the question for the foreseeable future, simply taking the effects of money supply movements on the other side of the Taiwan Straits into account when setting policy could be beneficial for the central banks of both China and Taiwan.

Will the ECFA become a trade pact under the WTO framework or one with unique 'Cross-Strait characteristics?' In Chapter 2, Yun-Wing Sung compares the two trade pacts signed between China–Hong Kong and China–Taiwan. The Closer Economic Partnership Arrangement (CEPA) between China and Hong Kong, and the ECFA between China and Taiwan are landmarks in the history of free trade agreements (FTAs). The economic integration of the Chinese Economic Area (CEA), which has developed rapidly since the opening of China in 1979 and was arguably market-driven initially without much governmental coordination, soon called for more formal coordination that cumulated in the CEPA and the ECFA.

This chapter covers the events leading to the CEPA and the ECFA, and their provisions in terms of market access for goods and for services. Sung examines the economic impact of the two agreements on trade in goods and services and on bilateral investments in the CEA. The CEPA and the ECFA are also compared in terms of legal issues such as intellectual property protection, dispute settlement mechanisms, and compliance with the WTO framework. In particular, the chapter examines the impacts of the ECFA and the opening of Cross-Strait direct links on Hong Kong's position as an intermediary in Cross-Strait trade, investment, shipping and passenger traffic.

Besides economic factors, political considerations are always important in FTAs. The chapter covers the impacts of the two agreements on the relations of Hong Kong and Taiwan with China as well as with other economies outside the CEA, focusing on the efforts of Hong Kong and Taiwan to cultivate FTAs with other economies. Lastly, it discusses the prospects of a pan-CEA FTA and the future of the two agreements in the context of the rivalry between the US-backed Trans-Pacific Partnership (TPP) and the China-centered network of East Asian FTAs.

Fragmentation of the manufacturing production process becomes prevalent in the drive for globalization. Cross-border production at different stages of the manufacturing process is especially significant in the information and communication technologies (ICT) industry. Will sector integration with China benefit Taiwanese firms? In Chapter 3, Winston T. Lin analyses with rigorous econometric methodology whether Taiwan's investment in the ICT sector in China has generated benefits. Based on the theory of production, Lin's research proposes to answer the critical question of whether the integration of the ICT investments of Taiwan and China has positive effects on productivity and economic growth in Taiwan. Lin applies a two-stage sequential procedure consisting of: (i) the two-equation time-varying stochastic production frontier approach derived from the theory of production and the productive efficiency derived from the frontier approach as the performance metric (Stage 1); and (ii) the concept of total factor productivity or Malmquist productivity index (Stage 2). Having followed the two-stage process, the study fits a panel data-set covering the period from 1990 to 2010 into four with the proposed models. Empirical evidence from Lin suggests that the answer to the research question is negative. Lin's contributions in this chapter will offer important implications for firms from Taiwan as well as policymakers in mapping out the globalization strategy.

Economic interactions across the Taiwan Strait are not limited to the trade-investment nexus but also extend to the service sector. In Chapter 4, Hong-Jen Abraham Lin addresses the banking sector. He begins by reviewing and summarizing the literature on Taiwan and China's commercial banks. Furthermore, based on the experience of geographic deregulation on the European continent and in the US, he discusses the trends of integration after Taiwan and China signed the ECFA.

From the existing literature of empirical studies on cost and profit efficiencies of the banking industry, the author has found that a scale economy is not the motivation for Taiwanese and Chinese banks to expand. No evidence implies that the acquisitions of banks could help major banks in either Taiwan or China to improve cost and profit efficiencies. In the experience of China, the gain from improved cost efficiency is mainly caused by minor foreign ownership and outside monitoring. The banking markets in the European Union and most of the states of the US are monopolistic competitive after deregulation and integration. Thus, the banking markets of Taiwan and China are expected to be monopolistic competitive after integration. Henceforth, when the banking industry is monopolistic competitive and the equity market is well developed, quality of services or relationships is the key to success for the integration of the banking industry across the Strait.

Financial integration accelerated after the Uruguay Round of trade liberalization. How extensive is the integration of equity markets in the 'Greater Chinese Economic Zone?' Wan-Jiun Paul Chiou, Chun-Pin Hsu, and Chin-Wen Huang study the equity markets of China, Hong Kong, and Taiwan in Chapter 5. Due to continuing wealth accumulation and economic integration in the region, understanding the development and cost–benefit of international diversification in China, Hong Kong, and Taiwan is an indispensable element of global asset management. The effectiveness of international diversification has been well documented in developed economies. However, the potential economic value of international diversification to investors in developing countries has not yet received the attention it deserves from academia. China, Hong Kong, and Taiwan differ especially from other emerging economies in terms of the development and interactions of their financial markets. Since the late 1980s, there has been increasing economic integration between China and Taiwan. China, with its swiftly growing economy and its substantial role in the global production network, drives the economy of East Asia, particularly the 'Chinese region,' within which countries are increasingly interdependent. On the other hand, the dynamics of economic interdependence in this region have been accompanied by periodic military and political tensions. Thus, several critical issues emerge. How would international diversification benefit local investors in the Sino market? Would the benefits of the regional diversification vanish in their home area? Would the economic values generated by the internationally diversifying portfolios shrink as the economy was increasingly integrated? If the benefits still existed, how would the effectiveness with respect to local investors diverge across China, Hong Kong, and Taiwan? Because of China's rising economic importance and wealth accumulation, an understanding of diversification strategies and cost–benefit analysis in this Chinese-cultural region has become an indispensable element in global asset management.

In this chapter, the authors first present the development of the economies and equity markets of this region and show that economic integration is associated with Taiwan's investment in China. They then discuss the roles of these countries in the international optimal portfolio. Using the mean-variance efficient frontier proposed by Markowitz, they analyse the benefits of international diversification from the perspective of local investors. The empirical findings suggest that the domestic investors, particularly those in Hong Kong and Taiwan, will benefit more if they consider diversifying their portfolios with the assets of developed countries in outside regions. The time-varying benefits of diversification exist even when the economy in this region is increasingly integrated. The same conclusion holds when various levels of home-bias are considered.

During recent decades, after piling up its foreign exchange reserves, China began to engage in outward foreign direct investment (FDI), including mergers and acquisitions. In Chapter 6, Monica Yang presents an analysis on cross-border mergers and acquisitions (CBMAs) made by China in Taiwan. According to *World Investment Report* (UNCTAD, 2010), emerging and transition economies accounted for a quarter of global FDI outflows in 2009. Take China as an example: by 2009, its outward FDI reached US $229.6 billion, an eight-fold increase over the year 2000 (UNCTAD, 2010). Sixty-two percent of China's outward FDI in 2008 was in the form of CBMAs (MOFCOM, 2008). Although emerging market firms have assumed a critical role in outward FDI, prior management literature has not given sufficient attention to these firms. Yang proposes two main questions in this chapter: what is the composition of CBMAs initiated by China in Taiwan from 1997 to 2010, and what is the major motivation for these CBMAs? Yang focuses on CBMAs by China in Taiwan because Taiwan, with its unique political and economic background, can provide an understanding of how emerging market firms (for example, in China) undertake international expansion strategies in emerging markets. The observation window of this study, 1997 to 2010, allows one to observe Taiwan's attitude toward CBMAs from China from closed to open. Yang specifically examines ninety completed CBMAs (twenty initiated by China and seventy by Hong Kong). Her findings show that the number of CBMAs increases over time despite the fact that the Taiwan government holds restrictive policies toward direct investment from China. Moreover, target firms are primarily from the financial sector, service, and manufacturing industries. Acquiring firms from Hong Kong are more willing to undertake unrelated deals than those from China. Finally, the major payment method in these deals is cash-only.

This chapter also has several implications for Taiwan and China. First, in terms of the number of CBMA deals from China and Hong Kong between 2008 and 2010, the Taiwanese government's positive attitude toward direct investment from China did not stimulate more CBMA deals. Therefore, if this trend continues, this finding will alleviate some concern that more Taiwanese firms will be merged with or acquired by Chinese firms after recent economic policy changes like the signing of the ECFA. Second, compared to the number of CBMAs by China in other countries, Taiwan is not a major target for Chinese firms. However, the motives behind those CBMAs from China are very similar to those by China in other developed markets (such as the United States and

European countries). When developed markets like the USA and the UK continue to raise security concerns over Chinese CBMA proposals and reject them (for example, the 3Com–Huawei merger in 2008 or the Huawei–Marconi merger in 2005), Taiwan may become an important target market for Chinese firms that want to obtain critical implicit assets (for example, brand name, management or marketing knowledge and skills). The Taiwanese government thus needs to prepare and consider how to manage these types of CBMA deals in the future.

While many multinational enterprises (MNEs) make direct investment in China, not all of them can successfully penetrate China's domestic market. China's 'socialist market economy with Chinese characteristics,' which is predominated by party–state rule of man rather than being ruled by law, caused many hazards for many MNEs in their efforts to penetrate China's domestic market. In Chapter 7, Chen and Hsieh analyse the strategic alliance between Japanese and Taiwanese firms by classifying them into various formats such as joint ventures, original equipment manufacture (OEM), and technological cooperation. They discuss how various formats of strategic alliances could complement their comparative advantages in the Chinese market, and how business enterprises between Japan and Taiwan could collaborate with each other on respective exports to China.

Their study focuses on the information technology (IT) industry by comparing Japan–Taiwan strategic alliances with non-allied Taiwanese enterprises in terms of operating performances. It provides a better understanding about the market competitiveness of Japan–Taiwan strategic alliances. The authors examine strategic alliances by questionnaires to study Taiwanese enterprises located in Kunshan city and Dongguan city as a case study, then proceed to survey the results with regression analysis. The results show that those firms which acquired technologies through strategic alliance or technical cooperation performed better than the non-allied ones. And the longer the cooperation duration was, the more productive it would be for their performance. The finding contributes to important information in international management and may offer some lessons for other multinational enterprises interested in exploiting the Chinese market.

Due to agglomeration effects, Taiwanese investment in China has generated several industrial clusters in China, especially in the Yantze River Delta and the Pearl River Delta. By using the concept of global production network, Chen and Ku study the rise and evolution of the Kunshan ICT cluster in the Jiangsu province of China in Chapter 8. They attribute the rise of Kunshan to three advantages: geographical proximity to Shanghai, a set of local institutions that are loosely coupled with national institutions, and an intimate connection to Taiwanese multinational corporations (MNCs). They highlight the interactions between local institutions and Taiwanese MNCs under a global production system. Essentially, Kunshan offered a set of investment-friendly institutions that allowed Taiwanese MNCs to reconstruct their production networks so as to cope with the changing conditions in the global ICT industry. These conditions, which began in the mid-1990s, necessitated more concentrated, more flexible, faster, and larger-volume production. The emergence of Kunshan created a cross-border linkage between ICT clusters in Silicon Valley in California, Hsinchu in Taiwan, and Kunshan in China. With this triangular connection, Taiwanese firms in Hsinchu Science Park were able to upgrade their position in the global production network.

Among the high-tech industries, semiconductor production is one which has dual usage for civilian and military purposes. In general, the semiconductor industry consists of three or four major stages – design, fabrication, testing, and assembly and shipment – with various factor intensities at each stage. With globalization, these production stages became fragmented across national boundaries in accordance with the comparative advantages of the host countries. In Chapter 9, Ming-chin Monique Chu addresses the subject by examining that industry's linkage between China and Taiwan. The territorial distribution of semiconductor manufacturing activities across national borders, often as a result of pertinent sectoral globalization, can potentially change the international balance of economic and military powers. This chapter adopts a firm-level case-study approach in order to conduct a nuanced analysis of one aspect of the sectoral globalization in the Cross-Strait context, namely the under-studied migration of the strategic Taiwanese semiconductor sector to China. Eight cases in integrated circuit (IC) design and fabrication are analysed. It is noteworthy that the author conducted more than 160 rounds of interviews with officials and industry insiders in the US, Taiwan, and China between 2004 and 2005 as well as in 2009 for her research project. In particular, senior executives at seven out of the top eight chip makers in China and Taiwan were interviewed. The conclusions are twofold. First, some non-state actors spearheading the migration have done so by circumventing or violating Taiwanese regulations, thereby eroding the capacity and autonomy of the Taiwanese state vis-à-vis non-state actors. Second, case analyses indicate a gradual shift in IC design and fabrication capability from Taiwan to China. Given the dual-use nature of semiconductors, such a trend is expected to contribute to the growth of China's comprehensive power and security, to the detriment of Taiwan's long-term survival.

The last chapter, written by Peter C.Y. Chow, addresses the emerging trade bloc and economic integration across the Taiwan Strait from both regional and global perspectives. The ECFA was signed just as FTAs were proliferating and economic integration was unfolding in East Asia. To some extent, the emerging trade bloc and the 'Greater China Economic Zone' can be considered as a subset of regional economic integration in East Asia. Chow points out that, unlike in the European Union, which is mainly based in intra-regional trade among member states, countries experiencing economic integration in East Asia rely heavily on external markets, mainly the US and EU, to sell their final products. The worldwide economic recession of 2007–2008, triggered by the global financial crisis, offered two important lessons for trade-dependent economies in East Asia: that economic integration through the trade-FDI nexus on only the production side is not durable, and that creating a trade bloc dependent on external markets as destinations for exports of final consumption goods is not sustainable. To rebalance the global economy, East Asian countries would need to redirect their exports to alternative markets, a process which will not be feasible in the near future.

Having examined the trade structures of the economies of East Asia and the OECD, with a focus on the US, Chow applies the hub–spoke model a la Krugman–Baldwin to identify three potential hubs – that is, the China-centric, Japan-centric and US-centric hubs – for the economic integration of East Asia. Chow analyses Taiwan's policy options and its future in pursuing globalization, and he strongly advocates that Taiwan not limit itself to the China-centric hub. Instead, Taiwan needs to sign bilateral and multilateral FTAs to reach the 'near-hub' status. Especially important for Taiwan's development is to join the Trans-Pacific Partnership Agreement to expand its international horizon and to diversify its current trade dependency on the single market of China. Other than the cost–benefits of economic integration, Taiwan's success or failure in its pursuit of globalization has strong political implications for its political autonomy, which will significantly affect the growth, stability and balance of power in the Asia-Pacific region. As Taiwan is an emerging young democracy, future relations between Taipei and Beijing will affect the trend of global democracy as well.

NOTES

1. For the topics of economic interests and national identity, see Chow (2012b).
2. Taiwan sent an 'early announcement' of the ECFA to the WTO 8 months after it took effect – see *Taipei Times* (2011). But early announcement is not an official registration as required by the WTO.

REFERENCES

Chow, Peter C.Y., 2012a. *Trade and Industrial Development in East Asia: Catching Up or Falling Behind.* Cheltenham, UK and Northampton, MA: Edward Elgar Publishing.

Chow, Peter C.Y., 2012b. *National Identity and Economic Interest: Taiwan's Competing Options and Their Implications for Regional Stability.* New York: Palgrave Macmillan.

Kawai, Masahiro, and Ganeshan Wignaraja, 2009. 'Asian FTA Trends and Challenges,' ADB Working Paper No. 144 at the website: www.adb.org.

MOFCOM, 2008. *2008 Statistical Bulletin of China's Outward Foreign Direct Investment.* Beijing: Ministry of Commerce.

Ozeki, Hiromichi, 2008. 'Development of *De Facto* Economic Integration in East Asian Trade', ch. 2 in Tereso S. Tullao, Jr and Lim Hong Hin, eds, *Deepening Economic Integration in East Asia: Developments and Challenges.* Economic Research Institute for ASEAN and East Asia (ERIA), available at: www.eria.org/research/images/pdf/PDF%20No. . ./No.1-2-part1-2.pdf.

Taipei Times, 2011. May 7, available at: http://www.taipeitimes.com/News/biz/archives/2011/05/07/2003502592.

UNCTAD, 2010. *World Investment Report: Investing in a Low-carbon Economy.* New York and Geneva: UNCTAD.

Wallace, William, 1982. 'Economic Divergence in the European Community,' in John M. Letiche, ed., *International Economic Policies and Their Theoretical Foundation.* New York: Academic Press, pp. 183–223.

1. Cross-Strait linkages: historical perspective and empirical evidence

Richard C.K. Burdekin, Yijing Shen, and Hsin-hui I.H. Whited

> Taiwanese capital and technology played a bellwether role in mainland China's entry into the global economy, while Taiwanese investors and professional managers earned mainland China its first pot of gold from foreign trade. Now, through the development of cross-strait relations, the Taiwan experience is exerting an even broader effect . . . (Lai Shin-yuan, Minister of the Mainland Affairs Council, Taiwan, July 7, 2011)

1.1 INTRODUCTION

In this chapter we detail the evolving economic ties between mainland China and Taiwan and provide an up-to-date picture of the trade and investment flows between the two economies. We assess macroeconomic interdependence between mainland China and Taiwan in terms of an array of output, price, money, and interest rate measures for each economy. This enables us to determine the extent to which the trade and investment nexus has been reflected in measurable economic symbiosis. We explore the interrelationship between our mainland China and Taiwan variables using data from January 1994 through April 2011. Our examination includes causality testing as well as consideration of a possible cointegrating relationship between the mainland China and Taiwanese series. We also allow for a possible structural break associated with the onset of the global financial crisis. Although some of the indicated effects of mainland China on Taiwan may well reflect China's influence on world markets generally, in addition to direct transmission effects (Yang and Shea, 2005), the empirical results generally seem consistent with the ties between the two economies suggested in trade and capital flow data. The idea of a unified 'Greater China' region including Taiwan as well as mainland China and Hong Kong indeed seems to be emerging economically in spite of the remaining political impediments.

1.2 GROWING TRADE AND INVESTMENT TIES

In the years following the flight of Chiang Kai-shek's Nationalist regime to Taiwan (then known as Formosa) in the face of defeat on the mainland at the end of the 1940s, Taiwan's export promotion strategy and close ties with the west contrasted sharply with mainland China's effective withdrawal from world markets. Even after US President Richard Nixon's visit to China in 1972 marked the beginning of a thawing in US–mainland China relations, there was still no immediate *rapprochement* between the People's Republic and Taiwan. Indeed, Taiwanese firms were expressly forbidden any involvement on the mainland under Taiwan President Chiang Ching-kuo's 1979 policy of 'no contact, no negotiation, no compromise.' Mainland China nevertheless began officially encouraging links with Taiwan, including the adoption of a zero tariff policy on imports from Taiwan in 1980 – but abandoned this policy after just one year for want of interest on the other side of the Taiwan Strait. A major thawing was seen in 1985, however, with the announcement by Taiwan's government of a 'Non-interference Principle of Indirect Exports to the Mainland' (Tung, 2004, p. 1). In turn, mainland China offered special incentives for Taiwanese investment. Two investment zones, with special tax privileges for Taiwan-invested enterprises, were established in Fujian province in May 1989, for example, followed by new legislation in 1994 protecting investment from Taiwan.

Estimated total trade between mainland China and Taiwan steadily increased, rising from US $5160.0 million in 1990 to US $120 784.5 million in 2010 (see Table 1.1). This includes a sharp rebound from the near-18 percent drop registered in 2009 following the onset of the global financial crisis. The 2010 estimated total bilateral trade was not only nearly 40 percent above the depressed levels of 2009 but also approximately 15 percent above the old 2008 highs. A majority of the trade flow comprises exports from Taiwan to mainland China, accounting for 70 percent of total 2010 bilateral trade. Overall Cross-Strait trade volumes increased by over 280 percent since World Trade Organization (WTO) membership was achieved by both mainland China and Taiwan around the end of 2001.[1] By 2010, Cross-Strait trade was accounting for 22.97 percent of Taiwan's total foreign trade and for 4.06 percent of mainland China's total foreign trade (Table 1.2). Taiwan's estimated trade surpluses with mainland China, incorporating indirect transit trade via Hong Kong, steadily increased over the 1990–2010 period. Despite direct trade links developing only gradually, and being disallowed entirely until after 2000, mainland China became Taiwan's second largest export market by 1993 and has been its top export market since 2002 (Tung, 2004). The only two

Table 1.1 The level of Cross-Strait trade between Taiwan and mainland China, 1990–2010

	Taiwan exports to mainland China	Mainland China exports to Taiwan	Total bilateral trade
1990	US $ 4394.6	765.4	5160.0
1991	7493.5	293.2	7786.7
1992	10547.6	747.1	11294.7
1993	13993.1	1015.5	15008.6
1994	16022.5	1858.7	17881.2
1995	19433.8	3091.3	22525.1
1996	20727.3	3059.9	23787.2
1997	22455.2	3915.3	26370.5
1998	19840.9	4113.9	23954.8
1999	21312.5	4528.9	25841.4
2000	25009.9	6229.3	31239.2
2001	24061.3	5903.0	31510.4
2002	31528.8	7968.6	39497.4
2003	38292.7	11017.9	49310.6
2004	48930.4	16792.3	65722.7
2005	56271.5	20093.7	76365.2
2006	63332.4	24783.1	88115.5
2007	74245.9	28015.0	102260.9
2008	73977.8	31391.3	105369.1
2009	62090.9	24423.5	86514.4
2010	84832.2	35952.2	120784.5

Notes: Figures are in US $ millions and are based on estimates by Taiwan's Mainland Affairs Council that include transit trade between Taiwan and Mainland China via Hong Kong.

Source: Mainland Affairs Council, Executive Yuan (2011, p. 24).

declines in trade volume occurred in the face of the Asian financial crisis in 1998 and the global financial crisis in 2009. The pre-Asian financial crisis trade level was surpassed by the year 2000 while the pre-global financial crisis trade level was already being superseded in 2010. The importance of Taiwan's trade surpluses with mainland China is reinforced by the fact that, in every year since 1992, these surpluses offset overall trade *deficits* with the rest of the world. This offset has become increasingly marked since WTO membership was achieved. In 2001, a surplus with mainland China of US $19 704.4 million was combined with an only slightly lower overall trade balance of US $18 343.7 million. By 2010, however, the surplus with mainland China of US $48 880.0 million combined with an

Table 1.2 *Cross-Strait trade relative to Taiwan and mainland China's overall world trade, 1990–2010*

	Taiwan's trade balance with mainland China	Taiwan's trade balance with the world	Cross-Strait trade as share of total Taiwan trade	Cross-Strait trade as share of total mainland China trade
1990	US $ 3629.2	US $ 12498.4	4.23 %	4.47 %
1991	7200.3	13420.6	5.57	5.74
1992	9800.5	9769.7	7.31	6.82
1993	12977.6	8563.9	9.19	7.67
1994	14163.8	8602.5	9.93	7.56
1995	16342.5	9330.4	10.36	8.02
1996	17667.4	14658.6	10.79	8.21
1997	18539.9	9214.8	11.03	8.11
1998	15727.0	7365.6	11.00	7.39
1999	16783.6	12537.3	11.00	7.17
2000	18780.6	11217.8	10.67	6.59
2001	19704.4	18343.7	13.45	6.18
2002	23560.2	22071.6	15.89	6.36
2003	27274.8	22590.4	17.70	5.79
2004	32138.1	13612.8	18.72	5.69
2005	36177.8	15817.3	20.04	5.37
2006	38549.3	21319.1	20.65	5.00
2007	46230.9	27425.4	21.95	4.70
2008	42586.5	15180.9	21.24	4.11
2009	37667.4	29304.1	22.88	3.92
2010	48880.0	23364.1	22.97	4.06

Notes: Figures in the first two columns are in US $ millions and in the third and fourth columns are percentages. Bilateral trade statistics are based on estimates by Taiwan's Mainland Affairs Council that include transit trade between Taiwan and Mainland China via Hong Kong.

Source: Mainland Affairs Council, Executive Yuan (2011, pp. 25–27).

overall surplus of just US $23 364.1 million implied a deficit of US $25 515.9 million with the rest of the world.

WTO membership has been accompanied by increased liberalization of mainland China–Taiwan trade. The gradual extension of direct trade and transport ties to replace indirect shipping via Hong Kong or, to some extent, Japan, is one factor significantly adding to the attractiveness of Cross-Strait trade as shipping costs are brought down. Transshipping goods via a third area may have added as much as US $1.51 billion to annual Cross-Strait transportation costs in 2001, or just over 5 percent of the total trade value (Lardy, 2002, p. 166). Taiwan's foreign direct investment (FDI) in China, like that of the largest contributor, Hong Kong and Macau, has itself been attracted by mainland China's pool of cheap labor as well as the incentives offered to FDI by the People's Republic of China. This Taiwanese FDI offers mutual benefits to both economies by augmenting mainland China's existing comparative advantage via technology transfers (in line with the 'comparative-advantage-augmenting' type of FDI described by Ozawa, 1992, pp. 40–42). The recent move toward larger-scale enterprises focusing on high-tech endeavors has also been accompanied by a more comprehensive presence on the mainland, with the upstream and downstream sectors alike moving to the mainland as part of a largely complete industrial supply chain transplanted over from Taiwan (Sun, 2011). Far from this increasing movement of Taiwanese manufacturing operations to the mainland dampening the level of exports coming from the remaining operations on Taiwan, as conventional theory regarding a tradeoff between outward investment and exports would predict (Li and Yu, 2010), export growth has continued to accelerate throughout.

The importance of Cross-Strait trade to mainland China is reflected in the fact that Taiwan became China's fourth-largest trading partner over the 1990s. Impressive as the ongoing growth in trade flows appears to be, the officially reported figures still do not capture the full picture, however. Actual Cross-Strait economic ties are bolstered not only by re-exporting from Taiwan to mainland China via Hong Kong but also by substantial Taiwanese investment via holding companies in tax-exempt locations like the British Virgin Islands and the Cayman Islands (both British Overseas Territories) that are not accounted for at all in the official data (Tung, 2004). The significance of Cross-Strait investment flows via third areas is reflected in the fact that the second-most important destination for outward investment from Taiwan is British Central America while the second-most important source of foreign investment in mainland China is the British Virgin Islands. As shown in Table 1.3, US $97 320.92 million in approved outward investment going from Taiwan to mainland China over the 1991–2010 period was combined with US $22 826.15 million reportedly destined for British Central America. This latter amount was more than double the amount approved for the United States, the next largest recipient, and more than three times the amount that went to Hong Kong or Singapore.

The same Caribbean region features prominently in mainland China's own foreign investment statistics. Table 1.4 shows that, in 2010 alone, there was an inflow of US $10 447.34 million to mainland China from

Table 1.3 Cumulative Taiwan-approved outward investment by country (or area), 1991–2010

	Cases	Amount	Percentage by amount
Mainland China	36 685	US $ 97 320.92	60.89 %
British Central America	2 002	22 826.15	14.28
USA	4 738	10 979.74	6.87
Singapore	428	5 438.53	3.40
Hong Kong	1 069	3 495.99	2.19
Vietnam	406	3 014.58	1.89
Thailand	286	1 736.90	1.09
Japan	492	1 316.50	0.82
Panama	64	1 270.70	0.79
Philippines	129	537.27	0.34
Korea	143	499.01	0.31
Germany	141	167.09	0.10
Others	2 078	11 238.07	7.03
Total	50 661	159 841.44	100.00

Notes: Figures in the first column are the absolute numbers, the second column is in US $ millions, and the third column is percentages.

Source: Mainland Affairs Council, Executive Yuan (2011, p. 31).

Table 1.4 Sources of realized foreign investment in mainland China in 2010

	Amount	Percentage
Hong Kong and Macau	US $ 61 222.01	57.90 %
British Virgin Islands	10 447.34	9.88
Singapore	5 428.20	5.13
Japan	4 083.72	3.86
Korea	2 692.17	2.55
USA	3 017.34	2.85
Taiwan	2 475.74	2.34
Germany	888.40	0.84
Others	15 480.08	14.64
Total	105 735.00	100.00

Notes: Figures in the first column are in US $ millions and the second column is percentages.

Source: Mainland Affairs Council, Executive Yuan (2011, p. 50).

the British Virgin Islands – an inflow that almost certainly includes the Taiwanese funds going (otherwise inexplicably) to this particular part of the world. This 'unofficial' inflow from Taiwan via the British Virgin Islands itself dwarfs the official inflow of foreign investment from Taiwan of just US $2475.74 million in 2010. Many of the funds directed to Hong Kong and Singapore in the official figures were also likely to be ultimately destined for mainland China. Taiwanese firms are attracted to this indirect route because, until President Ma Ying-jeou took office in May 2008, regulatory requirements for investing in China remained quite burdensome whereas the simple act of registering with the Investment Commission was enough to permit firms to invest anywhere else in the world (Rosen and Wang, 2011, p. 28). Restrictions on direct investment in mainland China were significantly eased afterwards, however. The upper limit on the percentage of a Taiwanese firm's total assets that can legally be invested in mainland China was increased from 40 percent to 60 percent, for example, while direct airline flights between Taiwan and mainland China were permitted for the first time in July 2008. Importantly, the signing of the Economic Cooperation Framework Agreement (ECFA) in August 2010 allowed capital inflows from mainland China for the first time (Chen, 2011). It is hoped that this may eventually lead to zero Cross-Strait trade tariffs, which the Taiwanese government estimates could boost annual economic growth by 1.65–1.72 percent (Liou, 2011, p. 173).[2] Meanwhile, Taiwan also stands to benefit from spillover effects arising from a series of megaprojects launched by the Beijing government since the onset of the global financial crisis (Chen, 2011).

The importance of the mainland China economy for Taiwanese industrial production is reflected in the number of sectors for which exports to China account for more than half of their total world exports. Rosen and Wang (2011, p. 79) identify ten such sectors generating US $33.7 billion in exports to mainland China in 2008, led by the optical display sector with US $16 billion a year in liquid crystal displays alone. Although exports to mainland China traditionally involved taking advantage of cheap labor for final assembly and re-export to the west, the mainland Chinese market has become increasingly important as a source of final demand as well – a trend that has only intensified with the coming of the global financial crisis and China's increase in relative strength vis-à-vis Europe and the United States (Rosen and Wang, 2011, p. 95). Evidence of strong business cycle linkages between mainland China and Taiwan is identified by Hughes Hallett and Richter (2009), who also find that this relationship is stronger than that between mainland China and any other Asian economy (or indeed the United States). Hughes Hallett and Richter's spectral analysis also points to a sharp increase in coherence since 2002, which coincides with the advent of WTO membership, along with greater concentration at longer business cycle frequencies. Hughes Hallett and Richter (2009, p. 848) attribute this uptrend to increased two-way trade in components and manufactures, coupled with the increased dependence of Taiwan on mainland China for investment opportunities, that leave Taiwan 'becoming part of a single Chinese economic zone.'

Greater integration between the two economies would also be expected to manifest itself in reduced price dispersion, as removal of trade barriers allows more scope for the law of one price to assert itself. Moreover, the transmission of inflationary or deflationary shocks from one economy to the other is likely insofar as, say, falling prices in mainland China necessitate price cuts by Taiwanese exporters if they are not to suffer a loss of competitiveness. Thus, co-movement in mainland China and Taiwanese price series as well as industrial production could quite naturally arise in conjunction with the increasing trade and investment flows between the two economies. The extent to which increased Cross-Strait ties have been accompanied by increased monetary and financial monetary integration is another testable proposition. Money supply co-movement could ensue from the transmission of monetary policy shocks from one economy to the other and would not necessarily require deliberate policy responses to events on the other side of the Taiwan Straits. Cheung et al. (2007) have already pointed to increased financial integration between mainland China and Taiwan being reflected in shrinking interest-rate differentials. In addition, Cheung et al. (2005) find some suggestions that integration between mainland China and the economies of Hong Kong and Taiwan during 1996–2001 was proceeding more rapidly than mainland China's integration with non-Chinese economies such as the United States and Japan.

Most prior studies of interactions between mainland China and Taiwan remained limited to either trade relationships or stock market interdependence alone. Significant linkages between the mainland Chinese and Taiwanese stock markets, as well as with Hong Kong, were consistently identified in such studies as Bahng and Shin (2004), Cheng and Glascock (2005), Chi et al. (2006), and Tian (2007). Although earlier studies typically found little evidence of longer-run integration, or cointegration, with the US market (Cheng and Glascock, 2005; Chi et al., 2006; Huyghebaert and Wang, 2010), Burdekin and Siklos (2012) find support for such a relationship in applying quantile cointegration methods to a dataset extending through 2010. It remains important, though, to allow for a broader range of potential interactions, and interdependence, between mainland China and Taiwan as reflected in output, money growth, and inflation variables in addition to stock market indices.[3] In the sections below we utilize mainland China data on output, prices, money supply, interest rates, and the stock market drawn from the Great China Database (http://www.finasia.biz/tejonline/tejonline.htm) and the Bloomberg terminal together with equivalent Taiwan data drawn from the Republic of China Statistical Database, the Central Bank of Taiwan, and the Bloomberg terminal.

1.3 MORE GENERAL MACROECONOMIC INTERDEPENDENCE

Although the 1997–98 Asian financial crisis exerted deflationary effects on the economies of both mainland China and Taiwan, Figure 1.1 shows that the upward trend in industrial production was maintained in each case. Mainland China industrial production also continued to rise through the global slowdown that accompanied the bursting of the Nasdaq bubble in 2000 and the terrorist attacks of September 11, 2001. There was a sharp fall in Taiwan's industrial production at this time, however. The Taiwanese economy was more exposed than mainland China to these events, in part

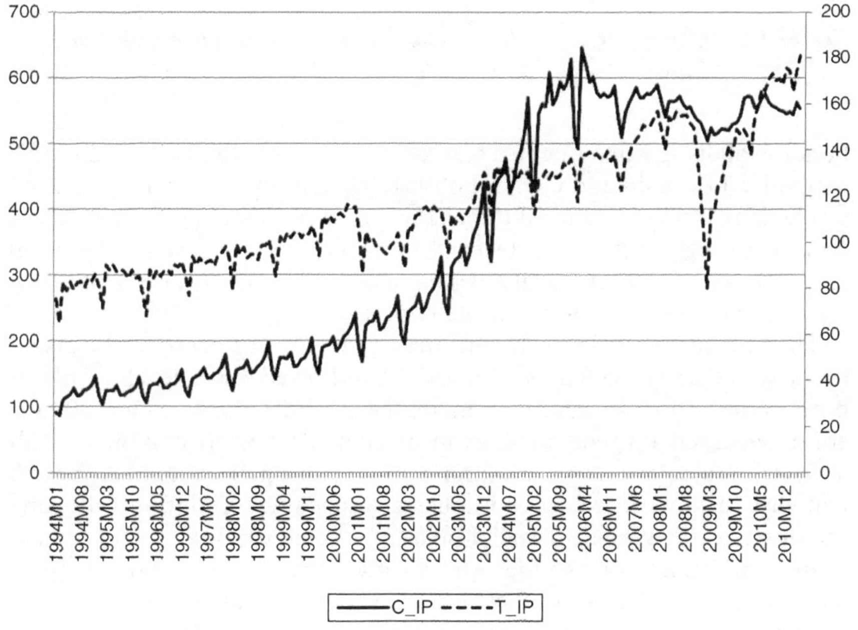

Figure 1.1 Industrial production in mainland China vs industrial production in Taiwan

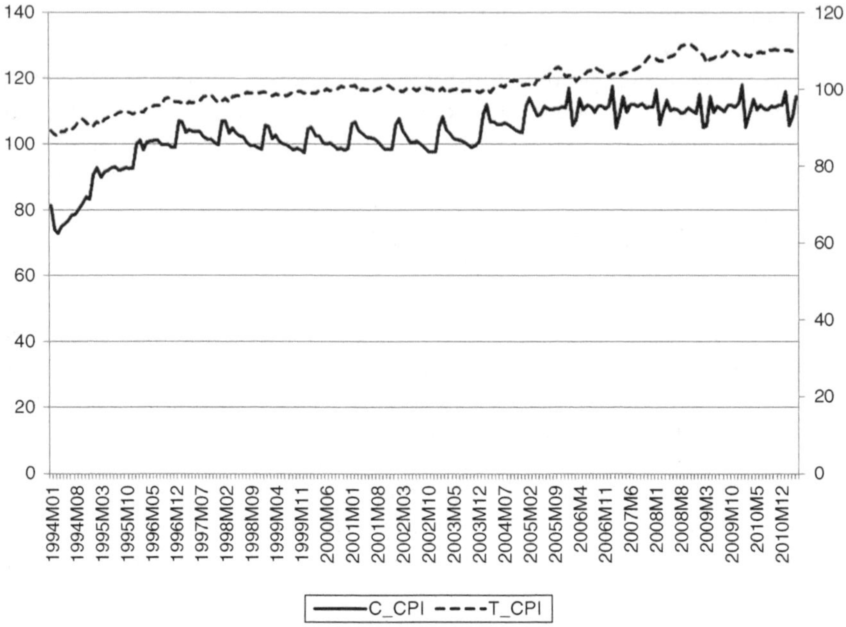

Figure 1.2 Consumer prices in mainland China vs consumer prices in Taiwan

because of its greater openness as compared with the capital controls maintained by mainland China. Political frictions in Taiwan likely played a role in exacerbating the 2001 weakness as well (Yang and Shea, 2005). Not surprisingly, both the industrial production series register a sharp fall in 2008 as the global financial crisis intensified. The drop in the Taiwanese series is once again the larger of the two.

The upward trend in both consumer price indices prior to the Asian financial crisis is evident in Figure 1.2 followed by a leveling off in both series prior to renewed increases in 2003–2004. After 2005 a continued mild uptrend in Taiwan consumer prices is combined with a flatter trajectory for mainland China consumer prices. Although neither consumer price series implies any sustained deflation following the onset of the global financial crisis, the same cannot be said for the Taiwan wholesale price index or the mainland China producer price index (Figure 1.3). Both these series experience an approximate 20 percent drop in 2007–2008 before rebounding. In each case, the pre-crisis levels were close to being regained at the end of our data sample in April 2011. Prior to the global financial crisis, the two series followed

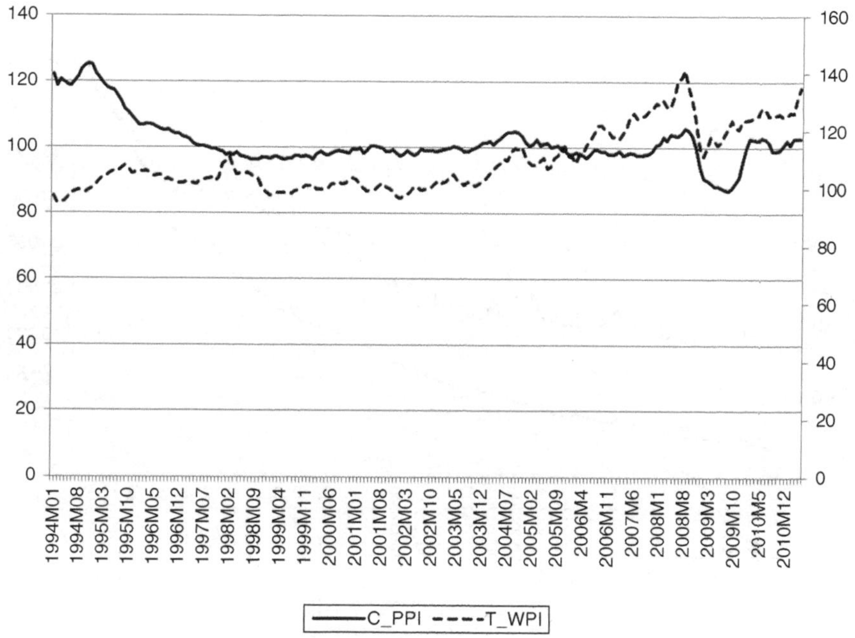

Figure 1.3 Producer prices in mainland China vs wholesale prices in Taiwan

somewhat divergent paths from 1994–98 but largely similar trends over 1998–2007.

We also take into account possible commonalities between money growth rates in mainland China and Taiwan, considering both M2 and M1 money supply measures – and in Taiwan's case an extended M1 money supply definition (M1B) that includes passbook savings deposits (Figures 1.4–1.6).[4] Although Taiwan's central bank, like mainland China's, emphasized M2 growth during the 1990s, the trends for broad and narrow money are actually very similar in each case. The different pairs of money supply measures appear to feature broadly similar upward movement over much of the sample period, but there is a slackening of Chinese money growth during 2005–2007 not shared by the Taiwanese series. This reflects the People's Bank of China's attempts to rein in liquidity at that time, as the economy showed signs of overheating. The mainland China money supply series, like the Taiwan money supply series, soon ratcheted up in 2008, however, reflecting the easing undertaken as each central bank expanded liquidity in the hope of cushioning the impact of the global financial crisis.

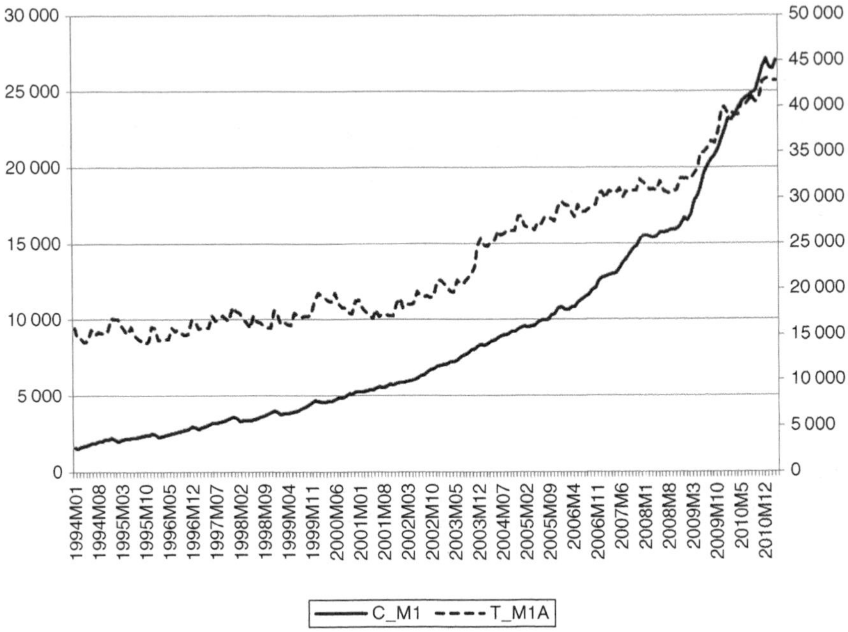

Figure 1.4 M1 money supply in mainland China vs M1A money supply in Taiwan

Interest rates in mainland China and Taiwan are represented by data on the one-month interbank rate (Figure 1.7). Although the mainland China series is much noisier, both series trend downward until 2003 and then rise almost in lockstep from 2003–2007. After this, the sudden spike in the mainland China interest rate in mid-2007 reflects moves aimed at curtailing asset price inflation reflected in soaring stock and real estate prices. Although both sets of interest rates were then cut sharply in 2008, the subsequent behavior was substantially different. The Taiwanese interbank rate, rather like the US federal funds rate, was quickly cut to nearly zero in an attempt to boost liquidity in the banking system and remained below half a percent through the end of the sample. These monetary policy moves were accompanied by a fiscal stimulus package that, like that initially adopted in mainland China, emphasized construction spending. In addition, the government provided consumption coupons worth around US $120 to each Taiwanese citizen and offered special unemployment benefits (Wang, 2010). While easy money policies remained in place in Taiwan through 2011, the mainland China interbank rate was moved back up as early as 2009 and exceeded pre-crisis levels by the end of 2010.

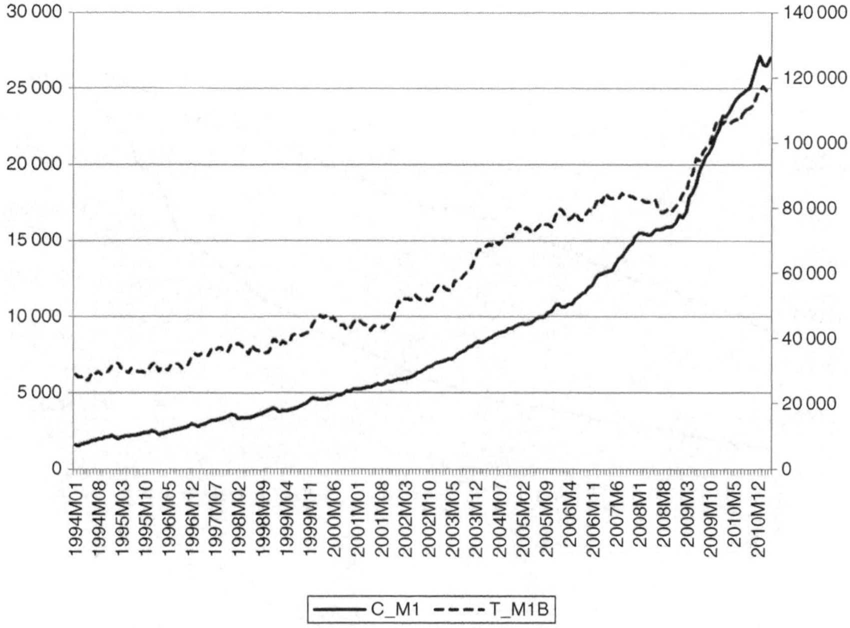

Figure 1.5 M1 money supply in mainland China vs M1B money supply in Taiwan

Such rising rates were part of the Chinese authorities' attempts to rein in renewed signs of asset price inflation. The very fact that inflation, rather than deflation, was a concern so early after the outbreak of the crisis is consistent with the relative resiliency of the Chinese real economy at this time – as reflected also in the industrial production series portrayed in Figure 1.1.

Finally, we consider respective stock market performance based on the Taipei stock market index and the Shanghai A-Share index (Figure 1.8). In this case, the two stock markets appear to follow a similar trajectory until 2000. After that point, the Taipei index breaks down sharply before recovering in 2002 and entering a rising phase that continues until 2007. Meanwhile, the Shanghai index peaks in early 2001 and then enters an extended downturn that persists until 2005. This is followed by the great bull market of 2005–2007, however, with the Shanghai A-Share index enjoying more than five-fold gains by the time of the peak reached in October 2007. Both markets plunge dramatically in the summer of 2008 before rebounding. In Taiwan's case, this rebound is sufficient to make up most of the lost ground by the end of 2010. The Shanghai market is not so

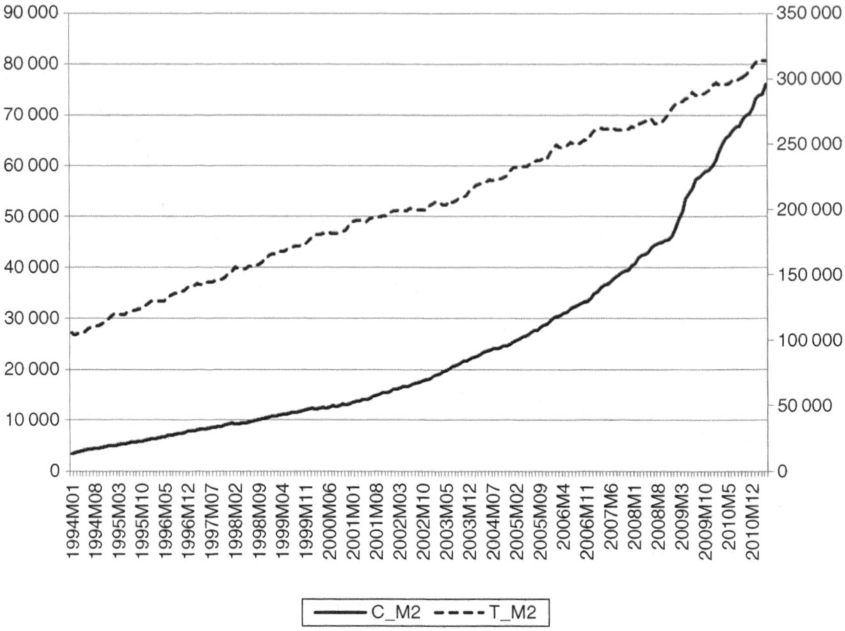

Figure 1.6 M2 money supply in mainland China vs M2 money supply in Taiwan

fortunate, however, and a new, more moderate, downturn sets in during 2009. This suggests that, even though the real economy might have been resilient enough to continue growing in spite of the interest rate hikes, the stock market was not.

1.4 CAUSAL RELATIONSHIPS BETWEEN THE CROSS-STRAIT VARIABLES

We begin by examining the simple correlation coefficients between our mainland China and Taiwan variables.[5] These data are all monthly series from January 1994 through April 2011.[6] These numbers generally reflect the correspondence suggested in the preceding figures. With the series specified in levels, Table 1.5 shows sample correlations between the mainland China and Taiwan series pairs to be 0.89 for industrial production, 0.83 for consumer prices, 0.94 or higher for the three money supply pairs, 0.72 for the interest rate pairs, and 0.45 for the stock market series. Only the mainland China PPI and Taiwan WPI fail to exhibit such conform-

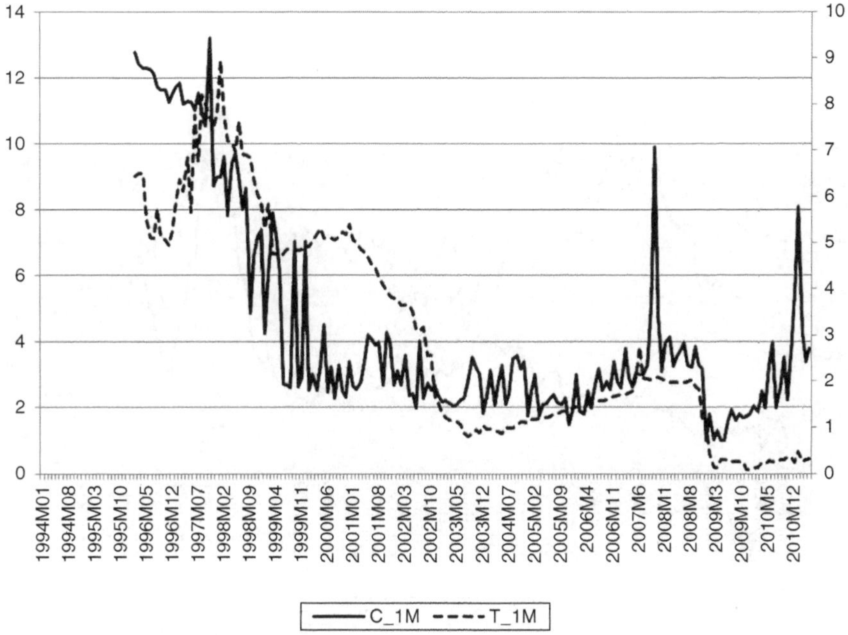

Figure 1.7 *One-month interest rate in mainland China vs one-month rate in Taiwan*

ity with a correlation of −0.21. The Table 1.5 correlations also suggest considerable degrees of co-movement between M2 growth and consumer price inflation in both mainland China and Taiwan. This is a Cross-Strait phenomenon and not just a within-country effect. There is, for example, a correlation coefficient of 0.90 between mainland China M2 growth and Taiwanese consumer inflation and a correlation of 0.80 between Taiwan's M2 growth and mainland China's consumer inflation. This suggests possible mutual sensitivity of inflation performance to monetary policy on the other side of the Taiwan Straits.

Granger-causality testing, with the data now transformed into (log) growth rates to assure stationarity, generally suggests that significant, bi-directional causal relationships underlie these correlations.[7] Table 1.6 shows significant bi-directional causality between mainland China and Taiwan industrial production, mainland China and Taiwan consumer prices, and each pair of narrow money supply measures. There is unidirectional causality in the case of the broad money supply series, with Chinese M2 Granger-causing Taiwanese M2 but not the reverse. The share price series also feature unidirectional causality, but this

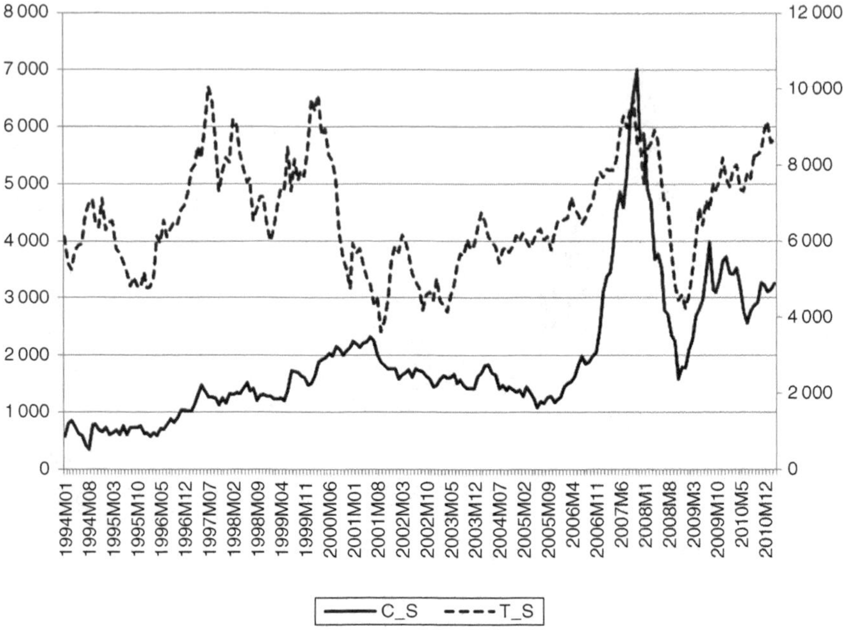

Figure 1.8 Shanghai stock market index in China vs Taipei stock market index in Taiwan

time the significant causal relationship runs from the Taiwanese series to the mainland China series. It is possible that this result is driven by the Taiwan share price index reflecting broader developments in world financial markets which then impact the Shanghai market. The producer price/wholesale price indices and interest rate series do not significantly Granger-cause each other.

Results for other significant combinations of mainland China and Taiwan variables follow in Table 1.7. In addition to co-determination amongst the different money supply series, these findings suggest that increased money growth in one economy tends to be followed by increased industrial production in the other. Such positive output effects could follow from monetary expansion boosting import demand via the wealth effect and thereby exerting a positive effect on foreign producers as well.[8] Taiwan M1A, M1B and M2 money growth all Granger-cause Chinese industrial production while mainland China M1 and M2 growth each have significant causal effects on Taiwanese industrial production. There is significant bidirectional causality between mainland China industrial production and Taiwanese consumer price inflation as well as between mainland China consumer price inflation and Taiwanese industrial production. Furthermore, mainland China consumer price inflation is found to Granger-cause Taiwanese industrial production and wholesale price inflation, but these causal relationships are unidirectional with no significant effects of the Taiwanese variables on mainland China consumer prices. Mainland China producer price inflation also Granger-causes Taiwanese industrial production and Taiwanese interest rates, again with no reverse feedback being present. Another unidirectional causal relationship runs from mainland China M2 growth to Taiwanese interest rates. There is somewhat less evidence of unidirectional effects running from the Taiwanese variables to the mainland China variables. There are, however, indicated causal effects of Taiwanese share-price movements on both mainland China consumer prices and mainland China producer prices, and a significant effect of Taiwanese M2 growth on mainland China share prices.

Evidence of bidirectional causality involving industrial production, consumer prices and the narrow money supply is consistent with growing integration in trade and investment flows being accompanied by more broad-based ties between the two economies. This is combined with a number of unidirectional relationships, generally with the direction of causality running from mainland China to Taiwan. Given the relative size of the two economies, and greater relative importance of Cross-Strait trade to Taiwan, it may seem surprising that all the relationships are not simply unidirectional. To some extent, the indicated causal effects of some of the Taiwanese variables on mainland China may actually be proxying for 'rest of the world effects.' Taiwan's economy remains more exposed to external shocks owing both to its being a small, open economy and to its not sharing the relative insulation afforded by the capital controls maintained by mainland China. Insofar as Taiwan's economy reacts faster to outside effects, the causality test results may embody reactions to such external effects rather than purely Taiwan-specific events. Another complication arises from the triangular nature of the global production network insofar as Taiwanese firms react to increases in global demand by increasing their production in mainland China and then exporting the finished product to western markets from there.[9] The quite pervasive causal relationships involving industrial production, consumer prices, and money supply remain important, however, in supporting the premise that Cross-Strait ties involve much more than trade and investment flows alone. Notwithstanding the qualification required for the (more limited) indicated causal effects running from Taiwan to mainland China, there is certainly quite consistent evidence of causal effects of mainland China output, price, and money supply movements on the Taiwanese economy.

Table 1.5 Means, standard deviations, and correlations for each series

Chinese variables:

	C_Y	C_CPI	C_PPI
Mean	337.18	103.42	101.63
Standard Deviation	186.85	8.58	7.25

Taiwanese variables:

	T_Y	T_CPI	T_WPI
Mean	115.43	101.08	109.51
Standard Deviation	26.40	5.61	10.77

Correlation table:

	C_Y	C_CPI	C_PPI	C_M1	C_M2	C_IR	C_S
C_Y	1						
C_CPI	0.73	1					
C_PPI	–0.39	–0.71	1				
C_M1	0.84	0.67	–0.38	1			
C_M2	0.85	0.68	–0.39	0.99	1		
C_IR	–0.59	–0.35	0.37	–0.46	–0.46	1	
C_S	0.64	0.57	–0.40	0.69	0.69	–0.30	1
T_Y	0.89	0.70	–0.37	0.89	0.88	–0.51	0.71
T_CPI	0.86	0.83	–0.63	0.90	0.90	–0.54	0.72
T_WPI	0.82	0.65	–0.21	0.85	0.85	–0.25	0.72
T_M1A	0.91	0.71	–0.36	0.98	0.98	–0.50	0.68
T_M1B	0.93	0.74	–0.43	0.97	0.97	–0.57	0.69
T_M2	0.93	0.80	–0.56	0.94	0.94	–0.66	0.72
T_IR	–0.86	–0.61	0.10	–0.77	–0.77	0.72	–0.41
T_S	0.16	0.30	–0.17	0.28	0.28	0.27	0.45

Notes:
C_Y and T_Y refer to mainland China and Taiwan industrial production;
C_CPI and T_CPI refer to mainland China and Taiwan consumer price indices;
C_PPI and T_WPI refer to mainland China and Taiwan producer price and wholesale price indices;
C_M1, T_M1A and T_M1B refer to mainland China and Taiwan narrow money supplies;
C_M2 and T_M2 refer to mainland China and Taiwan broad money supplies;
C_IR and T_IR refer to mainland China and Taiwan one-month interest rates; and
C_S and T_S refer to mainland Chin and Taiwan stock market indices.

Sources: Data sources are noted in the body of the paper.

C_M1	C_M2	C_IR	C_S
8 869.98	24 406.45	4.44	1 923.19
6 763.52	19 071.64	3.24	1 182.65

T_M1A	T_M1B	T_M2	T_IR	T_S
23 418.63	59 667.83	204 890.1	3.02	6 701.58
8 132.48	25 129.71	58 668.42	2.36	1 433.91

T_Y	T_CPI	T_WPI	T_M1A	T_M1B	T_M2	T_IR	T_S
1							
0.87	1						
0.84	0.82	1					
0.91	0.89	0.86	1				
0.92	0.91	0.83	0.99	1			
0.91	0.96	0.80	0.95	0.98	1		
–0.75	–0.74	–0.58	–0.81	–0.86	–0.87	1	
0.34	0.25	0.37	0.31	0.27	0.20	0.19	1

1.5 LONG-RUN RELATIONSHIPS AND COINTEGRATION

The causality-testing suggests particularly strong transmission effects arising from money growth on each side of the Taiwan Straits. Money growth in mainland China appears to exert significant causal effects not only on Taiwanese money growth but also Taiwanese inflation and industrial production. The much lesser evidence of causal relationships involving the wholesale price/producer price series, and to some extent the share price series, remains unsurprising given the smaller correlations evident in

Table 1.6 Granger-causality between Taiwan and China variable equivalents

Null hypothesis	F-statistic	Probability
T_Y does not Granger-cause C_Y	3.12	0.02
C_Y does not Granger-cause T_Y	14.57	0.01
T_CPI does not Granger-cause C_CPI	3.60	0.01
C_CPI does not Granger-cause T_CPI	5.70	0.01
T_WPI does not Granger-cause C_PPI	1.62	0.17
C_PPI does not Granger-cause T_WPI	1.42	0.23
T_M1A does not Granger-cause C_M1	10.83	0.01
C_M1 does not Granger-cause T_M1A	7.61	0.01
T_M1B does not Granger-cause C_M1	8.61	0.01
C_M1 does not Granger-cause T_M1B	10.00	0.01
T_M2 does not Granger-cause C_M2	1.04	0.39
C_M2 does not Granger-cause T_M2	4.53	0.01
T_IR does not Granger-cause C_IR	1.41	0.23
C_IR does not Granger-cause T_IR	0.99	0.41
T_S does not Granger-cause C_S	3.79	0.01
C_S does not Granger-cause T_S	0.94	0.44

Notes: All data series are in percentage change form to assure stationarity. Relationships significant at the 5 percent level or better are marked in bold.

Table 1.5 and the patterns shown in the plots. The lack of any significant causality between the two interest rate series appears to be at odds with the rather similar trends shown in Figure 1.7, however. In this respect, it must be borne in mind that Granger-causality deals with short-run impacts of one variable on another rather than long-run co-movement. We now address this latter question by applying cointegration analysis to the same set of mainland China and Taiwan variable pairs. The results reported in Table 1.8 are for the Johansen procedure under allowance for ten lags – and with the variables, of course, now entered in their original levels rather than the growth rate form required for the causality testing procedure.

Table 1.8 shows that evidence of cointegration over our 1994–2011 sample is limited to the interest rate and share price pairs. This former finding, in particular, is very much consistent with the similar trends evident in Figure 1.7 – but the apparent insignificance for the other pairings begs the question of why so many of the pairs found to be causally-related do not apparently feature any long-run co-movement. The answer seems to lie, in part, with the impact of the global financial crisis. Re-estimation with the sample curtailed in June 2007 reveals significant cointegration between the two consumer price series, Taiwanese M1A and mainland China M1,

Table 1.7 Other significant Taiwan and China variable pairs

Null hypothesis	F-statistic	Probability
T_CPI does not Granger-cause C_Y	3.80	0.01
C_Y does not Granger-cause T_CPI	4.26	0.01
T_M1A does not Granger-cause C_Y	24.61	0.01
C_Y does not Granger-cause T_M1A	26.47	0.01
T_M1B does not Granger-cause C_Y	10.57	0.01
C_Y does not Granger-cause T_M1B	16.94	0.01
T_M2 does not Granger-cause C_Y	5.96	0.01
C_Y does not Granger-cause T_M2	12.75	0.01
T_Y does not Granger-cause C_CPI	2.56	0.04
C_CPI does not Granger-cause T_Y	18.26	0.01
T_WPI does not Granger-cause C_CPI	0.29	0.88
C_CPI does not Granger-cause T_WPI	2.43	0.05
T_M1A does not Granger-cause C_CPI	14.05	0.01
C_CPI does not Granger-cause T_M1A	5.33	0.01
T_M1B does not Granger-cause C_CPI	8.17	0.01
C_CPI does not Granger-cause T_M1B	6.23	0.01
T_M2 does not Granger-cause C_CPI	8.89	0.01
C_CPI does not Granger-cause T_M2	6.56	0.01
T_S does not Granger-cause C_CPI	3.51	0.01
C_CPI does not Granger-cause T_S	0.13	0.97
T_Y does not Granger-cause C_PPI	1.42	0.23
C_PPI does not Granger-cause T_Y	6.47	0.01
T_IR does not Granger-cause C_PPI	0.82	0.52
C_PPI does not Granger-cause T_IR	5.10	0.01
T_S does not Granger-cause C_PPI	4.14	0.01
C_PPI does not Granger-cause T_S	1.54	0.19
T_Y does not Granger-cause C_M1	1.26	0.29
C_M1 does not Granger-cause T_Y	9.32	0.01
T_CPI does not Granger-cause C_M1	6.95	0.01
C_M1 does not Granger-cause T_CPI	5.04	0.01
T_M1A does not Granger-cause C_M1	10.83	0.01
C_M1 does not Granger-cause T_M1A	7.61	0.01
T_M1B does not Granger-cause C_M1	8.61	0.01
C_M1 does not Granger-cause T_M1B	10.00	0.01
T_M2 does not Granger-cause C_M1	6.12	0.01
C_M1 does not Granger-cause T_M2	6.29	0.01
T_Y does not Granger-cause C_M2	5.66	0.01
C_M2 does not Granger-cause T_Y	8.34	0.01
T_CPI does not Granger-cause C_M2	7.65	0.01
C_M2 does not Granger-cause T_CPI	3.51	0.01
T_WPI does not Granger-cause C_M2	4.04	0.01
C_M2 does not Granger-cause T_WPI	1.16	0.33

Table 1.7 (continued)

Null hypothesis	F-statistic	Probability
T_M1A does not Granger-cause C_M2	3.73	0.01
C_M2 does not Granger-cause T_M1A	6.33	0.01
T_M1B does not Granger-cause C_M2	3.68	0.01
C_M2 does not Granger-cause T_M1B	4.03	0.01
T_IR does not Granger-cause C_M2	2.38	0.06
C_M2 does not Granger-cause T_IR	3.03	0.02
T_M2 does not Granger-cause C_S	2.52	0.04
C_S does not Granger-cause T_M2	0.05	0.99

Note: See Notes to Table 1.6.

Table 1.8 Cointegration between Taiwan and China variable equivalents

Null hypothesis	Trace statistic
T_Y is cointegrated with C_Y over 1994–2011	0.93
T_Y is cointegrated with C_Y over 1994–2007	0.00
T_CPI is cointegrated with C_CPI over 1994–2011	0.78
T_CPI is cointegrated with C_CPI over 1994–2007	3.77
T_WPI is cointegrated with C_PPI over 1994–2011	0.21
T_WPI is cointegrated with C_PPI over 1994–2007	0.30
T_M1A is cointegrated with C_M1 over 1994–2011	3.34
T_M1A is cointegrated with C_M1 over 1994–2007	5.66
T_M1B is cointegrated with C_M1 over 1994–2011	1.20
T_M1B is cointegrated with C_M1 over 1994–2007	2.69
T_M2 is cointegrated with C_M2 over 1994–2011	1.64
T_M2 is cointegrated with C_M2 over 1994–2007	5.28
T_IR is cointegrated with C_IR over 1994–2011	7.00
T_IR is cointegrated with C_IR over 1994–2007	7.87
T_S is cointegrated with C_S over 1994–2011	6.01
T_S is cointegrated with C_S over 1994–2007	0.65

Notes: The trace statistics test for the presence of at least one cointegrating equation between each variable pair under allowance for 10 lags. Relationships that exceed the 5 percent critical value of 3.76 are marked in bold.

and Taiwanese M2 and mainland China M2. There is therefore considerable support for co-movement between the money and consumer price series that goes beyond a simple short-term causal effect. Although the evidence suggests that these relationships were not maintained after 2007, this could well prove to be a purely temporary dislocation owing to the extreme

Table 1.9 Significant cointegrating relationships for other Taiwan and China pairs

Null hypothesis	Trace statistic
T_S is cointegrated with C_CPI over 1994–2011	11.70
T_S is cointegrated with C_CPI over 1994–2007	8.06
T_S is cointegrated with C_PPI over 1994–2011	6.01
T_S is cointegrated with C_PPI over 1994–2007	4.40
T_Y is cointegrated with C_M1 over 1994–2011	8.99
T_Y is cointegrated with C_M1 over 1994–2007	14.38
T_CPI is cointegrated with C_M1 over 1994–2011	6.83
T_CPI is cointegrated with C_M1 over 1994–2007	11.32
T_M2 is cointegrated with C_M1 over 1994–2011	4.38
T_M2 is cointegrated with C_M1 over 1994–2007	4.20
T_S is cointegrated with C_M1 over 1994–2011	8.16
T_S is cointegrated with C_M1 over 1994–2007	5.23
T_Y is cointegrated with C_M2 over 1994–2011	7.25
T_Y is cointegrated with C_M2 over 1994–2007	11.65
T_CPI is cointegrated with C_M2 over 1994–2011	6.47
T_CPI is cointegrated with C_M2 over 1994–2007	12.94
T_WPI is cointegrated with C_M2 over 1994–2011	8.22
T_WPI is cointegrated with C_M2 over 1994–2007	1.22
T_M1A is cointegrated with C_M2 over 1994–2011	3.14
T_M1A is cointegrated with C_M2 over 1994–2007	5.72
T_S is cointegrated with C_IR over 1994–2011	6.63
T_S is cointegrated with C_IR over 1994–2007	5.97
T_M1A is cointegrated with C_S over 1994–2011	3.79
T_M1A is cointegrated with C_S over 1994–2007	0.07

Note: See Notes to Table 1.8.

pressures of the global financial crisis.[10] At the same time, co-movement between the share price series actually seems to have strengthened after 2007. Given that the Shanghai and Taipei market indices appear to be cointegrated over 1994–2011, but not over 1994–2007, it seems reasonable to infer that the full sample results were being primarily driven by a closer post-2007 relationship.[11]

In considering cointegration between other combinations of mainland China and Taiwanese variables, Table 1.9 shows that the pervasive role played by the money supply series with respect to prices and output on the other side of the Taiwan Straits found in the causality testing does, in fact, carry over into significant long-run relationships as well. In this case, however, the suggested influence of Chinese money is much more pervasive than the effects of the Taiwanese money supply aggregates. Mainland China M1 and mainland China M2 are both cointegrated with Taiwanese industrial production and Taiwanese consumer prices not only over 1994–2011 but also over 1994–2007. These output and inflation relationships suggests that positive effects on Taiwanese exporters arising from monetary expansion in mainland China may well extend beyond the short-run effects identified in the preceding Granger-causality analysis. Mainland China M2 is cointegrated with Taiwanese wholesale prices as well, but this relationship holds only for the full sample and not for the pre-2007 subsample. Although Taiwanese M1A is correlated with mainland China share prices, this relationship is significant only for the full sample and not for the 1994–2007 subsample. Taiwanese M2 and mainland China M1 are significantly cointegrated with each other over both intervals. Such money supply ties could be another manifestation of Cross-Strait trade and investment linkages but almost certainly also reflect common responses to outside shocks. Finally, there are a number of significant cointegrating relationships involving Taiwanese share prices. The Taipei market index is, in fact, cointegrated with mainland China consumer prices, producer prices, M1 money supply, and interest rates over both the 1994–2011 and 1994–2007 periods. Although it should be emphasized that these results say nothing about which variable is driving which, these significant relationships may well reflect sensitivity of Taiwanese stock prices to long-run trends on the mainland.

To the extent that significant cointegrating relationships become somewhat more prevalent after 2007, this likely reflects increased globalization influences as well as closer Cross-Strait ties. Mainland China's continued greater insulation from world events is reflected, however, in its relative resilience to the global financial crisis that allowed the People's Bank of China to begin raising rates in 2009 whereas Taiwan's central bank, like the US Federal Reserve, kept interest rates near zero through 2011 and beyond. This is not to say that mainland China was not significantly impacted by the crisis but rather that its vulnerability was simply much less than for most other world economies (Zhang et al., 2012). Meanwhile, as argued earlier, increased Cross-Strait trade flows and, in particular, increased dependence of Taiwanese exporters on the mainland China market, would be expected to lead to accompanying sensitivity of Taiwanese economic variables to developments on the mainland. Although we cannot prove that such Cross-Strait ties are the sole cause of the co-movement identified in the econometric testing, they are certainly very much consistent with it. Significant monetary and financial interdependence appears to have emerged over our sample period in conjunction with the rise in bilateral trade.

1.6 CONCLUSIONS

Consistent with past work identifying Cross-Strait business cycle ties (Hughes Hallett and Richter, 2009) and financial linkages (Cheung et al., 2005; 2007), we find evidence of quite broad-based economic linkages that seem to have gone hand-in-hand with the pronounced and well-documented increases in trade and investment flows. The transmission of money supply movements across the Taiwan Straits is perhaps the most striking feature of our econometric analysis. The extent of the interdependence evidenced in both the Granger-causality testing and the cointegration analysis suggests possible gains from monetary policy coordination. Although recent initiatives have led to valuable easing of the impediments to trade and investment flows between mainland China and Taiwan, this has not so far extended to any formal cooperation in the monetary policy arena. Although naturally remaining a purely hypothetical analysis, Yeh (2008) goes even further in considering the impact of a prospective full monetary union between mainland China and Taiwan. While this presumably would remain out of the question for the foreseeable future, simply taking the effects of money supply movements on the other side of the Taiwan Straits into account when setting policy could well be beneficial for the mainland China and Taiwan central banks alike.

ACKNOWLEDGEMENT

We are grateful to two anonymous referees for helpful comments.

NOTES

1. The People's Republic of China joined the WTO on December 11, 2001 and Taiwan followed on January 1, 2002.
2. The potential benefits arising from a full free trade agreement have been examined, based on a computable general equilibrium analysis, by Chen et al. (2009).
3. For an earlier application of this general approach, see Burdekin and Whited (2009) as well as Burdekin (2008, ch. 9). The present chapter goes beyond this, however, in not only covering more recent data going through the global financial crisis but also adding cointegration and interest rate analysis.
4. Taiwan's M1A contains currency held by the public plus checking accounts and passbook deposits of enterprises and individuals (including non-profit organizations) in monetary institutions. M1B is defined as M1A plus Passbook Savings Deposits of Individuals (including non-profit organizations) in monetary institutions.
5. We cannot directly incorporate Cross-Strait trade variables and investment flows in the empirical testing as, unlike the macroeconomic and share price series, such data are not generally available on a monthly basis.

6. Seasonality has been removed from the data by employing the Holt–Winters exponential smoothing method.
7. A lag length of four is imposed throughout.
8. Some support for such short-run effects of mainland China monetary expansion on output in Taiwan and other East Asian economies, as well as more sustained price-level effects, is provided by Koźluk and Mehrotra (2009).
9. Although expanding the empirical specification to explicitly allow for effects of changes in export demand associated with US and European income growth etc. lies beyond the scope of this chapter, we should acknowledge that the indicated bidirectional causality findings could scarcely fail to be influenced by such outside factors.
10. The Granger-causality results seem less affected by whether or not the sample period extends beyond 2007. Appendix Table A1.1 shows that the only changes from the causality between the counterpart variables depicted in Table 1.6 are (i) the causal relationship between mainland China M2 and Taiwanese M2 is bidirectional over 1994–2007 rather than unidirectional over 1994–2011; and (ii) the unidirectional relationship between Taiwanese shares and mainland China shares seen over 1994–2011 is not statistically significant over 1994–2007 (the significance level drops down to 12 percent).
11. There are too few observations to sensibly test cointegration over the post-2007 sample alone.

REFERENCES

Bahng, Seungwook and Seung-Myo Shin (2004). 'Interactions of Stock Markets within the Greater China Economic Bloc.' *Global Economic Review*, 33: 43–60.

Burdekin, Richard C.K. (2008). *China's Monetary Challenges: Past Experiences and Future Prospects*. New York: Cambridge University Press.

Burdekin, Richard C.K. and Pierre L. Siklos (2012). 'Enter the Dragon: Interactions between Chinese, US and Asia-Pacific Equity Markets, 1995–2010.' *Pacific-Basin Finance Journal*, 20 (June), 521–41.

Burdekin, Richard C.K. and Hsin-hui I.H. Whited (2009). 'Macroeconomic Interdependence between Mainland China and Taiwan: A Cross-Strait Perspective on Globalization.' *The Chinese Economy*, 42 (January–February): 5–39.

Chen, Hsiao-hung Nancy (2011). 'Political Economy of Cross-Strait Investments: The Taiwanese High-tech Industry as an Example.' *Seoul Journal of Economics*, 24 (Summer): 171–95.

Chen, Kun-Ming, Meng-Chia Tsai, Chia-Ching Lin, and Chow-hsia Tu (2009). 'Impact of Cross-Strait Trade Liberalization: A Computable General Equilibrium Analysis.' *China & World Economy*, 17 (November–December): 106–22.

Cheng, Hwahsin and John L. Glascock (2005). 'Dynamic Linkages Between the Greater China Economic Area Stock Markets – Mainland China, Hong Kong, and Taiwan.' *Review of Quantitative Finance and Accounting*, 24 (June): 343–57.

Cheung, Yin-Wong, Menzie D. Chinn, and Eiji Fujii (2005). 'Dimensions of Financial Integration in Greater China: Money Markets, Banks and Policy Effects.' *International Journal of Finance and Economics*, 10 (April): 117–32.

Cheung, Yin-Wong, Menzie D. Chinn, and Eiji Fujii (2007). *The Economic Integration of Greater China: Real and Financial Linkages and the Prospects for Currency Union*. Aberdeen, Hong Kong: Hong Kong University Press.

Chi, Jing, Ke Li and Martin Young (2006). 'Financial Integration in East Asian Equity Markets.' *Pacific Economic Review*, 11 (December): 513–26.

Hughes Hallett, Andrew and Christian Richter (2009). 'Economics in the Backyard: How Much Convergence is there between China and her Special Regions?' *World Economy*, 32 (June): 819–61.

Huyghebaert, Nancy and Lihong Wang (2010). 'The Co-Movement of Stock Markets in East Asia: Did the 1997–1998 Asian Financial Crisis Really Strengthen Stock Market Integration?' *China Economic Review*, 21 (March): 98–112.

Koźluk, Tomasz and Aaron Mehrotra (2009). 'The Impact of Chinese Monetary Policy Shocks on East and South-East Asia.' *Economics of Transition*, 17 (1): 121–45.

Lai, Shin-yuan (2011). 'The Republic of China's Mainland Policy: Piloting Cross-Strait Relations to Create a Peaceful Environment for Benign Interaction between the Two Sides of the Taiwan Strait.' Keynote speech at the international conference on 'Facing the Challenges of Cross-Strait Relations in 2012,' Washington, DC, July 7 (http://www.mac.gov.tw/public/data/1101715121671.pdf).

Lardy, Nicholas R. (2002). *Integrating China into the World Economy*. Washington, DC: Brookings Institution.

Li, Chu-Shiu and Chin-Ping Yu (2010). 'Analysis of the Economic Relationship Between China and Taiwan.' *The Chinese Economy*, 43 (January–February): 26–43.

Liou, To-hai (2011). 'Cross-Taiwan Straits Economic Relations and the ECFA.' In Kevin G. Cai (ed.), *China–Taiwan Straits Relations Since 1979*. Hackensack, NJ: World Scientific, pp. 155–85.

Mainland Affairs Council, Executive Yuan (2011). *Cross-Strait Economic Statistics Monthly*, No. 223, June (Taipei, Taiwan).

Ozawa, Terutomo (1992). 'Foreign Direct Investment and Economic Development.' *Transnational Corporations*, 1 (February): 27–54.

Rosen, Daniel H. and Zhi Wang (2011). *The Implications of China–Taiwan Economic Liberalization*. Washington, DC: Peterson Institute for International Economics.

Sun, Shengliang (2011). 'Economic Relations Across the Taiwan Straits and Beijing's Policy Adjustment.' In Kevin G. Cai (ed.), *China–Taiwan Straits Relations Since 1979*. Hackensack, NJ: World Scientific, pp. 51–86.

Tian, Gary Gang (2007). 'Are Chinese Stock Markets Increasing Integration with Other Markets in the Greater China Region and Other Major Markets?' *Australian Economic Papers*, 46 (September): 240–53.

Tung, Chen-Yuan (2004). 'Economic Relations between Taiwan and China.' UNISCI Discussion Papers (Madrid, Spain: Research Unit on International Security and Cooperation), No. 4, January (http://www.isn.ethz.ch/isn/Digital-Library/Publications/Detail/?ots591=0c54e3b3-1e9c-be1e-2c24-a6a8c7060233&lng=en&ord582=grp1&id=114748).

Wang, Jiann-Chyuan (2010). 'The Strategies Adopted by Taiwan in Response to the Global Financial Crisis, and Taiwan's Role in Asia-Pacific Economic Integration.' *Japan and the World Economy*, 22 (December): 254–63.

Yang, Ya-Hwei and Jia-Dong Shea (2005). 'Deflation and Monetary Policy in Taiwan.' NBER Working Paper 11244 (http://www.nber.org/papers/w11244).

Yeh, Kuo-chun (2008). 'Will a Taiwan–China Monetary Union be Feasible? Lessons from Europe.' *Peace Economics, Peace Science and Public Policy*, 14 (Issue 3, Article 1): 1–34.

Zhang, Nan, Thomas D. Willett, and Linyue Li (2012). 'The Effects of the Global Financial Crisis on China's Financial Market and Macroeconomy.' *Economics Research International*, Article ID 961694, doi:10.1155/2012/961694, 6 pages.

APPENDIX

Table A1.1 Granger-causality between Taiwan and China variable equivalents, 1994–2007

Null hypothesis	F-statistic	Probability
T_Y does not Granger-cause C_Y	3.52	0.01
C_Y does not Granger-cause T_Y	20.02	0.01
T_CPI does not Granger-cause C_CPI	3.93	0.01
C_CPI does not Granger-cause T_CPI	6.10	0.01
T_WPI does not Granger-cause C_PPI	0.98	0.42
C_PPI does not Granger-cause T_WPI	0.83	0.51
T_M1A does not Granger-cause C_M1	11.58	0.01
C_M1 does not Granger-cause T_M1A	6.94	0.01
T_M1B does not Granger-cause C_M1	11.35	0.01
C_M1 does not Granger-cause T_M1B	8.65	0.01
T_M2 does not Granger-cause C_M2	3.27	0.02
C_M2 does not Granger-cause T_M2	5.37	0.01
T_IR does not Granger-cause C_IR	0.38	0.82
C_IR does not Granger-cause T_IR	0.17	0.95
T_S does not Granger-cause C_S	1.86	0.12
C_S does not Granger-cause T_S	1.15	0.33

Notes: All data series are in percentage change form to assure stationarity. Relationships significant at the 5 percent level or better are marked in bold.

2. A comparison between the CEPA and the ECFA

Yun-Wing Sung

2.1 INTRODUCTION

Since the inauguration of reforms and opening in China in 1979, economic integration has evolved rapidly among the four economies of the Chinese Economic Area (CEA), namely the Chinese Mainland, Taiwan, Hong Kong, and Macau. The CEA rapidly became a heavyweight in world trade and investment, and the dynamism of the CEA reshaped the East Asian regional economy as well as the world economy.

For brevity, the Chinese Mainland will be referred to as the Mainland or China. Hong Kong and Taiwan will be referred to as the duo, and the duo plus the Mainland will be referred to as the trio. In this chapter, the CEA is often taken to be the economies of the trio. Strictly speaking, the CEA should be the quad, as it also includes the economy of Macau. However, as Macau's economy is very small, it is often ignored in our discussion.

Hong Kong and Macau reverted to Chinese rule in 1997 and 1999, and Beijing has long insisted that Taiwan is part of China. However, the quad involves four separate customs territories, and trade and investment among the four take the form of external trade and investment. In economic literature, China's economy usually means the Mainland's economy instead of the trio or the quad. It is thus necessary to designate the economy of the trio or quad as the CEA.

Initially, trade and investment flows among the quad grew largely through market forces without the benefit of formal bilateral or multilateral agreements. However, the rapid economic integration of the CEA calls for more formal arrangements such as free trade agreements (FTAs).

The first FTA in the CEA to emerge was the Closer Economic Partnership Arrangement (CEPA) between the Mainland and Hong Kong signed in June 2003. Mainland's CEPA with Macau followed in October in the same year. The China–Taiwan FTA, named Cross-Strait Economic Cooperation Framework Agreement (ECFA), was signed in June 2010.

This paper focuses on the comparison of the Mainland–Hong Kong

CEPA and the Cross-Strait ECFA. As Macau's economy is very small, and Mainland's CEPA with Macao is largely modeled on that with Hong Kong, we will focus on comparison between the Mainland–Hong Kong CEPA, and the Cross-Strait ECFA.

For brevity, the Mainland–Hong Kong CEPA and the Cross-Strait ECFA will be referred to simply as CEPA and ECFA respectively. The CEPA and ECFA are important in many ways. The CEPA is a landmark because it is China's first FTA,[1] and also Hong Kong's first FTA. It is the world's first FTA between two customs territories in the same country, and also the first FTA in the CEA. It sets a precedent for the other two FTAs in the CEA, namely the Mainland–Macau CEPA and the ECFA. Economically, the CEPA reinforces Hong Kong's position as China's gateway, and was also an important factor in the recovery of the Hong Kong economy then suffering from the aftermath of the Asian Financial Crisis and the SARS (Severe Acute Respiratory Syndrome) epidemic.

The ECFA is an even more prominent landmark than the CEPA. It is the world's first FTA between two rival political regimes with deep-seated and prolonged sovereign disputes. It is the most important agreement between the two regimes since 1949, the year when the People's Republic of China was established and the Nationalist government moved to Taiwan. The ECFA would institutionalize and transform the legal framework governing Cross-Strait relations. It would also accelerate integration in East Asia through the domino effect. For instance, the ECFA is likely to divert part of China's imports from South Korea to Taiwan, and this would spur South Korea to negotiate an FTA with China.

This paper is organized as follows. After the introductory section, Section 2.2 will cover the predominantly market-driven economic integration of the CEA before the conclusion of the CEPA and ECFA. Section 2.3 covers the events leading to the CEPA and ECFA, while Section 2.4 compares the provisions and impacts of the two. Section 2.5 focuses on the impacts of the ECFA on Hong Kong's position as an intermediary in Cross-Strait trade, investment, and finance. Section 2.6 concludes.

2.2 ECONOMIC INTEGRATION OF THE CEA BEFORE THE CEPA AND ECFA

In the Cold War era, economic links in the CEA were heavily restricted. The duo and the Mainland were in opposite camps. Hong Kong, along with West Berlin, were regarded as frontier showcases of the 'free world,' as both cities attracted large numbers of refugees from Communist areas. Mainland–Hong Kong economic exchanges, while substantial, were highly asymmetric: Hong Kong was open to Mainland exports and investment, but flows in the opposite direction were mostly banned by the Mainland. In terms of institutional barriers to movements of goods, capital, and people, Hong Kong was more closely integrated with most areas of the 'free world' than with the Mainland (Sung, 2005, pp. 49–50).

However, the Mainland has always been more open to Hong Kong than to the rest of the world; for example, even in the Cold War era, Hong Kong people could visit their relatives in the Mainland without a visa because they were regarded as Chinese. The Mainland has been benign towards Hong Kong most of the time since the establishment of the People's Republic in 1949. This is partly a result of Hong Kong's traditional position as China's gateway to the outside world.

While Mainland–Hong Kong relations were sometimes tense as a result of Beijing's ideological campaigns, Mainland–Taiwan relations were openly hostile, and armed conflicts in the Taiwan Straits were not infrequent. Economic exchanges in the Cold War era were non-existent except for Taiwan purchases of Mainland's herbal medicine indirectly via Hong Kong, as many of these herbs cannot be grown elsewhere (Sung, 2005, p. 61).

With the end of the Cold War in East Asia, a series of policy changes in the trio allowed economic integration in the CEA to proceed rapidly. The most important of these policy changes was China's opening and reform starting in 1979. The unilateral liberalizations in the Mainland were gradually reciprocated by policy changes in Hong Kong and Taiwan, cumulating in the signing of the CEPA and ECFA in 2003 and 2010 respectively. It should be stressed that, long before the signing of the CEPA and ECFA, the CEA was already a very successful example of economic integration.

In the early days of the Mainland's open-door era, the duo were very influential in the Mainland's development due to their huge lead in the level of economic development. The Mainland tailored its opening towards the duo, and gave Guangdong and Fujian special policy packages that vastly increased their autonomy. Guangdong established the three SEZs (special economic zones) of Shenzhen, Zhuhai, and Shantou, which were geared towards Hong Kong and Macau, while Fujian established the Xiamen SEZ geared towards Taiwan.

With very rapid economic development, the Mainland has gained the upper hand in its relationship with the duo since the early 2000s. To stay competitive, the duo have to strengthen their niches, and avoid areas where the Mainland is strong. Unlike the early 1980s, when the Mainland tailored its opening towards the duo, the duo have to recognize the strength of the Mainland. Since the early 2000s, the duo adjusted their policies accordingly to capture business opportunities from the Mainland.

Hong Kong proposed an FTA with the Mainland in late 2001, and the CEPA was signed in June 2003. Taiwan also proposed to establish direct transportation with the Mainland in 2000. The proposal was delayed by political problems which were solved with the change in government in Taiwan when the pro-independence DPP (Democratic Progressive Party) was replaced by the Nationalist Party in 2008. Direct air and shipping links were established in 2008, and the ECFA was signed in 2010.

2.2.1 Mainland–Hong Kong Integration before the CEPA

With the opening of China in 1979, economic integration proceeded rapidly between the Mainland and Hong Kong. Hong Kong manufacturing took advantage of the low wages in the Mainland, relocating to Guangdong starting in the early 1980s, and the process was largely spontaneous and market-driven. The Hong Kong government changed its policy from one of minimal contact with the Mainland to facilitating the market-driven economic integration. Transportation links with the Mainland were rapidly expanded. Hong Kong also lifted its restriction on civil servants to travel to the Mainland in the early 1980s. In line with Hong Kong's tradition of minimal government intervention, government policies generally followed rather than led the market (Sung, 2005, pp. 48–9).

Hong Kong investment rapidly transformed Guangdong into a world factory, and the Hong Kong–Guangdong economic nexus quickly became a big player in the world market. In 1992, Guangdong's exports surpassed Thailand's (Sung et al., 1995, p. 221). Guangdong's inward FDI (foreign direct investment) also surpassed that of Thailand in the same year (ibid., p. 67).

Economic integration between Hong Kong and the Mainland is asymmetric, as Hong Kong's economy is very open whereas the Mainland's is relatively closed. Hong Kong is much more open to the Mainland than vice versa, though the discrepancy has narrowed significantly since the Mainland's opening. However, as mentioned above, the Mainland has always been more open to Hong Kong than to the rest of the world. The CEPA is another example of the preferential opening of the Mainland to Hong Kong.

2.2.2 Cross-Strait Economic Integration before the ECFA

With the economic reforms and opening in 1979, the Mainland called for improvements in economic relations with Taiwan. Taiwan's initial response was a reaffirmation of the old 'Three Noes policy' (no contact, no negotiations, and no compromise). However, Hong Kong's rapid integration with the Mainland was one of the factors that nudged Taiwan towards gradual liberalization of Cross-Strait relations. The Hong Kong–Guangdong economic nexus served as a successful example to Taiwanese businessmen. The competitive exports of Hong Kong firms based in Guangdong also cut into Taiwan's market shares in overseas markets.

Taiwan's landmark decision in November 1987 to lift the ban on visits to the Mainland led to rapid growth in Cross-Strait trade and investment. However, Taiwan's liberalization of Cross-Strait economic links was very gradual due to political and security concerns.[2] As mentioned above, Taiwan's bans on direct air and shipping links with the Mainland continued till the change in political leadership in Taiwan in 2008. Despite Taiwan's bans on direct links, economic integration has proceeded rapidly between the Mainland and Taiwan, largely utilizing the efficient intermediary services of Hong Kong.

By 1992, only five years after Taiwan's landmark decision to liberalize visits to the Mainland, Taiwan surpassed Japan and the USA to become the second-largest investor in the Mainland (after Hong Kong). The Mainland surpassed the US as the foremost destination of Taiwan's outward FDI in the mid 1990s, and surpassed the USA to become the largest market for Taiwan in the early 2000s (Sung, 2005, p. 149). As in Hong Kong's case, Taiwan's export-oriented manufacturing also relocated rapidly to the Mainland. Taiwan's exports to the Mainland soared, partly because Taiwanese firms supply their Mainland subsidiaries with parts and components for further processing.

Flows of Mainland goods, investments, and visitors to Taiwan have been much smaller than the reverse flows due to Taiwan's restrictions. As a result, Taiwan has a large surplus in commodity trade with the Mainland that is largely balanced by deficits in bilateral investments and tourists' expenditures.

Development of Cross-Strait relations is very interesting as the two governments still do not recognize each other officially. Before the implementation of the ECFA, Cross-Strait policy coordination had been quite informal. Instead of official negotiations, policy interactions have often been a series of unilateral moves undertaken in the anticipation of reciprocal moves by the other party. For instance, in early 1991, Taiwan declared that, while it would continue to shun official contacts with the Mainland, it would nevertheless gradually develop unofficial exchanges. Bilateral issues would be dealt with by the Straits Exchange Foundation (SEF), a semi-official body established by Taipei. In late 1991, Beijing responded by establishing the Association for Relations Across the Taiwan Strait (ARATS) for dialogue (Sung, 2005, p. 64). Since then, Cross-Strait issues, including the negotiation of the ECFA, have been handled by the 'semi-official' SEF–ARATS process. While the process is cumbersome, it has achieved remarkable results in terms of trade and investment flows across the Taiwan Strait. Under the new ECFA framework, negotiations may be more expeditious, as will be detailed later.

2.2.3 WTO Membership and Integration of the CEA

Hong Kong has been a member of the WTO since 1995, the date of the founding of the organization. China became a member of the WTO towards the end of 2001, while Taiwan became a member at the beginning of 2002. The entry of China and Taiwan into the WTO is important for CEA integration in three ways. First, China and Taiwan have to liberalize their economies further according to their protocols of accession. This has stimulated intra-CEA trade and investment. Second, the WTO provides an institutional framework for handling economic interactions and disputes. This is particularly important for the Mainland and Taiwan as the two governments do not officially recognize each other. Third, the WTO allows its members to conclude FTAs, which are exceptions to the MFN (Most Favored Nation) principle of the WTO. The MFN principle stipulates that any tariff concessions or benefit granted by a member to any other country must be extended to all members. An FTA violates the MFN principle because, in an FTA, tariff exemption is only granted to members of the FTA instead of all WTO members. In the WTO framework, an FTA is allowed if it requires tariffs eventually to be abolished (not just lowered) for 'substantially all trade' (not just for some products). Both the CEPA and the ECFA come under the WTO framework for FTAs.

It has often been noted that both the Mainland and Taiwan have frequently violated WTO standards in their economic relations with each other.[3] For instance, Taiwan bans the importation of a large number of agricultural and industrial products from the Mainland. Such bans are inconsistent with the MFN principle as they are not imposed on other WTO members. However, Beijing and Taipei have gradually improved their compliance with WTO standards in Cross-Strait relations. The ECFA is particularly beneficial in this regard, as will be detailed later.

2.3 EVENTS LEADING UP TO THE CEPA AND THE ECFA

As a result of the rapid economic integration of the CEA, a 'Greater China' FTA has been advocated since the early 1990s. However, FTAs in the CEA have been slow to emerge. Political animosity and mistrust in Cross-Strait relations is an obvious problem. The other problem is that it took China 15 years of hard bargaining to enter the WTO. Before WTO entry, any FTA negotiations involving China would pose complications to China's WTO entry. A concession given by China to anyone in a prospective FTA could be taken as a precedent in China's negotiation to enter the WTO.

2.3.1 Events Leading up to the CEPA

When Hong Kong reverted to Chinese rule in 1997, 'one country, two systems' was an untried design. Beijing tried to interfere as little as possible, and Hong Kong had to take the initiative to shape its relations with the Mainland. Elites in Hong Kong were then very concerned about the possible adverse impacts of deep integration with the Mainland on Hong Kong's autonomy (Sung, 2005, pp. 186–7). Progress in policy coordination with the Mainland was extremely slow, for example extending the hours of operation of a Hong Kong–Mainland passenger checkpoint (the Lok Ma Chau–Huanggang crossing) to 24 hours, a very small step in integration, took a long time to accomplish. It was implemented in January 2003, more than five years after Hong Kong's reversion (Sung, 2005, pp. 191–2).

However, Hong Kong was severely hit by the Asian Financial Crisis that started in 1997. Economic recovery in 2000 was cut short by the terrorist attack on the US on September 11, 2001. Elites in Hong Kong wished to speed up integration with the Mainland as a strategy of economic development. In December 2001, right after China's WTO membership was approved by the November 2001 Doha Ministerial Conference of the WTO, the Hong Kong government proposed to Beijing to conclude a Mainland–Hong Kong FTA. Negotiations were started right away, but progress was slow until late 2002. However, the deepening economic crisis in Hong Kong spurred Beijing to act decisively to shore up the Hong Kong economy. The CEPA was signed in June 2003 (Sung, 2005, p. 199).

2.3.2 Events Leading up to the ECFA

After China entered the WTO in 2001, it concluded a substantial number of FTAs with other economies, including an FTA with the ASEAN (Association of Southeast Asian Nations), which is a very important trading partner of both China and Taiwan. Taiwan is increasingly marginalized as it has failed to conclude FTAs with its major trading partners,[4] largely because of Beijing's opposition. Without the ECFA, Taiwan's exports to the Mainland would suffer heavily from competition from the

ASEAN. As South Korea and Japan are also interested to conclude a multilateral FTA with China, Taiwan has the incentive to act decisively to reverse its marginalization.

In Taiwan, Ma Ying-jeou of the Nationalist Party took office as president in March 2008, replacing the pro-independence DPP, and producing a rapid breakthrough in Cross-Strait relations. The SEF–ARATS process resumed after 11 years' suspension. Two rounds of talks were held in June and November 2008, instituting direct Cross-Straits charter flights and direct shipping. The third and fourth rounds of talks were held in April and December of 2009, leading to agreements in financial and investment cooperation, customs inspection, and food safety. Negotiation on the ECFA took less than a year, and the ECFA was signed on June 29, 2010 (Hsieh, 2011, pp. 136–8). The Mainland was also motivated to make concessions as the ECFA would link Taiwan more closely to the Mainland, diluting the strong pro-independence sentiment in Taiwan.

2.4 PROVISIONS AND IMPACTS OF THE CEPA AND THE ECFA

The CEPA, when it was signed in mid 2003, was already a full FTA as it had abolished tariffs for 'substantially all trade' between the Mainland and Hong Kong. The CEPA also allowed for further developments and liberalizations. From 2003 to 2011, eight supplements were added, one each year.

In comparison with the CEPA, the ECFA is more tentative, as it is a 'framework agreement' or a roadmap to a comprehensive FTA down the road. Under the WTO, a framework agreement is an interim agreement leading to a full FTA (Hsieh, 2001, p. 140). The Early Harvest Program (EHP) of the ECFA would eliminate tariffs for selected products over 3 years, starting January 1, 2011. Though the EHP of the ECFA does not substantially cover all trade, it is still significant as it covers 15 percent of Cross-Strait trade. In comparison, the EHP of the China–ASEAN FTA covers only 1.8 percent of bilateral trade (Hsieh, 2011, p. 143). Moreover the EHP of the ECFA is the world's only EHP that covers liberalization of services (Hsieh, 2011, p. 143).

Due to political uncertainties and mistrusts across the Taiwan Strait, a step-by-step roadmap such as the ECFA is more suitable than a full FTA. Unlike the CEPA, a full Cross-Strait FTA would arouse a lot of opposition from domestic industries on both sides of the Taiwan Strait. The CEPA would not hurt domestic manufacturing in Hong Kong because Hong Kong has always been a free port. The CEPA poses very little harm to Mainland industries as Hong Kong is mostly service-oriented and its manufacturing is very small. While there is very little competition in manufacturing between the Mainland and Hong Kong, there is much more competition in manufacturing across the Strait. The ECFA, which is a gradual approach to a full FTA, allows domestic industries the time to adjust.

As expected, the CEPA and the ECFA are different in their statements on sovereignty issues. The CEPA explicitly recognizes 'one country, two systems' as a pre-condition, while the ECFA appeals to 'the principles of equality, reciprocity, and progressiveness' in the first sentence of its preamble.[5] On purpose, the term 'arrangement' instead of 'agreement' is used to name the CEPA, in order to avoid giving the impression that it has the status of an international agreement; while the term 'agreement' is used in the cross-strait case. In fact, the initial name of the proposed Cross-Strait agreement was 'Comprehensive Economic Cooperation Agreement' (CECA). As this acronym is too close to the CEPA, Taiwan insisted that the name be changed to the ECFA.

2.4.1 Provisions of the CEPA[6]

The CEPA was signed on June 29, 2003 and took effect on January 1, 2004. The scope of the CEPA has expanded every year with an additional supplement. To date, there have been eight supplements (usually named CEPA-1, 2, 3, etc.), with the last one signed by the end of 2011. The CEPA covers three broad areas, namely trade in goods, trade in services, and Trade and Investment Facilitation.

The CEPA involves two economies that are very asymmetric in size, in openness, and in level of development. The Hong Kong economy is small, highly developed, and very open, while the Mainland is large, less developed, and relatively closed. The benefits of the CEPA for Hong Kong are obvious as it involves the preferential opening of the vast Mainland market to Hong Kong. There are few gains for the Mainland in terms of market access as the Hong Kong market is small and already very open. However, as Hong Kong is by far the foremost investor in the Mainland, the Mainland is likely to gain from an increase in investment from Hong Kong through Investment and Trade Facilitation. Moreover, by opening its highly protected services sector selectively to Hong Kong ahead of WTO commitments, the Mainland may help its service industries to adapt and adjust to face the rigours of world competition. Lastly, the Mainland–Hong Kong CEPA symbolizes the union of Hong Kong to its motherland. The market access given to Hong Kong has considerable attraction for Taiwan. The CEPA would help to tilt opinion in Taiwan towards a Cross-Strait FTA.

2.4.1.1 Trade in goods

The CEPA initially granted zero tariffs to Hong Kong manufactures in 273 product categories, later expanded to over 1600 items. The 273 product categories already covered the main manufacturing industries of Hong Kong, namely: electrical and electronic products, textiles and clothing, plastic articles, watches and clocks, jewellery, and metal products.

As production costs are high in Hong Kong and Hong Kong manufacturing has declined for 2 decades, the CEPA was not expected to bring a massive revival of Hong Kong manufacturing. However, Hong Kong has better protection of intellectual property rights than the Mainland and the CEPA would benefit high value-added manufacturing, especially industries in which intellectual property rights protection is crucial. It would help Hong Kong to develop brand products targeting Mainland's middle class consumer market (Sung, 2005, p. 200).

2.4.1.2 Trade in services

The CEPA gave preferential access to Hong Kong companies in 18 service sectors initially, expanding to 47 sectors by the end of 2011. It also provides opportunities for Hong Kong professionals and residents to establish business or work on the Mainland. The detailed list of sectors and the preferential access in each can be found on the homepage of the Trade and Industry Department of Hong Kong. The 47 sectors cover the main service sectors of Hong Kong, namely: financial services, transportation and trade, tourism, and business and professional services (Table 2.1).

The preferential access takes one or more of the following forms (Sung, 2005, p. 201):

1. *Lower market access requirements*. The high entry thresholds set under China's WTO commitments are reduced for Hong Kong firms. For instance, the asset requirements of banks are greatly reduced; the annual sales and asset values of retailers are lowered; and the trading and capital requirements of import and export trade are also lowered. As service providers in Hong Kong tend to be small in size, the lowering of market access requirements allows many more Hong Kong companies to enter the Mainland market.
2. *Broader business scope*. The geographic restrictions set under China's WTO commitments are relaxed for Hong Kong firms under CEPA. For instance, in retail trade, only major cities (mostly provincial capitals) are open to foreign companies, while the CEPA permits Hong Kong companies to operate in all cities at the prefectural level, and all

Table 2.1 List of 47 sectors in China liberalized under the CEPA (end of 2011)

Service Sectors		
Accounting	Legal	Research and development
Advertising	Library, museum, and other cultural services	Road transport
Air transport	Logistics	Securities and futures
Audiovisual	Management consulting	Services incidental to manufacturing
Banking	Maritime transport	Services incidental to mining
Building cleaning	Market research	Services related to management consulting
Computer and related services	Medical	Social services
Construction and related engineering	Patent agency	Specialty design
Convention and exhibition	Photographic	Sporting
Cultural	Placement and supply services of personnel	Storage and warehousing
Distribution	Printing	Technical testing, analysis, and product testing
Environmental	Public utility	Telecommunications
Freight forwarding agency	Rail transport	Tourism
Individually-owned stores	Real estate	Trademark agency
Insurance	Related scientific and technical consulting services	Translation and interpretation
Interdisciplinary research and experimental development services		
Examinations for professional and technical qualification		

Source: Homepage of Trade and Industry Department, Hong Kong government.

cities at the county level in Guangdong province. In tourism, the geographic restrictions on foreign companies are lifted for Hong Kong companies.

3. *More corporate autonomy.* Hong Kong companies can establish wholly-owned ventures while other foreign companies are restricted to joint ventures in Convention and Exhibition, and in Real Estate services (architecture, engineering, survey).

There are many other significant concessions that cannot be captured by the above categorization. For example, imported films are restricted to 20 foreign films per year on a revenue-sharing basis, but Hong Kong-produced Chinese language films are free from the import quota. The requirements for co-production of films have also been relaxed significantly for Hong Kong.

Besides Hong Kong companies, Hong Kong professionals and residents will also benefit from CEPA. For instance, Hong Kong professionals in the securities and insurance industries can apply to practice on the Mainland, and Hong Kong permanent residents are permitted to sit the Mainland's legal qualifying examination (Hong Kong Trade Development Council, 2003, p. iv).

The CEPA has several provisions that aim to strengthen Hong Kong's cooperation with Guangdong. For instance, Hong Kong lawyers' residency requirements for operating in Guangzhou and Shenzhen are waived. Qualified Hong Kong retailers are allowed to set up operations in all cities at the county level in Guangdong, while Hong Kong residents are allowed to set up individually-owned retail stores in Guangdong.

2.4.2 Impact of the CEPA on the Hong Kong Economy

The benefits of zero tariffs for Hong Kong goods are small because Hong Kong manufacturing is small. The benefits would be larger in services as Hong Kong is a premier service hub in China's trade. According to the estimates of the Hong Kong government, CEPA-induced service receipts grew rapidly from HK \$1.5 billion in 2004 to HK \$14.7 billion in 2009, and the number of jobs created rose from 1415 in 2004 to 4425 in 2009.[7] However, such benefits are not large relative to the size of the Hong Kong economy. In 2009, CEPA-induced service receipts and employment were 0.9 percent of GDP and 0.3 percent of total employment.

It must be stressed that service liberalization is mostly a lengthy process. Though the CEPA has, in principle, opened many of the Mainland's service sectors, there are still many barriers in these sectors. The main channel to export services is for Hong Kong firms to set up shop in the Mainland. Setting up subsidiaries in the Mainland in sectors already opened under the CEPA still requires a number of permits or licenses from various departments of provincial or local authorities. Obtaining such licenses can be difficult and time-consuming.

In the long run, with substantial service liberalization in the Mainland, the benefits for Hong Kong in service receipts can be large. The CEPA strengthens Hong Kong's role as an international financial center, trading center, and service hub. The Mainland's financial liberalization will turn

Hong Kong into an offshore center for *Renminbi* business, which is of crucial importance to the position of Hong Kong as an international financial center. The 'Financial Services Cooperation' provisions in the CEPA also encourage Mainland banks to relocate their international treasury and foreign exchange trading centers to Hong Kong and to develop networks in Hong Kong through acquisition (Hong Kong Trade Development Council, 2003, p. 29). The CEPA also includes a clause that encourages more Mainland companies to seek listing in Hong Kong. The CEPA will strengthen the Hong Kong–PRD (Pearl River Delta) nexus, enabling the industrial powerhouse of the PRD to utilize the sophisticated supporting services of Hong Kong in logistics, distribution, financial services, and business services. In a nutshell, the CEPA will strengthen Hong Kong's position as the premier service hub of China.

It should be noted that the above estimates of CEPA-induced service receipts refer to business receipts from Hong Kong service suppliers on the Mainland. The very substantial expenditure of Mainland visitors in Hong Kong under the Individual Visit Scheme (IVS), which is also part of the CEPA, is estimated separately. Starting in July 2003, the IVS has allowed Mainland tourists to visit Hong Kong on an individual basis rather than joining group tours. In 2010, total visitors arriving in Hong Kong exceeded 36 million, of which 22.7 million were visitors from the Mainland. Of the visitors from the Mainland, 14.2 million visited Hong Kong under the IVS. This was nearly 40 percent of the 36 million total visitor arrivals in Hong Kong.

As the increase in visitors under IVS is partly at the expense of group tours, the Hong Kong government estimated the 'incremental IVS visitor arrivals' – that is, the additional number of visitors brought to Hong Kong by the IVS. In 2009, incremental IVS visitor arrivals were 6.07 million, bringing incremental value added of HK $16.1 billion (1 percent of GDP), and additional employment of 50 281 (1.4 percent of total employment).[8]

It is difficult to estimate the amount of CEPA-induced investment as the CEPA is only one of the many factors affecting the investment environment. However, there are many signs indicating that CEPA-induced investment is significant. The rapid conclusion of the CEPA signifies that China's new leadership gives a high priority to Hong Kong, and this is one of the main factors that reversed investor sentiment towards Hong Kong in late 2003. The CEPA has attracted foreign investment in both manufacturing and services. For manufacturing, the CEPA rules of origin are quite liberal, following mostly existing rules of origin used in Hong Kong. For products in which a value-added criterion is used, no more than 30 percent of the value added are required to be generated in Hong Kong. For services, the definition of a Hong Kong service company is quite liberal. The company must be registered in Hong Kong and have operated substantively in Hong Kong for the past 3 to 5 years. It must be liable to pay Hong Kong profit tax and must employ at least 50 percent of its staff locally. Foreign investors can easily acquire control of local companies to fulfil the above definition. Foreign banks have acquired a number of small and medium-size local Hong Kong banks as their asset requirements to enter the Mainland market are lower than foreign banks – for example, Taiwan's Fubon Bank acquired a small Hong Kong bank in 2003 to enter the Mainland market, leading to a quadrupling of Taiwan's approved investment in Hong Kong in that year (Sung, 2005, p. 203). Ultimately, the amount of investment attracted will be dependent on the export opportunities that the CEPA can generate.

There is a fear that the CEPA will increase the flow of Hong Kong entrepreneurs and professionals to the Mainland, leading to further hollowing-out in Hong Kong. However, increased flows of Hong Kong entrepreneurs and professionals northward will enlarge Hong Kong's business network on the Mainland, which is a great asset for Hong Kong as it strengthens its position as the foremost hub of China's commerce. Moreover, the CEPA will also increase the flow of Mainland skills southward. Ultimately, Hong Kong must maintain its lead in skills and service quality in order to retain its position as the premier service hub of China. Otherwise, the CEPA will only lead to the hollowing-out of Hong Kong services.

2.4.3 Impact of the CEPA on the Mainland Economy

As the Mainland economy is much bigger than that of Hong Kong, it is difficult to ascertain the impact of the CEPA on the Mainland. From Mainland statistics, the CEPA appears to have contributed to the very sharp increase of Hong Kong's FDI in China. As mentioned above, Hong Kong has consistently been the largest investor in China. From 1979–92, Hong Kong accounted for over 60 percent of China's inward FDI (Sung, 2005, p. 28). As the investment environment in China matured, China has been able to attract more FDI from beyond Hong Kong, and the share of Hong Kong in China's inward FDI declined sharply from 68 percent in 1992 to 29 percent in 2006. The decline was exaggerated as an increasing amount of Hong Kong's (and also Taiwan's) investment to China was channeled via the tax haven economies of the British Virgin Islands, the Cayman Islands, Samoa, Mauritius, and Barbados from 1993 to 2007.[9] Such flows were classified as investment from the tax haven economies in China's statistics of inward FDI.

Despite this statistical problem, there is evidently a dramatic rebound in Hong Kong's share of China's inward FDI in recent years. Since 2009, China has tried to trace the source of its inward FDI via the tax haven economies. According to China's statistics, Hong Kong accounted for well over half of China's inward FDI in 2011: including (excluding) Hong Kong's investment via the tax haven economies, Hong Kong's 2011 share was 64 percent (53 percent). The sharp rebound of Hong Kong's share in China's inward FDI seems to be related to the Mainland's efforts to raise capital on the Hong Kong stock exchange. The CEPA is likely to play a role here as the CEPA has improved market access to the Mainland for Hong Kong companies. Moreover, Trade and Investment Facilitation is an important part of the CEPA.

2.4.4 Provisions of the ECFA

The ECFA was signed by the SEF and ARATS on June 29, 2010 along with a Cross-Straits IPR (Intellectual Property Protection) Agreement. Both agreements took effect in September 2010. Tariff reduction of the EHP was effective from January 1, 2011. The ECFA also mandated further negotiations within six months of the effective date of the ECFA on four agreements to govern trade in goods, trade in services, investment agreement, and a dispute settlement mechanism (Hsieh, 2011, p. 138).

The ECFA established a 'Cross-Straits Economic Cooperation Committee' (CSEC Committee) to handle negotiations of the above four agreements. As Hsieh (2011, p. 142) has pointed out, the Committee, which comprises senior officials from both sides, 'will be the first "joint" organization in cross-straits relations.' Hopefully, this 'joint' Committee will work more expeditiously than the SEF–ARATS process. It may also provide a precedent in other areas of Cross-Strait relations.

As mentioned above, the EHP of the ECFA is very substantial. It is also highly asymmetric as concessions by China were nearly five times those of Taiwan in trade value. Table 2.2 summarizes the concessions of Taiwan vs the Mainland. The Mainland would abolish tariffs on 539 items with import values of US \$138.8 million or 16.1 percent of the Mainland's imports from Taiwan, while Taiwan would abolish tariffs on 267 items with import values of US \$28.6 million or 10.5 percent of Taiwan's imports from the Mainland (Hsieh, 2011, p. 143). The asymmetry in agricultural products is worth noting: 'While China agreed to accord preferential tariffs to 18 Taiwanese agricultural products, Taiwan will continue its MFN-inconsistent ban on the importation of 830 Chinese agricultural products and will not lower tariffs on 1415 such products' (Hsieh, 2011, p. 143).

Table 2.2 ECFA: early harvest concessions in trade

Sector	Concessions by China		Concessions by Taiwan	
	Items	Trade value	Items	Trade value
Petrochemical	88	59.44	42	3.29
Textile	136	15.88	22	1.16
Machineries	107	11.43	69	4.74
Transportations	50	1.48	17	4.09
Others	140	49.97	117	15.3
Agriculture	18	0.16	–	–
Total	539	138.38	267	28.58

Note: Units are US $10 million.

Source: Hsu, 2011.

Table 2.3 ECFA: early harvest commitments in services

	China's commitments	Taiwan's commitments
Business services	1. Accounting, auditing, and book-keeping	1. Research and development
	2. Software implementation and data processing	2. Convention
	3. Research and development	3. Exhibition
	4. Convention	4. Special design
	5. Special design	5. Motion picture
	6. Audiovisual services	6. Commission agent's services
	7. Hospital	7. Sporting and other recreational services
	8. Aircraft repair and maintenance	8. Computer reservation systems
Financial sector	1. Banking and other financial services	Banking and other financial services
	2. Insurance and related services	
	3. Securities, futures, and other related services	

Source: Hsu, 2011.

Liberalization of services in the EHP is more limited than that in goods. The sectors involved are shown in Table 2.3. Liberalization in the banking sector is significant. Mainland banks will be able to establish branches in Taiwan and conduct New Taiwan Dollar business, while Taiwanese banks will be allowed to set up branches and conduct RMB business on the Mainland (Hsieh, 2011, pp. 144–5).

2.4.5 Impacts of the ECFA

Before the signing of the ECFA, think tanks in Taiwan and the Mainland have studied the benefits of the ECFA. Taiwan's Chung-Hua Institution for Economic Research estimated that the ECFA would increase Taiwan's GDP by 1.65 percent to 1.72 percent, while the Mainland's Chinese Academy of International Trade and Economic Cooperation estimated that the Mainland's GDP would increase by 0.63 percent (Hsieh, 2011, p. 137).

The ECFA has eased Taiwan's efforts to conclude FTAs with other economies. Though Beijing had blocked Taipei's efforts to negotiate FTAs with other partners in the past, Beijing gave the green light to Taiwan's efforts after the conclusion of the ECFA. Singapore announced that it wanted to negotiate a bilateral FTA with Taiwan in August 2010 (Hsieh, 2011, p. 137). Taiwan and New Zealand announced in October 2011 that they wished to investigate the feasibility of a bilateral FTA.[10]

The EHP has been implemented for a year or so, and it is difficult to disentangle the economic effects of the EHP from other factors. However, the effect of the EHP on Cross-Strait trade has been quite evident in Taiwan's exports of agricultural products to the Mainland. In the first 7 months of 2011, exports of Taiwan agricultural products grew 33 percent, while the exports of the EHP items grew 262 percent.[11] It should be noted that other factors such as the opening of Cross-Strait direct flights and shipping probably also contribute to this stellar export performance.

Though the ECFA did appear to stimulate Taiwan's agricultural exports to the Mainland, it did not appear to have much effect on overall Cross-Strait trade and investment. In 2011, the Mainland's imports grew by 25 percent, but its imports from Taiwan only grew by 8 percent. In the same year, the Mainland's exports grew by 20 percent, but its exports to Taiwan only grew by 18 percent. As for investment, the Mainland's inward FDI grew by 10 percent, but its FDI from Taiwan (including investment via the tax haven economies) only grew by 0.4 percent. In a nutshell, Taiwan's shares of the Mainland's trade and inward FDI declined in 2011.

The impact of the ECFA is a hotly debated issue in Taiwan. As the ECFA has only been implemented for a year, and the EHP only initially accounted for 15 percent of Cross-Strait trade, it is too early to conclude that the ECFA is of little benefit for Taiwan. With the implementation of the China–ASEAN FTA in 2010, it can be argued that Cross-Strait trade and investment would be much lower were it not for the ECFA.

One bright spot in the Taiwanese economy in 2011 was the growth of inward FDI. In the first 11 months of 2011, Taiwan's approved inward FDI was US $4.5 billion, 35 percent higher than during the same period in 2010. As global economic growth slowed from 5.2 percent in 2010 to 3.8 percent in 2011 as a result of the European debt crisis (International Monetary Fund, 2012), the rise in FDI in Taiwan was significant. It should be noted that very few foreign companies issued Taiwan Depository Receipts (TDR) in Taiwan until the end of 2009, despite the fact that this has been allowed since 1999. With improvement in Cross-Strait relations, some 13 foreign companies announced their intent to be listed on the Taipei stock market through the issue of TDRs (Siew, 2010).

As the EHP of the ECFA was only implemented at the beginning of 2011, it might be argued that it happened too late to affect FDI in the same year. However, the negotiation and conclusion of the ECFA was known well in advance, and this expectation might have shifted investment sentiments towards Taiwan. It must be stressed that the ECFA was but part of the many breakthroughs that occurred in Cross-Strait relations since the Nationalist Party took office in March 2008. It is certainly likely that the improvements in Cross-Strait relations have significant effects on investor sentiments, but it is very difficult to disentangle the effects of ECFA from other breakthroughs.

2.4.6 Comparing the CEPA and the ECFA

Both the CEPA and the ECFA are asymmetric: the Mainland is large and the duo are small. In both cases, the Mainland has made many more concessions than the duo. In both cases, national reunification has been the prime motivation for the Mainland to make concessions.

While the CEPA is a full FTA and the ECFA is in the nature of an interim agreement to a full FTA, the ECFA is more far-reaching in some ways. The issue of removal of technical trade barriers is addressed in the ECFA but not in the CEPA. Technical barriers are important in Cross-Strait trade since a substantial share of the trade involves electrical and electronic equipment such as computers and mobile phones. Likewise, the issue of investment protection is addressed in the ECFA but not in the CEPA.

The DSM (Dispute Settlement Mechanism) of the ECFA, which is being negotiated, may be more substantive than that of the CEPA. The DSM under the CEPA is very informal. The CEPA provides for a Joint Steering Committee comprising senior representatives of the two sides (article

19.1). The two sides will resolve problems 'through consultation in the spirit of friendship and cooperation,' and 'The Steering Committee shall make its decisions by consensus' (article 19.5).[12] The dispute provisions of Cross-Strait agreements before the ECFA were likewise informal. China and Taiwan concluded 22 agreements from 1990 to 2010, and dispute settlement was only mentioned in 13 of them. As Hsieh (2011, p. 152) noted, these agreements merely stated that disputes 'shall be resolved by prompt negotiation'. There were no enforcement procedures.

While the DSM of the ECFA has not yet been concluded, Taiwan is in a stronger position than Hong Kong to negotiate a more formal DSM with the Mainland. Hopefully, the DSM of the ECFA will contain enforcement procedures and would put Cross-Strait exchanges on a firm footing.

2.4.6.1 The CEPA, the ECFA, and the WTO

To enhance the transparency of RTAs (Regional Trading Agreements), the WTO established a Transparency Mechanism in late 2006. The Mechanism mandates 'early announcement' (informing the WTO of newly-signed RTAs or RTAs under negotiation), and 'notification' (formally submitting details of the agreement to the WTO). Notification should occur before the implementation of preferential treatment. The RTA will be examined by WTO committees and also members of the WTO after notification.[13]

The CEPA was signed in June 2003 and was notified to the WTO promptly by the end of 2003. As for the ECFA, Taiwan and the Mainland provided the WTO with information on the ECFA in line with the 'early announcement' procedure on May 6, 2011, eight months after the ECFA took effect (*Taipei Times*, May 7, 2011). However, the ECFA is not yet notified to the WTO even though preferential treatment began in January 2011 with the EHP.

There are speculations that the ECFA is WTO-incompatible, and this accounts for the delay in notification. While it is true that the ECFA is an interim agreement rather than a full FTA, the WTO does allow interim agreements. While the ECFA does not specify a deadline for transition to a full FTA, there are quite a few FTAs with lengthy transitions of 12 years, or even 20 years as in the Korea–US FTA (Hsieh 2011: 149). While Taiwan's bans on importation of agricultural products from the Mainland certainly violate the MFN principle, agricultural products only constitute a small portion of cross-strait trade. Moreover it can be argued that such bans are temporary arrangements to be phased out in transition to a full FTA. With the specification of long term goals, the ECFA can be WTO compatible (Hsieh, 2011, pp. 148–51).

With notification, the ECFA will periodically come under the trade policy review of the WTO. This may spell trouble for Taiwan's farmers as the WTO may find Taiwan's bans on Mainland agricultural products objectionable. However, it is in the long-term interest of Taiwan to place Cross-Strait economic relations firmly within the WTO framework.

Notification to the WTO is a politically sensitive issue in Taiwan as the WTO is regarded as an international arena that would bolster Taiwan's status. There were worries in Taiwan that Beijing would obstruct WTO notification as Beijing might regard the ECFA as an internal Chinese matter. This worry may not be valid as the CEPA, which was signed under the 'one country, two systems' framework, was nevertheless notified to the WTO. However, it is noteworthy that the ECFA is conspicuously missing in the list of FTAs shown on the homepage of the Ministry of Commerce of China.[14] The homepage lists the CEPA, other FTAs involving China, and also FTAs that are 'under negotiation' and 'under consideration.' The ECFA is omitted even though it is already signed and implemented. The reason that Beijing omits the ECFA from China's list of FTAs is not clear.

2.5 THE IMPACT OF THE ECFA AND THE OPENING OF CROSS-STRAIT DIRECT LINKS ON HONG KONG

With the rapid thaw in Cross-Strait relations under Ma Ying-jeou, there has been a warming-up of relations between Hong Kong and Taiwan. Before 2008, Hong Kong and Taiwan had avoided official contact. Taiwan was represented in Hong Kong under the semi-offical Chung Hwa Travel Agency. Hong Kong did not even have a semi-official office in Taipei.

Since 2008, Hong Kong has dropped its no-official-contact policy with Taiwan. Senior Taiwanese officials were welcome in Hong Kong, and Hong Kong officials also visited Taiwan (Chu, 2010, p. 5). The Hong Kong Trade Development Council and the Hong Kong Tourism Board opened branch offices in Taiwan in 2010 and 2011 respectively. In April 2010, the Hong Kong–Taiwan Economic and Cultural Co-operation and Promotion Council (ECCPC) was established to represent Hong Kong in talks with its counterpart, the Taiwan–Hong Kong Economic and Cultural Co-operation Council (ECCC). The two Councils involve senior ministers. They are incorporated as legal entities but are empowered by the two governments to conclude pacts. This is similar to the SEF–ARATS arrangement.

There have been concerns about the impact of ECFA and Cross-Strait direct links on Hong Kong as an intermediary in Cross-Strait business. However, market reactions in Hong Kong to the improvement of

Cross-Strait relations were quite positive. With the opening of direct flights and shipping, Cross-Strait passenger numbers and trade in transit via Hong Kong are expected to fall, but Hong Kong is expected to gain by providing financial and businesses services to the rapid increase in Cross-Strait business.

Sung (2005, pp. 184–6) has estimated Hong Kong's direct losses in shipping and air passenger traffic from full-scale Cross-Strait direct links. Shipping and air passenger losses would amount to 0.74 percent and 0.12 percent of Hong Kong's GDP respectively. The combined loss would be 0.86 percent of Hong Kong's GDP, which is not insignificant, but not disastrous. While the volume of Cross-Strait transit trade via Hong Kong is quite large, the trade margin of transit trade is small. As for Cross-Strait transit passengers via Hong Kong, they only stay in Hong Kong for a short while to board a connecting flight. Their expenditure in Hong Kong is small. Cathay Pacific, the carrier based in Hong Kong, would lose airline revenue. This loss is small relative to GDP, but is substantial for Cathay Pacific.

Thus far, the losses from transit trade and transit passengers appear to be much less than the above estimates. Despite the opening of direct shipping since 2008, Cross-Strait trade re-exported via Hong Kong grew by 45 percent from 2009 to 2011, reaching a record US $30.5 billion in 2011. Hong Kong's highly efficient financial and trade-related services have contributed to the continual growth of Cross-Strait trade re-exported via Hong Kong.

Direct flights did have a substantial effect on Taiwanese travelling to Hong Kong. According to Taiwan's statistics, the number of Taiwanese travelling to Hong Kong declined from a peak of 3.0 million in 2007 to 2.9 million in 2008, and declined further to 2.2 million in 2011,[15] though Hong Kong remains an important tourist destination for Taiwan. It should be noted that the opening of Taiwan to Mainland tourists would benefit Hong Kong as the prosperous Pearl River Delta is an important source of tourists for Taiwan, and many of these tourists would visit Taiwan via Hong Kong. While direct Cross-Strait flights did have an adverse effect on Cathy Pacific, the airline has remained very profitable.

The liberalization of services in the ECFA would strengthen Taipei as a service hub or Regional Operation Center. Hong Kong service-providers would face more competition in Cross-Strait business. As there has been significant liberalization of the financial sector in the EHP of the ECFA, Hong Kong banks would face competition from Taiwan/Mainland banks in financing Cross-Strait business. Hong Kong may also face competition in other service sectors liberalized in the ECFA, for example conference and exhibition services, and accounting services.

The Hong Kong stock exchange is the prime market for the listing of Taiwan's mainland-based companies. With the financial sector liberalization under the ECFA, Taipei has tried to persuade these companies to launch their IPOs (Initial Public Offerings) on the Taiwan Stock Exchange (Chu, 2010, p. 3). However, these companies continue to prefer to be listed in Hong Kong. Hong Kong's position is very secure as the liquidity, infrastructure, and regulatory environment of the Hong Kong Stock Exchange are unsurpassed in Asia. Hong Kong was the world's number one stock exchange for IPOs in both 2009 and 2010. Hong Kong is also Asia's largest management center for venture capital.

The ECFA has created a level playing field in Cross-Strait business for companies of the trio. Hong Kong's companies would no longer be favored by artificial barriers of the pre-ECFA era. However, given the lead of Hong Kong as a service hub in finance, logistics, and business and professional services, Hong Kong should fare well in open competition. Hong Kong's tourism continues to boom, and the total number of visitor arrivals broke the record of 30 million in 2010. Moreover, the number of Taiwanese enterprises investing in Hong Kong has grown from 3000 in 2002 to around 5000 in 2009 (Choi, 2010, p. 5).

2.6 CONCLUSION

Since the signing of the ECFA, there has been speculation in Hong Kong about a Taiwan–Hong Kong FTA that may eventually lead to a pan-CEA FTA. As mentioned above, discussion of a 'Greater China' FTA has been popular since the 1990s. However, in terms of market access, Taiwan does not have a strong incentive to conclude an FTA with Hong Kong. The Hong Kong economy is small and already very open. Unlike Singapore (which is also small), Hong Kong is not a sovereign nation. A Taiwan–Singapore FTA will strengthen the international status of Taiwan. A Taiwan–Hong Kong FTA is likely to be politically sensitive in Taiwan as the Hong Kong government is only a local government. The FTA may be perceived as diminishing Taiwan's international status. Given the extreme political sensitivity in Taiwan on such issues, an FTA with Hong Kong is unlikely. A pan-CEA FTA is thus also unlikely.

The CEPA and the ECFA are part of the Mainland's network of China-centric FTAs that include the ASEAN Plus One (ASEAN plus China) FTA, the prospective ASEAN Plus Three (China, Japan, and South Korea) FTA, and the proposed ASEAN Plus Six (the Three plus India, Australia, and New Zealand) FTA. China also has a number of bilateral

FTAs with countries in Asia, Europe, and Latin America. China's FTA network is part of China's strategy to highlight China's commitments of its partners in order to promote a multi-polar world that would constrain the power of the US (Bergsten, 2008, p. 16).

After the signing of the CEPA and the ECFA, China has given the green light to Hong Kong and Taiwan to conclude FTAs with other countries. Hong Kong signed an FTA with New Zealand in March 2010, and signed another FTA in June 2011 with the EFTA (European Free Trade Association) comprising Iceland, Liechtenstein, Norway, and Switzerland. Hong Kong and Chile also conducted a joint study of the feasibility of an FTA in 2009, and negotiation is likely to start in 2012. As mentioned above, Taiwan is negotiating an FTA with Singapore, and is conducting a joint study with New Zealand on the feasibility of an FTA.

Besides FTAs involving Hong Kong or Taiwan, the CEPA and the ECFA also give an impetus to competitors of Hong Kong and Taiwan to conclude FTAs with China. As mentioned above, South Korea is likely to hasten its FTA negotiations with the Mainland for fear of losing its share of the Mainland market to Taiwan. This will strengthen the network of China-centric FTAs. While the CEPA and the ECFA are part of the network of FTAs in East Asia, they have also stimulated FTA formation in the region.

The US promotion of TPP (Trans-Pacific Partnership), and the US policy of re-engagement in East Asia starting in 2010 introduced a new dynamism into FTA formation in the Asia-Pacific region. The TPP was first formed in 2005. It was originally an FTA of four small nations in the Asian Pacific, namely, Brunei, Chile, New Zealand, and Singapore. The US entered the TPP negotiations in 2008, using the TPP as a platform to build a trans-Pacific FTA to counterbalance China's network of East Asian FTAs. The US entry to TPP negotiations was followed by Australia, Peru, Vietnam, and Malaysia, and the TPP expanded to nine nations in 2010. While the TPP is in principle open to any nation on the Pacific Rim, it would be difficult for China to join due to the high standards of the agreement.

Japan announced that it would join TPP negotiations in the Asian Pacific Economic Community (APEC) leaders' meeting in November 2011. A few days later, at the East Asian Summit, China, Japan, and South Korea agreed to speed up work on a Trilateral FTA of the three nations.[16] In May 2012, the three agreed to start negotiations on the Trilateral FTA within the same year (*Wall Street Journal*, May 13, 2012). Discussion on the Trilateral FTA has taken a long time, but rivalry between China and Japan has prevented progress. The dynamic introduced by the TPP has broken the ice as China is worried about the rapid progress of the US-backed TPP. Japan may end up joining both the US-backed TPP and the China-backed Trilateral FTA.

Taiwan is presently not involved in the negotiations of the TPP, but Taiwan has expressed preliminary interest in the TPP.[17] Singapore and New Zealand are founding members of the TPP, and they are considering bilateral FTAs with Taiwan. Participation of Taiwan in the US-backed TPP will be a sensitive issue in Cross-Strait relations, and China's reaction to Taiwan's possible participation in the TPP is not yet known. In any case, the TPP dynamic has accelerated FTA formation in East Asia.

Both the CEPA and the ECFA have been landmark FTAs. The CEPA is clearly a predecessor of the ECFA, and also provides an impetus for Taiwan to conclude the ECFA. Unlike the CEPA, which is a full FTA, the ECFA is more of an interim agreement with the goal of an eventual FTA. However, the ECFA has gone beyond the CEPA in IPR protection. The ECFA is also likely to go beyond the CEPA in investment protection and in dispute settlement mechanisms. These 'CEPA-plus' features of the ECFA may in turn lead to modifications and strengthening of the CEPA. In a nutshell, the CEPA and the ECFA are complementary and mutually reinforcing.

NOTES

1. China acceded to the Asia-Pacific Trade Agreement (previously known as the Bangkok Agreement) in 2001. However, this Agreement is a Preferential Trade Agreement (PTA) that falls short of a FTA. By WTO rules, a FTA requires tariffs to be eventually be abolished for "substantially all trade" while a PTA only requires tariff reduction (not abolishment) for some products that do not cover "substantially all trade".
2. For a detailed analysis of Taiwan's gradual liberalization of cross-strait links, see Sung (2005, pp. 61–8).
3. For a detailed description of WTO-inconsistent measures in Cross-Strait trade, see Hsieh (2011, pp. 123–30).
4. Taiwan has only been able to conclude FTAs with five small allies in Central America. These small countries accounted for less than 0.2 percent of Taiwan's exports (Hsieh, 2011, p. 134).
5. Text of ECFA (http://www.ecfa.org.tw/EcfaAttachment/ECFADoc/ECFA.pdf).
6. Detailed information on the CEPA is available from the homepage of the Trade and Industry Department of the Hong Kong government.
7. See '2010 Update of CEPA's Impact on the Hong Kong economy (Trade in Services),' http://www.tid.gov.hk/english/cepa/statistics/statistics_research.html.
8. See '2010 Update of CEPA's Impact on the Hong Kong economy (Individual Visit Scheme),' http://www.tid.gov.hk/english/cepa/statistics/statistics_research.html.
9. Many Hong Kong firms have moved their registration to the tax haven economies since the early 1990s as insurance against the 1997 handover of Hong Kong to China. Taiwanese subsidiaries in Hong Kong followed suit. Many Mainland subsidiaries in

Hong Kong (which invested in the Mainland to take advantage of preferences given to overseas companies) did the same, with the result that the tax haven economies became China's second-largest source of FDI since 2000, accounting for around 30 percent of China's inward FDI in 2007. However, channeling of investment via the tax haven economies has eased since 2007 as worries over the 1997 handover of Hong Kong have subsided and Taiwan has relaxed its restrictions on investment in the Mainland. Moreover, there is less incentive for Mainland companies to invest in the Mainland through overseas subsidiaries as the Mainland has abolished its preference for foreign investors under the principle of national treatment. For details, see Sung (2005, pp. 26–32).
10. http://taiwantoday.tw/ct.asp?xItem=178906&ctNode=426.
11. Council of Agriculture, Taiwan (http://eng.coa.gov.tw/content_view.php?catid=24199&hot_new=8790).
12. Trade and Industry Department of Hong Kong government (http://www.tid.gov.hk/english/cepa/).
13. http://www.wto.org/english/tratop_e/region_e/trans_mecha_e.htm.
14. http://fta.mofcom.gov.cn/english/index.shtml.
15. Homepage of Mainland Affairs Council of Taiwan (http://www.mac.gov.tw/public/Data/2399271071.pdf).
16. 'Asian giants inch toward major FTA,' *Global Times*, November 21, 2011.
17. http://www.ecfa.org.tw/ShowNews.aspx?id=383&year=all&pid=&cid=.

REFERENCES

Bergsten, C. Fred, Freeman, Charles, Lardy, Nicholas R., and Mitchell, Derek J., 2008. *China's Rise: Challenges and Opportunities*, Washington, DC: Peterson Institute for International Economics and Center for Strategic and International Studies.

Choi, Jonathan, 2010. 'ECFA Motivates Hong Kong to Redefine its Role,' *CGCC Vision*, September, Hong Kong (http://www.cgcc.org.hk/b5/chamber/bulletin/files/Booklet_1286436040.22592_CGCC%20VISION%20Sep10.pdf).

Chu, Yun-han, 2010. 'Taiwan and Hong Kong Re-embrace Each Other,' *Hong Kong Journal*, January (http://www.hkjournal.org/archive/2010_spring/3.htm).

Hong Kong Trade Development Council, 2003. *CEPA: Opportunities for Hong Kong Service Industries*, Hong Kong, September.

Hsieh, Pasha L., 2011. 'The China–Taiwan ECFA, Geopolitical Dimensions and WTO Law,' *Journal of International Economic Law*, 14(1), 121–56.

Hsu, Kristy, 2011. 'The Economic Cooperation Framework Agreement (ECFA) between China and Taiwan and Its Implications,' presentation in seminar on 'The Current Status and Future Prospects of India–Taiwan Relations,' ICRIER, India (http://www.icrier.org/pdf/Session%20IV-Kristy%20Hsu-Presentation.pdf).

International Monetary Fund, 2012. 'World Economic Outlook – Update,' January 24.

Siew, Vincent C., 2010. 'The Impact of ECFA on Cross-strait Trade and Investment,' November 3, in the homepage of the Asian Corporate Governance Association (http://www.acga-asia.org/public/files/The%20Impact%20of%20ECFA%20on%20Cross-Strait%20Trade%20and%20Investment.pdf).

Sung, Yun-Wing, 2005. *The Emergence of Greater China: The Economic Integration*

of Mainland China, Taiwan, and Hong Kong, Basingstoke and New York: Palgrave Macmillan.
Sung, Yun-Wing, Liu, P.W., Wong, Richard, and Lau, P.K., 1995. *The Fifth Dragon: The Emergence of the Pearl River Delta*, Singapore: Addison-Wesley.
Taipei Times, 2011. 'WTO notified of EFCA', May 7, p. 11.

3. Assessing the impacts of the integration of the ICT investments of Taiwan and China upon economic growth in Taiwan

Winston T. Lin

3.1 INTRODUCTION

Since the start of the 1980s, the investments on information technology (IT) and communications technology (CT) have rapidly increased. For instance, since the 1990s, Taiwan has invested approximately US $245 992 million on IT and CT; and in Taiwan, the CT investment is about 2.5 to 3.5 times that of IT (Chen and Lin, 2011). Indeed, ICT (used hereafter to denote IT and CT combined) has been used to procure state-of-the-art computer hardware, software, and services; to develop new communications systems for re-engineering business and innovative production processes in operations and production management; to train the production and information systems staff and end-users to become more skilled in using ICT; to build up computer networks for connecting manufacturers, suppliers and customers; etc. (see Chen and Lin, 2011; Lin and Shao, 2000). China is no different, meaning that – as in Taiwan – ICT spending in China has rapidly increased since the 1990s (see Figures 3.1 and 3.2, which show how ICT investments in Taiwan and China have evolved over time and by sector).

Moreover, because of the fact that in recent years contact between the two sides of the Taiwan Strait has become highly frequent and the fact that since many investors from Taiwan have engaged in investing and business activities in China, there is a perception that Taiwan's economic or productivity growth has been enhanced by China's ICT investments. In other words, there exists a notion that the integration of Taiwan's and China's ICT investments stimulates the economic or productivity growth of Taiwan.[1]

This research is devoted to investigating whether this notion is a misconception. More specifically, the goal of our research is to seek the answer to the question: Does the integration of the ICT investments of Taiwan and China have positive impacts upon the productivity or economic growth of Taiwan? To fulfil the goal, we follow Chen and Lin (2011) by adopting the theory of production as the theoretical basis and the two-stage sequential methodology with two built-in performance measures. We construct four research models fitted into a panel data-set at the sector level, covering the period from 1990 to 2010.

The rest of the paper is organized as follows. Section 3.2 describes the economic theory on which this research is based, the two-stage methodology, the performance measures, and the research models. Section 3.3 presents empirical evidence. Finally, Section 3.4 concludes the paper with some remarks and suggests some extensions.

3.2 THE THEORY OF PRODUCTION, TWO-STAGE RESEARCH METHODOLOGY, PERFORMANCE MEASURES, AND RESEARCH MODELS

This section in essence follows Chen and Lin (2011). Other references include, but are not limited to, Bakos and Kemerer (1992), Chen and Lin (2009), Coelli (1995), Fried et al. (1993), Grosskopf (1993), Lin (2009), Lin and Chen (2002), Lin et al. (2012), Lin and Chiang (2011), Lin et al. (2010), Lin and Shao (2000), Lin and Shao (2006a, b), Malmquist (1953, 1993), Schmidt (1986), Shao and Lin (2001, 2002, 2009), Shu and Lee (2003), and Tohidi and Tarokh (2006). Among these other references, Malmquist (1953, 1993) and Shao and Lin (2009) are relevant to Stage 2, while the rest are useful for Stage 1.

3.2.1 The Theory of Production

As mentioned in Chen and Lin (2011), economic theory has been particularly emphasized in the research of IT value and the related issues of the productivity paradox and productivity growth (Bakos and Kemerer, 1992; Chen and Lin, 2009; Lin and Shao, 2000; Lin, 2009; Lin et al., 2010; Lin et al., 2012). The productivity paradox is a phenomenon that was coined in the late 1970s to describe the issue of the apparent lack of productivity improvements that are expected to occur as a result of IT investment (Lin and Shao, 2006a). Here, the productivity paradox means the lack of a substantial and statistically significant contribution of ICT investments to sector output.

This research is again based on the well-established theory of production. We define Y_{jt} = the actual (observed) ouput, tangible goods or intangible services, produced by production factors (inputs) in sector j at time t,

K_{jt} = the ordinary (non-ICT) capital used by j at time t,
L_{jt} = the ordinary labor used by j at time t,
I_{jt} = the ICT capital invested by j at time t,
$\mathbf{X}_{jt}$ = a vector of inputs = (K_{jt}, L_{jt}) in the absence of I_{jt}
= (K_{jt}, L_{jt}, I_{jt}) in the presence of I_{jt}, and
$f(\mathbf{X}_{jt}; \boldsymbol{\beta})$ = the production function representing the maximum (desired or expected) output, where $\boldsymbol{\beta}$ = a vector of unknown coefficients.

Equipped with these notations, the theory of production is characterized by three components, namely: (a) a production process in which a production unit utilizes inputs to produce Y_{jt}; (b) the production frontier that specifies that in reality the observed output must be smaller than or equal to the maximum output due to technological, management and other constraints – that is, $Y_{jt} \leq f(\mathbf{X}_{jt}; \boldsymbol{\beta})$; and (c) the productive (technical) inefficiency (u_{jt}), defined as the difference between the maximum and the actual output given by $u_{jt} = f(\mathbf{X}_{jt}; \boldsymbol{\beta}) - Y_{jt}$ or

$$Y_{jt} = f(\mathbf{X}_{jt}; \boldsymbol{\beta}) - u_{jt}, \quad j = 1, \ldots, n, \quad t = 1, \ldots, m \tag{3.1}$$

where u_{jt} is random and non-negative; hence, it is assumed to be one-sided and normally distributed according to $|N(0, \sigma_u^2)|$. Thus, the production unit either operates on the frontier (if productively or technically efficient, meaning $u_{jt} = 0$) or below the frontier (if productively or technically inefficient, meaning $u_{jt} > 0$).

3.2.2 A Two-Stage Sequential Methodology

Based on the production theory, we can derive two research approaches in a two-stage sequential process to carry out the proposed research as well as two performance measures that follow immediately from the research approaches.

3.2.2.1 Stage 1, the time-varying stochastic production frontier approach and productive efficiency: a one-equation model

Adding a traditional random error (v_{jt}) to the right-hand side of Equation (3.1) leads to the one-equation time-varying stochastic production frontier model described by

$$Y_{jt} = f(\mathbf{X}_{jt}; \boldsymbol{\beta}) - u_{jt} + v_{jt}, \quad j = 1, \ldots, n, \quad t = 1, \ldots, m \tag{3.2}$$

where $X_{jt} = (K_{jt}, L_{jt})$ and $X_{jt} = (K_{jt}, L_{jt}, I_{jt})$ without and with ICT investments respectively, and v_{it} is assumed to follow the distribution according to $N(0, \sigma_v^2)$. Note that Lin (2009) has cited and discussed several tests on the normal assumption underlying the frontier model; and the present research selects such an assumption. Then, the productive inefficiency can readily be transformed into the productive (technical) efficiency given by

$$PE_{jt} = \exp(-u_{jt}), \; j = 1, \ldots, n, \; t = 1, \ldots, m \tag{3.3}$$

which lies between one and zero, implying that as $u_{jt} = 0$ (no inefficiency), $PE_{jt} = 1$ (the highest efficiency); and as u_{jt} tends to infinite (the largest inefficiency), PE_{jt} tends to zero (no efficiency). Thus, u_{jt} and PE_{jt} have a one-to-one correspondence relationship.

3.2.2.2 Stage 1, the generalized time-varying stochastic production frontier approach: a two-equation model

The one-equation frontier model can be generalized to form a two-equation model (Chen and Lin, 2009; Lin and Chen, 2002; Lin and Chiang, 2011; and Lin et al., 2012) as described by Equations (3.4) and (3.5):

$$Y_{jt} = f(X_{jt}; \boldsymbol{\beta}) - u_{jt} + v_{jt} \tag{3.4}$$

$$u_{jt} = g(Z_{jt}; \boldsymbol{\alpha}) + w_{jt}, \; j = 1, \ldots, n, \; t = 1, \ldots, m \tag{3.5}$$

where w_{jt}, like u_{jt}, is a one-sided normally distributed random variable, Equation (3.4) is equivalent to Equation (3.2), Z_{jt} is a vector, and $\boldsymbol{\alpha}$ is another vector of unknown coefficients. Here, the random productive inefficiency u_{jt} is constituted by two components, the deterministic $g(Z_{jt}; \boldsymbol{\alpha})$ and the random w_{jt} (cf. Chen and Lin, 2009 and Lin and Chen, 2002 for more details). In particular, according to Chen and Lin (2009), Lin and Chen (2002), and Lin and Chiang (2011), Z_{jt} represents a broad set of sector-, firm-, or country-specific characteristics, observable and/or unobservable, that cause or explain the differences in productive (in)efficiencies. For example, Z_{jt} = (per capita consumer expenditure, time, government bond yields, the ratio of foreign exchange reserves to imports, the unemployment rate, and the inflation rate) used in Chen and Lin (2009); and Z_{jt} = (growth options, external balances, national savings, return on assets, and vertical integration) as used in Lin and Chiang (2011). Here, in this study, $Z_{jt} = (I^c_{jt} \text{ or } I_{jt})$ that drives the productive (in)efficiency of a sector.

Furthermore, as indicated in Lin et al. (2012), in Equation (3.5) there is a constant term, α_0, separated from the $\boldsymbol{Z}_{jt}$ terms, unless it is statistically insignificant. In other words, the $g(\cdot)$ function consists of the intercept term, regardless of whether $g(\cdot)$ is linear or nonlinear. In the two-step nonlinear maximum-likelihood (2SNML) estimation (see Section 3.2.5 below), Equations (3.4) and (3.5) are combined into a one-equation model. The constant of (3.4) and that of (3.5) can be combined into one constant or separated (Lin and Chen, 2002). In presenting the estimates (Table 3.1), we did not separate them because there is no need to do so. Note that after having combined Equations (3.4) and (3.5) into one-equation, $-w_{jt}$ plays the role of $-u_{jt}$ in the combined one-equation model. In the likelihood ratio (LR) test conducted in Section 3.3.3.2 (below), $\boldsymbol{\alpha}_0$ is counted as one towards the degree of freedom.

3.2.2.3 Stage 2, productivity or economic growth

As indicated in Chen and Lin (2011), in the literature there has been a lot of attention paid to Stage 1, the values of ICT, but little to Stage 2: do the ICT values contribute to the productivity (or economic) growth of a decision-making unit? It is generally accepted that the economic growth (EG) of a country may be measured by its productivity growth (PG) (Chen and Lin, 2011; Fried et al., 1993; etc.). Thus, Stage 1 and Stage 2 can be connected together to analyse the impacts of ICT investments upon the PG or EG of a country by means of the following relationship (see for example Chen and Lin, 2011; Jorgenson and Stiroh, 1999; and Shao and Lin, 2001; 2009): *PG* or *EG* at t = (Productive efficiency change at t) × (Technological progress at t), that is,

$$PG_t \text{ (or } EG_t) = PEC_t \times TP_t. \tag{3.6}$$

According to Equation (3.6), PEC_t and TP_t are two decisive contributing factors of the country's PG or EG at time t.

Conventional wisdom (see for example Chen and Lin, 2011; Fried et al., 1993; Shao and Lin, 2009) also refers to PG as total factor productivity (TFP) and, based on the concept of the Malmquist productivity index (Malmquist, 1953, 1993; and Shao and Lin, 2009), two indexes (the productive efficiency-change index denoted by $I_{PEC,jt}$ and the technological progress index denoted by $I_{TP,jt}$) can be calculated using the estimated results of PE_{jt} and the coefficient estimates from Stage 1 as shown below:

$$I_{PEC,jt} = PE_{jt}/PE_{j,t-1} \tag{3.7}$$

where PE_{jt} is given by Equation (3.3) from Stage 1, and

Table 3.1 Estimates of the stochastic frontier models: Stage 1

Model	Coefficient Estimates							R^2
	β_0 (t-value)	β_1 (t-value)	β_2 (t-value)	β_3 (t-value)	α_0 (t-value)	α_1 (t-value)	α_{1c} (t-value)	
1	2.6039*	.4273*	.0472*	.0680	–	–	–	.9891
	(84.6)	(55.1)	(6.40)	(17.8)				
2	2.3347*	.4129*	.1144*	–	–.0737	.0678*	–	.9700
	(40.2)	(28.4)	(9.01)		(–.724)	(5.62)		
3	1.9179*	.4222*	.0527*	–	–.2159	–	.0486*	.9715
	(105.0)	(29.1)	(4.33)		(–1.49)		(2.75)	
4	2.9385*	.1138*	.0369*	.0226*	.0540	–	–.0088	.9823
	(46.7)	(27.0)	(8.19)	(14.1)	(–.807)		(–.853)	

Notes:

* denotes significance at the 1% level and Δ at the 5% level.

a Cf. Table 3 in Chen and Lin (2011).

b The optimal transformation parameters are $\delta^* = -0.1$ and $\theta^* = -0.04712$ for Model 1; $\delta^* = -0.1$ and $\theta^* = 0.13673$ for Models 2 and 3; and $\delta^* = 0.2$ and $\theta^* = 0.2272$ for Model 4.

$$I_{TP,jt} = \left\{\left[1 + \frac{\partial F(\boldsymbol{X}_{jt}; \hat{\boldsymbol{\beta}}, \hat{\boldsymbol{\alpha}})}{\partial(t-1)}\right] \times \left[1 + \frac{\partial F(\boldsymbol{X}_{jt}; \hat{\boldsymbol{\beta}}, \hat{\boldsymbol{\alpha}})}{\partial(t)}\right]\right\}^{\frac{1}{2}}, \qquad (3.8)$$

where $\hat{\boldsymbol{\beta}}$ and $\hat{\boldsymbol{\alpha}}$ are the estimates of $\boldsymbol{\beta}$ and $\boldsymbol{\alpha}$, respectively. When $I_{PEC,jt}$ is $> 1 (< 1)$, country (sector) j would experience a productive efficiency gain (loss) at time t, and if $I_{TP,jt}$ is $> 1 (< 1)$, country (sector) j would benefit a positive technological progress (repression) at time t as a result of the ICT investments.[2]

Then, the productivity growth (PG) or economic growth (EG) can be assessed by using the Malmquist total factor productivity or PG index (or EG index). In other words, we have

$$I_{TFP,jt} = I_{PEC,jt} \times I_{TP,jt} \qquad (3.9)$$

If $I_{TFP,jt}$ is $> 1 (< 1)$, the ICT investments would have positively (adversely) contributed to the productivity or economic growth. Normally, the higher than 1, the better the PG will be. Equation (3.9) is defined as the product of Equations (3.7) and (3.8). Based on this definition, the Malmquist index measures the contribution of ICT incorporating the BT production frontier (Shao and Lin, 2009).

Furthermore, if we define $AI_{PEC,j} = \Sigma_t I_{PEC,jt}/m$ and $AI_{TP,j} = \Sigma_t I_{TP,jt}/m$, then we can calculate the economic contribution of ICT to sector j via

$$EC_j = AI_{PEC,j} \times AI_{TP,j}, \quad j = 1, \ldots, n. \qquad (3.10)$$

Similarly, defining $AI_{PEC,t} = \Sigma_j I_{PEC,jt}/n$ and $AI_{TP,t} = \Sigma_j I_{TP,jt}/n$, we can compute the productivity or economic growth at t using

$$PG_t \text{ (or } EG_t) = AI_{PEC,t} \times AI_{TP,t}, \quad j = 1, \ldots, n. \qquad (3.11)$$

As emphasized in Lin (2009) and Lin and Chuang (2011), the productivity paradox is a phenomenon of average – it is not a one period phenomenon. To be consistent with this concept, Equations (3.10) and (3.11) are needed. Just because the product of two averages as defined by Equations (3.10) and (3.11) is not the same as the average of the product that is given by Equation (3.9), the simple average given by $AI_{TFP,j} = \Sigma_{t=1}^{m} I_{TFP,jt}/m$ and $AI_{TFP,t} = \Sigma_{j=1}^{n} I_{TFP,jt}/n$ are not valid for explaining or determining whether the productivity paradox exists or not.

3.2.3 Research Models for Stage 1 and Stage 2

Following Chen and Lin (2009) and Lin et al. (2011), we consider two cases. In Case 1, Taiwan's ICT capital (represented by I_{jt}) is treated as an actual output-affecting variable to enter the $g(.)$ function, the second equation of the two-equation approach. In Case 2, I_{jt} is treated as a desired output-influencing input to enter the $f(.)$ function, the production function which represents the desired or maximum output. In order to achieve the objective of the research, we propose four research models as follows.

First, we consider Case 2 in which I_{it} appears in the $f(\cdot)$ function along with K_{jt} and L_{jt}. This results in a one-equation-three-factor model given by

$$\text{Model 1: } Y_{jt} = f(K_{jt}, L_{jt}, I_{jt}; \boldsymbol{\beta}) - u_{jt} + v_{jt}$$

in which I_{jt} stands alone in the $f(\cdot)$ function, serving as a desired output-affecting input along with K_{jt} and L_{jt}.

Second, we consider Case 1 in which I_{jt} appears in the $g(\cdot)$ function, leading to a two-equation-two-factor model described by

$$\begin{aligned}\text{Model 2: } Y_{jt} &= f(K_{jt}, L_{jt}; \boldsymbol{\beta}) - u_{jt} + v_{jt}\\ u_{jt} &= g(I_{jt}; \boldsymbol{\alpha}) + w_{jt},\end{aligned}$$

in which I_{jt} stands alone in the $g(\cdot)$ function, serving as an observed output-influencing variable.

Third, we can evaluate the impacts of the integration of the ICT investments of Taiwan and China by proposing the following Model 3, again a two-equation-two-factor model:

$$\begin{aligned}\text{Model 3: } Y_{jt} &= f(K_{jt}, L_{jt}; \boldsymbol{\beta}) - u_{jt} + v_{jt}\\ u_{jt} &= g(I^c_{jt}; \boldsymbol{\alpha}_c) + w_{jt},\end{aligned}$$

where I^c_{jt} is China's ICT capital and it stands alone in the $g(\cdot)$ function, being treated as Taiwan's observed output-influencing variable.

Fourth and finally, we can evaluate the impacts of the integration of the ICT investments of Taiwan and China by extending Model 1 for Case 2 by incorporating I^c_{jt}, which yields a two-equation-three-factor model:

$$\begin{aligned}\text{Model 4: } Y_{jt} &= f(K_{jt}, L_{jt}, I_{jt}; \boldsymbol{\beta}) - u_{jt} + v_{jt}\\ u_{jt} &= g(I^c_{jt}; \boldsymbol{\alpha}_c) + w_{jt}\end{aligned}$$

in which Taiwan's ICT investments are integrated with China's ICT investments in the production process.

3.2.4 Specification of the Production Frontier Function

The $g(.)$ function is assumed to be linear for the same reasons as described in Lin et al. (2011). The frontier function $f(.)$ is represented by the Box–Tidwell (BT) transformation function (Box and Tidwell, 1962; Lin and Shao, 2000; 2006a; 2006b; Lin et al., 2012) for the same reasons as given in Lin et al. (2011).

The stochastic production frontier of the three-factor BT transformation is represented by

$$\frac{Y_{jt}^{\delta} - 1}{\delta} = \beta_0 + \beta_1\left(\frac{K_{jt}^{\theta} - 1}{\theta}\right) + \beta_2\left(\frac{L_{jt}^{\theta} - 1}{\theta}\right) + \beta_3\left(\frac{I_{jt}^{\theta} - 1}{\theta}\right) - u_{jt} + v_{jt}, \tag{3.12}$$

where the optimal values, denoted by δ^* and θ^*, of the two transformation parameters (δ and θ) are used to normalize the distributions of dependent variable Y_{jt}.[3]

Several remarks are in order. First, the SPF approach incorporating the BT production frontier pools panel data (cross-sectional (j) and time-series (t) data combined). Therefore, the econometric approach can be applied at different levels of study, for example firms, sectors, industries, states, or countries (cf. Chen and Lin, 2009; Grosskopf, 1993; Lin and Chen, 2002; Lin and Chuang, 2011; Lin and Shao, 2000; 2006a; 2006b; Lin, 2009; Lin et al., 2011; Shao and Lin, 2001; 2002; 2009; and Shu and Lee, 2003). In other words, the cross-sectional data (j) may be generated by firms, sectors, or industries at the microeconomic level or by states or countries at the macroeconomic level. The present study is limited to Taiwan and China only; sectors are the best choice for the cross-sectional index j, and the data at the sectoral level are available.

Second, according to the studies at the firm level (for example, Brynjolfsson and Hitt, 1996; Dewan and Min, 1997; Hitt and Brynjolfsson, 1996; Lin and Chuang, 2011; Lin and Shao, 2000; 2006a; 2006b; Shao and Lin, 2001; 2002; among others) and the research at the country level (for example, Chen and Lin, 2009; Lin and Chen, 2002; Lin, 2009; Lin et al., 2010; Lin and Chiang, 2011; Lin et al., 2012; Shu and Lee, 2003; etc.), although firms and countries, like sectors, differ substantially in the capital, labor, and ICT intensities, dummy variables were not added for firms or countries. Here, we have added dummy variables for sector to the estimated production function; however, they not only appear to be statistically insignificant but also affect the significance of other major variables such as K_{jt}, L_{jt}, I_{jt} and I_{jt}^{c}.

Third and finally, as stated above, the stochastic production frontier is specified to be the Box–Tidwell (1962) transformation function represented by Equation (3.12) for the three-factor case. Mathematically, it can be shown (Lin and Shao, 2006a) that as δ^* tends to be equal to θ^*, the BT transformation function collapses to the Box–Cox (1964) transformation function – that is, BC would become a special case of BT; and as δ^* and θ^* tend to zero, the limit of the BT transformation function is the Cobb–Douglas (CD) production function – that is, CD would become a special case of BT (Lin and Chiang, 2011; Lin and Shao, 2006a; Lin, 2009; Lin et al., 2011). Thus, although the dependent variable is not ln(output) but rather output transformed with a BT transformation, the limit of the BT transformation is equivalent to ln(output). Accordingly, defining $\exp(-u_{jt})$ for PE_{jt} as given by Equation (3.3) is valid mathematically and empirically (Fried et al., 1993; Grosskopf, 1993; Lin, 2009; Lin and Shao, 2000; 2006a; 2006b; Lin et al., 2011; and Schmidt, 1986;) which guarantees that $0 \leq PE_{jt} \leq 1$. Furthermore, computing PE_{jt} using $\hat{Y}_{jt}/\hat{Y}^0_{jt}$, where $\hat{Y}_{jt}$ is the predicted (estimated) output with the value of u_{jt} lying in $(0, \infty)$ and $\hat{Y}^0_{jt}$ is the predicted output with $u_{jt} = 0$, does not ensure that $PE_{jt} \in [0, 1]$.

3.2.5 Estimation in Stage 1

The four frontier models (one-equation and two-equation) were estimated by the iterative two-step nonlinear maximum likelihood (2SNML) method using the statistical software LIMDEP (Chen and Lin, 2009; Lin and Shao, 2000; Lin, 2009; Lin et al., 2012; Schmidt, 1986; among others).

3.3 EMPIRICAL EVIDENCE

The two-stage sequential methodology was applied to the data of Taiwan at the sector level. The methodology can be applied at the firm level, at the industry level, and at the country level as well. Taiwan was ranked in the group of developed countries with high income by The World Bank (Lin, 2009; and Lin and Chiang, 2011).

3.3.1 Major Economic Sectors of the Taiwan Economy

Following *Digital Planet 2002*, *2004*, *2006*, and *2008* (published by The World Information Technology and Service Alliance), the economy of Taiwan is divided into eleven economic sectors. These sectors are: Agriculture (AG); Construction (CT); Consumer (CS); Finance & Business Services (FB); Government (GV); Manufacturing (MF); Mining (MN);

Table 3.2 A brief description of the 11 economic sectors of Taiwan

j	Sector	Description
1	Agriculture (AG)	Agriculture, forestry, fishing and animal husbandry, and their products (for example, grain, and farm and fishery products)
2	Construction (CT)	Residential, industrial, and commercial constructions
3	Consumer (CS)	Accommodation and food services; professional, scientific and technical services; support services; human health and social work services; arts, entertainment and recreation services; clothing; etc.
4	Finance & Business Services (FB)	Finance, insurance, real estate; rental and leasing services; and other business services
5	Government (GV)	Services provided by government, for example public administration; defense; compulsory social security; education; etc.
6	Manufacturing (MF)	Food; textiles; furniture; paper and pulpwood; machinery and equipment; chemical products; etc.
7	Mining (MN)	Mining and quarrying; minerals; coal; petroleum; metal products; etc.
8	Other Services (OS)	Personal and social services; industrial services; and commercial services
9	Transportation and Communications (TC)	Transportation and storage; information and communications, including telephone and Internet; etc.
10	Utilities (UT)	Electricity and gas supply; water supply and remediation services; and natural gas
11	Wholesale & Retail Trade (WR)	Commodities or items traded at wholesale prices; and commodities or items traded at consumer prices

Note: The sector divisions follow Digital Planet 2002, 2004, 2006, and 2008, The Global Information Economy. (See Chen and Lin, 2011.)

Other Services (OS); Transport & Communications (TC); Utilities (UT); and Wholesale & Retail Trade (WR) (see Chen and Lin, 2011). Table 3.2 presents a brief description of these economic sectors.

3.3.2 Variables and Sources of Data

The variables needed for this research consist of: (i) capital; (ii) labor; (iii) ICT investments = IT investment + CT investment; and (iv) information systems (IS) investment, which is the expenses for IS staffing. Thereby, the independent variables consist of: (v) ordinary (non-ICT) capital (K_{jt})

= capital – ICT investments; (vi) ordinary labor (L_{it}) = labor – IS investment; and (vii):

$$\text{ICT capital } (I_{jt}) = \text{ICT spending} + 3 \times \text{IS staffing spending} \quad (3.14)$$

(Brynjolfsson and Hitt, 1996; Chen and Lin, 2009; 2011; Dewan and Min, 1997; Hitt and Brynjolfsson, 1996; Lin, 2009; Lin and Chen, 2002; Lin et al., 2011; Lin and Chiang, 2011; Lin and Shao, 2000; 2006a; 2006b), where the multiplier of 3 in the calculation of I_{jt} is the assumed service life of the asset created by IS labor and has been commonly practiced in the literature. ICT capital in China, denoted by I^c_{jt}, is defined in the same way as I_{jt} in Taiwan. The dependent variable Y_{jt} refers to the value added by the input factors. To rule out the influence and other possible factors, the data have been transformed into 2000 US dollars by deflating the data by the US consumer price index (CPI) with base 2000 = 1.00. The time period covers 1990 to 2010.[4, 5]

The principal sources of data on the dependent and independent variables are summarized in Table A3.1 of the Appendix along with the major variables involved and their definitions. Figures 3.1 and 3.2 show how the ICT investments of Taiwan and China, respectively, have evolved over time and by sector.

3.3.3 Discussions and Implications

3.3.3.1 Stage 1: the LR test

The two-step nonlinear maximum likelihood method (2SNML) of estimation has recorded the log-likelihood values.[6] Therefore, we can perform the likelihood ratio (LR) test (Coelli, 1995; Greene, 2003; Lin et al., 2012) on the hypothesis constituted by the null hypothesis H_0: model parameter magnitude differences do not exist against the alternative hypothesis H_1: model parameter magnitude differences do exist. This is meaningful because we would like to determine whether the differences in the parameters associated with any two research models differ significantly from zero. Thus, if H_1 is not rejected, it would indicate that a comparison of the two models is appropriate.

The test statistic (see for example Coelli, 1995 and Lin et al., 2012) is given by:

$$LR = -2[\log(L_0) - \log(L_1)] \quad (3.15)$$

where log (L_0) and (L_1) are the log-likelihood values under H_0 and H_1 or with and without restrictions on the parameters to be estimated,

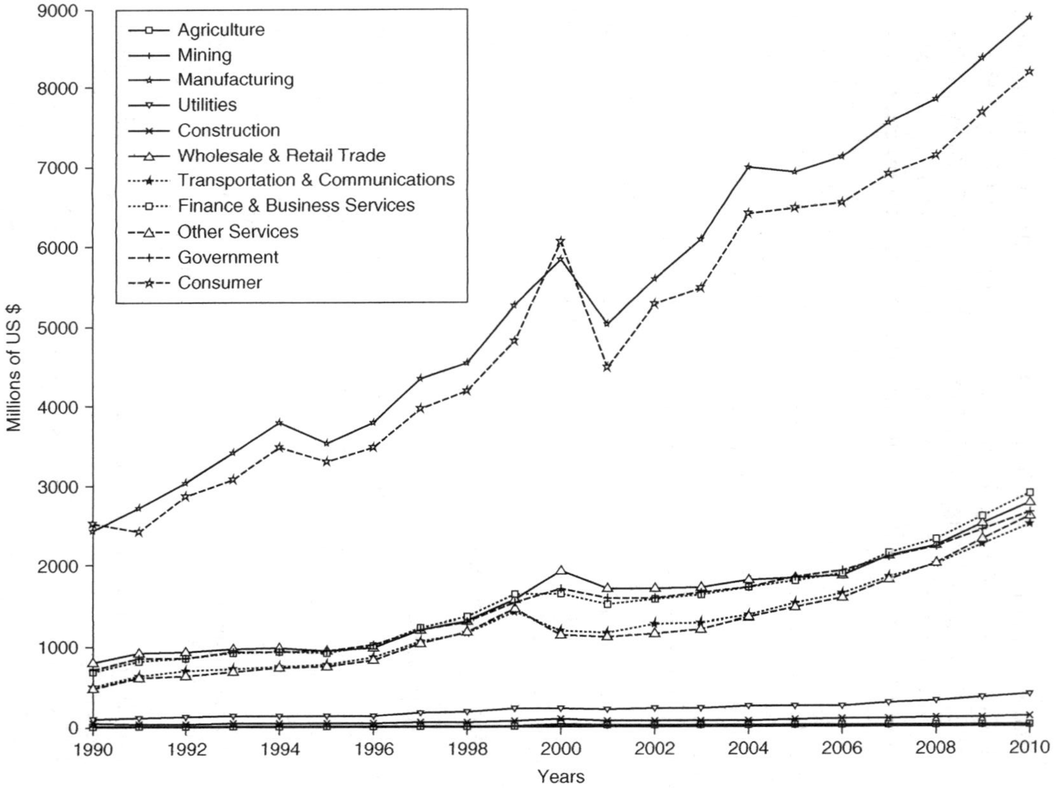

Figure 3.1 ICT capital: Taiwan

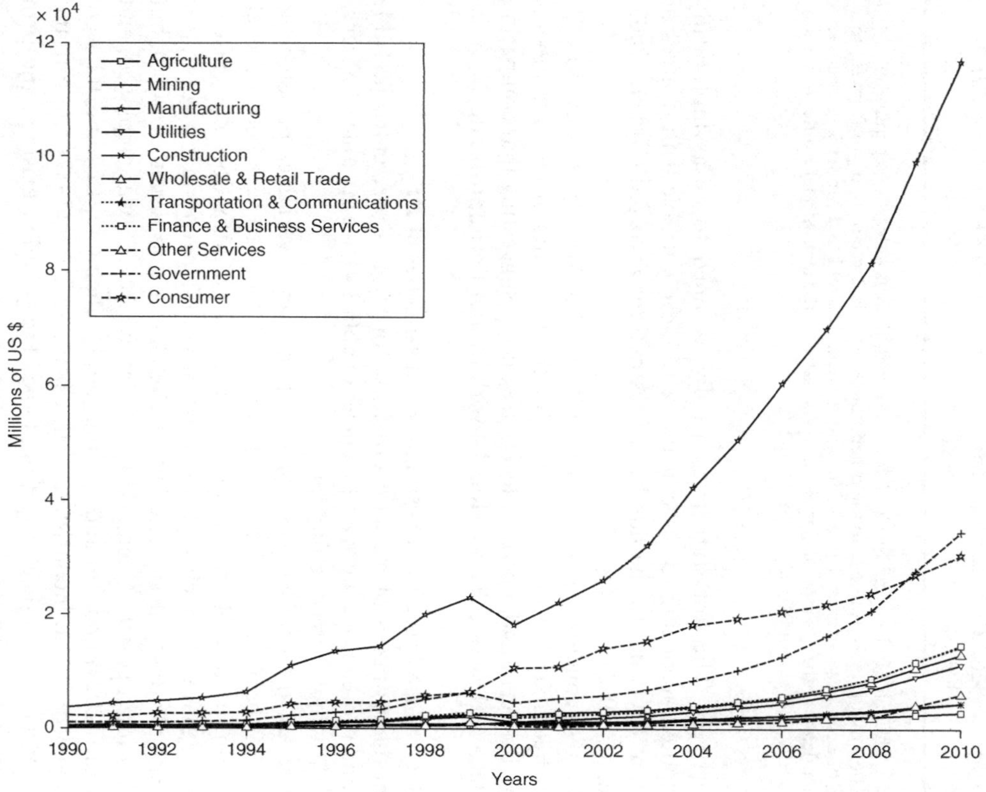

Figure 3.2 ICT capital: China

Table 3.3 The likelihood ratio (LR) test: Stage 1

Model	The observed value of the LR test statistic	The critical value at the 1% level	The critical value at the 5% level	Conclusion
2 vs 3	426.13	6.63	3.84	H_1
1 vs 4	302.70	9.21	5.99	H_1

Notes: Though Model 2 and Model 3 are not nested, there is at least one parameter restriction that gets us from one to the other model – that is, from α_1 to α_{1c} or from α_{1c} to α_1. As one can observe from Table 3.2, α_1 and α_{1c} from Model 2 and Model 3, respectively, are significant at the 1% level of significance. As stated in the text, Model 2 differs statistically and econometrically from Model 3.

respectively. The test statistic is usually assumed to be asymptotically distributed according to the chi-square random variable with degrees of freedom (k) equal to the number of restrictions involved (Greene, 2003; Lin et al., 2011).

The test conclusions are shown in Table 3.3. We can readily observe from this table that the conclusions for the two pairs of research models at the 1 percent and 5 percent levels are all H_1, suggesting that comparing Model 3 with Model 2 and Model 4 with Model 1 is appropriate.

3.3.3.2 Stage 1: coefficient estimates and estimates of PE_{jt}

From the estimates of model coefficients for Stage 1 (presented in Table 3.1) and those of productive efficiencies (Table 3.4), we are able to observe the following interesting findings.

First, all the coefficient estimates of the input variables presented in Table 3.2 bear positive signs and are significant at the 1 percent level, suggesting that, collectively, the productivity paradox does not exist in Taiwan; and this conclusion is consistent with conventional wisdom (see for example Brynjolfsson and Hitt, 1996; Dewan and Kraemer, 2000), but is contradictory with Chen and Lin (2009) when CES was employed, and with Lin (2009) and Lin and Chiang (2011) when CD, BC, and BT were deployed. It is also inconsistent with Chen and Tang (1987) and Pitt and Lee (1981), who respectively found that the paradox exists at the firm and the industry level.

Second, the LR test is appropriate for Model 2 vs Model 3 since there is one parameter restriction that gets us from one to the other model – that is, from α_1 and α_{1c} (or from α_{1c} to α_1). Both α_1 and α_{1c} are significant (see Table 3.1). Thus, it does not preclude a comparison of Model 2 and Model 3 because, as we can observe from Table 3.1, both the coefficient estimate

Table 3.4 Estimates of PE_{jt}*: Stage 1 and Model 1 only*

t	j	PE_{jt}	j	PE_{jt}	j	PE_{jt}	j	PE_{jt}	j	PE_{jt}	j	PE_{jt}
1990	1	.8812	3	.9781	5	.9386	7	.9801	9	.9594	11	.9327
1991	(AG)	.8781	(CS)	.9778	(GV)	.9280	(MN)	.9758	(TC)	.9337	(WR)	.9599
1992		.8822		.9838		.9315		.9828		.9704		.9653
1993		.8863		.9804		.9411		.9828		.9940		.9656
1994		.8807		.9826		.9272		.9816		.9797		.9439
1995		.8735		.9823		.9314		.9800		.9803		.9516
1996		.8735		.9685		.9137		.9492		.9629		.9044
1997		.8735		.9634		.9295		.8997		.9355		.8735
1998		.8862		.9762		.9540		.9555		.9655		.9439
1999		.8873		.9777		.9671		.9746		.9624		.9024
2000		.9588		.9811		.9824		.9827		.9807		.8753
2001		.9030		.9257		.9465		.9302		.8995		.8735
2002		.8907		.9046		.9403		.9070		.8735		.8735
2003		.9016		.9018		.9513		.9051		.8735		.8735
2004		.9395		.9526		.9827		.9607		.9213		.8788
2005		.9132		.9504		.9802		.9504		.8955		.8903
2006		.9074		.9461		.9776		.9437		.8746		.8929
2007		.9177		.9486		.9784		.9328		.8735		.8948
2008		.9295		.9565		.9807		.9458		.8735		.9311
2009		.9327		.9493		.9777		.9285		.8735		.9242
2010		.9411		.9445		.9787		.9232		.8737		.9336
1990	2	.9860	4	.9637	6	.9814	8	9398	10	.9528		
1991	(CT)	.9802	(FB)	.9668	(MF)	.9803	(OS)	.9404	(UT)	.9487		
1992		.9919		.9718		.9847		.9529		.9613		
1993		.8735		.9716		.9886		.9734		.9717		
1994		.9801		.9692		.9831		.9514		.9655		
1995		.9790		.9688		.9823		.9496		.9723		
1996		.9724		.9503		.9686		.9294		.9557		
1997		.9129		.9605		.9692		.9300		.9549		
1998		.9104		.9785		.9790		.9556		.9708		
1999		.9266		.9818		.9802		.9638		.9741		
2000		.9769		.9851		.9836		.9697		.9784		
2001		.9347		.9499		.9449		.9200		.9285		
2002		.9134		.9358		.9323		.9091		.9149		
2003		.9349		.9383		.9333		.9092		.9173		
2004		.9614		.9813		.9721		.9536		.9648		
2005		.9568		.9770		.9671		.9482		.9588		
2006		9499		.9776		.9657		.9489		.9569		
2007		.9410		.9777		.9661		.9518		.9559		
2008		.9512		.9770		.9714		.9599		.9644		
2009		.9504		.9743		.9686		.9564		.9614		
2010		.9562		.9671		.9681		.9560		.9604		

($\hat{\alpha}_1$ = .0678) of I_{jt} in Model 2 and that ($\hat{\alpha}_{1c}$ = .0486) of I^c_{jt} in Model 3 are significant at the 1 percent level. As pointed out by Chen and Lin (2009) and Lin et al. (2011), the two-equation SPF modeling methodology suggests two ways to change u_{jt} and, hence, PE_{jt}, EC_j, and PG_t, one way from each of the two equations. In other words, these two ways represent two major sources of PE_{jt}, hence, EC_j, and PG_t. No unobservable factors are involved in Model 2 or Model 3. Obviously, Model 2 and Model 3 distinguish the contribution of I_{jt} of Taiwan from the contribution of I^c_{jt} of China to the economic growth of Taiwan through the second equation of the two-equation time-varying SPF modeling approach. It should be emphasized that the second equation distinguishes Model 2 from Model 3, even though the first equation is the same for Model 2 and Model 3. Statistically and econometrically, Model 2 differs from Model 3 and Model 2; and Model 3 facilitates the comparison of the contributions of $I_{jt}$and I^c_{jt} to the economic growth of Taiwan.

Third, the coefficient estimated (−.0088) of I^c_{jt} in Model 4 is not statistically significant and bearing a wrong sign, suggesting that I^c_{jt} from China is not important to Taiwan, given that Taiwan has already engaged in ICT investments; in contrast, I^c_{jt} becomes important to Taiwan in the absence of I_{jt} because the coefficient estimate (.0486) of I^c_{jt} in Model 3 is significant.

Fourth, the coefficients of determination (R^2s) are very high, ranging from .9700 for Model 2 to .9891 for Model 1.

Fifth and finally, the productive efficiency (PE) estimates presented in Table 3.4 indicate that the FB sector is most productively efficient, whereas the WR sector is least productively efficient. They also indicate that the sectoral productive efficiencies in Taiwan tend to fluctuate dynamically over time and that the changing paths of productive efficiencies differ from sector to sector.

3.3.3.3 Stage 2: answers to the focal question

To seek the answer to the critical question posited, namely 'Does the integration of the ICT investments of Taiwan and China have positive impacts upon the productivity (or economic) growth of Taiwan?', we compare the results of Model 3 and Model 2 (Tables 3.5 and 3.6) and the results of Model 4 and Model 1 (Tables 3.7 and 3.8). Each comparison is made on the basis of two productivity (or economic) growth indexes – that is, EC_j and PG_t.

In the first place, we consider Taiwan's and China's ICT investments in two separate models. Thus, we proceed to compare the results of Model 3 with their counterparts in Model 2 by referring to Tables 3.5 and 3.6. (i) On the basis of EC_j (Table 3.5), the answer to the question is obviously negative, if Taiwan's ICT investments were replaced by China's ICT

Table 3.5 Estimates of the productive (economic) growth indexes based on EC_j*, Model 3 vs Model 2: Stage 2*

Sector	1 (AG)	2 (CT)	3 (CS)	4 (FB)	5 (GV)	6 (MF)	7 (MN)	8 (OS)	9 (TC)	10 (UT)	11 (WR)
Model 3	.98852	.99564	.99583	.99119	.99686	.100649	1.00104	1.00442	.99814	1.00448	1.00045
Ranking	11	9	8	10	7	1	4	3	6	2	5
Model 2	.98276	.99227	.99771	.98502	.99667	1.01611	1.00579	1.01452	.99774	1.01526	1.00491
Ranking	11	9	7	10	8	1	4	3	6	2	5
Difference	.00576	.00337	(.00188)	.00617	.00019	(.00962)	(.00475)	(.01010)	.00040	(.01078)	(.00446)

Table 3.6 Estimates of the productive (economic) growth indexes based on PG_j*, Model 3 vs Model 2: Stage 2*

Year	1992	1993	1994	1995	1996	1997	1998	1999	2000	2001
Model 3	1.02176	1.01666	1.01158	1.00923	.99081	.97086	1.00507	1.02402	1.00883	.95083
Model 2	1.04000	1.03541	1.02914	1.02362	.99285	.94245	.99885	1.04956	1.01313	.89968
Difference	(.01824)	(.01875)	(.01756)	(.01439)	(.00204)	.02841	.00622	(.02554)	(.00430)	.05115
Year	2002	2003	2004	2005	2006	2007	2008	2009	2010	
Model 3	.93552	.98967	1.02616	1.01424	.99899	.99406	1.00037	1.00194	1.00167	
Model 2	.89607	.98194	1.05007	1.03696	1.00203	.99409	1.00640	1.01447	1.01198	
Difference	.03945	.00774	(.02391)	(.02242)	(.00304)	(.00003)	(.00603)	(.01253)	(.01031)	

Table 3.7 Estimates of the productive (economic) growth indexes based on EC_j, *Model 4 vs Model 1: Stage 2*

Sector	1 (AG)	2 (CT)	3 (CS)	4 (FB)	5 (GV)	6 (MF)	7 (MN)	8 (OS)	9 (TC)	10 (UT)	11 (WR)
Model 4	.97901	1.19339	1.21217	.99634	1.18026	1.30522	1.21873	1.29596	.99802	1.28848	1.22557
Ranking	11	7	6	10	8	1	5	2	9	3	4
Model 1	.98099	1.19548	1.21418	.99421	1.18213	1.30712	1.22066	1.29794	.99984	1.29104	1.22845
Ranking	11	7	6	10	8	1	5	2	9	3	4
Difference	(.00198)	(.00209)	(.00201)	.00213	(.00187)	(.00190)	(.00193)	(.00198)	(.00182)	(.00256)	(.00288)

Table 3.8 Estimates of the productive (economic) growth indexes based on PG_j, *Model 4 vs Model 1: Stage 2*

Year	1992	1993	1994	1995	1996	1997	1998	1999	2000	2001
Model 4	1.02634	1.02376	1.01769	1.01246	.99432	.97757	1.00906	1.02703	1.01673	.95891
Model 1	1.03025	1.02489	1.01888	1.01356	.99551	.97878	1.01019	1.02814	1.01782	.95996
Difference	(.00391)	(.00113)	(.00119)	(.00110)	(.00119)	(.00121)	(.00113)	(.00111)	(.00109)	(.00105)
Year	2002	2003	2004	2005	2006	2007	2008	2009	2010	
Model 4	.95381	.99564	1.02917	1.02089	1.00581	1.00097	1.00533	1.00812	1.00757	
Model 1	.95480	.99671	1.03743	1.02188	1.00678	1.00202	1.00641	1.00921	1.00869	
Difference	(.00099)	(.00107)	(.00826)	(.00099)	(.00097)	(.00105)	(.00108)	(.00109)	(.00112)	

investments. We can use the difference row in Table 3.5 to get the total difference that is equal to (.0257), meaning that China's ICT investments, if used in the production operations of Taiwan, would have reduced Taiwan's productivity (economic) growth by 2.57 percent during the time period considered. Specifically, China's ICT investments may have little positive impact on the AG, CT, FB, GV, and TC sectors, but exert negative effects on the other six sectors. (ii) On the basis of PG_t (Table 3.6), the answer to the question is again negative, if Taiwan's ICT undertakings were substituted by China's ICT investments. As we did in (i) above, we can use the difference row in Table 3.6 to obtain the total difference of (.04612) or (4.612 percent), suggesting that if China's ICT investments were integrated with Taiwan's ICT investments in the production operations, Taiwan's productivity (economic) growth would have decreased by 4.612 percent for the time period under study. As a matter of fact, China's ICT investments appear to have positive (in 1997, 1998, 2001, 2002, and 2003) and negative (in the other 14 years) impacts on Taiwan's productivity (economic) growth.

In the second place, we integrate Taiwan's ICT investments with China's ICT investments. Therefore, we now must compare the results of Model 4 with those of Model 1 by referring to Tables 3.7 and 3.8, again on the basis of the same two productivity (economic) growth indexes. (i) On the basis of EC_j (Table 3.7), the answer to the question is certainly negative. We can calculate the total difference using the difference row in Table 3.7, which is (.01889) or (1.889 percent), meaning that integrating the ICT investments of Taiwan and China together would decrease the productivity (economic) growth rate of Taiwan by 1.889 percent. Specifically, the integration of the ICT investments of Taiwan and China in Taiwan's production process would have a positive effect on the FB sector only and have negative effects on the other ten sectors. (ii) On the bass of PG_t (Table 3.8), the integration impacts are again negative. Numerically, we can calculate the total difference by using the difference row in Table 3.8, which is (.03073) or (3.073 percent), implying that integrating Taiwan's ICT investments with those of China would reduce the productivity (economic) growth rate of Taiwan by 3.073 percent during the time period considered. Specifically, the integration has negative impacts on the productivity growth of Taiwan in every year during the time period studied.

3.4 CONCLUSIONS AND EXTENSIONS

The objective of this research is to pursue the answer to the question concerning whether the integration of the ICT investments of Taiwan and China has positive impacts on the economic (or productivity) growth of Taiwan. Following Chen and Lin (2011), we used the theory of production as the theoretical foundation, the two research approaches that follow immediately from the theory and the two performance metrics that are built in the research approaches, in a two-stage sequential process, to achieve the objective. The two stages are interrelated and intertwined.

From the perspective of empirical validation, four research models were constructed and fitted into a panel data-set from Taiwan, covering the time period from 1990 to 2010. Empirical evidence strongly suggests that the answer to the above question is evidently negative.

As mentioned in Chen and Lin (2011), there are several extensions to this research for future research. For example, the two-stage methodology may be applied to conduct firm-level and country-level research. Another example requires applying the constant elasticity of substitution (known as CES) production frontier (Chen and Lin, 2009; Lin and Shao, 2006b). As such, it becomes possible to analyse how the substitution and complement relationships among ordinary capital (non-ICT capital), ordinary labor, and ICT capital affect productive efficiencies and productivity growth. A third instance involves the theory of partial adjustment that leads to the partial adjustment approach (Lin et al., 2010). This alternative is much easier to apply than the stochastic production frontier approach since the one-sided normally distributed inefficiency variable is not present in the partial adjustment model.

ACKNOWLEDGEMENTS

The author thanks the anonymous referees for their constructive and helpful comments and suggestions which led to the rigor and improvement of the research. Financial supports granted by the Chiang Ching-Kuo Foundation for International Scholarly Exchange (USA), the School of Management at The State University of New York at Buffalo, and National Sun Yat-sen University (Taiwan) are gratefully acknowledged.

NOTES

1. By integration, we mean to integrate ICT capital (stock) of Taiwan (I_{jt}) and ICT capital (stock) of China (I^c_{jt}) in our research models (see Models 3 and 4 on p.63) to reveal the impacts of I_{jt} and I^c_{jt} upon Taiwan's output in the production process and, hence, upon Taiwan's economic growth. Of course, it is not possible to integrate I_{jt} and I^c_{jt} into a single variable. It is conceivable that many investors from Taiwan have invested in China; as such, part, if not all, of the ICT investments of Taiwan are located in China and the

impact of the interaction between I_{jt} and I^c_{jt} upon Taiwan's economic growth cannot be ignored. The mechanism by which I^c_{jt} impacts the economy of Taiwan is through the production and operations processes which are structured by the two-equation stochastic production frontier (SPF) approach (Chen and Lin, 2009; Lin and Chiang, 2011) derived from the theory of production and by the formulation of research models derived from the two-equation SPF approach. The built-in productivity efficiency measure in cooperation with the Malmquist productivity index concept (Malmquist, 1953; 1993; Shao and Lin, 2009) becomes a well-established metric that can be used to judge the effect of the ICT investments of Taiwan and China upon the economic growth of Taiwan.

2. The derivatives in Equation (3.8) for CD, BC, and BT have been presented in Chen and Lin (2011).
3. δ and θ are solved based on the result of the ordinary least squares without the inefficiency term u – that is:

$$\frac{Y^{\delta}_{jt} - 1}{\delta} = \beta_0 + \beta_1\left(\frac{K^{\theta}_{jt} - 1}{\theta}\right) + \beta_2\left(\frac{L^{\theta}_{jt} - 1}{\theta}\right) + \beta_3\left(\frac{I^{\theta}_{jt} - 1}{\theta}\right) + v_{jt}, \qquad (3.12')$$

by maximizing the following equation given by

$$L_{\max}(\delta, \theta) = -\left(\frac{nm}{2}\right) ln\left(\frac{SSE}{nm}\right) + (\delta - 1)\sum_{j,t} ln\, Y_{jt} \qquad (3.13)$$

where θ is a hidden parameter in the calculation of SSE.
Then, δ^* and θ^* found in equations (3.12′) and (3.13) are used to transform the data for Equation (3.12). Note that the BT (Box and Tidwell, 1962) involves two transformation parameters (δ and θ) as shown in Equation (3.12), while BC (Box and Cox, 1964) involves only one transformation parameter. Thus, expression (3.13) is correct for BT in the absence of u_{jt} as originally suggested and as done in the first step of LIMDEP (see Box and Tidwell, 1962; Lin and Shao, 2000; 2006a; Lin, 2009; Lin and Chiang, 2011; and Lin et al., 2011). The estimates of equation (3.12′) also serve as the starting values to solve the SPF equation (3.12).
4. See notes in this chapter's Appendix for the reason why the US CPI index was used to deflate the nominal values.
5. Both I_{jt} and I^c_{jt} are a concept of stock rather than flow as given by Equation (3.14). The procedure of transforming flow into stock (capital) is commonly practiced in the literature as reflected by the references cited below Equation (3.14). Therefore, ICT per se is not treated as a stock.
6. Equation (3.13) is designed to obtain the optimal values (δ^* and θ^*) of the transformation parameters of BT (δ and θ). The log-likelihood values used for the LR test were not generated by Equation (3.13); instead, they were recorded by the iterative two-step nonlinear maximum-likelihood (2SNML) method of estimation (as stated in Section 3.2.5 above). Consequently, the LR test is valid and reliable.

REFERENCES

Bakos, J.Y. and Kemerer, C.F., 1992. Recent applications of economic theory in information technology research, *Decision Support Systems*, 8, 365–86.

Box, G.E.P. and Cox, D.R., 1964. An analysis of transformation, *Journal of the Royal Statistical Society*, Series B, 26, 211–43.

Box, G.E.P. and Tidwell, P.W., 1962. Transformation of the independent variables, *Technometrics*, 4, 531–50.

Brynjolfsson, E. and Hitt, L.M., 1996. Paradox lost? Firm-level evidence on the returns to information systems spending, *Management Science*, 42, 541–58.

Chen, T. and Tang, D., 1987. Comparing technical efficiency between imported-substitution-oriented and export-oriented foreign firms in a developing economy, *Journal of Development Economics*, 26, 277–89.

Chen, Y.H. and Lin, W.T., 2009. Analyzing the relationships between information technology, inputs substitution and national characteristics based on CES stochastic frontier production models, *International Journal of Production Economics*, 120, 552–69.

Chen, Y.H. and Lin, W.T., 2011. The values of information and communications technologies and their contributions to productivity growth with evidence from Taiwan, Working Paper, revised, 57 pp.

Coelli, T., 1995. Estimators and hypothesis tests for a stochastic frontier function: a Monte Carlo analysis, *Journal of Productivity Analysis*, 6, 247–68.

Dewan, S. and Kraemer, K.L., 2000. Information technology and productivity: evidence from country-level data, *Management Science*, 46, 548–62.

Dewan, S. and Min, C., 1997. The substitution of information technology for other factors of production: a firm level analysis, *Management Science*, 43, 1660–75.

Fried, H.O., Lovell, C.A.K., and Schmidt, S.S. (Eds), 1993. *The Measurement of Productive Efficiency: Techniques and Applications*, New York, NY: Oxford University Press.

Greene, W.H., 2003. *Economic Analysis*. Upper Saddle River, NJ: Pearson Education.

Grosskopf, S., 1993. Efficiency and productivity. In: H.O. Fried, C.A.K. Lovell, and S.S. Schmidt (Eds.), *The Measurement of Productive Efficiency: Techniques and Applications*, New York, NY: Oxford University Press, pp. 160–94.

Jorgenson, D.W. and Stiroh, K.J., 1999. Productivity growth: current recovery and long-term trends, *American Economic Review* (Papers and Proceedings), 89, 109–15.

Hitt, L.M. and Brynjolfsson, E., 1996. Productivity, business profitability, and consumer surplus: three different measures of information technology values, *MIS Quarterly*, 20, 121–42.

Lin, W.T., 2009. The business value of information technology as measured by technical efficiency: evidence from country-level data, *Decision Support Systems*, 46, 865–74.

Lin, W.T. and Chen, Y.H., 2002. *Productive Efficiency of Major Industries from Taiwan and China*, Buffalo, NY: The State University of New York at Buffalo, and Kaohsiung, Taiwan: National Sun Yat-sen University.

Lin, W.T., Chen, Y.H., and Chuang, C.H., 2012. Evaluating the business values of e-commerce and information technology independently and jointly, Working Paper, revised, 38 pp.

Lin, W.T. and Chiang, C.Y., 2011. The impacts of country characteristics upon the value of information technology as measured by productive efficiency, *International Journal of Production Economics*, 132, 13–33.

Lin, W.T. and Chuang, C.H., 2012. Investigating and comparing the dynamic patterns of the business value of information technology over time, Working paper (invited to submit a revision for 2nd review by the *European Journal of Operational Research*), revised, 28 pp.

Lin, W.T., Chuang, C.H., and Choi, J.H., 2010. A partial adjustment approach

to assessing and measuring the business value of information technology, *International Journal of Production Economics*, 127, 158–72.
Lin, W.T. and Shao, B.B.M, 2000. Relative sizes of information technology investments and productive efficiency: their linkage and empirical evidence, *Journal of the Association for Information Systems*, 1, Article 7, 1–35.
Lin, W.T. and Shao, B.B.M., 2006a. Assessing input effect on productive efficiency in production systems: the value of information technology capital, *International Journal of Production Research*, 44, 1799–819.
Lin, W.T. and Shao, B.B.M., 2006b. The business value of information technology and inputs substitution: the productivity paradox revisited, *Decision Support Systems*, 42, 493–507.
Malmquist, S., 1953. Index numbers and indifference surfaces, *Trabajos de Estadistica*, 4, 209–42.
Malmquist, S., 1993. Index numbers and demand functions, T*he Journal of Productivity Analysis*, 4, 251–60.
Pitt, M.M. and Lee, L., 1981. The measurement and sources of technical inefficiency in the Indonesian weaving industry, *Journal of Development Economics*, 9, 43–64.
Schmidt, P., 1986. Frontier production functions, *Econometric Reviews*, 4, 289–328.
Shao, B.B.M. and Lin, W.T., 2001. Measuring the value of information technology in technical efficiency with stochastic production frontiers, *Information and Software Technology*, 43, 447–56.
Shao, B.B.M. and Lin, W.T., 2002. Technical efficiency analysis of information technology investments: a two-stage empirical investigation, *Information & Management*, 39, 391–401.
Shao, B.B.M. and Lin, W.T., 2009. Evaluating information technology industry performance: a stochastic production frontier approach. In: R.J. Kauffman and P.P. Tallon (Eds), *Economics, Information Systems and Electronic Commerce: Empirical Research*, New York, NY: M.E. Sharpe.
Shu, W.S. and Lee, S., 2003. Beyond productivity – productivity and the three types of efficiencies of information technology industries, *Information and Software Technology*, 45, 513–24.
Tohidi, H. and Tarokh, M.J., 2006. Productivity outcomes of team work as an effect of information technology and team size, *International Journal of Production Economics*, 103, 610–15.

APPENDIX

Table A3.1 Variables, definitions, and sources

Variable	Definition	Data source (issue)
Capital_{jt}	Total expenses on capital stock	Monthly Statistics of the R.O.C. (various issues); Statistical Yearbook of China (various issues); UN Common Database
Labor_{jt}	Total wages paid to all employment workers	Monthly Bulletin of Labor Statistics (various issues); Statistical Yearbook of China (various issues); UN Common Database
ICT spending_{jt}	Computer hardware + software + computer services + communications	Digital Planet (2002, 2004, 2006, & 2008); Digital Planet Update (2004, 2006)
IS staffing spending_{jt}	ICT services + internal ICT expenses	Proxy: ICT spending_{jt} / $\text{Capital}_{jt} = q_{jt}$; IS staffing $\text{spending}_{jt} = \text{Labor}_{jt} + q_{jt}$
K_{jt}	Capital_{jt} – ICT capital_{jt}	
L_{jt}	Labor_{jt} – IS staffing spending_{jt}	
I_{jt}	ICT capital_{jt} (stock) obtained by applying Equation (3.14)	
Y_{jt}	Gross domestic product (GDP)	Monthly Statistics of the R.O.C. (various issues from 1/1990 to 12/2009); UN Common Database; OECD Database; and Statistical Yearbook of China (various issues)

Notes: The data on ICT spending collected from Digital Planet were expressed in millions of US dollars. For this research, the data on Capital, Labor, and IS staffing spending collected from the official statistical publications in Taiwan and China were transformed into millions of US dollars using the officially-published exchange rates between NT$ and US$ and between RMB and US$. Then, all the data of millions of US dollars were transformed into millions of US 2000 dollars using the US CPI index rather than the CPI of Taiwan and China. (See Chen and Lin, 2011.)

4. Trends for future integration of commercial banking between Taiwan and China after the ECFA

Hong-Jen Abraham Lin

4.1 INTRODUCTION

4.1.1 Background

China is the one of the fastest-growing economies worldwide and is the first choice for Taiwanese foreign direct investments. By the end of 2010, Taiwan invested US $159.84 billion in China. Major industries between Taiwan and China have integrated or become horizontally and vertically connected. Nevertheless, no such integration exists in the banking industry, owing to regulatory and political issues.

Since Taiwan and China joined the WTO (World Trade Organization) in 2002 and 2001 respectively, and China promised open banking and insurance markets in 2006, major Western banks have invested shares in major Chinese state-owned banks (see details in Hong and Zheng, 2009; Kuan et al., 2009). Taiwan's banks may also grasp this opportunity to expand their business in China, whereas China can demonstrate its economic power in Taiwan by establishing its banking branches.

The promise of opening financial markets was fulfilled in the Memorandum of Understanding (MOU) and the Economic Cooperation Framework Agreement (ECFA) between Taiwan and China. The MOU was signed on November 16, 2009, and became valid on January 16, 2010. The MOU and the ECFA further integrate financial markets between Taiwan and China. Within 3 to 5 years after the ECFA, Taiwan and China will open their banking and insurance markets to each other to establish cross-border branches.

Table 4.1 East Asia's Banks in 2004

Country	Market share % (top five)	ROE % (top three)	Relative size compared with banks in Taiwan
Taiwan	37	3.57	1
Singapore	89	4.30	2.78
Korea	73	5.83	4.67
Hong Kong	76	10.88	2.12

Source: Wu (2008).

4.1.2 The Perspective of Banks in Taiwan

Banks in Taiwan have experienced intense competition for more than a decade. From 1990 to 2001, the number of banks increased from 24 to 53, and the return on equity was reduced by a margin of 29.28 percent to 5.5 percent (Lieu et al., 2005, p. 925). Lin et al. (2009, pp. 6111–12; 6613) studied 24 Taiwan publicly-traded banks and found high cost efficiency to accompany low profit efficiency for the whole industry. Homogeneous products and price-cut competitions among banks may cause the reasons behind this phenomenon. These banks do not have strong markets outside of Taiwan, and most compete primarily in the Taiwan domestic market.

Table 4.1 (according to Wu, 2008, p. 77) shows that Taiwan's banks are comparatively small in terms of size, market share, and return on equity in East Asia according to the data in the year 2004. The top three banks in Taiwan earned 3.57 percent return on equity while the counterparts in Hong Kong yielded as much as 10.88 percent. And the size of banking assets in Hong Kong was only 2.12 times that in Taiwan. In market share, Taiwan's top banks are less concentrated. That is, they own less market power compared with banks in Singapore, Korea, or Hong Kong. Obviously, the banking market in Taiwan is 'over-banking,' where the market is highly competitive and the profit margin is low.

Because efficiency analysis is a very effective tool to explore the operations and performance of a bank, the results of a previous study (Huang, 2004, p. 433) of Taiwan's banks are displayed as follows. In Table 4.2 (according to Huang, 2004), from 1981 to 2000, the cost efficiency of Taiwan's banks has been improved from 0.9159 to 0.9243 but their total factor productivity stayed as −0.0047, which means a minor decrease in productivity. The improvement in efficiency does not guarantee an improvement in total factor productivity, when negative technological

Table 4.2 Mean total factor productivity and cost efficiency of Taiwan's banks

	Total factor productivity	Cost efficiency
1981–1990	–0.0153	0.9159
1991–1996	0.0076	0.9213
1997–2000	–0.0047	0.9243

Source: Huang (2004).

changes offset the effect of this efficiency improvement. In addition, the return on equity remained low after 2000, according to Table 4.1. Thus, Taiwan's banks are facing severe competition and struggling for survival.

After opening its doors to banks in other countries, will China be an opportunity or a threat to Taiwan's banks? Hong and Zheng (2009) compared and showed that Taiwan's bank branches in Mainland China profited more than their counterparts in Taiwan did. The opportunity for banks in Taiwan to expand to China may increase in the future. Lu et al. (2005, p. 1073) stated that China's banks are still in favor of lending loans to state-owned enterprises. Numerous small- and medium-sized businesses in China cannot obtain sufficient funding because of this biased policy, and rely on funds from underground finance or family borrowings for their capital investments and working capital. This could be an alternative market for Taiwan's banks in China if Taiwan's banks cooperated with experienced local players.

Banks in China will establish branches in Taiwan to serve more tourists and investors from China to Taiwan. Will Chinese banks in Taiwan become a threat to Taiwanese banks? Answering this question requires a discussion from China's perspective.

4.1.3 The Perspective of Banks in China

Hsu (2006) compared financial reforms in China and those in Taiwan and concluded that the experience in Taiwan may help future banking development in China. Particularly after the ECFA, the foreseeable cooperation of financial institutions and communications across the Taiwan Strait will become more convenient and less costly. Financial institutions such as credit unions in China may learn from Taiwan on reforms in local and underground finance. China may not learn this type of knowledge and practical experience from major foreign bankers.

Empirical work from Lin (2010) shows the cost efficiency of China's

Table 4.3 Cost and profit efficiencies of China's banks before and after 2000

	Cost efficiency			Profit efficiency		
	Half normal	Exponential	Gamma	Half normal	Exponential	Gamma
1996–2000	0.7772	0.8047	0.7760	0.6524	0.6526	0.5329
2001–2005	0.7447	0.7847	0.6873	0.6542	0.6541	0.5326

Source: Lin (2010).

banks became weaker after 2000 and the profit efficiency in general improved. Table 4.3 displays the results. Cost efficiency measures the performance of a bank on the cost side and profit efficiency assesses the profit side performance. When a bank is able to save more costs, its cost efficiency will increase. However, if its profitability reduces, its profit efficiency may not improve at the same time.

The research lists the cost and profit efficiencies of banks under three different assumptions on the distributions of the random inefficiency term: half normal, exponential, and Gamma,[1] respectively, since the efficiency estimates are subject to change depending upon the different assumptions on the distributions of the inefficiency term. In terms of cost efficiency, the half normal one falls from 0.7772 to 0.7447 after year 2001 in the sample under study. The exponential cost efficiency decreases from 0.8047 to 0.7847. The Gamma distributed cost efficiency also shows a decreasing trend from 0.7760 to 0.6873. All the changes in cost efficiencies are significant at 5 percent.

On the other hand, profit efficiencies under the assumptions of half normal and exponential distributions increase. The half normal one improves from 0.6524 to 0.6542 and the exponential one moves up from 0.6526 to 0.6541. Nevertheless, the Gamma distributed one decreases from 0.5329 to 0.5326, though the magnitude of this decrease is tiny (0.0003) and statistically insignificant. An interpretation to these outcomes is that the Chinese market is 'under-banking.' When China opened its door to foreign banks in 2001 and the protection from the government had been removed, the cost efficiency of its banks could not catch up with the foreign competitors and so their cost efficiency went down. However, the profit efficiency of China's banks could have been improved because of deregulation and financial reforms. After deregulation and financial reforms, China's banks could expand their business to profit more when the overall banking market was still underdeveloped.

4.1.4 The Structure of this Article

This chapter reviews literature on commercial banking in China and Taiwan and analyses strengths and weaknesses using two different approaches: (1) efficiency analysis; and (2) strategic analysis. Efficiency analysis includes cost efficiency, profit efficiency, scale economy, and scope economy of the banking industry. The analysis is based on industrial organization tools. Strategic analysis incorporates the threat or opportunity for Taiwan's banks, how they can face the 'giant' Big Four in China, and where the benefit lies for this banking cooperation or integration. According to the above research and analysis, this work summarizes previous findings, addresses possible implications, and indicates directions for future studies.

Because the financial integration is stilll in progress, the data that directly record the path of this Cross-Strait change are not readily available. Hence, the author depicts the possible future trends simply based on the existing literature of research. The evidence supporting all the arguments of this chapter awaits future studies.

This chapter differentiates itself from other related studies in the following ways. First, it centers on the potential impacts of economic integration of Taiwanese and Chinese banks. Previous research explored either China or Taiwan. To the best of my knowledge, none of them has discussed both, needless to say the integration across the Strait. Second, this chapter successfully links previous theoretical achievements and empirical evidence (including my own previous empirical tests) regarding the prediction of future Cross-Strait integration. Thus, it is not purely a review article. Third, this chapter does not test any hypothesis since the data are not available. Nevertheless, it has provided timely references for policymakers as well as future researchers who are interested in empirical testing.

The remainder of this chapter is organized as follows. Section 4.2 analyses the existing literature on scale economy, scope economy, efficiency, and productivity. Section 4.3 summarizes the strategic approaches of relationship banking, e-banking, and consumer banking. Section 4.4 reviews the history and literature of geographic integration of the banking industry in the US and Europe. Finally, Section 4.5 summarizes the findings above. The structure of the analysis is illustrated by Figure 4.1, where the relationships between outlines are depicted. Subsection 4.3.4's regulations and reforms affect almost all the factors in the analysis. And Subsection 4.3.1's e-banking and Subsection 4.2.4's information and telecommunication technologies interact and intertwine with each other. In addition, Subsection 4.2.3's cost and profit efficiencies and Subsection 4.2.4's technological change jointly affect the productivity of a bank (see Lin and Lin, 2009, p. 80).

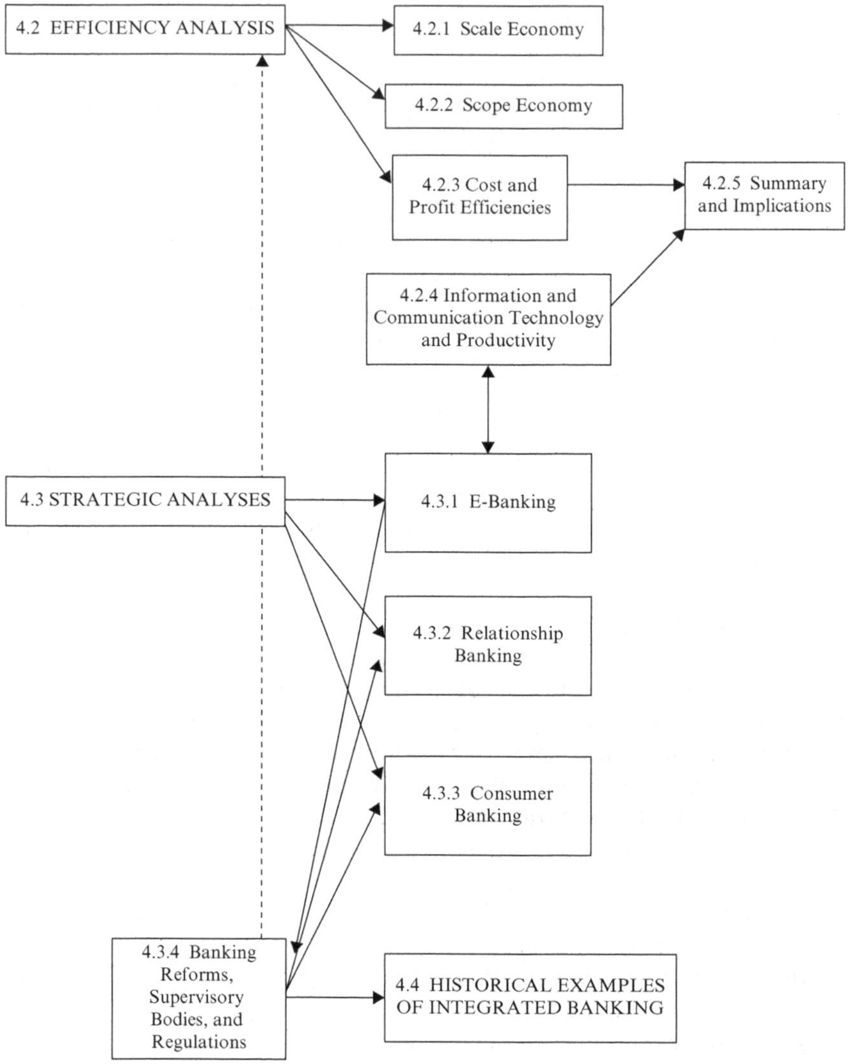

Figure 4.1 Research structure of this chapter

4.2 EFFICIENCY ANALYSIS

This section explores the strengths and weakness of banks in China and Taiwan from an industrial organization perspective, mainly efficiency analysis. The concepts include scale economy, scope economy, cost and profit efficiencies, and information and communication technologies (ICT) and productivity.

4.2.1 Scale Economy

The measure of scale economy indicates the existence of scale economy. The indicator used by Jagtiani et al. (1995, p. 1177) measures economy of scale. If a company operates at the level of increasing return to scale, this indicator is greater than one. If it operates at the constant return to scale or decreasing return to scale, the Jagtiani indicator is equal to or smaller than one. The existence of scale economy also means that, as output increases, the average cost per unit of output decreases. That is, the more a bank produces, the more it saves per unit of output.

Traditionally, the output variables of commercial banking have included financial investments, demand deposits (if demand deposit is not available, use total deposits), and total loans, according to the intermediary approach. Following this tradition and the method of Jagtiani et al. (1995), Taiwan's banks fall in the range of constant return to scale (Huang et al., 2009; Lin et al., 2009). Huang et al. (2007, p. 105) found all banks in Taiwan operate in the increasing scale of economy in the long run (over 22 years). Nevertheless, this scale economy has decreased in recent years. Lieu et al. (2005) found that Taiwan's banks are in the range of increasing return to scale. Most researchers and practitioners observe no scale economy (that is, constant return to scale or decreasing return to scale) in the banking market in Taiwan. In other words, enlarging the size of a commercial bank does not lower the average cost.

4.2.2 Scope Economy

Willig (1979) estimated the scope economy for multiproduct firms. This methodology appropriately applies to the field of banking. Scope economy means that the wider the variety of products a bank sells, the more it saves on the average cost per product. For instance, bank holding companies (or universal banking in the UK) that include both commercial banking and investment banking may enjoy a scope economy. The concept of 'bankassurance' that incorporates or merges both banking products and insurance products into one financial institution is another example.

Based on the method of Willig (1979), the estimations by Lin and Lin (2009) and by Lin et al. (2009) support the existence of scope economy. Fu and Heffernan (2008, pp. 345 and 353) indicated that joint stock banks enjoy a higher scope economy. In practice, Taiwan's second financial reform moved toward the bank holding company system to increase scope economy in banking. Although the scope economy of China's banks is found in previous literature, the financial industries in China are specialized because of regulations that each financial firm should concentrate on only one area of the industry: commercial banking, investment banking or insurance. It is difficult to fully utilize scope economy by expending different production lines across different financial industries. Further development of the scope economy of China's banks awaits future deregulations in the banking industry. However, I believe that expanding a wider product mix within the scope of each individual financial industry is still feasible.

4.2.3 Cost and Profit Efficiencies

This subsection discusses and summarizes the literature of cost and profit efficiencies in banking based upon Data Envelopment Analysis (DEA) or the stochastic frontier approach. The various methodologies are not the focal point; instead, only the insights and implications from the empirical literature are highlighted and compared. Efficiency analysis is essential in the field of financial institutions. For instance, Berger and Humphrey (1991, p. 117) emphasized the importance of efficiency analysis, which dominates the scope and scale economies in the assessment of the banking industry.

Lin et al. (2009) indicated that Taiwan's publicly-traded banks were more cost-efficient than their Chinese counterparts before 2000. Taiwan's banks were featured with higher transparency than their Chinese counterparts. Kumbhakar and Wang (2007) found that joint-stock banks in China are more efficient and productive than state-owned ones.

Fu and Heffernan (2007) indicated that joint-stock banks in China enjoy higher cost efficiency. Shen and Lu (2008, p. 22) also posited that joint-stock and city commercial banks in China are most profitable; and following Wu et al. (2007, p. 343), the return on assets for partial foreign-owned banks is higher. Berger et al. (2010, p. 3) estimated China's bank efficiencies and found that the Big Four are the least profit-efficient, and that foreign ownership significantly improves efficiency. In summary, although various papers have explored efficiencies from diverse angles, joint-stock banks are the most profitable or efficient among all the types of banks.

Lieu et al. (2005) investigated cost efficiency and off-balance sheet activities and found that old banks have easier accessibility to off-balance sheet transactions and thus their cost efficiency is higher. Liang et al. (2008, p. 287) related non-performing loans to operational efficiency of banks in Taiwan. Lin et al. (2009) studied bank efficiencies from 1995 to 1999 and estimated higher cost efficiencies for old banks. Their findings indicated that newly-established banks operated at a lower efficiency level than old banks did. The main reason why old banks in Taiwan operate efficiently is market monitoring. That is, most government-owned banks are partially publicly-traded on the Taiwan Stock Exchange and become transparent to the market. Hence, they also make efforts toward minimizing cost (or maximizing profit) by following the market mechanism.

4.2.4 Information and Communication Technology and Productivity

The constant return to scale and the existence of scope economy in commercial banking may be ascribed to intensive use of information and communication technologies (ICT). Before the 1990s, most bank information technology centered on the mainframe computer system. In a bank, the most common ICT structure is a group of terminals linked to a mainframe computer (a centralized computing system). A bank operating on this type of system may not own massive extra capacity to manage more transactions because all transactions rely on the mainframe.

Today, one personal computer can handle more transactions and difficult tasks than a mainframe of 20 years ago. A bank operating on this 'distributional computation' system owns extra capacity to handle more products and transactions. The average cost per product or per unit of output is also extremely low. Therefore, the use of ICT and e-commerce models has shifted and reshaped cost and profit frontiers worldwide (Lin and Lin, 2009).

Banks in Taiwan and China have also transitioned to ICT systems. After decentralizing the ICT system and lowering the cost per computer, the ICT cost of a small bank may not differ from that of a big bank. The ICT system capacity for a bank has grown sufficiently to handle multi-product businesses easily. The computing system transition explains why there is no scale economy and justifies the existence of scope economy in Taiwan and China. The evidence was supporting the theory that IT inputs make banks more productive in Taiwan (Huang, 2005, p. 251) while such evidence in China has not yet been explored. Although in theory there may exist huge potential for this ICT integration (Lin, 2007; Lin and Lin, 2009), the compatibility of the ICT systems and the banking systems across the Strait remains unknown. This awaits future discussions in the related fields.

4.2.5 Summary and Implications

The literature review indicates that most studies conclude that there is no scale economy in China and Taiwan, but scope economy. This implies that further development of multi-product businesses such as universal banking, bank holding companies, or 'bankassurance' will help banks acquire more scope economy. Large size will not automatically reduce the average cost of bank outputs. The concept of 'too-big-to-fail' is only a myth if a big bank does not possess any strength other than its size. This coincides with the phenomena of the 1990s economic downturn in Japan and the 2008–2009 financial crisis in the US.

Minor foreign ownership helps enhance bank efficiency in China. According to the features of Taiwanese banks, such as governance, management, market monitoring, transparency, and comparatively solid regulation, Taiwan's banks are foreign to China in practice. It is expected that Taiwanese banks that enter the Chinese market and acquire shares from Chinese banks will improve the cost efficiency of banks in China in future. In addition, ICT investments are positively associated with the productivity of banks in Taiwan, but this impact is uncertain in their counterparts in China.

Even though Taiwan has gained higher efficiency, its strength is gradually fading after increasing numbers of Western and Japanese banks have entered the Chinese market. Long-standing political issues have closed the door of cooperation between Taiwan and China for decades. This has led to delayed involvement of Taiwan in China's financial markets following Taiwan's long history of direct investment in China. However, regulations in China currently prevent commercial banks from selling insurance and other financial securities. Thus, expanding scope economy across financial industries is impossible at present but could be possible after further deregulation in China in future.

4.3 STRATEGIC ANALYSES

This session includes various strategic analyses including e-banking, relationship banking, consumer banking and bank regulations.

4.3.1 E-Banking

China has more Internet users (in terms of the absolute number) than any other country in the world. As of 2009, 384 million persons use the Internet in China, including some urban and rural labor workers. A large web population implies huge e-banking potential. Taiwan's development using Internet technologies and applying e-commerce models has preceded China's, and it is thus more advanced in e-banking.

On the other hand, the demand for loans is strong and the supply is short in the loan market in China, particularly in regions where very few financial institutions can effectively outreach enterprises. In some rural areas, only agricultural credit unions exist and operate following government policies. Whenever the government tightens money supplies, limited funding flows to urban areas and fast-growing rural or village enterprises suffer from insufficient funding. E-banking brokers in China try to match the asymmetric demand and supply of funds.

An e-banking opportunity exists for Taiwanese banks, which works for village enterprises and matches the demand and supply while banks in Taiwan have a savings surplus.

Dobson and Kashyap (2006, p. 105) stated that the financial system in China is still fragmented where local branches have more decision-making power compared with their counterparts in Western countries. Conceptually, e-banking might help find new opportunities when current markets are segmented. E-banking enables borrowing across geographic or policy barriers because of different interest rates, conditions, or loan policies of different banks across borders.

Berger and DeYoung (2006, p. 1510) further explored bank efficiency and found that headquarter control over remote branches increases over time following geographic integration. In the meantime, the agency cost of bank branches decreases. This phenomenon is mainly because of technological change. The use of information and communication technology contributes significantly to lower agency cost in remote bank branches and better control ability from bank headquarters (see also Lin and Lin, 2009).

4.3.2 Relationship Banking

Relationship banking is banking businesses based on specialized products and terms for each related customer. Both borrowers and lenders can negotiate the terms, requirements, and interest rates according to the unique needs of customers.

Boot and Thakor (2000, p. 708) and Boot (2000, p. 7) investigated how European commercial and savings banks survived or even thrived when American-style transaction banking and capital markets prevailed on the European continent. When the publicly-traded bond or equity market develops, the amount of total loan-lending via commercial banking reduces. When interbank competition is simultaneously more serious, relationship banking adds higher value for borrowers. The market share of relationship banking increases among all loan-lending.

The situation stated by Boot and Thakor is similar to that in China: the equity market has been booming and foreign and domestic banks are increasing. Because Taiwan's entry into Chinese financial markets has been delayed, Taiwanese banks should focus on relation-oriented businesses in Taiwan's corporations in Mainland China.

Kuan et al. (2009) and Hong and Zheng (2009) stated that Taiwanese corporations and entrepreneurs have a preference towards financial services in Taiwanese banks. This is because most Taiwanese corporations in China are medium-small businesses that have difficulty obtaining funding from major banks in China. However, banks in China have difficulty assessing credit records of Taiwanese borrowers. Taiwanese banks should start businesses in China with relationship banking among Taiwanese firms.

On the other hand, fragmented markets in China (see Dobson and Kashyap, 2006, p. 105) offer opportunities for relationship banking. The three geographic segments of the Yantze River Delta, the Pearl River Delta, and the Beijing Capital region are not integrated in terms of the decision-making of financial institutions. A discrepancy exists in interest rates and loan quality across different segments. The research by Berger et al. (2010) also implies that geographic or product diversification does not improve the cost and profit efficiencies of China's banks. If Taiwan's banks can effectively integrate businesses across various segments and regions, the chance of successful entry will increase. Moreover, 'relationship' in Chinese is 'GuanXi,' which is highly emphasized in Chinese business connections. Hsu (2006) suggested that Taiwanese banks in China have contributed to the growth of Taiwanese corporations in China, and will continue to foster further growth of these corporations. Leung et al. (2003, p. 30) indicated that Asian banks have particular strengths in entering and surviving the Chinese market. Hence, Taiwanese banks might have a higher possibility of surviving and thriving in China than some foreign banks, particularly in more localized, segmented, smaller markets.

4.3.3 Consumer Banking

Consumer banking in Taiwan has grown rapidly. Taiwanese banks experiencing overexpansion and saturation in the domestic market have sought new markets overseas. The governmental policies of China also encourage consumption, particularly in inland provinces and rural areas (there are stimulus plans for rural areas). Therefore, Taiwanese banks may develop consumer banking businesses in China. However, Hong and Zheng (2009) did not support expansion of the consumer banking business in China because Taiwan has suffered from bad debts due to rapid growth of consumer banking such as credit card businesses. In addition, China's regulators restrict banks from the development of consumer banking such as wealth management, personal finance and unsecured consumer lending. There exist barriers for the domestic banks and foreign banks in China to enter the consumer banking markets.

4.3.4 Banking Reforms, Supervisory Bodies, and Regulations

Taiwanese banks and Chinese ones are under two different supervisory systems. Banks in Taiwan operate across different financial sectors (deposit and loan, securities, insurance, etc.) while banks in China focus on the deposit and loan business. The regulatory body in China follows a similar philosophy. In China, the People's Bank is responsible for macroeconomic monetary control and the banking regulatory commission is dedicated to monitoring at the firm level. A Chinese commercial bank cannot involve non-commercial banking businesses. The Taiwanese banking market is saturated while the Chinese banking market still has many potentials and unsatisfied needs for future development. In other words, Taiwanese banks are 'overbanking' and Chinese banks are 'underbanking.'

Several different viewpoints include banking reforms and capital adequacy. Kwong and Lee (2005, pp. 1 and 12) highlighted a problem of current bank reforms in China. When required adequate capital is higher, funding from Chinese banks will be tighter, so loanable funds will flow to major big cities. Then fast-growing village and rural enterprises face the problem of insufficient working capital for doing business.

Here is an opportunity for Taiwan's banks, which can cooperate with some local deposit and loan institutions in towns, villages, or in second- and third-line cities where enterprises have difficulty getting funds. Taiwan's banking market has already been too competitive and 'overbanked.' Taiwan banks can use the channels of local institutions in China to finance town and village enterprises, when major banks in China provide loans that are limited to big state-owned or well-known companies. Particularly since the privatization of the township and village enterprises since mid-1990s, Taiwan's banks and China's local and regional financial institutions may have more opportunities to expand their customer bases. For China, investing in Taiwan (buying or establishing bank branches in Taiwan) could help diversify its own risk geographically or even politically by 'putting its eggs in several baskets.' However, this does not solve monitoring and regulating problems. In other words, 'Who is watching the eggs in the basket?' (Amihud et al., 2003, p. 857).

China's large enterprises have long preferred the investment banking business models of Hong Kong to the commercial banking business model, despite the fact that, in practice, commercial banking is more important in China (Hsu, 2006). The British/American investment banking model adopted by Hong Kong calls for a sound accounting system, reliable auditing, transparency of operations and in-time disclosure to the public. Unfortunately, most firms in China do not possess these desirable features when they consider financing from investment bankers.

Hence, Hsu suggested that China learn from the business models and experiences of Taiwan instead of the Hong Kong model, since the banking system in Taiwan has dealt with underground finance and the transition from underground finance to organized commercial banking. The experience in Taiwan may help bank reform in China, particularly in the transformation of local deposits and loan institutions.

Risk and regulation issues are also barriers to cross-border integration of the banking industry between Taiwan and China. First, as mentioned above, monitoring banks and enterprises across the Strait is risky. Second, the capital control and foreign exchange system in China may hinder the progress of Taiwanese banks' entry. China's regulatory authority sees capital control as the core of financial stability and foreign exchange pegging as its major strength in international trade. Either one of them may wipe out the profits that Taiwan or foreign banks earn.

Third, Taiwan and China are still 'rival regimes:' China still claims its sovereignty over Taiwan. This unfriendly political environment could heat up investor anxiety and cause a riskier Cross-Strait integration than cases in Europe. This Cross-Strait political hostility will also lead to difficulty in the reconciliation of banking supervision.

4.4 HISTORICAL EXAMPLES OF INTEGRATED BANKING

Before 1970, commercial banking in the US was restricted to the state where the bank headquarters was located. Several states began to deregulate by removing geographic restrictions on inter-state branching. Hence, the 1970s, 1980s, and 1990s have witnessed upheaval in the landscape of the commercial banking industry in the US. In 1994, the Riegel-Neal Interstate Banking and Branching Efficiency Act allowed out-of-state bank holding companies to operate across states without geographic restrictions. This long deregulation process may help to explain the difficulties involved in banking industry integration between Taiwan and China.

Berger and Humphrey (1991) and Berger et al. (1987, p. 501) carried out some early work in the study of scope and scale economies related to the integration of the US banks. Zardkoohi and Fraser (1998, p. 97) proved that the geographic deregulation in the US banking system fostered more competition. Hence, the key question is: 'Would the more competitive market structure induce higher efficiency (or better performance) from a bank?' DeYoung et al. (1998) discovered that the cost efficiency of local banks deteriorated right after out-of-state entry and improved after 6 years of deregulation. Jayaratne and Strahan (1998) showed that after the state-entry restriction is lifted, operating cost and loan loss of banks decreases. That is, better banks grow and weaker banks disappear. Berger et al. (2000, p. 27) indicated that in international mergers, domestic banks enjoy higher cost and profit efficiencies over their foreign counterparts while some countries such as the US may own limited global advantages in the world banking markets. Stiroh and Strahan (2003, p. 801) also found that large banks would have gradually earned higher market share and gained higher cost efficiency after cross-state integration. Shaffer (1993, p. 423) simulated the cost efficiency of bank megamergers in the US and found significant efficiency gains in cross-state megamerger cases. Yildirim and Mohanty (2010, p. 63) described the market structure of the commercial banking industry for 50 states after deregulation. They found that in most states in the US, the banking industry operates under monopolistic competition. The commercial banking market has become less competitive in recent years because large banks have gained more market power and small banks have become less competitive. This conclusion supports Subsection 4.3.2, that quality competition could be more essential than price competition. The banking markets for both Taiwan and China will likely stay monopolistic competitive after integration. Nevertheless, I conjecture that the allocation of funding and other resources will be more efficient.

Another well-known example was banking market integration in Europe in the 1990s. European Market Unification (EMU) fostered integration of the banking industry across countries in Europe. Altunbas and Molyneux (1996, p. 217) measured the economy of scale prior to EU integration. They found that French, German, and Spanish banking markets enjoy the economy of scale. That is, large-size banks tend to be more cost-efficient. Yildirim and Philippatos (2007, p. 123) explored the market structure and cost and profit efficiencies of banks in Europe from 1993 to 2000. They addressed the issue that a competitive market structure leads to higher cost efficiency and causes lower profit efficiency. Therefore, the removal of geographic restrictions will not automatically enhance cost and profit efficiencies simultaneously. Epstein and Johnson (2010, p. 1237) highlighted the differences between Eastern European nations and Central European nations after integration. Koutsomanoli-Filippaki and Mamatzakis (2010, p. 9) found that the speeds of adjustment toward long-term equilibrium vary from country to country in European Union nations. Boot (1999, p. 609) also stated the existence of national protection over domestic banks after integration. And Houben et al. (2008, p. 242) showed evidence that integrated EU banks tend to be nationally-oriented and regionally clustered, where the market structures are 'differentiated' and 'tailor-made.' These results from Europe coincide with those from Taiwan and China by Lin et al. (2009), where cost efficiency increases and profit decreases after banks integrate more within the boundary of each economy. According to the simulation results, Altunbas et al. (1997, p. 317) found that the mergers across EU countries are not always cost-saving. We may infer that, in addition to cost saving, there should be other motivations for bank mergers. Bandt and Davis (1999, p. 21) stated that country barriers remain significant after integration and integrated markets are monopolistic competitive. Their conclusion is the same as the example of the US explored by Yildirim and Mohanty (2010).

Moreover, geographic integration in either the EU or the US would diversify the risk a bank faces (see for example Shaffer, 1993; Goldberg and Levi, 2000; and Meon and Weill, 2005, p. 315; Morgan et al., 2004, p. 1580).

Based on the literature of integration in the banking industry in the US and Europe, this chapter finds that the banking market does not automatically march towards the perfect competitive market. Instead, a monopolistic competitive market structure is common after banking industry integration.

4.5 SUMMARY

This chapter reviews and compares literature on commercial banking in Taiwan and China. Differences will continue to exist and the domestic bank will still possess certain strengths and market power. This chapter further compares the different systems of Taiwan and China in terms of efficiency analysis and strategic analysis and discusses the integration experience of the banking industry in the US and Europe. From these analyses and literature review, this work predicts or conjectures how Taiwan's banks survive and how China's banks respond to the dramatic change in financial integration across the Taiwan Strait following the ECFA.

The banking market literature shows no scale economy in either Taiwan or China. However, most literature supports the existence of scope economy. Privately-owned banks in China also tend to be more cost- and profit-efficient than their state-owned counterparts. No such evidence exists in Taiwan because most Taiwanese banks in the sample are publicly-traded and monitored by investors.

Taiwan's banks enjoy higher cost efficiency, e-banking strengths, and relationship banking for Taiwanese corporations. However, because the financial market in Taiwan is so small, the profit efficiency of banks has been decreasing when the market is more competitive. The e-banking potential includes integrating fragmented Chinese markets and online loan agents, and cooperations after the ECFA. Taiwanese banks and financial institutions in China may adopt Taiwanese models and develop new consumer banking markets in China. Taiwan can help fund- insufficient village enterprises to obtain loans, while major large banks in China focus on state-owned and large enterprises in first-tier cities. Institutions in China may learn institutional knowledge in 'underground finance,' 'financial products,' and 'insurance.' Small credit unions and cooperative units that form strategic alliances or mergers with robust Taiwanese banks could also gain efficiency quickly.

The history of banking integration in the US and Europe implies that banking markets in most states are comparatively monopolistic. Quality competition is essential in a monopolistic comparative market; therefore, the commercial banking industry should compete by providing higher quality services and differentiated fees. European bankers have built 'relationship banking' to compete in financial markets against big international commercial banks and growing capital markets. Bank integration does not remove all legal or geographic barriers between nations or states. Instead, local banks still possess specific strengths in local markets.

In addition to all the factors above, we have to pay attention to the differences between Taiwan and China. Currently China has capital control and foreign exchange pegging systems. And it is difficult to monitor the banks and investments across the Taiwan Strait from either side. The political tension and the reconciliation of regulation between two regimes are not easy. It is a time-consuming process.

In summary, banking industry integration will lead to a monopolistic competitive market structure where quality competition, instead of price competition, is the key to success. The concepts of relationship banking in local markets, e-banking, and scope economy may contribute to higher bank efficiency after integration. Based on previous experiences and studies, this work infers and conjectures that: (1) Taiwan's banks possess strengths in the local Taiwanese market; (2) Taiwan's banks will not acquire a big market share in China but it helps Taiwanese enterprises in China when Taiwan's banks extend businesses and branches across the Strait; and (3) because Taiwan has developed and reformed its commercial banking market earlier than China, China may learn from Taiwan about financial reforms. Taiwan's banks in China will definitely help the continuous growth of Taiwan's corporations in China.

NOTE

1. Half normal distribution, exponential distribution, and Gamma distribution are different probability distributions that depict the shape of the random cost or profit inefficiency. The estimates of the inefficiencies are affected by the different assumed probability distributions.

REFERENCES

Altunbas, Y. and P. Molyneux (1996), 'Cost Economies in EU Banking Systems,' *Journal of Economics and Business*, 48 (3), 217–30.

Altunbas, Y., P. Molyneux, and J. Thornton (1997), 'Big Bank Mergers in Europe: An Analysis of the Cost Implications,' *Economica*, 64, 317–29.

Amihud, Yakov, G. DeLong, and A. Saunders (2003), 'The Effects of Cross-Border Bank Mergers on Bank Risk and Value', *Journal of International Money and Finance*, 21, 857–77.

Bandt, O. d. and P. Davis (1999), 'A Cross-Country Comparison of Market Structures in European Banking by September 1999', Working paper no. 7, European Central Bank Working Paper Series. 22 typed pages.

Berger, A.N. and R. DeYoung (2006), 'Technological Progress and the Geographic Expansion of the Banking Industry,' *Journal of Money, Credit, and Banking*, 38 (6), 1483–513.

Berger, A.N., R. DeYoung, H. Genay, and G.F. Udell (2000), 'Globalization of Financial Institutions: Evidence from Cross-Border Banking Performance,' *Brookings-Wharton Papers on Financial Services*, 3, Robert E. Litan and Anthony Santomero, eds, 23–158.

Berger, A.N., G.A. Hanweck, and D.B. Humphrey (1987), 'Competitive Viability in Banking: Scale, Scope and Product Mix Economies in Banking,' *Journal of Monetary Economics*, 20, 501–20.

Berger, A.N., I. Hasan, and M. Zhou (2010), 'The Effects of Focus Versus Diversification on Bank Performance: Evidence from Chinese Banks,' BOFIT–Institute for Economies in Transition, Bank of Finland, BOFIT Discussion Papers 4/2010, 52 typed pages.

Berger, A.N. and D.B. Humphrey (1991), 'The Dominance of Inefficiencies over Scale and Product Mix Economies in Banking,' *Journal of Monetary Economics*, 28, 117–48.

Boot, A.W.A. (1999), 'European Lessons on Consolidation in Banking,' *Journal of Banking and Finance*, 23, 609–13.

Boot, A.W.A. (2000), 'Relationship Banking: What Do We Know?' *Journal of Financial Intermediation*, 9 (1), 7–25.

Boot, A.W.A. and A.V. Thakor (2000), 'Can Relationship Banking Survive Competition?' *Journal of Finance*, 55 (2), 679–713.

DeYoung, R., I. Hasan, and B. Kirchhoff (1998), 'The Impact of Out-of-State

Entry on the Cost Efficiency of Local Commercial Banks,' *Journal of Economics and Business*, 50 (2), 191–203.

Dobson, Wendy and A.K. Kashyap (2006), 'The Contradiction in China's Gradualist Banking Reforms,' *Brookings Papers on Economic Activity*, 2, 103–48.

Epstein, R.A. and J. Johnson (2010), 'Uneven Integration: Economic and Monetary Union in Central and Eastern Europe,' *Journal of Common Market Studies*, 48 (5), 1237–60.

Fu, X. and S.A. Heffernan (2007), 'Cost X-efficiency in China's Banking Sector,' *China Economic Review*, 18, 35–53.

Fu, X. and S.A. Heffernan (2008), 'Economies of Scale and Scope in China's Banking Sector,' *Applied Financial Economics*, 18, 345–56.

Goldberg, Michael A. and Maurice D. Levi (2000), 'The European Union as a Country Portfolio," *European Journal of Political Economy*, 16 (3), 411–27.

Hong, Y.M. and Ming Zheng (2009), 'Capital Markets Integration and Regulation across Strait,' Special Study Report, published by Taiwan Securities Association, 198 pages, available at: http://www.csa.org.tw/downdoc/doc/98%E5%B9%B4%E8%AD%89%E5%88%B8%E5%85%AC%E6%9C%83%E7%A0%94%E7%A9%B6%E5%A0%B1%E5%91%8A/%E5%85%A9%E5%B2%B8%E8%B3%87%E6%9C%AC%E5%B8%82%E5%A0%B4%E6%95%B4%E5%90%88%E8%88%87%E7%9B%A3%E7%AE%A1.pdf.

Houben, A., I. Schrijvers, and T. Willems (2008), 'Supervising Cross-Border Banks in Europe,' *Journal of Banking Regulation*, 9, 227–46.

Hsu, C.-M. (2006) (in Chinese), 'The Cross Strait Financial Cooperation between Taiwan and China based on the Taiwan Experience,' available at: http://wenku.baidu.com/view/d6fdb4691eb91a37f1115cc1.html.

Huang, M.H. (2004), 'Banking Reforms Productivity and Risk Management in Taiwan's Banking Industry,' *Academia Economic Papers*, 32 (3), 413–39.

Huang, T.-H. (2005), 'A Study on the Productivities of IT Capital and Computer Labor: Firm-Level Evidence from Taiwan's Banking Industry,' *Journal of Productivity Analysis*, 24, 241–57.

Huang, T.-H., B.-G. Chang, and Y.-F. Chiu (2009), 'An Examination of Banks' Efficiency for Six Asian Countries Using the Metafrontier Cost Function', *Academia Economic Papers*, 37 (1), 61–100.

Huang, T.-H., Y.-H. Chen, and P.-S. Chen (2007), 'Estimating Long-Run Efficiency Levels of Taiwan's Commercial Banks Using a Dynamic Cost Frontier Model,' *Academia Economic Papers*, 35 (1), 83–114.

Jagtiani, J., A. Nathan, and G. Sick (1995), 'Scale Economics and Cost Complementarities in Commercial Banks' On- and Off-Balance-Sheet Activities,' *Journal of Banking & Finance*, 19, 1175–89.

Jayaratne, Jith and Philip E. Strahan (1998), 'Entry Restrictions, Industry Evolution and Dynamic Efficiency: Evidence from Commercial Banking,' *Journal of Law and Economics*, 41, 239–74.

Koutsomanoli-Filippaki, A. and E.C. Mamatzakis (2010), 'Estimating the Speed of Adjustment of European Banking Efficiency Under a Quadratic Loss Function,' *Economic Modeling*, 27 (1), 1–11.

Kuan, C.M., Y.L. Huang, and R.C. Yang (2009), *Special Study Report*, Taiwan Securities Association, 42 typed pages.

Kumbhakar, S.C. and D. Wang (2007), 'Economic Reforms, Efficiency and Productivity in Chinese Banking,' *Journal of Regulatory Economics*, 32, 105–29.

Kwong, C.C.L. and P.K. Lee (2005), 'Bad Loans Versus Sluggish Rural Industrial Growth: A Policy Dilemma of China's Banking Reform,' *Journal of the Asia Pacific Economy*, 10 (1), 1–25.

Leung , M.K., D. Rigby, and T. Young (2003), 'Entry of Foreign Banks in the People's Republic of China: A Survival Analysis,' *Applied Economics*, 35 (1), 21–31.

Liang, C.-J., M.-L. Yao, D.-Y. Hwang, and W.-H. Wu (2008), 'The Impact of Non-Performing Loans on Banks' Operating Efficiency for Taiwan Banking Industry,' *Review of Pacific Basin Financial Markets and Policies*, 11, 287–304.

Lieu, P.-T., T.-L. Yeh and Y.-H. Chiu (2005), 'Off-Balance Sheet Activities and Cost Inefficiency in Taiwan's Banks,' *Service Industries Journal*, 25 (7), 925–44.

Lin, H.-J. (2007), 'The Strategies of International E-Finance under Basel II: A Complementary Asset Approach,' *Journal of Internet Banking and Commerce*, 12 (3), 10 pages, available at: http://www.arraydev.com/commerce/jibc/.

Lin, H.-J. (2010), 'Banks in China: An Analysis of Cost and Profit Efficiencies,' available at SSRN: http://ssrn.com/abstract=1692974.

Lin, H.-J. and W.T. Lin (2007), 'International E-Banking: ICT Investments and the Basel Accord,' *Journal of Comparative International Management*, 10 (1), 23–39. available at: http://findarticles.com/p/articles/mi_hb3249/is_1_10/ai_n28566768/.

Lin, H.-J. and W.T. Lin (2009), *IT and Efficiency Analysis of Commercial Banks and Insurance Firms: A Global Comparison,* Saarbrücken, Germany: VDM Publishing Company.

Lin, W.T., H.-J. Lin, and S.K. Mohanty (2009), 'The Cost and Profit Efficiencies and Scope Economies of Commercial Banks: Evidence from Taiwan and China,' *International Journal of Finance*, 21 (2), 6097–123.

Lu, D., S.M. Thangavelu, and Q. Hu (2005), 'Biased Lending and Non-Performing Loans in China's Banking Sector,' *Journal of Development Studies*, 41 (6), 1071–91.

Meon, P.-G. and L. Weill (2005), 'Can Mergers in Europe Help Banks Hedge Against Macroeconomic Risk?' *Applied Financial Economics*, 15, 315–26.

Morgan, D., B. Rime, and P.E. Strahan (2004), 'Bank Integration and State Business Cycles,' *Quarterly Journal of Economics*, 119 (4), 1555–84.

Shaffer, S. (1993), 'Can Megamergers Improve Bank Efficiency?' *Journal of Banking and Finance*, 17, 423–36.

Shen, C.-H. and C.-H. Lu (2008), 'Is There a Silver Lining in the Cloudy Performance of Chinese Banks? An Empirical Investigation into the Determinants of Profitability and Risk,' in E.J. Fuchs and F. Braun (eds), *Emerging Topics in Banking and Finance*, Hauppauge, NY: Nova Science Publishers.

Stiroh, K.J. and P.E. Strahan (2003), 'Competitive Dynamics of Deregulation: Evidence from U.S. Banking,' *Journal of Money, Credit and Banking*, 35 (5), 801–28.

Willig, R.D. (1979), 'Multiproduct Technology and Market Structure,' *American Economic Review*, 69, 346–51.

Wu, H.-L., C.-H. Chen, and M.-H. Lin (2007), 'The Effect of Foreign Bank Entry on the Operational Performance of Commercial Banks in the Chinese Transitional Economy,' *Post-Communist Economies*, 19 (3), 343–57.

Wu, W.-H. (2008), 'The Second Financial Reform and the Development of Financial Industry in Taiwan,' *Review of Pacific Basin Financial Markets and Policies*, 11 (1), 75–97.

Yildirim, H.S. and Sunil K. Mohanty (2010), 'Geographic Deregulation and Competition in the US Banking Industry,' *Financial Markets, Institutions and Instruments*, 19 (2), 63–94.
Yildirim, H.S. and George C. Philippatos (2007), 'Efficiency of Banks: Recent Evidence from the Transition Economies of Europe, 1993–2000', *European Journal of Finance*, 13 (2), 123–43.
Zardkoohi, A. and D. Fraser (1998), 'Geographic Deregulation and Competition in U.S. Banking Markets,' *Financial Review*, 33, 85–98.

5. Development and international diversification benefits of equity markets in China, Hong Kong, and Taiwan

Wan-Jiun Paul Chiou, Chun-Pin Hsu, and Chin-Wen Huang

5.1 INTRODUCTION

The effectiveness of international diversification has been well documented in rich economies.[1] However, the potential economic value of international diversification to investors in developing countries has not yet received the attention it deserves from academia. Among emerging countries, the development and interaction of financial markets between China, Hong Kong, and Taiwan differ notably from the others. Since the late 1980s, there has been an increase in the cross-Taiwan Strait economic integration between China and Taiwan, which is evident from broad economic indicators such as trade in goods, services and investments. The growth of the Chinese economy and the development of China in the global production chain network drive the economy in East Asia, particularly the 'Chinese region,' increasingly interdependent with each other. On the other hand, the dynamics of economic interdependence in this region has been accompanied by time-swinging military and political tensions. Thus, several critical issues emerge: What international diversification benefits local investors in the Sino market? Do the benefits of regional diversification vanish in their home region? Do the economic values generated by internationally diversifying portfolios shrink as the economy is increasingly integrated? If the benefits still exist, do their effectiveness to local investors diverge across China, Hong Kong, and Taiwan? Because of its rising economic importance and wealth accumulation, understanding the diversifying strategies and benefits in this Chinese-cultural region has become an indispensible element in global asset management. In this chapter, we study the economic development of these countries/districts and the benefits of diversification with other countries in the world from a local investor's point of view.

Recent studies have paid a great deal of attention to the related issues of diversification of financial markets in the same area, particularly in Europe, due to the trend of regional integration. Flavin (2004) and Moerman (2008) investigate size in the benefits of cross-industry diversification and international diversification in European countries. Carrieri et al. (2004) and Hardouvelis et al. (2006) document the time-varying market integration in the Eurozone. However, research on the effectiveness of internationally diversifying in other areas that are at an early stage of integration, such as the so-called 'pan-Chinese markets,' is relatively silent so far.

Understanding the benefits of diversification and portfolio allocation in this Mandarin zone is crucial in four respects. First, the three countries or districts have experienced the highest growth in the world in the last five decades respectively and, more notably, are believed to continue in this way in the future. Although a small amount of recent research (for example, Allen et al., 2005; Bhabra et al., 2008; Fan et al., 2007; and Gul et al., 2009) has documented the specialties of the Chinese market, the upsurge in economic integration makes understanding the characteristics of the optimal asset allocations in this area significant. More importantly, China has signed the Closer Economic Partnership Arrangement (CEPA) with Hong Kong and Macau in 2003 and the Economic Cooperation Framework Agreement (ECFA) with Taiwan in 2010.[2] Our analysis contributes to the literature by investigating this timely issue from an angle of the *potential* benefits of diversification.

Second, previous research suggests that both investors and corporations have a propensity to implement home-biased asset allocations. Investors tend to invest more in their home markets than the optimum, at both domestic and international levels.[3] On the other hand, multinational enterprises (MNEs) also tend to diversify their foreign direct investment (FDI) and expand their business and sales intra-regionally rather than globally.[4] For instance, Rugman (2005) surveys the top 500 MNEs in the world, which represent more than 90 percent of FDI and over half of international trade in the world, and finds that more than 80 percent of their sales were performed in their home regions. The economic interactions between China, Hong Kong, and Taiwan particularly follow the above patterns. The analysis of this diversification with home-bias provides an insight into portfolio management regarding the influence of regional integration on diversification strategies and benefits.

Third, the economic integration of Taiwan and China differs from the typical models that are primarily liaised by treaties between the governments. Unlike other split countries, such as Korea, the private investment from Taiwan to China plays the key role in fashioning economic integration under long-term political hostility and military tension. Such developments also influence the industrial structures and the economic growth in these countries. Recent literature suggests that the correlations and integration in the international market increased (Bekaert et al., 2007; Bekaert et al., 2005; Goetzmann et al., 2005; Pukthuanthong and Roll, 2009; Stulz and Williamson, 2003) and the domestic expected returns in most countries declined (Ang et al., 2009; Bekaert and Harvey, 2003; Bekaert et al., 2005; and Bekaert et al., 2009) during past decades. The former has a negative effect, while the latter has a positive impact on the global diversification benefits to domestic investors. Moreover, Eun and Lee (2010) also find a convergence in risk-adjusted returns across countries in the past 4 decades. Given the mixed effects discussed above, the long-term trend of international diversification benefits is not clear *a priori*. Thus, a thorough time-series analysis of potential gains helps to determine how international diversification benefits domestic investors when this regional market is increasingly integrated.

The major findings of this analysis are as follows. The inclusion of assets in developed economies, particularly those in Europe and North America, provide a better improvement in mean-variance efficiency than those in emerging markets. The diversification strategies that include other two countries/districts in this Sino region do not benefit the local investors. To ensure the robustness of our finding, we consider home-bias investment in constructing portfolios and obtain a similar conclusion, although the benefits tend to be less when the portfolios are more home-biased. The time-varying benefits of diversification are determined by the dispersion of the mean-variance efficiency of domestic assets in these countries.

This chapter is organized as follows: Section 5.2 discusses the development and impact of the free trade agreements in this area; Section 5.3 reports the economic background and industries of the region; and Section 5.4 describes the data. The measurement of the benefits of cross-nation diversification under various investment constraints are presented in Section 5.5. Section 5.6 discusses the empirical results. Section 5.7 presents the conclusions.

5.2 FREE TRADE AGREEMENTS IN THIS REGION

In recent years, there has been a rapid growth in enhancing economic integration and cooperation. As of the end of July 2010, according to the World Trade Organization, there are 283 free trade agreements (FTAs) and regional trade agreements (RTAs) in force in the world. Their locations include Europe (European Union, Central European Free Trade Agreement, European Free Trade Association, Baltic Free Trade Area, etc.), the Americas (North American Free Trade Agreement, Southern Common Market, etc.), Asia (Association of Southeast Asian Nations, Asia Pacific Trade Agreement, etc.), former Soviet Union republics, and Africa (West African Economic and Monetary Union, etc.). This trend is particularly important to emerging nations due to high economic growth and increasing interdependence.

The effects of regional integration on promoting international trade are mixed. Baldwin (1997) comments that regional integration triggers pressures for such multilateral agreements and suggests that such liberalization strengthens the hand of exporters and pro-trade forces. On the other hand, trade agreements intensify the intra-regional dependence, generating a substitution effect on actual globalization. Bhagwati (1992) suggests that regionalism brought by regional trading agreements (RTAs) stress the benefits of free trade but may divert attention from the inter-regional trading system and eventually threaten the multilateral trading system. The empirical studies of Qian et al. (2008) and Rugman (2005) confirm that firm investment behavior tend to be home-region biased.

The term 'free trade agreement' conventionally refers to a 'preferential trade agreement (PTA) with tariffs eliminated entirely on goods produced in member countries.' However, 'FTA' is increasingly used simply to refer to an assortment of economic agreements, such as closer economic partnership agreements, comprehensive economic partnership agreements, or economic partnerships. The benefits of FTAs are promoting interdependence of regional economy, promoting political goodwill, and promoting economic or political integration.

The trend of trade treaties in the Chinese region is strengthened by the other countries' RTAs that are currently in force or under negotiation, particularly those in Asia. The primary competitors of the export of the Chinese countries, such as the ASEAN of ten countries, Japan, South Korea, and India, have signed FTAs with their major common importers. Due to the diplomatic issue, China is the only political entity that can successfully engage in pacts with other major countries, although Taiwan had completed FTAs with four Latin American countries by 2010. Other than negotiating with countries outside this region, Hong Kong and Macau signed the CEPAs in 2003 and Taiwan signed the ECFA in 2010 with China, respectively.[5]

The major motivations for signing trade agreements vary across countries in this Mandarin-language market. For small economies like Hong Kong and Taiwan, to maintain economic interest in the development of 'core–periphery' relations is a major concern. Since the unification with China in 1997 and 1999 respectively, the difference in income per capita and the unemployment rate in Hong Kong and Macao have increased. The marginalization of local manufacturers in small markets is consistent with Krugman (1991). The major objective for the two Special Administrative Regions (SARs) is to promote economic growth by strengthening trade and investment cooperation with China.

Expected economic interest and political influence from China are the major reasons for Taiwan to sign the agreement. Although Taiwan is a larger economy than the two former colonies, the move of domestic production lines to China also has caused de-industrialization. Export has played a vital role in Taiwan's economic development and has accounted for around 60–70 percent of the source of economic growth over recent decades. Therefore, Taiwan's government believes that its international competitiveness will be improved once the trade barriers with China are eliminated. In addition, after taking power in 2008, China-friendly Ma Ying-jeou's administration intends to ease Cross-Strait tensions by enhancing economic ties. This political incentive is regarded as fitting with China's strategy to achieve its goal to merge with Taiwan, or to achieve so-called peaceful reunification.[6]

China's political benefits are no less significant than its economic profits from the agreements. FTAs are often used to signal importance in the political relationship between the two states. Using the pacts that remove implications of sovereignty, China gains more *de facto* control over the other Chinese regions, financially and politically. In particular, Beijing intends to make unification with Taiwan take place through economic integration and to eventually encompass political integration.

The legal ambiguity is the key factor determining whether the agreements in this region can effectively yield benefits to companies. Under the World Trade Organization (WTO) structure, any commercial disputes should be settled in an international setting. Given that China sees Hong Kong and Taiwan as part of China, the Chinese insist that it is a domestic issue and, thus, the cases ought to be handled by the Chinese courts. The uncertainties in the political environment, legal procedures, and judicial outcome will dissuade investments in this region.

5.3 MACROECONOMIC BACKGROUND AND REGIONAL INTEGRATION

Since 1990, economic growth in this region has been higher than in the rest of the world. One of the most important indicators is the development of

Table 5.1 Growth of markets in China, Hong Kong, and Taiwan

Date	Number of companies listed			Capitalization (US $ billion)		
	China	Hong Kong	Taiwan	China	Hong Kong	Taiwan
12/31/1990	8	284	199	0.1	83.4	100.7
12/31/1991	14	333	221	0.5	122.0	124.9
12/31/1992	52	386	256	1.0	172.1	101.1
12/31/1993	183	450	285	40.6	385.2	192.2
12/31/1994	291	529	313	43.5	269.5	246.5
12/31/1995	323	518	347	42.1	303.7	187.2
12/31/1996	540	561	382	113.8	449.2	273.6
12/31/1997	764	658	404	206.4	413.3	287.8
12/31/1998	853	665	437	231.3	343.6	260.0
12/31/1999	950	717	462	330.7	608.2	376.0
12/31/2000	1086	779	531	581.0	623.4	247.6
12/31/2001	1160	857	584	524.0	506.1	292.6
12/31/2002	1235	968	638	463.1	463.1	261.2
12/31/2003	1296	972	669	681.2	714.6	379.0
12/31/2004	1384	1014	697	639.8	861.5	443.1
12/31/2005	1387	1020	1201	780.8	1055.0	476.0
12/31/2006	1440	1021	1222	2426.3	1715.0	594.7
12/31/2007	1530	1029	1248	6226.3	2654.4	663.7
12/31/2008	1604	1017	1260	2793.6	1328.8	356.7
12/31/2009	1700	1319	755	3573.2	2305.1	657.6
12/31/2010	2063	1396	752	4027.8	2711.3	818.5

Notes: The number of companies listed and the capitalization in US $ billion of each country as of the end of each year are reported. China includes the exchanges of Shanghai and Shenzhen.

Source: World Federation of Exchanges.

equity markets in this region. Table 5.1 reports the number of companies listed and capitalization in US $ billions for each country as of the end of each year from 1990 to 2010. The numbers suggest that the stock markets in these countries and districts grew considerably, particularly in China. The average annual growth of market value in Hong Kong and Taiwan are 17.4 percent and 10.5 percent respectively, but 53.2 percent in China. However, the volatility in China's equity markets is also greater than in the other two markets. For example, Chinese markets lost 55 percent of their value in the 2007–2008 financial crisis but could have gained at most 3500 percent in the early 1990s. In addition, the number of companies listed in China also boomed from 8 in 1990 to 2063 in 2010. In addition, many Chinese companies also list shares in both the Hong Kong and SH/

SZ markets. Such developments provide a financing channel to enterprises and investing opportunities to local investors in China.

The economic integration in this area is associated with Taiwan's investment in China. Primarily lured by low factor costs, taxation benefits, and access to the domestic market in China, Taiwan's industries have reallocated their production lines to China. Figure 5.1 shows the chronological change in Taiwan's direct investment (DI) in China and its weight in overseas investment. The total amount has grown substantially and reached US $9.7 billion in 2007. For Taiwan's overall international investment, more than half of the Taiwanese private sector's overseas investment flowed to China after 2000. On the other hand, China had no direct investment in Taiwan during this period. Taiwan's US $64.9 billion cumulative DI to China from 1991 to 2007 indicates that the Cross-Strait economic linkage is close but unbalanced.

Comparing with other countries, the direct investment amounts from Taiwan into China grow hugely. Table 5.2 shows the major origins of FDI in China in 2008 and 2009. Taiwan not only represents the second-largest investor in China but is also the fastest grower in 2009. Consider the investment amounts from Hong Kong, Japan, Singapore, and South Korea: more than 90 percent of international investments in China are regional and within the Chinese cultural area. The fact is consistent with the findings of Qian et al. (2008) and Rugman (2005).

The substantial increase in the investment amount from Taiwan to China also reflects variation in the structure of its industries. Table 5.3 shows the top five Taiwanese industries investing in China and their proportions in total investment amount. The percentage of investment of capital-intensive and high-technology industries, such as non-financial services, high-tech and electronic-product related companies, rises while the percentage of investment of light industries, such as textiles, clothing, and food, decreases during the period. In particular, the investment from Taiwanese firms of electronic products, machines, parts and components, computers, and optical products represents more than half of total investment after 1999. The shifts are consistent with the rapid growth of the Chinese economy and the increasing share of products in the international market during the last two decades.

As shown in Table 5.4, the industrial structures are different in each country. In Hong Kong, banking, real estate, and non-financial services represent more than half of the stock market value. In contrast, electronics represents more than half of equity market capitalization in Taiwan, while in China the major manufacturing industries are mining, quarrying, food and beverages, and metallic mineral products. Due to the divergence in economic developmental stages, the bilateral relation of overlapping

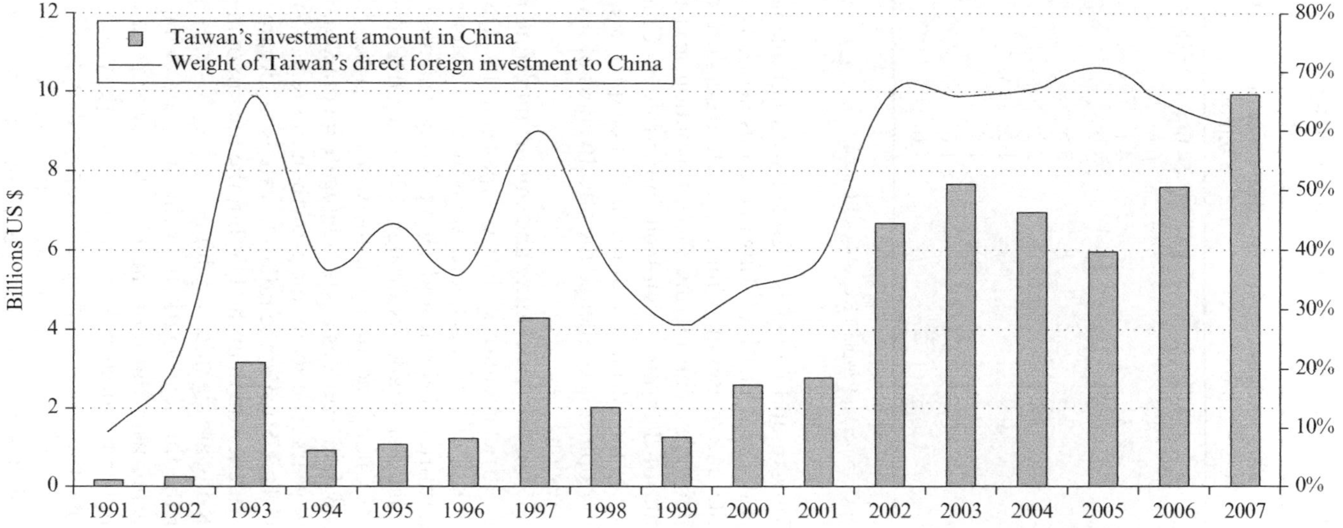

Note: This figure shows the investment amount in US $ billions (bar) from Taiwan to China and the weight of Taiwan's investment to China in all overseas investment amounts (line).

Figure 5.1 Taiwan's direct investment to China

Table 5.2 China's major origins of foreign direct investment

Country of origin	2008 amount (US $ billion)	2009 amount (US $ billion)	Growth (%)
Hong Kong	41.0	54.0	31.6
Taiwan	1.9	6.6	245.7
Japan	3.7	4.1	12.7
Singapore	4.4	3.9	–12.4
United States	2.9	3.6	21.5
South Korea	3.1	2.7	–13.8
United Kingdom	0.9	1.5	60.7
Germany	0.9	1.2	36.3
Macao	0.6	1.0	71.9
Canada	0.5	1.0	76.5

Data Source: Ministry of Commerce, People's Republic of China.

industries between Taiwan and China is blended with complement and competition. In general, the strength of Taiwanese businesses is research and innovation, while enterprises in China benefit from low costs of production factors. However, considering the information in Table 5.1, the direct investments of Taiwan's high-tech industries in China may enhance the similarity of industrial structure. In this chapter, we investigate whether such developments challenge the effectiveness of investment diversification in this region.

Table 5.5 reports the country risk rating and important economic indicators of these three districts/countries. For comparison, the US data is shown. The sovereign risk of China is higher than in other countries. The two small economic entities, Taiwan and Hong Kong, maintain higher dependence on international trade. Although China's GDP per capita is still low, the role of China's economy in the world is increasingly significant due to its growth in overseas trade, aggregate income, and capital market value in recent years. The economic growth in this region in general is higher than that of the US while the inflation rate is moderate. Taiwan has a lower unemployment rate than the US, but the unemployment rates in China and Hong Kong are significantly higher.

The indicators for the financial markets in this area are demonstrated in Table 5.4. Comparing with those of the US, the lower price/earnings (P/E) ratios imply higher required risk premiums of equity securities in this region. Observing the stock market development index suggested by Beck et al. (2003), the Chinese market is less mature than the ones in Hong Kong or Taiwan. The greater opaqueness, lack of transparency of

Table 5.3 The top 5 industries of direct investment from Taiwan to China

Year	#1 Industry	%	#2 Industry	%	#3 Industry	%	#4 Industry	%	#5 Industry	%
1991	Electronic products and machines	20.41%	Rubber products	18.34%	Textiles mills, leather, fur, and clothing	16.66%	Plastic products	12.91%	Food, beverages, and tobacco	11.09%
1992	Electronic products and machines	21.28%	Food, beverages, and tobacco	18.79%	Plastic products	18.20%	Textiles mills, leather, fur, and clothing	14.86%	Chemical material and products	5.17%
1993	Electronic products and machines	23.16%	Plastic products	11.90%	Textiles mills, leather, fur, and clothing	10.67%	Food, beverages, and tobacco	10.28%	Metallic mineral products	5.87%
1994	Electronic products and machines	20.97%	Food, beverages, and tobacco	15.20%	Metallic mineral products	9.41%	Chemical material and products	9.31%	Non-metallic mineral products	8.61%
1995	Electronic products and machines	22.42%	Transpor-tation vehicles and parts	12.44%	Food, beverages, and tobacco	10.78%	Metallic mineral products	10.72%	Chemical material and products	8.68%
1996	Electronic products and machines	25.78%	Transpor-tation vehicles and parts	13.51%	Metallic mineral products	10.43%	Food, beverages, and tobacco	9.91%	Textiles mills, leather, fur, and clothing	8.74%

Table 5.3 (continued)

Year	#1 Industry	%	#2 Industry	%	#3 Industry	%	#4 Industry	%	#5 Industry	%
1997	Electronic products and machines	25.96%	Metallic mineral products	9.16%	Non-metallic mineral products	8.87%	Textiles mills, leather, fur, and clothing	8.41%	Non-financial services	8.26%
1998	Electronic products and machines	41.03%	Non-financial services	8.67%	Textiles mills, leather, fur, and clothing	8.41%	Transpor-tation vehicles and parts	7.46%	Chemical material and products	7.23%
1999	Electronic products and machines	45.17%	Chemical material and products	11.42%	Metallic mineral products	8.34%	Plastic products	7.91%	Transpor-tation vehicles and parts	5.04%
2000	Electronic products and machines	59.56%	Non-financial services	8.13%	Plastic products	7.10%	Metallic mineral products	7.07%	Transpor-tation vehicles and parts	4.37%
2001	Electronic products and machines	33.51%	Electronic parts and components	14.58%	Computers, electronic and optical products	12.27%	Electrical equipment	6.43%	Non-financial services	5.55%
2002	Electronic products and machines	32.47%	Computers, electronic and optical products	11.86%	Electronic parts and components	11.57%	Electrical equipment	6.70%	Non-financial services	5.43%

2003	Electronic products and machines	26.40%	Computers, electronic and optical products	9.18%	Electronic parts and components	7.67%	Transportation vehicles and parts	7.21%	Food, beverages, and tobacco	7.15%
2004	Electronic products and machines	32.54%	Electronic parts and components	14.39%	Computers, electronic and optical products	11.07%	Metallic mineral products	6.94%	Electrical equipment	5.76%
2005	Electronic products and machines	25.46%	Computers, electronic and optical products	15.12%	Electronic parts and components	10.34%	Metallic mineral products	7.71%	Transportation vehicles and parts	7.54%
2006	Electronic products and machines	28.81%	Electronic parts and components	15.09%	Computers, electronic and optical products	13.72%	Non-financial services	7.77%	Electrical equipment	6.20%
2007	Electronic products and machines	29.42%	Electronic parts and components	17.35%	Computers, electronic and optical products	12.07%	Electrical equipment	7.48%	Non-financial services	7.01%
2008	Electronic products and machines	31.26%	Electronic parts and components	18.45%	Computers, electronic and optical products	10.22%	Electrical equipment	8.39%	Non-financial services	6.23%

Source: Mainland Affairs Council, Republic of China – Taiwan.

Table 5.4 Major industries

China	(%)	Hong Kong	(%)	Taiwan	(%)
Financial services	19.28	Financial services	35.49	Electrics	55.02
				Financial services	13.25
Mining and quarrying	17.59	Real estate and construction	13.85	Non-financial services	7.54
Food, beverages, and tobacco	8.98	Telecommunications	10.36	Chemical materials and products	6.91
		Public utility	10.19		
Non-metallic mineral products	8.20	Non-financial services	6.65	Plastic products	4.20
				Textiles mills, leather, fur, and clothing	3.45
		Toy, watch, and clock	4.60		
Metallic mineral products	6.70				
		Textiles mills, leather, fur, and clothing	4.45	Non-metallic mineral products	3.09
Electrical equipment	6.17				
Textiles mills, leather, fur, and clothing	5.52	Electrical equipment	4.35	Transportation vehicles and parts	2.13
		Food, beverages, and tobacco	2.45		
Non-financial services	3.74			Food and beverages	1.56
		Wood and bamboo products	2.03		
Real estate and construction	3.57			Others	2.85
Chemical material and products	3.49	Others	5.58		
Transportation vehicles and parts	3.23				
Public utility	2.15				
Others	11.38				

Notes: The percentages of market capitalization of publicly-listed companies of industry in each country as of November 2009 are reported. China is calculated by a combination of the Shanghai and Shenzhen Stock Exchanges.

Source: Websites of Shanghai, Shenzhen, Hong Kong, and Taipei Stock Exchanges.

information and investors' protection, leads to high R^2 and synchronicity among domestic portfolios.[7] On the other hand, given the higher returns in China, it is not a straightforward matter to determine the magnitude of diversification benefits for local investors in this Mandarin-language

Table 5.5 Indicators of economic development and markets

		China	Hong Kong	Taiwan	US
Long-term currency rating [a]	(Dec. 2008)	A–	A+	AA–	AAA
GDP per capita (PPP) [b,e]	(US $, 2008)	5970	43847	30912	47440
Real GDP growth rate [b,e,f]	2001–2008	8.92%	4.20%	3.06%	1.38%
	2008	7.66%	–4.49%	–5.11%	–3.67%
	2009–2014	8.48%	1.90%	2.09%	0.46%
Weight of world capitalization [d]	1997	0.89%	1.79%	1.25%	48.92%
	2008	4.48%	3.16%	1.10%	35.84%
Market cap growth (%) [d]	2001–2008	35.87%	27.65%	15.24%	6.99%
Stock market development [d,b,e]	2001–2008	32.54%	430.15%	117.99%	129.21%
	2008	17.78%	593.62%	137.42%	135.80%
Unemployment rate [b,e]	2001–2005	10.60%	9.00%	4.90%	5.40%
	2005	10.00%	9.20%	4.60%	5.10%
International trade dependence [b,e]	2001–2008	56.47%	286.18%	99.88%	24.36%
	2008	69.33%	332.98%	108.46%	23.65%
Inflation rate [b,e,f]	2001–2008	2.11%	–0.27%	1.16%	2.85%
	2008	–0.06%	–1.00%	–0.50%	–0.39%
	2009–2014	1.28%	1.25%	1.32%	1.61%
Control of corruption index (–2.50 to 2.50) [b]	2001–2005	–0.50	1.47	0.71	1.74
	2005	–0.70	1.68	0.70	1.56
P/E ratio [c]	2001–2008	18.22	11.33	10.08	23.46
	2008	13.90	12.21	9.41	20.36
Foreign exchange rate volatility [c]	2001–2008	0.46%	0.60%	7.66%	14.48%
	2008	2.57%	0.83%	10.07%	13.13%

Notes: The country risk rating and development indicators of economy and financial markets in China, Hong Kong, Taiwan, and the US are presented. The long-term currency rating is by Standard and Poors in December 2008. International trade dependence is the sum of export and imports of goods and services divided by GDP. Inflation rate is the change in consumer price index within a year. Following Beck et al. (2003), stock market development is market capitalization divided by GDP. Foreign exchange rate volatility is the highest minus the lowest exchange rate of local currency to the US dollar divided by the average of open and closed exchange rate within a year. US dollar volatility is measured by using the Dollar Trade Weighted Index.

Sources: The data sources are: a. Standard and Poors; b. the World Development Indicators by the World Bank; c. Global Financial Data; d. the World Federation of Exchanges; e. the National Statistics of Republic of China – Taiwan; f. International Monetary Fund forecasting.

Table 5.6 Comparison of financial markets

	MV/ GDP (%)	GDP (US$ billion)	Dividend yield (%)			Turnover ratio (%)		
			2007	2008	2000–2008	2007	2008	2000–2008
China	68.41	4327.00	0.36	0.90	1.19	264.46	153.49	137.01
Hong Kong	616.88	215.40	2.20	5.40	4.18	94.10	86.04	60.72
Taiwan	94.86	376.04	4.20	9.80	6.06	153.28	145.45	180.45
Developed countries								
Japan	63.29	4923.30	1.40	2.70	1.28	138.40	151.20	99.68
Korea	50.67	929.10	1.40	2.60	3.39	192.60	196.27	202.62
US	80.36	14441.40	1.91	3.00	1.81	167.10	240.16	121.04
UK	69.61	2683.60	3.10	4.40	5.51	154.20	152.73	112.83
Singapore	145.67	181.90	2.90	6.20	5.29	77.60	63.67	61.56
Germany	30.26	3669.80	1.84	4.10	1.99	205.44	421.30	186.29
Asian developing countries								
Thailand	37.74	273.25	3.10	6.90	3.16	59.99	113.42	84.61
Malaysia	85.17	222.20	2.69	6.30	3.27	52.18	49.60	35.81

Notes: The ratios of stock market value (MV) with the GDP of a country as of December 2008 are reported. The mean of dividend yield and turnover ratio (trading value divided by market value) between 2000 and 2008 are demonstrated. China is calculated by a combination of Shanghai and Shenzhen Stock Exchanges. The US is a combination of NYSE and Nasdaq market value and used the S&P 500 dividend yield. The other countries include UK (London), Germany (Deutsche Börse), Thailand (Thailand SE), and Malaysia (Bursa Malaysia).

Data sources: World Development Indicators by the World Bank and the World Federation of Exchanges.

region. From the perspective of currency risk, the Taiwanese dollar is the most volatile among the three economies due to its greater liberalization in the currency market. Since the factors determining the gains from investing optimal regional portfolios show various directions among markets, the benefits of diversification for local investors in these countries requires an empirical study.

Table 5.6 compares the three countries with other similar financial markets. In terms of ratio of market capitalization with GDP, Hong Kong's situation is similar to that of Singapore but is different from other countries. This ratio also suggests that the stock markets in China and Taiwan have been relatively comparable to those in mature economies. In addition, the dividend yields in this region, particularly in Taiwan, are higher than other stock markets in the world. The security market turnover in this Chinese-speaking region is, on average, similar to the one in developed countries and higher than their neighbors at a similar developmental stage. Given the above qualities, an analysis of the diversification strategies in these three markets is significant to financial economists and practitioners.

5.4 DATA

The US Dollar-denominated monthly returns of the Morgan Stanley Capital International (MSCI) indices for China, Hong Kong, Taiwan and another 32 countries are used in this study. We classify them as developed (21, including Hong Kong) and developing (14, including China and Taiwan) economies. The US 90-Day T-Bill yield is a proxy for the risk-free interest rate. The market capitalizations are obtained from the World Federation of Exchanges. The sample period is from January 1988 to December 2010.

Table 5.7 presents the sample countries in this study, the average growth rates of their market value from December 1992 to November 2008, and the region in which each country is located. They are grouped into eight geographical areas: East Asia, North America, Latin America, North Europe, West/Central Europe, South/East Europe, and Oceania. For this sample, the countries with the largest growth in market value were Finland, Brazil, Turkey, and Greece. There is considerable variation in the growth of market value within each group of countries at a given developmental stage and in various geographical regions.

Table 5.7 also summarizes the performance and dynamics of the monthly Sharpe ratio for each market. Since our sample period includes periods of financial crises, the raw return of the stock markets in developing economies, in general, is lower than that of the stock markets in developed countries. There are considerable cross-regional differences among the equity returns of these markets. Specifically, the equity securities in the Americas and Europe outperformed the ones in other countries, while the stock markets of East Asia performed below average. These findings agree with the fact that the risk-adjusted returns of developed countries, on average, are higher than those in emerging markets. The countries with the highest average of mean-variance efficient domestic portfolios are the Netherlands, Switzerland, the US, and Belgium. This is consistent with the previous findings that the mean-variance efficiency of equity prices in emerging markets is lower due to their higher volatility (Bekaert and Harvey, 2003).

Table 5.7 also displays the time-varying risk-adjusted performance of

Table 5.7 Data of international markets

Panel A: Developed Countries												
Country	Cap growth (%)	Mean return (%)	Region	Sharpe ratio								
				Median	St. dev	Skewness	Kurtosis	Max	Mo-Yr	Min	Mo-Yr
Australia	17.64	12.13	Oceania	0.080	0.149	1.28	0.96	0.5826	Oct-07	0.0768	Oct-01
Austria	19.21	7.88	C/W Europe	–0.026	0.229	1.07	–0.23	0.6345	Oct-07	–0.1474	Jun-00
Belgium	10.05	13.46	C/W Europe	0.108	0.154	0.11	–0.90	0.4814	Aug-06	–0.1600	Apr-09
Canada	17.03	10.98	N. America	0.074	0.136	0.99	0.68	0.5651	Nov-06	–0.1013	Aug-94
Switzerland	14.58	16.42	C/W Europe	0.175	0.156	–0.11	–0.94	0.4437	Mar-98	–0.1761	Mar-03
Germany	13.75	9.09	C/W Europe	0.080	0.130	0.36	–0.14	0.4263	Jan-08	–0.1817	Apr-03
Denmark	17.98	14.00	C/W Europe	0.097	0.148	1.13	1.17	0.6147	Oct-07	–0.1176	Apr-03
Spain	22.94	11.58	C/W Europe	0.075	0.148	0.74	–0.01	0.5552	Oct-07	–0.1151	Aug-93
Finland	31.26	10.01	N. Europe	0.092	0.150	–0.05	–0.94	0.3894	Apr-00	–0.2306	Jan-93
France	15.66	10.68	C/W Europe	0.104	0.114	0.52	0.03	0.4369	Oct-07	–0.1215	Mar-03
UK	10.70	11.30	C/W Europe	0.100	0.150	–0.01	–0.69	0.4550	Oct-07	–0.2397	Apr-03
Hong Kong	21.59	9.90	E. Asia	0.058	0.131	0.34	–1.07	0.4203	Nov-07	–0.1160	Oct-02
Ireland	5.20	8.74	C/W Europe	0.063	0.153	0.22	–0.74	0.4253	Apr-09	–0.2346	Mar-98
Italy	16.32	6.45	S. Europe	0.042	0.117	0.79	0.13	0.4183	Oct-07	–0.1343	Apr-03
Japan	5.12	–4.22	E. Asia	–0.062	0.111	1.09	0.58	0.2590	Nov-07	–0.2288	Sep-98
Netherlands	13.80	15.01	C/W Europe	0.182	0.167	–0.20	–1.14	0.4257	May-98	–0.1839	Apr-09
Norway	23.77	8.47	N. Europe	0.024	0.146	0.87	–0.11	0.4855	Oct-07	–0.1555	Oct-03
New Zealand	8.75	7.67	Oceania	0.067	0.170	0.20	–1.09	0.4504	Oct-07	–0.1948	Nov-00
Singapore	18.70	7.63	E. Asia	0.041	0.157	0.83	0.16	0.5229	Aug-07	–0.1756	Sep-98
Sweden	19.51	11.52	N. Europe	0.071	0.138	0.35	–1.13	0.4515	Oct-07	–0.1228	Oct-02
USA	11.61	15.55	N. America	0.163	0.178	–0.09	–1.27	0.4454	May-98	–0.1862	Apr-09

Panel B: Emerging Markets

Country	Cap growth (%)	Mean return (%)	Region	Sharpe ratio							
				Median	St. dev	Skewness	Kurtosis	Max	Mo-Yr	Min	Mo-Yr
Argentina	8.33	5.21	L. America	0.050	0.132	0.59	0.59	0.4440	Jun-07	–0.2165	Jun-02
Brazil	27.55	9.77	L. America	0.065	0.134	1.16	1.85	0.5234	Oct-07	–0.1550	Aug-02
Chile	15.14	13.71	L. America	0.112	0.197	0.17	–1.24	0.5439	Oct-07	–0.1913	Aug-02
China	38.76	1.03	E. Asia	–0.022	0.234	0.97	0.45	0.5432	Sep-07	–0.3489	Apr-02
Greece	25.74	7.43	S. Europe	0.066	0.140	0.65	–0.06	0.4590	Nov-07	–0.1488	Jul-95
Indonesia	22.73	2.89	E. Asia	0.014	0.179	0.69	–0.26	0.4906	Feb-08	–0.2710	Oct-98
Korea, S.	18.23	3.19	E. Asia	–0.002	0.128	0.79	–0.26	0.3371	Oct-07	–0.2268	Jan-98
Malaysia	9.49	5.95	E. Asia	0.093	0.149	–0.10	–0.87	0.3727	Jan-08	–0.2648	Nov-98
Mexico	7.81	13.46	L. America	0.074	0.163	0.72	–0.74	0.4989	Mar-08	–0.1203	Feb-99
Philippines	14.56	1.35	E. Asia	0.002	0.187	0.15	–1.35	0.4170	Nov-07	–0.2641	Nov-01
Portugal	21.01	6.11	C/W Europe	0.013	0.152	0.43	–0.47	0.4687	Oct-07	–0.2081	Jan-93
Thailand	9.23	3.09	E. Asia	0.060	0.173	–0.07	–1.22	0.3538	Oct-07	–0.2611	Sep-98
Turkey	27.31	4.35	S. Europe	0.030	0.086	0.56	–0.31	0.2873	Jan-08	–0.1091	Feb-95
Taiwan	14.46	–1.05	E. Asia	–0.019	0.085	0.60	0.13	0.2332	Oct-07	–0.1662	Oct-02

Notes: The table reports the growth rate of capitalization from December 1992 to November 2010. The mean of return is annualized. Additionally, the table presents the mean, median, standard deviation, maximum, and minimum of the time series of the monthly Sharpe ratio for each market. The table reports the growth rate of capitalization from December 1992 to December 2008.

each market. The unit-risk return changes considerably over time. For most countries, the highest domestic Sharpe ratio occurred in 1998 and 2007. The local investors in most emerging markets generated the lowest risk-adjusted performance in 1997 and 1998 due to the Asian financial crises of that period. Investors in developed countries experienced the largest loss in 2002 and 2003 because of the evaporation of high-tech bubbles after 2000 and the fact that the recession worsened after the terrorist attacks in 2001. Also displayed by this table are non-synchronous movements of mean-variance efficiency across countries, which imply potential gains for domestic investors who diversify their portfolios globally. For instance, in 1998, there are three markets of the maximum mean-variance efficiency and seven markets of the minimum. This suggests that cross-country performances can differ drastically in the same year and that local investors may avoid losses in their home markets by allocating their funds *optimally* in other countries.

Figure 5.2 shows the change of correlation coefficients between each country in this Chinese-speaking region and all other markets over the sample period. Hong Kong, in general, demonstrates higher correlations with the other markets than the other two countries. All these markets are also more correlated with the other countries in the rest of the world in recent years, particularly during the financial crisis period of 2007 to 2008. Furthermore, the fact that some markets are less correlated with the countries in this region indicates potential diversification benefits from inter-continental investments.

The means of the correlations between each market and all other countries in the recent period are persistently greater than the means in the earlier period. Figure 5.2 shows that, in the first period, some markets are negatively correlated or almost uncorrelated with markets in this region, particularly in China. The increase of correlation is particularly significant after 2002. All correlation coefficients in the second period are increasing and positive. These results display the increasing integration of the global financial market over the past 2 decades. The cross-temporal comparison of correlation challenges the effectiveness of globally diversified portfolios.

The above dynamics of international market returns highlight the need of a time-series analysis of the strategies and benefits of diversification for investors in these Sino countries and districts. The non-synchronous movement of risk-adjusted returns among international markets suggests that local investors have a chance to improve the mean-variance efficiency of their portfolios by investing in foreign assets.

a)

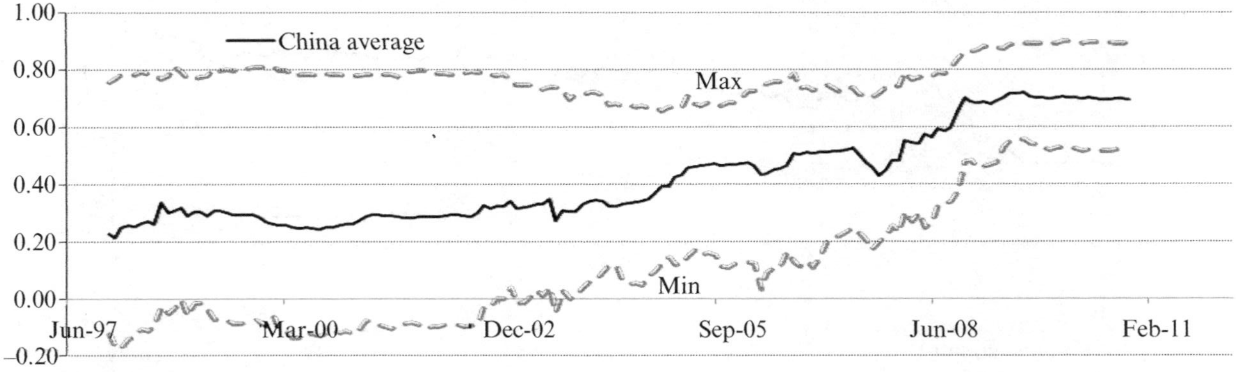

Note: The average, maximum, and minimum correlations of China, Hong Kong, and Taiwan with other countries from Dec. 1997 to Nov. 2010 are reported.

Figure 5.2 Correlation with other countries

b)

c)

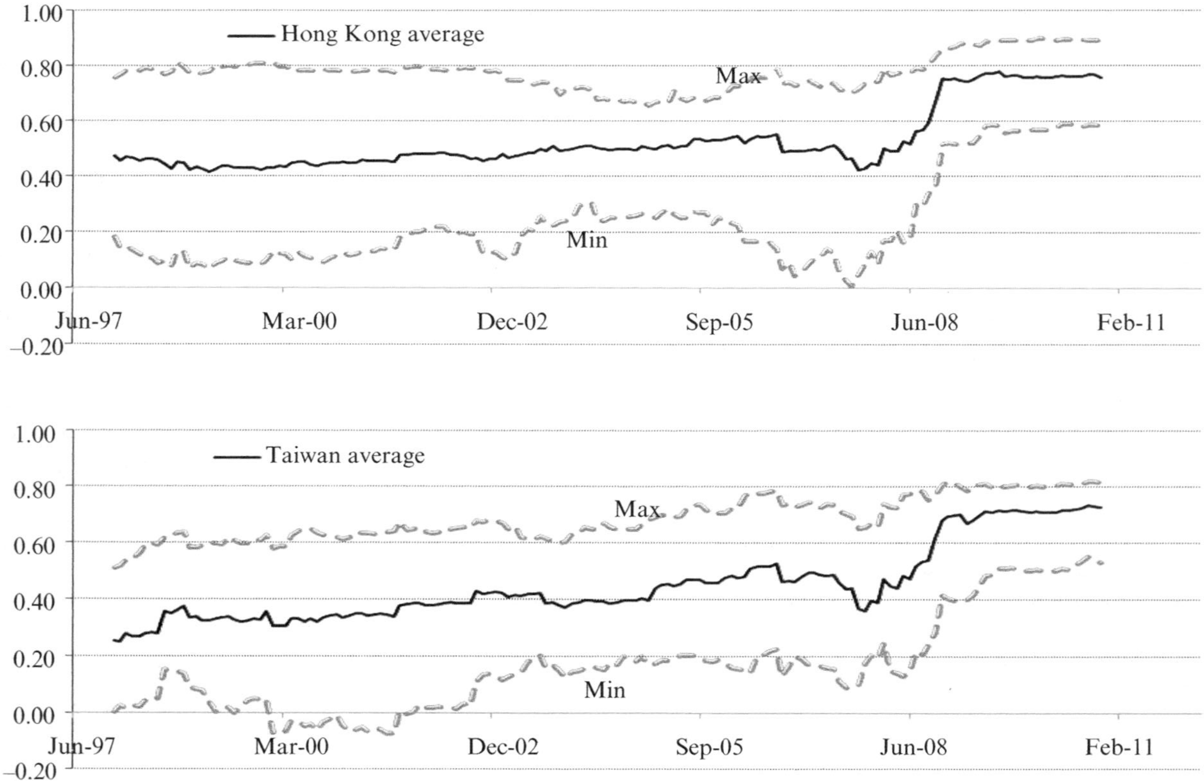

Figure 5.2 (continued)

5.5 METHODOLOGY

We use the improvement of mean-variance efficiency and the reduction in volatility of diversified portfolios of local markets with international assets to measure the effectiveness of diversification in the three countries. The effect of short-sales (SS) constraints and home bias (HB) investing behavior is considered in our analysis.

Suppose a representative local investor wants to minimize the volatility of her portfolio and gain the same return by allocating funds among various international markets. The expected returns in excess of the risk-free interest rate and the variance-covariance of N international asset returns, $\mathbf{R}$, can be expressed as a vector $\boldsymbol{\mu}^T = [\mu_1, \mu_2, \ldots, \mu_N]$ and a positive definite matrix $\mathbf{V}$, respectively. Let S be the set of all real vectors of weighting $\mathbf{w}^T$ such that $\mathbf{w}^T\mathbf{1} = w_1 + w_2 + \ldots + w_N = 1$, where $\mathbf{1}$ is an N-vector of ones. The investor thus follows the method of Markowitz (1952) to form the global efficient frontier. The problem of the unconstrained optimal portfolio selection is then expressed as a Lagrangian:

$$\min_{\{\mathbf{w},\phi,\eta\}} \Xi = \frac{1}{2}\mathbf{w}^T\mathbf{V}\mathbf{w} + \phi(\mu_p - \mathbf{w}^T\mu) + \eta(1 - \mathbf{w}^T\mathbf{1}), \qquad (5.1)$$

where μ_p denotes the value-weighted mean return on the portfolio and the shadow prices ϕ and η are two positive constants.

We take into account the feasibility of portfolio in the model. First, short-selling is not allowed for international investors in some countries.[8] Since short-selling is not allowed for foreign investors in many countries, including Taiwan and China, it is not unreasonable to include these constraints. Second, it has been well documented that investors tend to invest in domestic securities above the optimal level. Though home bias is not a constraint in investing, such behavior can be modeled as upper bounds in the optimal portfolio. For the home bias analysis, we set up several scenarios (50 percent to 90 percent) to analyse the benefits of diversification. Since portfolio weights are between 0 and 1, it makes sense to set domestic portfolio weight as greater than 50 percent but less than 100.

Given the multiple bounds described above, the Kuhn-Tucker conditions are then applied to solve the multiple-constraint optimization. The subset of portfolio weights $P_{L,D}$ with short-sales constraints and home-biased investments (SS+HB(L)) in country D can be described as:

$$P_{L,D} = \{\mathrm{w_p} \in \Omega : 0 \leq \mathrm{w}_i \leq 1, \mathrm{w}_D \geq L, \boldsymbol{i} = \mathbf{1}, \mathbf{2}, \ldots, \boldsymbol{N}\},\ 0 < L < 1, \qquad (5.2)$$

where w_D is the proportion of the domestic assets, and L is the minimum portfolio weight that the investor places in the home market. A greater L implies a stronger home-bias tendency when the investor forms a portfolio strategy. For our analysis, we set the scenarios of home-bias from 50 percent to 90 percent. The constrained optimal weights can be solved by applying the Kuhn-Tucker conditions when the complementary slackness conditions, primal constraints, and gradient equations are fulfilled.

The benefits of diversification can be measured in two ways. The first is the maximum increase in mean-variance efficiency caused by diversifying a portfolio internationally while still holding a certain portion of domestic assets. Since the incentives of diversification are not only to seek higher yields but also to reduce a portfolio's volatility, the maximum Sharpe ratio (MSR) represents the highest mean-variance efficiency that can be achieved by the international efficient frontier. Specifically,

$$MSR_{L,D} = \max_{\mathbf{w}_p}[(\mathbf{w}_p^T\mu)/(\mathbf{w}_p^T\mathbf{V}\mathbf{w}_p)^{\frac{1}{2}}|\mathbf{w}_p^T \in P_L]. \tag{5.3}$$

For the domestic investor, therefore, the greatest improvement in unit-risk return brought by global diversification is

$$\delta_{SS+HB(L),D} = MSR_{L,D} - SR_D, \tag{5.4}$$

where SR_D is the Sharpe ratio for the domestic portfolio in country D.

The second assessment of diversification benefits is shown by the reduction in volatility that results from international investing. Elton et al. (2007) suggest that investors may choose to minimize the risk of a portfolio due to the unpredictability of the expected returns. Thus, investors may want to construct a minimum-variance portfolio (MVP). Let σ_D and $\sigma_{MVP,SS+HB(L),D}$ represent the standard deviations of a domestic portfolio and the MVP under different scenarios of home bias for investors in country D, respectively. The maximum decline in volatility achieved by diversifying a portfolio internationally is

$$\varepsilon_{SS+HB(L),D} = \sigma_D - \sigma_{MVP,SS+HB(L),D}. \tag{5.5}$$

In this study, the global efficient frontiers and the return per risk are estimated by using monthly returns over the previous 5 years. Since the returns and risks are time-varying, it is important to note that the intertemporal comparison of diversification benefits should be based on relative values. The time-series of the diversification benefits and the weights with various bounds can be generated by rolling over the asset returns.

5.6 EFFECTIVENESS OF INTERNATIONAL DIVERSIFICATION

Figure 5.3 exhibits the no-short-sales efficient frontiers of the global portfolio, Great China market efficient frontier, and the domestic portfolios of selected countries from 1992 to 2010. In general, developed countries demonstrate higher mean-variance efficiency than the emerging markets. The only exception is Japan because of a long-term economic recession. In the Sino region, the equity market in Hong Kong has the highest risk-adjusted return but China's market demonstrates the worst performance. All these markets are also more volatile than in the developed countries.

Figure 5.3 also suggests that the investor in the Great China region also benefits from global diversification. Although regional diversifying portfolios outperform domestic investments in Hong Kong, China, and Taiwan, the global frontier demonstrates improved mean-variance efficiency. However, it is not clear which countries outside the Sino region will yield *most* diversification benefits for investor in each of these Chinese-culture countries. We will analyse the effectiveness of diversification, country by country.

Figure 5.4 shows the time-series of Sharpe ratio of national market portfolios in the Chinese region. The mean-variance efficiency of China's equity market is lower than those in Hong Kong and Taiwan before 2005 but is higher after 2005. All these markets demonstrate significant variation in mean-variance over time. Because of the chronological deviation of mean-variance efficiency and correlations among markets, the shape and size of these efficient frontiers vary drastically. The dynamics of *ex ante* efficient frontiers reflects the intertemporal evolution of mean-variance efficiency, cross-country correlations, and the business cycle of the world economy.

Table 5.8 reports the benefits of international diversification of these three markets with the other countries in the world. In general, China's domestic investor benefits from international diversification more strongly than do those in Hong Kong or Taiwan. Shown in Panel A, in the long term, except investing in the Philippines, Ireland, and Japan, the Chinese investor can enhance her portfolio's performance by investing overseas. As the portfolio strategies become increasingly home-biased – for example, from 50 percent to 90 percent – the diversification benefits become smaller but still exist. Though investing in other countries can decrease risk by a greater or lesser amount, the strategies that Chinese investor include the assets in developed countries provide greater benefits of risk reduction than those of emerging markets.

For the domestic investor in Hong Kong, as demonstrated in Panel B,

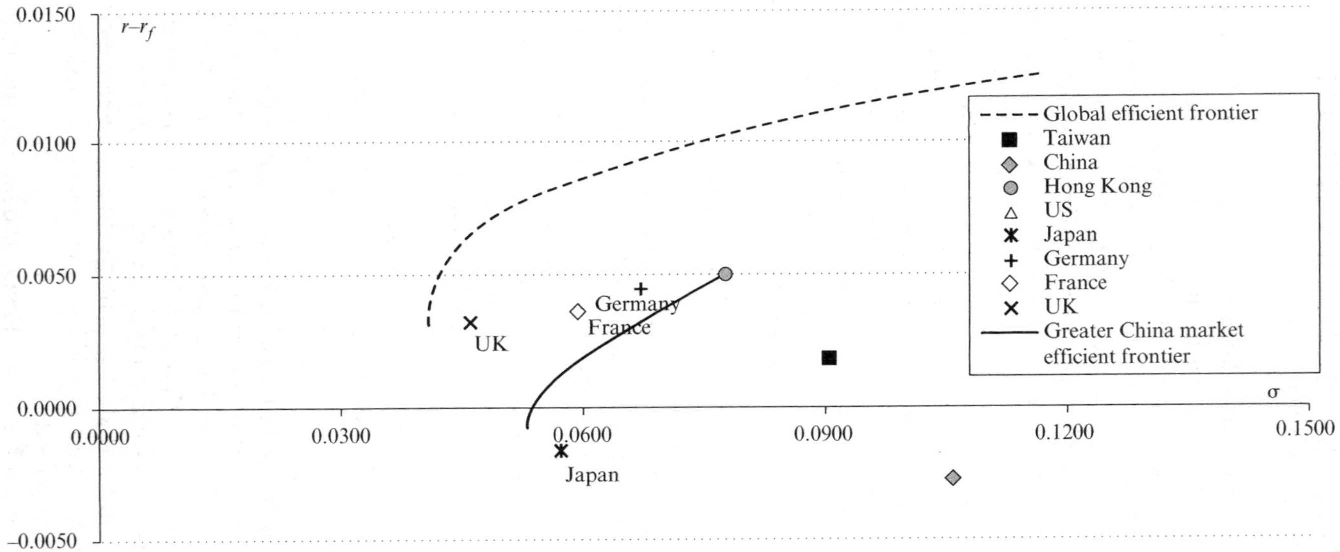

Notes: The global efficient frontier is formed by the monthly returns of the MSCI indices of 35 countries during the period of 1992.12–2010.11. The mean-variance efficiency of some countries is presented.

Figure 5.3 Global efficient frontier

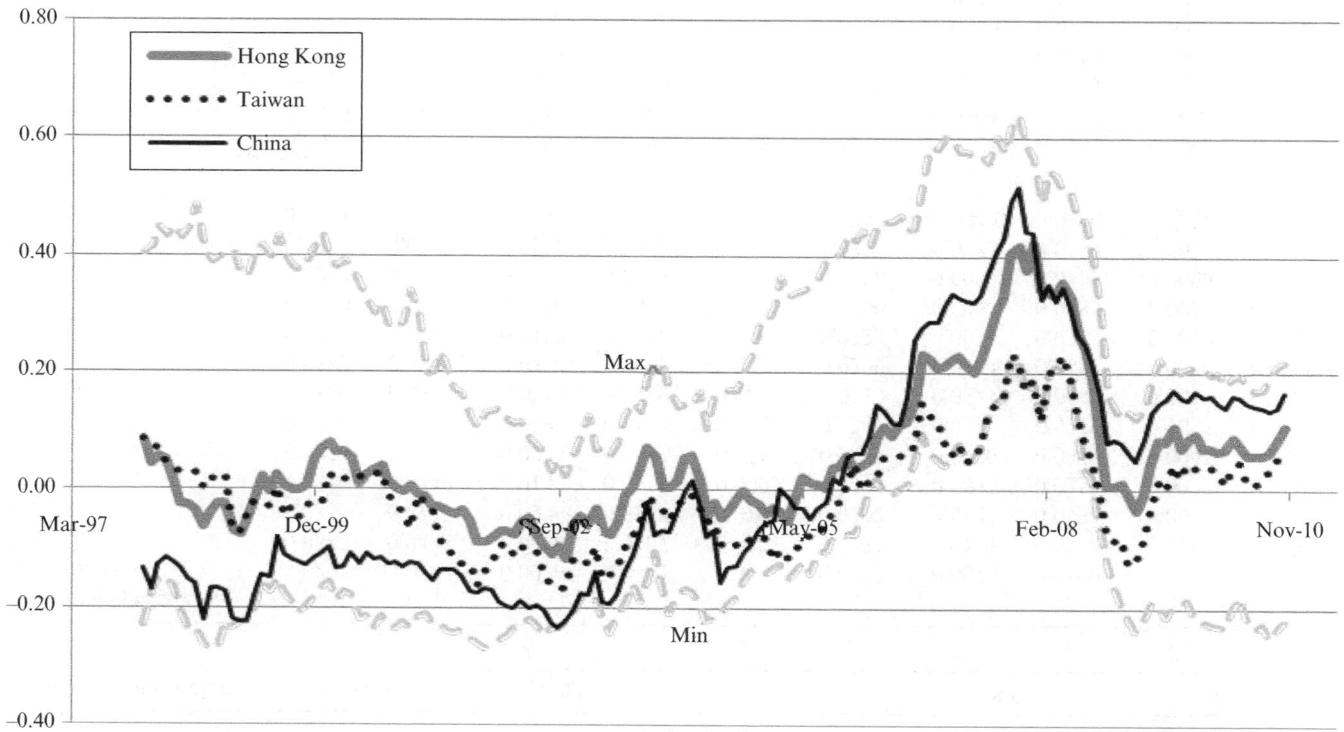

Figure 5.4 Sharpe ratio of national portfolios

Table 5.8 The benefits of international diversification

Panel A: China										
Home portfolio weight	50%		60%		70%		80%		90%	
L	δ	ε	δ	ε	δ	ε	δ	ε	δ	ε
Emerging markets										
Argentina	0.0095	0.0437	0.0076	0.0352	0.0061	0.0272	0.0046	0.0190	0.0027	0.0101
Brazil	0.0512	0.0402	0.0406	0.0307	0.0301	0.0221	0.0199	0.0144	0.0098	0.0073
Chile	0.0350	0.0328	0.0270	0.0267	0.0194	0.0202	0.0123	0.0134	0.0059	0.0067
Greece	0.0226	0.0740	0.0149	0.0558	0.0093	0.0396	0.0053	0.0251	0.0023	0.0119
Indonesia	0.0279	0.0646	0.0223	0.0583	0.0162	0.0482	0.0100	0.0345	0.0046	0.0179
Korea, S.	0.0255	0.0578	0.0187	0.0464	0.0127	0.0347	0.0077	0.0229	0.0035	0.0112
Malaysia	0.0169	0.0383	0.0118	0.0299	0.0075	0.0219	0.0041	0.0142	0.0017	0.0069
Mexico	0.0589	0.0358	0.0454	0.0282	0.0324	0.0209	0.0204	0.0138	0.0096	0.0068
Philippines	–0.0143	0.0462	–0.0102	0.0404	–0.0067	0.0323	–0.0039	0.0223	–0.0018	0.0113
Portugal	0.0170	0.0601	0.0116	0.0437	0.0078	0.0300	0.0047	0.0185	0.0022	0.0086
Thailand	0.0004	0.0603	–0.0003	0.0503	–0.0008	0.0390	–0.0009	0.0265	–0.0006	0.0133
Turkey	0.0244	0.0662	0.0178	0.0489	0.0119	0.0326	0.0072	0.0189	0.0034	0.0083
Taiwan	0.0121	0.0492	0.0099	0.0361	0.0075	0.0247	0.0049	0.0150	0.0024	0.0068
Developed countries										
Australia	0.0404	0.0385	0.0297	0.0297	0.0207	0.0214	0.0128	0.0137	0.0060	0.0065
Austria	0.0335	0.0955	0.0247	0.0743	0.0170	0.0536	0.0104	0.0341	0.0048	0.0162
Belgium	0.0128	0.0625	0.0082	0.0465	0.0052	0.0328	0.0031	0.0207	0.0014	0.0098
Canada	0.0446	0.0343	0.0328	0.0246	0.0226	0.0168	0.0140	0.0103	0.0065	0.0048
Switzerland	0.0317	0.0478	0.0222	0.0332	0.0148	0.0220	0.0089	0.0132	0.0040	0.0060
Germany	0.0118	0.0520	0.0074	0.0370	0.0045	0.0249	0.0026	0.0151	0.0012	0.0069

Denmark	0.0487	0.0415	0.0354	0.0310	0.0244	0.0220	0.0150	0.0139	0.0070	0.0066
Spain	0.0484	0.0528	0.0350	0.0378	0.0239	0.0257	0.0146	0.0157	0.0067	0.0072
Finland	0.0433	0.1070	0.0306	0.0779	0.0200	0.0527	0.0117	0.0316	0.0052	0.0142
France	0.0202	0.0464	0.0135	0.0324	0.0088	0.0215	0.0052	0.0129	0.0023	0.0059
UK	0.0141	0.0483	0.0095	0.0342	0.0062	0.0230	0.0037	0.0139	0.0017	0.0064
Hong Kong	0.0178	0.0321	0.0132	0.0235	0.0091	0.0161	0.0056	0.0099	0.0026	0.0046
Ireland	–0.0024	0.0849	–0.0028	0.0634	–0.0024	0.0444	–0.0016	0.0277	–0.0007	0.0130
Italy	0.0221	0.0537	0.0148	0.0385	0.0095	0.0263	0.0055	0.0161	0.0024	0.0075
Japan	–0.0265	0.0249	–0.0193	0.0195	–0.0130	0.0144	–0.0078	0.0094	–0.0035	0.0046
Netherlands	0.0123	0.0589	0.0078	0.0415	0.0048	0.0276	0.0028	0.0165	0.0013	0.0075
Norway	0.0301	0.0464	0.0223	0.0361	0.0157	0.0264	0.0099	0.0172	0.0048	0.0084
New Zealand	0.0169	0.0680	0.0126	0.0521	0.0088	0.0372	0.0055	0.0235	0.0026	0.0111
Singapore	0.0185	0.0244	0.0139	0.0192	0.0097	0.0141	0.0060	0.0092	0.0028	0.0045
Sweden	0.0351	0.0623	0.0245	0.0439	0.0163	0.0294	0.0097	0.0177	0.0044	0.0082
USA	0.0163	0.0653	0.0109	0.0457	0.0070	0.0303	0.0041	0.0181	0.0018	0.0082

Panel B: Hong Kong

Home portfolio weight	50%		60%		70%		80%		90%	
L	δ	ε	δ	ε	δ	ε	δ	ε	δ	ε
Emerging markets										
Argentina	–0.0025	0.0516	0.0007	0.0481	0.0033	0.0422	0.0045	0.0325	0.0035	0.0183
Brazil	0.0417	0.0506	0.0373	0.0453	0.0312	0.0382	0.0232	0.0286	0.0128	0.0160
Chile	0.0262	0.0603	0.0226	0.0500	0.0179	0.0384	0.0125	0.0260	0.0064	0.0130
China	–0.0263	0.0658	–0.0212	0.0557	–0.0157	0.0439	–0.0102	0.0306	–0.0048	0.0158
Greece	0.0208	0.0713	0.0170	0.0587	0.0128	0.0449	0.0085	0.0303	0.0042	0.0152
Indonesia	0.0055	0.0974	0.0066	0.0865	0.0066	0.0716	0.0055	0.0519	0.0032	0.0276
Korea, S.	0.0099	0.0627	0.0094	0.0527	0.0083	0.0410	0.0065	0.0280	0.0038	0.0141

Table 5.8 (continued)

	Panel B: Hong Kong									
Home portfolio weight	50%		60%		70%		80%		90%	
L	δ	ε	δ	ε	δ	ε	δ	ε	δ	ε
Emerging markets										
Malaysia	–0.0032	0.0616	–0.0025	0.0511	–0.0020	0.0392	–0.0014	0.0265	–0.0008	0.0132
Mexico	0.0490	0.0511	0.0411	0.0438	0.0319	0.0346	0.0217	0.0238	0.0109	0.0121
Philippines	–0.0352	0.0831	–0.0255	0.0733	–0.0170	0.0595	–0.0101	0.0417	–0.0045	0.0213
Portugal	0.0207	0.0604	0.0169	0.0477	0.0128	0.0351	0.0086	0.0229	0.0043	0.0111
Thailand	–0.0188	0.0891	–0.0140	0.0771	–0.0097	0.0621	–0.0060	0.0439	–0.0029	0.0229
Turkey	0.0066	0.0381	0.0067	0.0321	0.0064	0.0250	0.0055	0.0172	0.0036	0.0091
Taiwan	–0.0329	0.0269	–0.0261	0.0213	–0.0193	0.0158	–0.0125	0.0103	–0.0060	0.0051
Developed countries										
Australia	0.0457	0.0520	0.0365	0.0421	0.0271	0.0316	0.0178	0.0209	0.0087	0.0102
Austria	0.0386	0.1156	0.0318	0.0930	0.0239	0.0692	0.0156	0.0452	0.0075	0.0219
Belgium	0.0191	0.0650	0.0145	0.0508	0.0104	0.0375	0.0067	0.0247	0.0032	0.0122
Canada	0.0471	0.0322	0.0374	0.0268	0.0277	0.0206	0.0181	0.0140	0.0088	0.0070
Switzerland	0.0356	0.0505	0.0273	0.0380	0.0196	0.0269	0.0124	0.0169	0.0059	0.0080
Germany	0.0139	0.0504	0.0110	0.0395	0.0083	0.0292	0.0057	0.0192	0.0029	0.0095
Denmark	0.0569	0.0472	0.0446	0.0384	0.0326	0.0291	0.0211	0.0194	0.0102	0.0096
Spain	0.0535	0.0512	0.0424	0.0406	0.0312	0.0301	0.0203	0.0197	0.0099	0.0097
Finland	0.0367	0.0958	0.0291	0.0754	0.0214	0.0548	0.0139	0.0350	0.0068	0.0166
France	0.0247	0.0435	0.0192	0.0334	0.0139	0.0241	0.0090	0.0156	0.0044	0.0075
UK	0.0176	0.0495	0.0133	0.0373	0.0095	0.0264	0.0060	0.0167	0.0029	0.0080
Ireland	–0.0046	0.0854	–0.0038	0.0675	–0.0028	0.0500	–0.0017	0.0328	–0.0008	0.0160

Italy	0.0240	0.0498	0.0191	0.0393	0.0140	0.0289	0.0090	0.0189	0.0043	0.0092
Japan	–0.0372	0.0283	–0.0268	0.0240	–0.0179	0.0188	–0.0106	0.0129	–0.0047	0.0065
Netherlands	0.0135	0.0563	0.0101	0.0422	0.0073	0.0298	0.0048	0.0188	0.0024	0.0089
Norway	0.0321	0.0536	0.0272	0.0451	0.0215	0.0354	0.0150	0.0246	0.0077	0.0127
New Zealand	0.0113	0.0784	0.0104	0.0629	0.0086	0.0467	0.0060	0.0305	0.0031	0.0148
Singapore	0.0039	0.0405	0.0037	0.0333	0.0031	0.0254	0.0023	0.0171	0.0012	0.0086
Sweden	0.0346	0.0563	0.0272	0.0435	0.0201	0.0317	0.0132	0.0206	0.0065	0.0101
USA	0.0130	0.0649	0.0093	0.0476	0.0063	0.0328	0.0038	0.0202	0.0018	0.0094

Panel C: Taiwan

Home portfolio weight	50%		60%		70%		80%		90%	
L	δ	ε	δ	ε	δ	ε	δ	ε	δ	ε
Emerging markets										
Argentina	0.0325	0.0652	0.0277	0.0572	0.0218	0.0463	0.0150	0.0325	0.0075	0.0166
Brazil	0.0744	0.0669	0.0619	0.0580	0.0476	0.0464	0.0321	0.0325	0.0160	0.0167
Chile	0.0473	0.0708	0.0368	0.0562	0.0265	0.0413	0.0169	0.0267	0.0080	0.0129
China	–0.0043	0.0848	–0.0026	0.0701	–0.0013	0.0538	–0.0005	0.0363	–0.0002	0.0182
Greece	0.0491	0.0734	0.0375	0.0593	0.0262	0.0440	0.0161	0.0287	0.0074	0.0138
Indonesia	0.0354	0.1200	0.0274	0.1027	0.0190	0.0809	0.0111	0.0554	0.0047	0.0278
Korea, S.	0.0365	0.0707	0.0288	0.0577	0.0211	0.0436	0.0136	0.0288	0.0066	0.0141
Malaysia	0.0176	0.0714	0.0119	0.0574	0.0073	0.0428	0.0038	0.0282	0.0015	0.0138
Mexico	0.0678	0.0616	0.0530	0.0493	0.0384	0.0365	0.0246	0.0238	0.0117	0.0115
Philippines	–0.0110	0.0931	–0.0092	0.0768	–0.0074	0.0581	–0.0053	0.0383	–0.0028	0.0187
Portugal	0.0428	0.0611	0.0319	0.0473	0.0221	0.0339	0.0136	0.0214	0.0063	0.0101
Thailand	0.0047	0.0996	0.0020	0.0832	–0.0001	0.0644	–0.0011	0.0438	–0.0011	0.0220
Turkey	0.0475	0.0331	0.0408	0.0300	0.0323	0.0256	0.0222	0.0195	0.0111	0.0110

Table 5.8 (continued)

Panel C: Taiwan										
Home portfolio weight	50%		60%		70%		80%		90%	
L	δ	ε	δ	ε	δ	ε	δ	ε	δ	ε
Developed countries										
Australia	0.0590	0.0548	0.0445	0.0422	0.0313	0.0303	0.0196	0.0193	0.0092	0.0092
Austria	0.0483	0.1107	0.0358	0.0844	0.0247	0.0598	0.0151	0.0374	0.0069	0.0176
Belgium	0.0385	0.0636	0.0275	0.0487	0.0185	0.0349	0.0111	0.0222	0.0050	0.0106
Canada	0.0672	0.0406	0.0506	0.0319	0.0356	0.0233	0.0222	0.0149	0.0104	0.0072
Switzerland	0.0505	0.0515	0.0367	0.0385	0.0250	0.0268	0.0152	0.0166	0.0070	0.0077
Germany	0.0401	0.0490	0.0301	0.0383	0.0211	0.0278	0.0131	0.0179	0.0061	0.0086
Denmark	0.0741	0.0534	0.0550	0.0416	0.0382	0.0300	0.0236	0.0191	0.0109	0.0091
Spain	0.0750	0.0548	0.0568	0.0424	0.0399	0.0305	0.0249	0.0193	0.0116	0.0091
Finland	0.0721	0.0865	0.0560	0.0680	0.0398	0.0491	0.0247	0.0311	0.0114	0.0146
France	0.0458	0.0438	0.0338	0.0334	0.0233	0.0237	0.0143	0.0149	0.0066	0.0070
UK	0.0352	0.0511	0.0252	0.0377	0.0170	0.0261	0.0103	0.0161	0.0047	0.0074
Hong Kong	0.0276	0.0293	0.0212	0.0234	0.0151	0.0174	0.0096	0.0114	0.0045	0.0056

Ireland	0.0157	0.0774	0.0102	0.0600	0.0061	0.0435	0.0032	0.0280	0.0012	0.0135
Italy	0.0441	0.0496	0.0329	0.0387	0.0228	0.0279	0.0139	0.0177	0.0064	0.0084
Japan	–0.0175	0.0407	–0.0130	0.0316	–0.0090	0.0228	–0.0055	0.0144	–0.0025	0.0068
Netherlands	0.0373	0.0529	0.0272	0.0396	0.0187	0.0277	0.0114	0.0173	0.0053	0.0081
Norway	0.0537	0.0636	0.0419	0.0518	0.0304	0.0390	0.0196	0.0258	0.0094	0.0126
New Zealand	0.0274	0.0750	0.0204	0.0577	0.0141	0.0411	0.0087	0.0259	0.0040	0.0122
Singapore	0.0245	0.0553	0.0184	0.0432	0.0128	0.0315	0.0080	0.0203	0.0037	0.0098
Sweden	0.0630	0.0552	0.0480	0.0429	0.0340	0.0311	0.0213	0.0199	0.0100	0.0095
USA	0.0347	0.0597	0.0247	0.0433	0.0166	0.0295	0.0100	0.0180	0.0045	0.0083

Notes: The table reports the benefits of international diversification under various sets of short-sale plus home-bias (SS+HB(*L*)) investment constraints to the local investor in each country. The increase in the risk-adjusted premium and the decrease in volatility of domestic portfolios by international diversification are $\delta_{SS+HB(L),D} = MSR_{SS+HB(L),D} - SR_D$ and $\varepsilon_{SS+HB(L),D} = \sigma_D - \sigma_{MVP,SS+HB(L),D}$, respectively.

the ability to diversify her portfolio with emerging markets is generally poor, particularly those neighboring Southeast Asian countries. Similar to the results of China, diversifying with the portfolios in Ireland and Japan does not improve the mean-variance efficiency to Hong Kong's investor. Instead, the assets in the majority of developed countries, particularly in Canada and Australia, bring greater benefits to the locals in Hong Kong than those in emerging markets. In most cases, the home-bias investment decreases but does not eliminate the diversification benefits.

The results of benefits for Taiwan's investor, shown in Panel C, also suggest a low effectiveness of regionally international diversification. The Sharpe ratio will decrease if Taiwan's investor includes securities in China, the Philippines, Thailand, and Japan in the portfolios. On the other hand, Taiwan's investor still benefits from the diversification with Hong Kong's assets.

The comparative position of mean-variance efficiency for domestic assets shapes the time-variation of benefits of diversification. Dispersion of Sharpe ratio is a better measure of the benefits of diversification since it accounts for the effects of both correlation and standard deviation. Figure 5.4 shows dynamic revolutions of risk-adjusted returns in these three countries and indicates the time-variation of performance in each stock market. The non-synchronous fluctuating patterns imply that there are potential gains to domestic investors if they diversify their portfolios over time. The existence of domestic investments with superior performance than foreign securities challenges the need to seek overseas assets to improve a portfolio's mean-variance efficiency. The rotation of performance of domestic portfolios for these countries leaves investors in other countries with an opportunity to offset the loss of their domestic portfolios.

5.7 CONCLUSION

Due to rising economic power and integration in the so-called Greater China region, it is critical to understand the development of equity markets and the global diversification benefits to local investors. The analysis is critical to both financial academics and to Wall Street. This chapter responds to this crucial issue by empirically exploring the 'Greater China market,' one of the fastest-growing economies in the world. We have constructed time-rolling international optimal portfolios while considering short-sales and home-bias investment. We first discussed the development and impact of the economic integration in this area and reported on the economic background and industrial structure in this region. Our results suggest that investors in this Greater Chinese market benefit more from international diversification that includes assets in other regions than assets in this region, even though the returns in this region are higher. The empirical results suggest that the inclusion of assets in developed economies, particularly those in Europe and North America, provide a higher increase in mean-variance efficiency than those in emerging markets. The diversification strategies that include the other two countries in this Sino region do not benefit the local investors. This is because of the increasingly integrated economy in this area, particularly in Hong Kong and Taiwan. To ensure the robustness of our findings, we considered home-bias investment in constructing portfolios and obtained a similar conclusion, although the benefits tend to be less when the portfolios are more home-biased. The time-varying benefits of diversification are determined by the dispersion of the mean-variance efficiency of domestic assets in these countries.

This chapter adds to the current literature by investigating the benefits to the local investor in an economically more powerful and integrated region. Home-bias investing and no-sales are considered in asset strategies when we evaluate the portfolio performance. The conclusions support the proposition that cross-country diversification in outside regions benefits local investors more than the portfolios in the same region. In addition, investing in developed countries provides stronger improvement in mean-variance efficiency than in the emerging markets. Future research of the benefits of international diversification strategies may take into account the dynamics in expected returns, volatilities, and correlations among assets and the demands of hedging market exposure and exchange-rate risk. Future studies may address the importance of the diversification benefits of sub-portfolios in the greater Chinese market with other countries. Such sub-portfolio analysis will provide more understanding regarding the role of Chinese markets in global portfolio management.

NOTES

1. For a more detailed discussion, see Cosset and Suret (1995); De Roon et al. (2001); De Santis and Gerard (1997); Fletcher and Marshall (2005); French and Poterba (1991); Goetzmann et al. (2005); Griffin and Karolyi (1998); Harvey (1995); Li et al. (2003); Novomestky (1997); and Obstfeld (1994).
2. These treaties are similar to a free trade agreement (FTA).
3. For more detailed discussion, please see Coval and Moskowitz (1999) and Parwada (2008) for intranational empirical findings, and Chan et al. (2005); Cooper and Kaplanis (1994); Errunza et al. (1999); French and Poterba (1991); and Hau and Rey (2008) for international results. Graham et al. (2009) and Lau et al. (2010) investigate the factors determining home bias.

4. For more detailed discussion, please see Bae et al (2008); Denis et al. (2002); Qian et al. (2008); and Rugman (2005).
5. The names of these pacts avoid the term 'FTA' owing to China's core international guideline, One-China policy. The CEPAs have been in effect since January 2004 and the ECFA since January 2011.
6. In 2012, Ma Ying-jeou was re-elected as Taiwan's president. In many reports, he is described as China-friendly. See the Reuters report after the election: http://www.msnbc.msn.com/id/45997749/ns/world_news-asia_pacific/t/taiwan-re-elects-china-friendly-president/.
7. For a more detailed discussion, please see Jin and Myers (2006) and Morck et al. (2000).
8. See De Roon et al. (2001); Harvey (1995); Li et al. (2003); and Pástor and Stambaugh (2000).

REFERENCES

Allen, F., Qian, J., and Qian, M. (2005). Law, finance, and economic growth in China. *Journal of Financial Economics*, 77, 57–116.

Ang, A., Hodrick, R.J., Xing, Y., and Zhang, X. (2009). High idiosyncratic volatility and low returns: international and further U.S. evidence. *Journal of Financial Economics*, 91, 1–23.

Bae, K., Stulz, R., and Tan, H. (2008). Do local analysts know more? A cross-country study of the performance of local analysts and foreign analysts. *Journal of Financial Economics*, 88, 581–606.

Baldwin, R.E. (1997), The causes of regionalism. *The World Economy*, 20, 865–88.

Beck, T., Demirgüç-Kunt, A., and Levine, R. (2003). Law, endowments, and finance. *Journal of Financial Economics*, 70, 137–81.

Bekaert, G. and Harvey, C.R. (2003). Emerging markets finance. *Journal of Empirical Finance*, 10, 3–56.

Bekaert, G., Harvey, C., Lundblad, C., and Siegel, S. (2007). Growth opportunities and market integration. *Journal of Finance*, 62, 1081–138.

Bekaert, G., Harvey, C.R., and Ng, A. (2005). Market integration and contagion. *Journal of Business*, 78, 39–70.

Bekaert, G., Hodrick, R.J., and Zhang, X. (2009). International stock return comovements. *Journal of Finance*, 64, 2591–626.

Bhabra, H., Liu, T., and Tirtiroglu, D. (2008). Capital structure choice in a nascent market: evidence from listed firms in China. *Financial Management*, 37, 341–64.

Bhagwati, J. (1992). Regionalism versus multilateralism. *The World Economy*, 15, 535–55.

Carrieri, F., Errunza, V., and Sarkissian, S. (2004). Industry risk and market integration. *Management Science*, 50, 207–21.

Chan, K., Covrig, V., and Ng, V. (2005). What determines the domestic bias and foreign bias? Evidence from mutual fund equity allocations worldwide. *Journal of Finance*, 60, 1495–534.

Cooper, I. and Kaplanis, E. (1994). Home bias in equity portfolios, inflation hedging, and international capital market equilibrium. *Review of Financial Studies*, 7, 45–60.

Cosset, J.-C. and Suret, J.-M. (1995). Political risk and the benefits of international portfolio diversification. *Journal of International Business Studies*, 26, 301–18.

Coval, J.D. and Moskowitz, T.J. (1999). Home bias at home: local equity preference in domestic portfolios. *Journal of Finance*, 54, 2045–73.

Denis, D., Denis, D.K., and Yost, K. (2002). Global diversification, industrial diversification, and firm value. *Journal of Finance*, 57, 1951–79.
De Roon, F.A., Nijman, T.E., and Werker, B.J. (2001). Testing for mean-variance spanning with short sales constraints and transaction costs: the case of emerging markets. *Journal of Finance*, 56, 721–42.
De Santis, G. and Gerard, B. (1997). International asset pricing and portfolio diversification with time-varying risk. *Journal of Finance*, 52, 1881–912.
Elton, E.J., Gruber, M.J., Brown, S.J., and Goetzmann, W.N. (2007). *Modern Portfolio Theory and Investment Analysis*. New Jersey: John Wiley & Sons.
Errunza, V., Hogan, K., and Hung, M. (1999). Can the gains from international diversification be achieved without trading abroad? *Journal of Finance*, 54, 2075–107.
Eun, C. and Lee, J. (2010). Mean-variance convergence around the world. *Journal of Banking and Finance*, 34, 856–70.
Fan, J.P., Wong, T.J., and Zhang, T. (2007). Politically connected CEOs, corporate governance, and post-IPO performance of China's newly partially privatized firms. *Journal of Financial Economics*, 84, 330–57.
Flavin, T.J. (2004). The effect of the Euro on country versus industry portfolio diversification. *Journal of International Money and Finance*, 23, 1137–58.
Fletcher, J. and Marshall, A. (2005). An empirical examination of the benefits of international diversification. *Journal of International Financial Markets, Institutions and Money*, 15, 455–68.
French, K.R. and Poterba, J.M. (1991). Investor diversification and international equity markets. *American Economic Review*, 81, 222–6.
Goetzmann, W., Li, L., and Rouwenhorst, G. (2005). Long term global market correlations. *Journal of Business*, 78, 1–38.
Graham, J., Harvey, C., and Huang, H. (2009). Investor competence, trading frequency, and home bias. *Management Science*, 55, 1094–106.
Griffin, J. and Karolyi, A. (1998). Another look at the role of the industrial structure of markets for international diversification strategies. *Journal of Financial Economics*, 50, 351–73.
Gul, F.A., Kim, J., and Qiu, A.A. (2009). Ownership concentration, foreign shareholding, audit quality, and stock price synchronicity: evidence from China. *Journal of Financial Economics*, 95, 425–42.
Hardouvelis, G.A., Malliaropulos, D., and Priestley, R. (2006). EMU and European stock market integration. *Journal of Business*, 79, 365–92.
Harvey, C. (1995). Predictable risk and returns in emerging markets. *Review of Financial Studies*, 8, 773–816.
Hau, H. and Rey, H. (2008). Home bias at the fund level. *American Economic Review*, 98, 333–8.
Jin, L. and Myers, S.C. (2006). R^2 around the world: new theory and new tests. *Journal of Financial Economics*, 79, 257–92.
Krugman, P. (1991). Increasing return and economic geography. *Journal of Political Economy*, 99, 483–99.
Lau, S., Ng, L., and Zhang, B. (2010). The world price of home bias. *Journal of Financial Economics*, 97, 191–217.
Li, K., Sarkar, A., and Wang, Z. (2003). Diversification benefits of emerging markets subject to portfolio constraints. *Journal of Empirical Finance*, 10, 57–80.
Markowitz, H. (1952). Portfolio selection. *Journal of Finance*, 7, 77–91.

Moerman, G. (2008). Diversification in euro area stock markets: country versus industry. *Journal of International Money and Finance*, 27, 1122–34.
Morck, R., Yeung, B., and Yu, W. (2000). The information content of stock markets: why do emerging markets have synchronous stock price movements? *Journal of Financial Economics*, 58, 215–60.
Novomestky, F. (1997). A dynamic, globally diversified, index neutral synthetic asset allocation strategy. *Management Science*, 43, 998–1016.
Obstfeld, M. (1994). Risk-taking, global diversification, and growth. *American Economic Review*, 84, 1310–29.
Parwada, J. (2008). The genesis of home bias? The location and portfolio choices of investment company start-ups. *Journal of Financial and Quantitative Analysis*, 43, 245–66.
Pástor, L. and Stambaugh, R. (2000). Comparing asset pricing models: an investment perspective. *Journal of Financial Economics*, 56, 335–81.
Pukthuanthong, K. and Roll, R. (2009). Global market integration: a better way to measure it and its application. *Journal of Financial Economics*, 94, 214–32.
Qian, G., Li, L., Li, J., and Qian, Z. (2008). Regional diversification and firm performance, *Journal of International Business Studies*, 39, 197–214.
Rugman, A. (2005). *The Regional Multinationals.* Cambridge: Cambridge University Press.
Stulz, R.M. and Williamson, R. (2003). Culture, openness, and finance. *Journal of Financial Economics*, 70, 313–49.

6. Cross-border mergers and acquisitions by China in Taiwan 1997–2010

Monica Yang

6.1 INTRODUCTION

Since the 1990s, the volume of foreign direct investment (FDI) has grown massively and become an important engine for global economic growth. The majority of FDI is created through cross-border mergers and acquisitions (CBMAs), which is an international expansion strategy that provides quick access to new foreign markets (Hitt and Pisano, 2003). For example, in 2005, 78 percent of global FDI inflows were through global CBMAs (UNCTAD, 2006, p. xvii). It is also noteworthy that emerging markets have gradually played an active role in initiating foreign investment activities. According to the *World Investment Report* (UNCTAD, 2010, p. xix), emerging and transition economies accounted for a quarter of global FDI outflows in 2009. Take China as an example: by 2009, its outward FDI reached US $229.6 billion, an eight-fold increase over the year 2000 (UNCTAD, 2010). Sixty-two percent of China's outward FDI in 2008 was in the form of CBMAs (MOFCOM, 2008). Although emerging market firms have assumed a critical role in outward FDI, prior management literature has not given sufficient attention to these firms. Therefore, our understanding of the international expansion strategies of firms from emerging markets is very limited (Buckley et al., 2007).

Recent research on CBMAs by emerging markets primarily focuses on the motives and challenges that firms from emerging markets have (Boateng et al., 2008; Buckley et al., 2007; Deng, 2004; Luo and Tung, 2007; Wei, 2010). Following this research trend, I propose the following questions in this study: (1) What is the composition of CBMAs initiated by China in Taiwan from 1997 to 2010? and (2) What is the major motivation for these CBMAs? The reason why I chose CBMAs by China in Taiwan is that Taiwan, with its unique political and economic background, will enhance our understanding of how firms in emerging markets (for example, China) undertake international expansion strategies in other emerging markets. The rivalry between China and Taiwan has persisted from 1949 to the present. While it seems no solution to the Taiwan problem in the immediate future, the economic ties between China and Taiwan are growing dramatically (Tung, 2004). Based on Taiwan's Mainland Affairs Council estimates, Taiwan's indirect trade with China via Hong Kong was only US $460 million in 1981, however, Cross-Strait trade increased tremendously to US $37.4 billion in 2002. Between 1981 and 2002, Taiwan's trade with China increased 134-fold. Since 1993, China has become Taiwan's third-largest trading partner, after the United States and Japan (Tung, 2004). Although the economic trade between China and Taiwan is growing, Taiwan's government was not friendly toward direct investment from China until 2008. The observation window of this study, from 1997 to 2010, will allow us to observe Taiwan's attitude toward CBMAs from China from closed to open.

6.2 HISTORICAL BACKGROUND BETWEEN CHINA AND TAIWAN

The conflict between China and Taiwan originally began in 1949 and has continued into the early twenty-first century (Chen, 2007). The political tension between China and Taiwan has dominated their economic relations (Bush, 2010). From 1996 to 2000, the economic exchanges between China and Taiwan were suppressed by the Taiwan government's policy of 'don't be hasty, be patient.' This policy imposed many restrictions on the economic exchanges between China and Taiwan. Although China started the 'go abroad' policy in 1999 to encourage Chinese firms to invest in foreign markets, Taiwan was not an interesting target for firms from China that did go abroad. Most Chinese firms at that time were state-owned giants interested in natural resources (Boateng et al., 2008; Wei, 2010), and Taiwan is not rich in such resources.

From 2001 to 2007, Taiwan's government replaced the 'don't be hasty, be patient' policy with the 'active openness and effective management' policy. Meanwhile, starting in 2002, Taiwan had amended its inward FDI regulations to comply with World Trade Organization (WTO) commitments. These revised regulations allowed in principle for mainland investors to enter real estate and designated service industries, with case-by-case approval from Taiwan's authorities. Although both policies were more open to the level of the economic exchanges between China and Taiwan, investment from China still did not show a significant change. The economic interdependence between China and Taiwan during this time was an asymmetrical one: an excess of domestic capital outflow from Taiwan to China, the latter gaining relatively more than the former (Deng, 2000). Because of this, some Taiwanese political leaders were worried that Taiwan's growing asymmetrical economic dependence on China might have a negative effect on Taiwan's national security. As a result, Taiwan's government actually refused the request for more openness.

From 2008 to now, current President Ma Ying-jeou has undertaken a systematic effort to stabilize political and economic relations with China and reduce the level of mutual fear. Both Taiwan and China have made significant progress on the economic side, removing obstacles and facilitating broader cooperation (Bush, 2010). In the summer of 2008, several polices supportive of Chinese investment in Taiwan were announced. Later in May 2009, the Ministry of Commerce in China issued regulations specifically governing outward FDI to Taiwan, encouraging such investment as long as it passed special scrutiny by Beijing. The biggest development came in June 2009: the Economic Cooperation Framework Agreement (ECFA) (Rosen and Wang, 2010; Shaw, 2009). This agreement was to ease the process for mainland firms to set up branches and offices in Taiwan, opening 192 sectors to Chinese investors (64 in manufacturing, 117 in services, and 11 in infrastructure).

To conclude, China's direct investment in Taiwan was virtually zero from 1990 until the early 2000s. Taiwan did not permit investment from China, ostensibly on national security grounds. Recent changes in Taiwan's inward investment rules and the increasing motivation and readiness of China's firms to invest abroad are expected to bring the mainland's FDI flows (including mergers and acquisitions) to Taiwan in the near future.

6.3 THEORETICAL EXPLANATIONS FOR MOTIVES BEHIND CBMAs AND HYPOTHESES

Dunning (1993) argues that multinational enterprises (MNEs) will decide in which country to undertake FDI or international production according to the endowments of location-specific advantages of the host country. Specifically, MNEs going abroad are motivated by the need to access resources (natural resources, favorable host country government policies, etc.), the market (supplier networks, special clusters, customers), and cost efficiencies (saving on cheap labor and production costs). These motives are often applied to explain CBMAs. However, it is pertinent to note that there is a difference between CBMA flows from developing countries to developed countries and those from developed countries to developing countries. For example, CBMAs involving firms from developed countries are likely to possess monopolistic and internationalization advantages compared with the firms from developing countries. While firms from developed countries may be motivated to engage in CBMAs to exploit their own resources abroad, firms from developing countries may cross borders to invest in order to explore or seek another country's resources (Boateng et al., 2008). Therefore, it is argued that the internationalization of MNEs from emerging markets is not based on the possession of domestic assets which can be 'exploited' abroad; rather, they enter international business to 'explore' their needed ownership advantages (Luo and Tung, 2007; Wei, 2010). In other words, MNEs from developing countries that lack ownership advantages present a more prevalent case of asset-seeking/augmenting. Technology transfer, learning managerial skills, and access to international markets constitute a major set of strategic motivations for developing-country firms to engage in international activities.

Recent studies on Chinese outward FDI have highlighted the fact that Chinese firms are lagging behind western firms in their development of firm-specific advantages, especially in technology and experience in innovative activities, managerial capabilities, and marketing skill (Wei, 2010). Thus, strategic asset-seeking, both tangible and intangible, has been widely discussed as the motive behind Chinese outward FDI. China has been well known as having a cost advantage when competing in simple products and lower income markets. In order to compete in higher value-adding markets and to develop a differentiation advantage, one of the main firm-specific advantages they need is foreign knowledge of technology-intensive production (UNCTAD, 2003). Chinese enterprises have established R&D centers in high-income countries to assist in the development of technologically advanced, knowledge-intensive products manufactured in China (Buckley et al., 2007). Chinese MNEs have also increasingly sought brand and distribution networks (Deng, 2007). Foreign firms' willingness to sell or share their brands owing to financial exigency or restructuring needs makes it possible for latecomer MNEs such as China to access the foreign market immediately (Luo and Tung, 2007).

In the case of CBMAs by China in Taiwan, I argue that Chinese firms are most likely to acquire Taiwanese firms by the motives of market and strategic asset-seeking. Market-seeking investment is intended to sustain existing markets and exploit new markets (Dunning, 1981). When China's domestic market faces fierce competition, Chinese firms will like to seek sales abroad in response to diminishing profits at home (Taylor, 2002). Because Taiwan and China are proximate, culturally and geographically, it is a natural step for Chinese MNEs that aim to get a larger share in the market to acquire companies with an applicable distribution network and brand name in Taiwan. Moreover, firms in Taiwan, as opposed to those in China, possess tangible and intangible knowledge in technology innovation and management. For instance, the high-technology industry, one of the critical industries in Taiwan, is strong in keeping 'strategic assets' such as human capital, brand reputation and managerial capabilities to a high standard. The financial services industry is another example. The distortion of the Chinese capital market has greatly contributed to the majority of Chinese outward foreign direct investment (OFDI) flowing into Hong Kong and tax havens such as the British Virgin Islands and the Cayman Islands. Because the financial services industry in Taiwan is relatively mature and full of experience with well-trained human capital, this industry is likely to be chosen as a target market for CBMAs by Chinese firms. Therefore, driven by the motive of strategic asset-seeking, Chinese firms are likely to acquire firms in certain industries where Taiwan possesses better knowledge and skills, such as manufacturing (technology) or financial services.

As to the motive of efficiency-seeking, this occurs when some mature MNEs with comparative advantages in economies of scale/scope seek 'low cost' locations for their operation and production activities (Dunning, 2001). Because the average household income and the cost of living in Taiwan are much higher than in China, the production cost in Taiwan will cost Chinese firm more in terms of the cost of labor, land, and other factors. Therefore, the motive behind CBMAs by China in Taiwan will not be efficiency-seeking. Finally, Taiwan does not possess abundant natural resources. The motive behind CBMAs by China in Taiwan thus will not be seeking natural resources. Altogether, I argue that Chinese firms are likely to merge with or acquire Taiwanese firms under the motives of market and strategic asset-seeking. They are likely to enter technologically-advanced or knowledge-intensive industries such as manufacturing (technology) or financial service industries.

Hypothesis 1: The target industries of CBMAs by China in Taiwan are technology-advanced or knowledge-intensive.

In addition to the specific motives that characterize Chinese outward FDI, the Chinese government's support has been acknowledged as a major driver of Chinese OFDI (Deng, 2007; Luo et al., 2010). Financial support provided by the Chinese government has played a crucial role in Chinese firms' globalization and their acquisition of strategic assets from overseas (Rui and Yip, 2008). For example, China Development Bank and the

China Export and Import Bank, together with other state-owned banks, provide credit funds (with low lending rates, fast approval processes, and extensible terms) every year to support key outward FDI projects. Other forms of financial support include tax exemptions in relation to the export of equipment, raw materials, and intermediate products; double taxation avoidance treaties with host nations, and freedom from foreign exchange controls (Luo et al., 2010). Meanwhile, the shares of most Chinese MNEs are held by a mix of the state, legal persons, foreign financial service institutions, and individual investors. The State Council owns shares in most cases and legal personal shares are mainly controlled by the regional and central government and their ministries. Consequently, the business operations of Chinese companies engaged in outward FDI are largely controlled by government (Wei, 2010; Chen and Young, 2010). The dominant position of the state in Chinese OFDI allows the government to determine the type of investment it would like to encourage. Therefore, investment decisions in the case of MNEs from developed countries are governed by a mix of political and economic objectives, rather than just profit-maximization (Deng, 2009; Buckley et al., 2007). Support provided by the Chinese government towards outward FDI is thus intertwined with strong political considerations, including natural resource security, innovation promotion (for example, improving the competitiveness of Chinese firms), and building relationships with other countries. Existing examples here are that the Chinese government uses overseas investments as a channel to strengthen its relationship with those in Africa and South Asia and to maintain the prosperity of Hong Kong and Macao during their transition periods (Deng, 2004). When it comes to the case of Taiwan, political considerations will certainly be involved in the decision-making process of CBMAs by Chinese MNEs. In order to continue and deepen the economic interdependence between China and Taiwan, I argue that with the support of the Chinese government, the number of CBMAs by Chinese firms in Taiwan will increase over time despite Taiwan's restrictive policies from 1997 to early 2008.

Hypothesis 2: The number of CBMAs by China in Taiwan increases over time.

6.4 DATA AND METHODS

The major data source of this study is 'Thomson One Banker' produced by Thomson Financial Corporation. This company collects information about mergers and acquisitions using a variety of sources such as financial news articles, Reuters Textline, the *Wall Street Journal*, Dow Jones, and so forth. This database is well known for its comprehensive lists of mergers and acquisitions (M&As) valued at US $1 million or more. My goal is to study all completed cross-border M&As initiated by China and Hong Kong-based organizations that merge with or acquire firms in Taiwan. Since the early 1990s, more and more Chinese firms have acquired weak corporations in Hong Kong to raise equity capital and have transformed themselves into MNEs overnight (Hong and Sun, 2004; Woo and Zhang, 2006; Globerman and Shapiro, 2009). Therefore, in the case of China and Taiwan, Hong Kong has evolved as a major transshipment location, the largest re-export hub in the region and a doorway to the south China economy. I thus decided to include Hong Kong-based firms in the sample. Because the first CBMA by China in Taiwan recorded in this database was 1997, I decided to collect all completed deals from 1997 to 2010. This observation window will allow us to observe important economic (for example, joining the WTO) and regulatory transitions (for example, 'go global' or 'ECFA' polices) in both countries. The final sample size was 90 cross-border M&A deals, 20 from China and 70 from Hong Kong. In terms of statistical analysis, I used frequency tables to illustrate critical features of these deals.

6.5 RESULTS AND DISCUSSIONS

In this section, I analyse the number and the nature of these CBMA deals over time. First, in terms of the number of deals, Table 6.1 shows that 20 deals (22 percent) are initiated by firms from China and 70 deals (78 percent) by firms from Hong Kong. Considering the historical background between China and Taiwan, I decided to examine these deals in three different time periods: before 2000; 2001 to 2007; and 2008 to 2010; representing the Taiwanese government's different attitudes toward direct investment from China. Before 2000, Taiwan held a very restrictive attitude toward direct investment from China. As a result, the total number of CBMA deals was only 10. From 2000 to 2007, Taiwan replaced those restrictive policies with somewhat more open ones. The total number of CBMA deals increased dramatically to 61, six times higher than the previous time period. Finally, between 2008 and 2010, the most open environment for direct investment from China, the total number of deals dropped back to 19. Thus, the number of CBMA deals initiated by China in Taiwan from 1997 to 2010 increased first, then decreased, displaying an inverted U-shape. Hypothesis 2, which argues that the number of CBMAs in Taiwan increases over time, is not supported.

Table 6.1 Number of cross-border mergers and acquisitions in Taiwan from China and Hong Kong, 1997–2010

Year	From China	From Hong Kong	Total
1997	1	2	3
1998	1	2	3
1999	1	3	4
2000	1	5	6
2001	0	8	8
2002	0	7	7
2003	0	5	5
2004	0	8	8
2005	4	5	9
2006	2	3	5
2007	3	10	13
2008	2	5	7
2009	3	5	8
2010	2	2	4
Total	20	70	90

To further understand the pattern of the number of these deals over time, I compared CBMA deals from China against those from Hong Kong. Before 2000, both China and Hong Kong had initiated a low number of deals. From 2000 to 2007, China and Hong Kong showed very different patterns. As shown in Table 6.1, there was no deal from China to Taiwan between 2001 and 2004. As mentioned earlier, I understand that this is possibly due to the Taiwanese government's restrictive policies toward economic trade with China. When those restrictive policies were replaced later by more open ones, deals from China increased but still remained low, averaging two to three deals per year between 2005 to 2007. By contrast, Hong Kong was very active between 2000 and 2007 in initiating CBMAs to enter Taiwan. It maintained more than five deals every year except in the year 2006. The highest number of deals was ten in 2007. I thus confirm that Hong Kong was still the major bridge of CBMAs from China to Taiwan during this period of time.

To understand the reason behind the decreasing pattern of CBMAs from 2008 to 2010, I examined the overall foreign direct investment (approved cases and amount) in Taiwan from 1997 to 2010 (see Table 6.2). Similar to the pattern of CBMAs, the number of approved cases and the amount of foreign investment in Taiwan increased to their highest point in 2007 and then declined in 2008 and 2009. Accordingly, during that period of time, Taiwan faced shrinking investment from foreign

Table 6.2 Approved foreign investment in Taiwan

Year	Total		From Hong Kong
	Case	Amount[a]	Amount
1997	683	4266.63	73.52
1998	1140	3738.76	18.76
1999	1089	4231.40	85.99
2000	1410	7607.76	27.32
2001	1178	5128.52	17.94
2002	1142	3271.75	1.42
2003	1078	3575.67	3.69
2004	1149	3952.15	2.60
2005	1131	4228.07	0.65
2006	1846	13969.25	4.64
2007	2267	15361.17	0.68
2008	1845	8237.11	1.74
2009	1711	4797.89	0.55
2010	2042	3811.57	2.95

Note: a. Unit: US $ millions.

Sources: Investment Commission, Ministry of Economic Affairs, R.O.C., Statistics on Overseas Chinese & Foreign Investment, Outward Investment, Indirect Mainland Investment, R.O.C., April 2011.

investors all over the world, not just from China. When I checked the total number of global CBMA deals by China in my database, I also found that the global M&A activities of China reached their peak in 2008 (128 completed deals) and then declined in 2009 (118 completed deals) and 2010 (98 completed deals). Therefore, Taiwan, as a CBMA target market for Chinese firms, was not treated differently from other target markets. I believe that the decreasing CBMA pattern between 2008 and 2010 is a normal response corresponding to the general investment environment in Taiwan.

In addition to the analysis of the number of deals, I examine the nature of these deals along the following dimensions: the industry of acquiring firms and target firms; related vs unrelated deals; the payment method and major players. In terms of the industry of acquiring firms, within the valid 80 deals, 42 (52.5 percent) of them are from the financial services industry, followed by 11 deals (18.8 percent) from the service industry and 10 deals (12.5 percent) from the manufacturing industry and wholesale trade industry. This result is very similar to that of the sub-sample of China. Within the 14 valid deals from China, 5 (35.7 percent) of them are from the financial services industry, followed by 4 deals (28.6 percent) from the service industry and two (14.3 percent) from the manufacturing industry. In the Hong Kong sample, of the 66 valid deals, 37 (56.1 percent) of them are from the financial services industry, followed by 9 deals (13.6 percent) from the wholesale trade industry and 8 deals (12.1 percent) from the manufacturing industry.

As to the industry of target firms, of the 80 valid deals, 21 (26.3 percent) of them are entering the financial service industry, followed by 16 deals (20 percent) entering the manufacturing industry and 13 deals (16.3 percent) entering the service industry. In the sample from China, of the 14 valid deals, 5 (35.7 percent) of them are entering the financial services industry, followed by 4 deals (28.6 percent) entering the service industry and 2 (14.3 percent) entering the manufacturing industry. In the sample from Hong Kong, 16 deals (24.2 percent) are entering the financial services industry, followed by 13 deals (19.7 percent) entering the manufacturing industry and 11 deals (16.7 percent) entering the wholesale trade industry. Currently Taiwan does not permit Chinese banks any presence on the island. To pave the way for expanded financial flows, we see the number of CBMAs in the financial services industry has increased. The first hypothesis which argues that Chinese firms are driven by the motives of market and strategic asset-seeking is supported because the target industries here are considered as knowledge-intensive or technology-intensive.

The third dimension of CBMAs is 'related vs unrelated.' Relatedness refers to the situation when both acquiring and target firms are in the same industry. I coded it 0 if both firms are in the same industry; 1 otherwise. Within the 80 valid deals, 47 deals (58.8 percent) were related deals. In particular, firms from Hong Kong, as opposed to those from China, were more likely to take risks in exploring different industries. In the sample from China, 12 deals (85.7 percent) were related. However, in the sample from Hong Kong, 35 deals (53 percent) were related and 31 deals (47 percent) were unrelated. Figure 6.1 shows the number of related and unrelated deals by HK firms over time. As indicated, unrelated deals were most active between 1999 and 2005 (except 2003).

Furthermore, in terms of the payment method, I found that 28 (80 percent) of the 35 valid deals were cash-only. The rest of the deals adopted a combination of cash and other methods such as debt and stock. Firms from both China and Hong Kong displayed the same preference here, as 7 (87.5 percent) of valid deals by China and 21 (77.8 percent) by Hong Kong were cash-only deals.

Finally, I investigated those active players in these CBMAs. Tom Group Limited is the most active player, initiating six deals, followed by

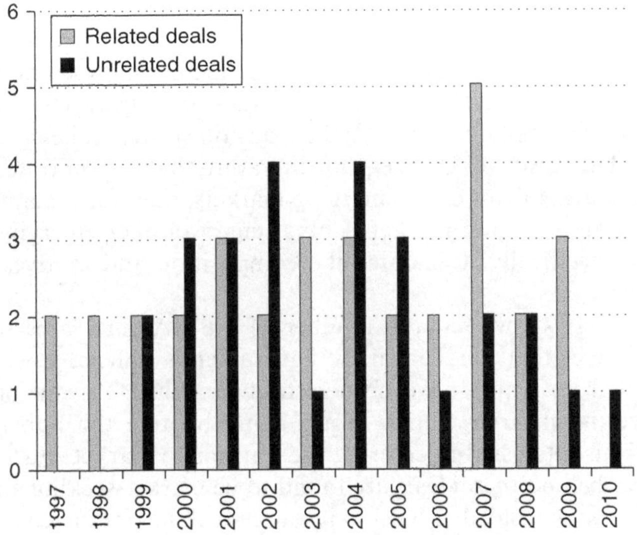

Figure 6.1 *The number of related and unrelated cross-border mergers and acquisitions in Taiwan from Hong Kong, 1997–2010*

Fox Conn (four deals), TPV Technology (four deals) and HSBC (three deals). All of them are based in Hong Kong except FoxConn. These four firms are scattered in industries like manufacturing, financial services and business services. Tom Group Limited, with around 3000 employees, is a leading Chinese-language media conglomerate in Greater China, which has diverse business interests in Internet, e-commerce, outdoor media, publishing, television, and entertainment. TPV Technology Limited, on the other hand, is a leading display solution provider producing a wide spectrum of desktop monitors and LCD TVs. Both companies were established in 1999, so all of their M&A deals were done in the latest 10 years. Foxconn Technology group, a trusted name in contract manufacturing services in the world, came in third. Hon Hai Precision Industry Company Limited, the anchor company of Foxconn Technology Group, was founded in Taiwan in 1974. The M&As initiated by Foxconn in Taiwan can thus be seen as the example for those Taiwanese firms who return their investment back to Taiwan. Lastly, HSBC is one of the world's largest banking and financial service organizations. It has been very active in the Asia-Pacific region since 1865. Foreseeing the expanded financial flows among China, Hong Kong, and Taiwan, HSBC actively engaged in CBMAs and prepared to be an influential player in this region.

6.6 CONCLUSIONS

Emerging markets like China have attracted increasing research attention on their outward direct investment activities and strategies. This study focuses on one specific international expansion strategy, the cross-border merger and acquisition. Unlike prior literature that concentrates on how developed market firms enter emerging markets, this study examines how firms from an emerging market (China) enter another emerging market (Taiwan). Specifically, I examine the composition and motives of these CBMA deals.

The findings show that the number of CBMAs increases over time despite the fact that the Taiwanese government's policies toward direct investment from China have been restrictive. While Taiwan prohibited direct investment from China, Hong Kong became the hub for those Chinese firms interested in entering the Taiwanese market. Furthermore, the motives behind these deals are found to be market-seeking and strategic asset-seeking, instead of natural resource-seeking or efficiency-seeking. Consequently, most target firms of these deals are in the financial services industry, service industry, and manufacturing industry. Compared to firms from China, acquiring firms from Hong Kong were more willing to undertake unrelated deals. Finally, both firms from China and Hong Kong prefer cash-only as the major payment method in CBMA deals.

Taiwan started to open up to inbound direct investment from China under memoranda of understanding (MOUs) signed in 2008. One relevant and interesting question is: 'Will the annual value of China-to-Taiwan investment be likely to rise significantly after significant regulatory changes?' I didn't see that in the case of CBMAs. It is probably that CBMAs, compared to imports/exports, is a complicated strategy which involves higher commitment of management and resources. Therefore, it may take more years to see the numbers of CBMAs surge. Because the observation window of my sample ranges from 1997 to 2010, it may be too early to capture the immediate impact of significant regulatory changes in Cross-Strait direct investment such as the ECFA. The unique contribution of this study is thus to offer a better understanding of direct investment from China to Taiwan, particularly on the issue of CBMAs, from the period of time that the Taiwanese government's attitude switched from negative to positive.

This study has several implications for Taiwan and China. First, in terms of the number of CBMA deals from China and Hong Kong between 2008 and 2010, the Taiwan government's positive attitude toward direct investment from China did not stimulate more CBMA deals. Therefore, this result will alleviate some concern that more Taiwanese firms will be merged with or acquired by Chinese firms after recent economic policy changes like the ECFA. Second, compared to the number of CBMAs by China in other countries, Taiwan is not a major target for Chinese firms. However, the motives behind those CBMAs from China are very similar to those by China in other developed markets (such as the United States and European countries). When developed markets like the USA and the UK continue to raise security concerns over Chinese CBMA proposals and reject them (for example, the 3Com–Huawei merger in 2008 or Huawei–Marconi in 2005), Taiwan may become an important target market for Chinese firms to obtain critical implicit assets (for example, brand name, management, or marketing knowledge and skills). The Taiwanese government thus needs to prepare and consider how to manage these types of CBMA deals in the future. Finally, the success of CBMAs is largely determined by how an acquiring firm manages its target firm after the transaction. Although Taiwan and China have shared a similar language and tradition, it is still unclear whether the performance of CBMAs by China in Taiwan is generally satisfactory. It thus becomes a challenge for those top management teams of Chinese firms in CBMAs to handle relevant conflicts such as managing different corporate cultures and management practices.

The limitation of this study is the low availability of data. Due to limited access to the information of Chinese investors, I have difficulties further analysing the background of the acquiring firms (that is, the ownership structures). Therefore, acquiring firms like Fox Conn, which are originally from Taiwan, deserve further data-collecting and investigation. Likewise, to understand whether these CBMA deals are successful or not after their completion, more data of post-M&A performance will rely on other reliable databases (for example, *Taiwan Economic Journal* and *InfoTimes*.)

With regard to additional directions for future research, I first propose several suggestions that would better explore the influence of important economic policy such as the ECFA. One suggestion is to conduct a comparative study that focuses on the similarities and difference of CBMAs before and after the ECFA. This research direction is very similar to the current one but requires a longer observation time. The other research direction is to investigate the impact of the ECFA on Taiwan's economy. For instance, this research can focus on the relationships between the activity of CBMAs and other critical variables such as market structure, employment opportunities, and technology transfer. Finally, future researchers can expand current studies to embrace more emerging markets and developed markets. One possible research direction is to examine whether the determinants of CBMAs from emerging markets in developed markets are the same as those in emerging markets.

REFERENCES

Boateng, A., Wang, Q., and Yang, T., 2008. 'Cross-border M&As by Chinese Firms: An Analysis of Strategic Motives and Performance.' *Thunderbird International Business Review*, 50, 259–70.

Buckley, P., Clegg, L., Cross, A., Liu, X., Cross, H., and Zheng, P., 2007. 'The Determinants of Chinese Outward Foreign Direct Investment.' *Journal of International Business Studies*, 38, 499–518.

Bush, R., 2010. 'China–Taiwan: Recent Economic, Political, and Military Developments Across the Strait, and Implications for the United States.' Brookings Institution. Available at: http://www.brookings.edu/research/testimony/2010/03/18-china-economy-bush.

Chen, C., 2007. 'China and Taiwan: A Future of Peace?' *Josef Korbel Journal of Advanced International Studies*, 1, 14–25.

Chen, Y. and Young, M., 2010. 'Cross-border Mergers and Acquisitions by Chinese Listed Companies: A Principal–principal Perspective.' *Asia Pacific Journal of Management*, 27, 523–39.

Deng, P., 2000. 'Taiwan's Restriction of Investment in China in the 1990s: A Relative Gains Approach.' *Asian Survey*, 40, 895–908.

Deng, P., 2004. 'Outward Investment by Chinese MNCs: Motivations and Implications.' *Business Horizons*, 47, 8–16.

Deng, P., 2007. 'Investing for Strategic Resources and its Rationale: The Case of Outward FDI from Chinese Companies.' *Business Horizons*, 50, 71–81.

Deng, P., 2009. 'Why Do Chinese Firms Tend to Acquire Strategic Assets in International Expansion?' *Journal of World Business*, 44, 74–84.

Dunning, J., 1981. *International Production and the Multinational Enterprise*. London: George Allen & Unwin.

Dunning, J., 1993. *Multinational Enterprise and the Global Economy*. New York: Addison-Wesley.

Dunning, J., 2001. 'The Eclectic (OLI) Paradigm of International Production: Past, Present and Future.' *International Journal of the Economics of Business*, 8, 173–90.

Globerman, S. and Shapiro, D., 2009. 'Economic and Strategic Considerations Surrounding Chinese FDI in the United States.' *Asia Pacific Journal of Management*, 26, 163–83.

Hitt, M. and Pisano, V., 2003. 'The Cross-border Mergers and Acquisition Strategy.' *Management Research*, 1, 133–44.

Hong, E. and Sun, L., 2004. *Go Overseas via Direct Investment: Internationalization Strategy of Chinese Corporations in a Comparative Prism*. London: Center for Financial and Management Studies, University of London.

Luo, Y. and Tung, R., 2007. 'International Expansion of Emerging Market Enterprises: A Springboard Perspective.' *Journal of International Business Studies*, 38, 481–98.

Luo, Y., Xue, Q., and Han, B., 2010. 'How Emerging Market Governments Promote Outward FDI: Experience from China.' *Journal of World Business*, 45, 68–79.

MOFCOM, 2008. *2008 Statistical Bulletin of China's Outward Foreign Direct Investment*. Beijing: Ministry of Commerce.

Rosen, D. and Wang, Z., 2010. 'Deepening China–Taiwan Relations through the Economic Cooperation Framework Agreement.' Peterson Institute for International Economics. Available at: http://www.iie.com/publications/pb/pb10-16.pdf.

Rui, H. and Yip, G., 2008. 'Foreign Acquisitions by Chinese Firms: A Strategic Intent Perspective.' *Journal of World Business*, 43, 213–26.

Shaw, J., 2009. 'China and Taiwan Deepen Economic Ties.' *Wall Street Journal*, April 27.

Taylor, R., 2002. 'Globalization Strategies of Chinese Companies: Current Developments and Future Prospects.' *Asian Business and Management*, 1, 209–25.

Tung, C., 2004. 'Economic Relations between Taiwan and China.' UNISCI Discussion paper.

UNCTAD, 2003. *FDI Policies for Development: National and International Perspectives*. New York and Geneva: UNCTAD.

UNCTAD, 2006. *World Investment Report 2006: FDI from Developing and Transition Economies*. New York and Geneva: UNCTAD.

UNCTAD, 2009. *Transnational Corporations, Agricultural Production and Development*. New York and Geneva: UNCTAD.

UNCTAD, 2010. *World Investment Report 2010: Investing in a Low-carbon Economy*. New York and Geneva: UNCTAD.

Wei, Z., 2010. 'The Literature on Chinese Outward FDI.' *Multinational Business Review*, 18, 73–112.

Woo, Y. and Zhang, K., 2006. *China Goes Global: The Implications of Chinese Outward Direct Investment for Canada*. Vancouver: Asia-Pacific Foundation of Canada.

7. Strategic alliance between Japan and Taiwan on the Chinese market: an empirical analysis of the IT industry

Chih-Ping Chen and Kai-Wen Hsieh

7.1 INTRODUCTION

The rapid economic growth of China after its economic reform has been and still is an irresistible attraction for many foreign investors. But not all of them know how to complement one another or to penetrate the Chinese market successfully. In fact, some have encountered serious problems and even failure, as reported in economic and financial news. One of the most significant obstacles has been China's legal and bureaucratic oversight (Weller, 1998). From foreign investors' perspective, China's legal system and bureaucratic structure causes uncertainty far greater than that of the ordinary business environment they encounter in other countries, whether developed or not. In addition, multinational enterprises (MNEs) have faced difficulties overcoming the cultural and societal barriers in managing their subsidiaries in China. Hence, successfully penetrating the vast market potential of China has become one of the hottest topics in international management.

Due to language and cultural similarities between peoples on both sides of the Taiwan Strait, Taiwanese managers know better than other foreigners how to emphasize the social network so as to capitalize on their relationship (Guanxi) with China's localities and overcome the Chinese legal system and bureaucratic structure.[1] In contrast, Japanese firms are more used to relying on their industrial conglomerates of Keiretsu (business–industrial conglomerates with both vertical and horizontal integration between firms) to manage the supply chain globally. A strategic alliance between Taiwanese and Japanese firms, mainly in the information technology (IT) industry, may thus generate stronger competitive advantages than other MNEs in China. Whether strategic alliances between Japanese and Taiwanese IT-related firms have a distinctive advantage in penetrating the Chinese market has attracted much attention in the field of international business.

Literature on international alliances addresses several different aspects; the resource-based theory focuses on the importance of firms' internal resources and claims that differences in performance are results of asymmetric knowledge and knowledge-related resources rather than opportunism. Firms can obtain the key resources and improve their own strategic positions in the market through the formation of strategic alliances. In that regard, Japanese and Taiwanese firms could complement one another and perform better in the Chinese market than if they were alone. In fact, when Taiwan's investment in China was expanding, Japanese firms began to establish different operating strategies and partnerships with Taiwanese firms, which were more familiar with Chinese language, culture, and society. Taiwanese firms are also more experienced in absorbing technological transfer from Japanese firms than from other MNEs in China. Through their strategic alliance with Japanese firms, Taiwanese enterprises in China could not only cut the transaction cost but could also obtain technical skills and managerial expertise from Japanese partners.

The strategic alliances between Taiwanese and Japanese firms were initiated because of complementary advantages in the Chinese market. And the profit incentives for both the Taiwanese and Japanese firms have led to numerous joint ventures in recent decades. Through various forms of their strategic alliance, Taiwanese firms could enhance their production technology and competitiveness while Japanese firms could have access to relatively low-priced components. Hence, the partnership is mutually beneficial and will allow them to expand the scale of production in China.

This study has chosen the Taiwanese firms operating in China in the IT industry from two major industrial clusters: Kunshan City of Jiangsu Province, and Dongguan City of Guangdong Province. The reason for choosing the IT industry in our surveys is justifiable because more than 40 percent of US imports of IT-related products, such as consumer electronics and computers, came from Asia, mainly China, Japan, Korea, and Taiwan, as reported in Chapter 10 of this book by Chow. Among those foreign-invested enterprises (FIEs) in China, the IT-related industry is particularly significant, as evidenced by the fact that six of Taiwan's IT-related firms were ranked among the top ten export firms in China in 2009.[2] Therefore, among those FIEs in China, Taiwan's IT-related firms could be considered as models for strategic management in international business.

This study is a modest attempt to offer a case study on the joint venture of Japanese and Taiwanese firms to overcome their difficulties penetrating the Chinese market. The main objective is to explore the strategic alliances between Taiwan's and Japan's firms and to evaluate their effect on the growth of firms by examining the relative performances of sales between the allied and non-allied firms in China. By using survey data and regression analysis technique, this study concludes that the unique pattern of strategic alliance between Taiwanese and Japanese firms has enabled them to perform better than those without alliances. This finding may offer some lessons for other multinational enterprises interested in exploiting the Chinese market.

The remainder of this paper is as follows. Section 7.2 reviews the formation and patterns of the strategic alliance between Taiwanese and Japanese firms, their developments in the past decade, and the assessments of the strategic alliance's probable benefits. Section 7.3 reviews recent literature on strategic alliances, presents models with descriptions of data and variables under study, and reports the empirical results. The final section presents a summary and conclusions.

7.2 THE DEVELOPMENT OF THE STRATEGIC ALLIANCE BETWEEN JAPAN AND TAIWAN

The flow of foreign direct investment into China in the 1980s and 1990s followed a trend to either license technology to a local partner or establish a joint venture (Evans et al., 2002). During this period, the cooperation between Japanese and Taiwanese firms indicates that strategic alliances between them were gradually maturing (Liu, 1998). It is noted that these developments are motivated by the profit incentives at the level of individual firms rather than at a macro level of national planning for both countries to penetrate the third market in China.

7.2.1 Status of Taiwanese Firms in China

Taiwanese firms initiated their investment through sole proprietorships, mergers and acquisitions (M&A), and original equipment manufacturers (OEMs). Most of the manufacturing industry produces goods either for export or to satisfy the domestic demands of China's market. Among all the investments made by Taiwan, the IT industry accounted for the greatest proportion in China. Table 7.1 shows Taiwanese investments in China from 1991 to 2010. As one can find from column 2, a great percentage of these investments lies in the manufacturing industry. Among all the invest-

Table 7.1 Taiwan's investment in China

Year	Total amount	Manufacturing amount	Electronic parts and components manufacturing amount	Computer, electronic, and optical products manufacturing amount
1991	174158	173058	4995	13926
1992	246992	246382	1528	11269
1993	3168411	2955618	110666	140821
1994	962209	886492	40769	48264
1995	1092713	998576	101889	55175
1996	1229241	1115905	88429	115059
1997	4334313	3902660	283525	313645
1998	2034621	1830689	281402	341687
1999	1252780	1166098	154029	271529
2000	2607142	2384246	412348	698776
2001	2784147	2513959	600559	492948
2002	6723058	6077594	1087523	1062716
2003	7698784	6807514	815821	976452
2004	6940663	6284971	1482225	1139980
2005	6006953	5281921	850106	1243497
2006	7642335	6649291	1618566	1472132
2007	9970545	8765998	2426286	1688385
2008	10691390	8761185	2051917	1783302
2009	7142593	5892078	1801294	1019404
2010	14617872	10840822	4854424	1235374

Note: Units: US $1000.

Source: Investment Commission, MOEA.

ment in manufactures, the IT industry accounts for the highest percentage. At the industry level, IT contains two major sectors: manufacturing of electronic parts and components; and manufacturing of computer, electronic, and optical products. Since 2000, the IT firms had begun expanding their business scale in China by increasing 36 percent of total capital investment in 1999, followed by 46 percent growth of investment in 2000, and 56 percent growth in 2010.

Taiwanese IT firms in China mostly received original equipment manufacturing (OEM) orders from foreign vendors, manufactured and processed them in China, and then exported them to final markets, primarily in OECD countries. During this production process, Japanese firms took roles on top of entire IT supplier chains. Japanese enterprises placed their orders to Taiwanese producers and purchased electronic parts and components, computers, peripherals, and electrical machinery. Furthermore, purchases from Japanese firms in recent years included the thin film transistor liquid crystal display (TFT-LED), integrated circuit (IC) semiconductors, etc. Notebooks, computer peripherals, and machinery were produced in Taiwan at the primary level of production and then exported as intermediates or semi-finished products to China for further processing before being sold to Japan and other industrialized countries.

7.2.2 The Formation and Patterns of the Strategic Alliance

The strategic alliance of Japan and Taiwan, according to Zhu (2010), can be classified into five major categories:

1. firms of joint ventures set up in Taiwan and performing investment in China;
2. joint ventures set up in China to run business and share benefits;
3. production alliances, especially the supply chains of components and supplements;
4. subsidiaries of Japanese firms in China recruiting cheap but diligent Taiwanese staff and technicians;
5. the Taiwanese market as the testing field for Japanese firms to learn and acquire experience before moving to China.

Taiwan was one of the pioneers of industrial clusters and supply chains in East Asia, and it formed easy access channels for purchasing materials and parts. Taiwanese firms are better than their Chinese counterparts at understanding Japanese firms, probably due to the influence of Japan's culture during the colonial period. Moreover, the Taiwanese are more familiar than the Japanese with Chinese culture and society (Liu, 2003). This unique socio-cultural factor may provide Taiwanese enterprises with a 'dual comparative advantage' in doing business in Taiwan, and their experiences could offer some lessons in international management.

Essentially, the relationship between Taiwanese and Japanese firms belongs to the subset of the global production network and supply chain mainly tied with the OEM orders from world-class firms in Japan. But the Japan–Taiwan relationship is far more complicated than the conventional one between providers and clients. Zhu (2004) argues that for the products exported to Japan, Japanese clients would require a much stricter standard of quality control. Hence, Japanese firms would demand that Taiwanese suppliers meet the high quality standard. Unlike western firms, Japanese firms usually offer technological assistance for quality improvement if foreign firms cannot meet the quality standard. But western firms will usually drop those firms from the production chain if they cannot meet the quality standard as expected. For that purpose, Japanese Keiretsu (a set of companies with interlocking business relationships and shareholdings) will establish an OEM relationship with Taiwanese firms in China and maintain their comparative advantage in the global market.

Through cross-border cooperation, investment, and emerging technological support, those Taiwanese firms allied with Japanese partners have reduced business uncertainty and increased their competitiveness in China's market. On the other hand, Japanese firms can also seek to adapt to the local business environment and to absorb cheap and diligent Taiwanese employees through their strategic alliances with Taiwanese counterparts. Nevertheless, some Japanese firms – those which focused on brand-name marketing – still retain production capabilities at home and choose to produce upper-market goods and high-end technological products in Japan. Hence, only low-end goods were sub-contracted to Taiwanese OEM producers, which then engaged most of their production in China. This is one reason why Japan could maintain its dynamic comparative advantage in the world market while transferring technology to other less developed countries, as Bernard and Ravenhill (1995) argue in their explanation of Japan's leadership by Akamatsu's 'flying geese' pattern of industrial developments in East Asia. Empirically, Chow (2012) examined Japan's comparative advantages and proved that other followers in the flock of flying geese – the eastern NICs, notably Korea and Taiwan – did not fully catch up with the mother goose of Japan in high-end products in the world market. Hence, Japanese firms are willing to transfer technology, cut the cost of production, and meet the necessary quality standards to penetrate China's market. Therefore, the strategic alliance between Japanese and Taiwanese firms has become more and more significant in recent years.

From the perspective of Japanese firms, Taiwanese partners could provide them with components of better quality, with faster delivery and lower cost than most local Chinese firms. Taiwanese firms in many ways are more effective than other foreign companies in terms of prices, and are more committed to the required delivery dates. As a result, Japanese firms took advantage of Taiwanese IT production chains in China by allying with them. Based on Mizuho's investigative report (Itou, 2009), there were at least 415 strategic alliances between Japan and Taiwan by June 2009, among which 91 were in the IT industry.

Zhu (2010) found that the Japanese enterprises purchased components and products from Taiwan's suppliers while providing technical and management skills. The partnership led to the enhancement of Taiwan's production capabilities, especially during the period when many Japanese firms had suffered from Japan's 'lost decade' of the Heisei recession. The strategic alliance could also be considered as part of the effort for Japanese firms to carry out an organizational restructuring and downsizing operation in its economic downturn.

For some high-tech industries such as semiconductors and LCDs, it is critical for Japan to develop its own indigenous IT industries and to survive global competition. Throughout the entire period of economic recession, Japanese firms continued to make investment in these sectors. As a result, many of these investments were involved with strategic alliances with Taiwanese firms. According to a report by the Japan External Trade Organization (JETRO) conducted by Yosimura (2010), there were cases, such as Xiroku's,[3] in which Japan transferred its newly-developed LCD touch panels to Taiwanese firms for production.

7.2.3 Benefits of Strategic Alliances

Most of the research which looks into the outcomes of Japan–Taiwan joint ventures in China adopts complementary resources as its analytical basis. Liu (2010) argues that the joint ventures integrated the advantages of Taiwanese firms' efficient production and market-exploration techniques with Japanese firms' outstanding production capabilities. They were thus able to explore new markets with great success. Some major conclusions from previous research on this benefit are summarized as follows.

In the field of IT industries, Japan benefits from alliances in several ways. First of all, with the manufacturing capabilities of Taiwanese firms, Japanese partners could focus on basic research for new products and shorten the time required for market penetration. The second benefit relates to costs. Japanese products, though functional with reliable quality, are more expensive than those produced in China and Taiwan. Taiwanese firms not only possess the capability of supplying similar goods but can also maintain the quality with lower production cost. Third, allying enables Taiwanese firms to have a better competitive edge on pricing similar products than Japan's rivals. Therefore, strategic alliances with Taiwanese firms enable Japanese firms to produce the same goods with lower cost and to enhance their competitiveness in the global market.

The benefits from alliance on Taiwan's side include the following. First, there are technology transfers from Japanese firms to Taiwanese partners through joint ventures, and the former even supply the components that promote production quality. Second, an alliance creates more opportunities for Taiwanese firms to take orders from Japanese firms, which helps them enlarge scales of production and generate more profits. Therefore, a strategic alliance is a 'win–win' for both partners.

7.3 COMPARISONS BETWEEN JAPANESE–TAIWANESE STRATEGIC ALLIANCES AND NON-ALLIED TAIWANESE ENTERPRISES IN RESPECT OF OPERATION

7.3.1 Review of Literature

Liu (2003) classifies six types of strategic alliance between Taiwanese and Japanese enterprises by market orientations (local versus global markets) and control types (Japanese control, Taiwanese control, and shared control). Based on interviews with the top corporate executives, Liu finds that 'there is a niche for each type' of alliance strategy. Then he explores how both Japanese and Taiwanese enterprises benefit from the complementary advantages of strategic alliances.[4]

Other studies focus on technological transfer and cooperation. Hagedoorn and Jos (1994) argue that the crucial relationship between strategic technology partnering and the profitability of firms apparently takes place through indirect channels, which, to a large extent, can be explained by the different characteristics of firms and industrial sectors in terms of technological transfers. Frederico (1999) points out that the technological cooperation could be explained by the need of the firm to acquire complementary competencies.

Based on those analyses of strategic alliances, one can understand why those Taiwanese enterprises allied with Japanese partners were benefiting the most in upgrading, reinforcing, or transferring production technology. Having been injected with Japan's technology, Taiwan's enterprises can upgrade their production technologies, enlarge production scales, and thereby increase their profits. Though the empirical results in literature show that more profits were achieved for those firms with strategic alliances with Japanese firms, comparisons between the profits and performance of both the Japanese and Taiwanese sides are rare in the existing literature.

This research is intended to compare Japanese–Taiwanese strategic alliances with non-allied Taiwanese enterprises in terms of operating performances and to demonstrate that strategic alliances contribute to the growth of sales of Taiwanese enterprises. It is expected to provide empirical support for the notion that strategic alliances with Japanese enterprises are truly a better option for Taiwanese firms. Instead of personal interviews, this study uses questionnaires, surveys, and regression analyses of the results. To the best of our knowledge, this study is the first modest attempt to bridge the gap on quantitative assessment on strategic alliance in existing literature on international management.

7.3.2 Rationales and Basic Assumptions of the Model

Since previous research had indicated that Taiwanese enterprises benefited the most from acquiring Japan's technologies, this study will analyse whether Taiwanese enterprises which received technology reinforcements and transfers from Japanese partners gained more profits than those without alliances. It is generally anticipated that those firms with technology support from Japan would perform better than non-allied ones in the Chinese market. Hence, we used capital and technologies from Japan as the independent variables in the regression model. Moreover, there is a dummy variable *JC*, which indicates whether the Taiwanese firms have capital investments from Japanese firms. The dummy variable *BT* indicates whether the Taiwanese firm buying technologies from Japanese firms has a significant effect on firms' performance. Two other variables are used as proxies of the effect of the technological relationship between Taiwan and Japan; *NT* stands for the number of technical supports, and *PT* stands for the years of strategic alliance.

Numerous measurements of the growth of firms appear in some previous studies. Evans (1987) and Audretsch et al. (1999) argue that a firm's growth is measured only by the number of employees. Heshmati (2001) defines the growth of a firm in terms of its number of employees, sales, and assets. Nevertheless, Storey (1994) points out that employment growth is less significantly related to firm growth than profitability. Honjo (2004) also examines the relationship between the sales and growth of the firm. This index can be considered as a weak proxy for efficiency measurement.

Because most of the firms surveyed in this study declined to reply to our questionnaires on labor employment, we cannot measure differences in the number of employees and the value of assets between allied and non-allied firms. On the other hand, sales are more likely to reflect the changes in a firm's employment rate. As Brush et al. (2000) argue, most firms value sales growth, and sales growth may enhance the welfare of managers instead of employees. Sales growth provides opportunities for

Table 7.2 Definitions of the variables

Independent variable	Definition
JC	Dummy variable if Japanese firm's capital jointed Taiwanese firms during the observation period (in thousands of NT$)
BT	Dummy variable for buying technologies from Japanese firms
NT	Number of firms providing technical support
PT	Period of technical cooperation (year)
Dependent Variable	
Y	Difference of the logarithm sales growth rate between 2009 and 2010 (in thousands of NT$)

Note: Each dummy variable takes the value 1 if the stated condition holds and 0 otherwise.

economics of scale and learning curve benefits. Thus, this study measures the performance of firms by sales growth. The data source provides sales for the recent 2 years based on their accounting periods. Table 7.2 describes the definitions of the variables. Here, a model of firm growth is written as:

$$\text{Growth of } Y = f(JC, BT, NT, PT)$$

7.3.3 Results of Empirical Analysis

Taiwanese investment in China is mostly concentrated in coastal areas, especially in the Yangtze River Delta and the Pearl River Delta. In particular, many Taiwanese firms are concentrated in Kunshan City in Jiangsu Province and in Dongguan City in Guangdong Province. According to the local associations of Taiwanese enterprises in Kunshan, there were about 4000 Taiwanese firms in 2011. On the other hand, the number of Taiwanese firms is around 3000 according to an announcement of the local associations of Taiwanese enterprises in Dongguan City in 2011.

The survey questionnaires were sent to Taiwanese enterprises located in Kunshan city in Jiangsu province, and Dongguan city in Guangdong province to provide case studies of Taiwanese firms operating in China. Four hundred questionnaires were delivered to the Taiwanese firms

Table 7.3 Summary statistics for covariates

Variable	Mean	Median	S.D.
Y	–7.55	18	4.426
JC	0	1	0.355
BT	0	1	0.106
NT	0	5	1.073
PT	0	10	2.384

Note: S.D. represents the standard deviation

Table 7.4 Correlation matrix

Abbreviation	*Y*	*JC*	*BT*	*NT*	*PT*
Y	1				
JC	0.369	1			
BT	0.074	–0.044	1		
NT	0.58	0.296	0.022	1	
PT	0.507	0.295	0.138	0.525	1

in each city listed by local enterprise associations. One hundred and one responded. The number of effective questionnaires was 89, which accounts for 11 percent of our delivered questionnaires. The returning rate was lower than anticipated, hence any conclusions must be qualified.

Among these 89 respondents, 24 could be defined as Japanese–Taiwanese strategic alliances, which included 12 Japanese–Taiwanese joint ventures, 1 with technology purchased from Japan, and 11 with technical cooperation with Japanese enterprises.

We employed regression as our analytical method, and the results are reported below. Table 7.3 shows the summary of descriptive statistics for each variable. Table 7.4 shows the correlation between all variables, and Table 7.5 shows the regression results.

Table 7.5 shows the estimated results from ordinary least squares (OLS). The coefficient of *JC* is significantly positive in the model of firm growth, although the coefficient of *BT* is not significant. This result suggests that when capital from Japanese firms joins Taiwanese partners, sales of Taiwanese firms are more likely to grow. The estimated coefficient of *BT* implies that buying technologies from Japanese firms has a positive

Table 7.5 Estimation results

Covariate	
Constant term	3.8881***
	(0.4890)
JC	2.2735**
	(1.1013)
BT	1.6634
	(3.5125)
NT	1.653***
	(0.4080)
PT	0.439**
	(0.1859)
R^{-2}	0.3953
Number of observations	89

Notes:
Significance: ***1%; **5%; and *10% levels.
Robust standard errors are in parentheses.

but not significant effect on firms' sales performance. Hence, it is unclear whether buying technology from Japanese firms is significant enough to directly affect sales growth. Plausibly, Taiwanese firms would have benefited more from Japanese capital than simply purchasing technical support.

On the other hand, the coefficients of *NT* and *PT* – the number of firms providing technical support and the duration of strategic alliance, respectively – are both significantly positive determinants of the growth of firms. The results imply that not only does cooperation with many firms improve sales, but so does longer duration of the cooperation. This finding could provide significant policy implications for strategic management of Taiwanese multinational enterprises operating in China.

7.4 CONCLUSION

In this study we discussed the effects of strategic alliances between Japanese and Taiwanese enterprises in the IT industry on the growth of firms. The pattern of strategic alliances includes joint ventures with transferred production technologies from Japan to Taiwan and technical cooperation and reinforcement acquired through OEM. This report also compared allied and non-allied Taiwanese enterprises in terms of sales performance. The regression results showed that those firms which acquired technologies through strategic alliance or technical cooperation from Japan performed better than the non-allied ones. And the longer the duration of cooperation, the more productive it would be for their performance. This finding is consistent with Itou (2010), who points out that the higher survival rates of Japanese–Taiwanese joint ventures in China were partly due to the trustful relationship. Accordingly, this study concludes that strategic alliances play a crucial role in creating sales for Taiwanese firms operating in China.

One word of caution is that, as with any survey results, one must recognize the analytical limit of the sample size due to the technical constraint of the number of respondents to our questionnaires. Further study with more samples and wider geographic areas is needed to improve understanding of the effect of Japanese–Taiwanese strategic alliance on firms' performance in China.

ACKNOWLEDGEMENTS

We are grateful to the local associations of Taiwanese enterprises of Kunshan City in Jiangsu Province, and Dongguan City in Guangdong Province, for providing access to the employment database for this study. We wish to thank anonymous referees for their valuable suggestions that significantly improved the quality of article. We also thank Peter C.Y. Chow for his precious comments, and the provision of invaluable research assistance. Needless to say, any remaining errors are our own.

NOTES

1. Many Taiwanese subsidiaries recruited retired party cadres to work as their liaison officers to deal with Chinese government officials. Arguably, China is still a country 'ruled by man, not by law.' Therefore, interpersonal relations (Guanxi) enabled Taiwanese managers to better manage the social network to build better social infrastructures than other foreign-invested enterprises in China.
2. According to statistics of Chinese Ministry of Commerce Reported in 2009. There enterprises are Quanta, Hong-Hai, Foxconn, Campal, Wistron, and Asus.
3. Xiroku Inc. was established as a business entity in Tsukuba city in February 2001. It is a new venture enterprise, and mainly produces touch-screens with the CMOS camera system.
4. The industries covered are in machinery, optical and other technology-intensive sectors. They are mostly located in the coastal area of China: Tailien Optical, Ricoh Eleme (Dong-guan), Nikon (Guan-dong), Liufeng, Toyota Industry, Fujiwa Machinery, Pioneer (Dong-guan) and Ding Yi/Sanyo Foods.

REFERENCES

Audretsch, D.B., E. Santarelli, and M. Vivarelli (1999), 'Start-up size industrial dynamics: some evidence from Italian manufacturing,' *International Journal of Industrial Organization*, 17, 965–83.

Bernard, Mitchell and John Ravenhill (1995), 'Beyond the flying geese and product life cycle,' *World Politics*, 47 (2), 171–210.

Brush, T.H., P. Bromiley, and M. Hendrickx (2000), 'The free cash flow hypothesis for sales growth and firm performance,' *Strategic Management Journal*, 21, 455–72.

Chow, Peter C.Y. (2012), *Trade and Industrial Development in East Asia: Catching up or Falling Behind.* Northampton, Massachusetts: Edward Elgar, chs 2 and 3 on the revealed comparative advantages.

Evans, D.S. (1987), 'Tests of alternative theories of firm growth,' *Journal of Political Economy*, 95, 657–74.

Evans, P., J.L. Barsoux, and V. Pucik (2002), *The Global Challenge: Frameworks of International Human Resource Management*. New York: McGraw-Hill.

Frederico, Rocha (1999), 'Inter-firm technological cooperation: effects of absorptive capacity, firm-size and specialization,' *Economics of Innovation and New Technology*, 8 (3), 253–71.

Hagedoorn, John and Jos Schakenraad (1994), 'The effect of strategic technology alliances on company performance,' *Strategic Management Journal*, 15, 291–309.

Heshmati, Almas (2001), 'On the growth of micro and small firms: evidence from Sweden,' *Small Business Economics*, 17 (3), 213–28.

Honjo, Yuji (2004), 'Growth of new start-up firms: evidence from the Japanese manufacturing industry,' *Applied Economics*, 36, 343–55.

Itou, Singo (2009), 'Chaiwan time of Japan and Taiwan alliance,' *Mitsuho Research*, 1–33.

Itou, Singo (2010), 'Taiwan–Japan joint venture in China,' *Practices and Case Studies, INK Issue*, The Strategic Alliance of Taiwanese and Japanese Businessmen in China, pp. 31–47.

Liu, Ren-Jye (1998), 'The new movement of strategic alliance between Taiwanese and Japanese enterprises after financial crisis,' *Commercial Times* (in Chinese).

Liu, Ren-Jye (2003), 'An Empirical Study of Strategic Alliances between Taiwanese and Japanese Enterprises in Mainland China,' *Journal of Asian Business* (Michigan), 19 (3), 71–94.

Liu, Ren-Jye (2010), 'FFG marketing strategy in China and Taiwan–Japan alliance,' *Practices and Case Studies, INK Issue*, The Strategic Alliance of Taiwanese and Japanese Businessmen in China, pp. 87–138.

Storey, D.J. (1994), *Understanding the Small Business Sector*, London: Thomson Learning.

Weller, D.L. (1998), 'The bureaucratic heavy hand in china, legal means for foreign investors to challenge agency action,' *Columbia Law Review*, 98 (5), 1238–82.

Yosimura, Syou (2010), 'See the case of small and medium enterprises alliance,' Japan–Taiwan Business Alliance Study Group Report, JETRO Issue, 51–64.

Zhu, Yan (2004), 'Japan–Taiwan enterprise alliance in China business,' *Economic Research*, Fujitsu Research Issue, 1–23 (in Chinese).
Zhu, Yan (2010), 'Taiwan–Japan business strategic alliance,' *Practices and Case Studies, INK Issue*, The Strategic Alliance of Taiwanese and Japanese Businessmen in China, pp. 181–98.

APPENDIX

Table A7.1 The strategic alliance pattern

Taiwanese Firm	Japanese Firm	Product	Strategic Alliance Pattern	Since
Thai Lin Semiconductor Corp.	Asahi Kasei Micro devices	Wafer Test	Original Equipment Manufacturer	2011
Wah Hong Industrial Corp.	Gumze Corporation	Optical film for Touch Panel use Invisible ITO Film	Technical Cooperation	2008
Power Quotient International Co. Ltd	Sino-JP Investments Co. Ltd	Flash Card, USB Flash Drive, DRAM Module, Hard Disk Drive, Solid State Disk, Industrial Product, Apple Accessory.	Joint Capital with Japanese Firms	2005
Optotech Corporation	Nichia Corporation, Hitachi Cable Corporation	LED Product	Joint Capital with Japanese Firms and Management	2005

Sources:
http://tw.stock.yahoo.com/news_content/url/d/a/111123/3/2wl6o.html
http://www.moneydj.com/kmdj/wiki/wikiviewer.aspx?KeyID=df70c3cd-e013-4cd3-89f1-6e08ac7c882c&Version=5
http://www.gocharter.com.tw/m2/detail.asp?main_id=1755
http://www.moneydj.com/kmdj/wiki/wikiviewer.aspx?keyid=ec87133c-3f10-4804-a02c-74d8e7aaf04a

8. Global production networks and the Kunshan ICT cluster: the role of Taiwanese MNCs

Tain-Jy Chen and Ying-Hua Ku

8.1 INTRODUCTION

The most outstanding feature of Kunshan as an emerging ICT (information and communications technologies) cluster in the world is its rapid transformation from farmland into a powerhouse of industrial production within 2 decades or so. Before the transformation, there was no apparent endowment of skilled labor in the region, and skilled workers are considered to be a precondition for the birth of a high-tech cluster (Bresnahan et al., 2001). Most observers of the dramatic rise of Kunshan pointed to the role of global connections, whereby Kunshan was largely seen as a relocation and reconstruction of the ICT cluster that previously existed in Taiwan. This view is over-simplified. It provides little explanation as to how these global connections have worked wonders for Kunshan, what circumstances have induced the relocation of the cluster from Taiwan to China, and what local conditions have made the relocation possible. Without answers to these questions, the rise of Kunshan can only be attributed to pure luck. The main purpose of this paper is to find these answers. The work is based on a field study in Kunshan conducted in April 2007 and a follow-up trip in October 2011.

We will study the rise and the evolution of the Kunshan cluster, using the concept of the global production network (GPN) (Gereffi, 1995; Ernst and Kim, 2002; Henderson et al., 2002), and focus on local institutions that underscore the working of global production networks. GPNs view global production as being accomplished by a set of differentiated and networked producers, who are globally dispersed, but may be locally clustered. GPNs posit that these multi-actor transnational production systems have an important bearing on the development and clustering dynamics of a region (Coe et al., 2008). Previous studies on GPNs have shown that the local environment, such as government policy and local institutions, shape the geographical configuration of a GPN (see for example Dicken, 1998; Liu and Dicken, 2006). Moreover, the configuration of a GPN evolves overtime, driven by technological innovations and changing patterns of competition in the market. Technology matters because it conditions the ability of related firms in the network to coordinate and integrate extraordinarily intricate operations across countries (Coe et al., 2008). Market competition matters because it defines the inter-relations between firms, and a GPN is fundamentally a relational view of the world (Dicken, 2004; Yeung, 2005). When a GPN evolves due to technological or market changes, the opportunity for a region to develop or upgrade its industry also evolves. A region with foresight can therefore prepare itself for the emerging opportunities by adopting a set of 'right' policies and institutions.

Our working hypothesis is: the rise of Kunshan is caused by a combination of a reconfiguration of a GPN in the ICT industry and a set of 'right' policies and institutions. The reconfiguration of the GPN was precipitated by technological innovations and demand-shifts in recent years. In terms of technology, the widespread diffusion of the Internet that began in the early 1990s drove the revolution in production methods. The new technology enabled a new production model known as 'build to order' (BTO) that replaced the traditional 'build to forecast' model. On the demand side, the increasing popularity of ICT products, particularly personal computers (PCs), around the world translated into a need for producers to offer low-priced yet innovative models in order to avoid commoditization (Schrage, 2007). In response to this trend, GPNs had to be reconstructed to create responsiveness, differentiation, and low costs at the same time. Geographical concentration of supply chains gave rise to responsiveness, and co-location of similar producers in the same industry gave rise to differentiation. Low cost was to be found in a location that provided abundant supply of labor that could be assimilated to global production cultures.

The advantage of Kunshan is understood to be low-cost labor, on which no discussion is needed. But low-cost labor is not sufficient to make Kunshan a viable player in the global production chains, as there are plenty of similar places in the world, including many in China. If we consider the trade-related infrastructures of Kunshan in the early 1990s when the agglomeration process began, it is hard to imagine that Kunshan could out-compete southern China in terms of the facilities that enable responsiveness in global production. For one thing, southern China is adjacent to Hong Kong, which is one of the most efficient seaports and financial centers in the world that allow efficient transportation and financial transactions. Therefore it must be something else that underscores the superiority of Kunshan over the other potential locations for a new cluster in the 'China Circle' that started to take shape in the early 1990s (Borrus, 1997).

We found that Kunshan's success hinges on three advantages. The first advantage is its geographical proximity to Shanghai which gives it the ability to attract skilled labor into the region (labor pooling) and to export notebook PCs in large volumes and in a flexible fashion to accommodate the newly-invented BTO scheme. The second advantage is the ability of the local government to create local institutions that are loosely coupled with domestic institutions but tightly coupled with international institutions. This special institutional arrangement allows Kunshan to leverage international resources for regional growth. The third advantage is Kunshan's close tie to Taiwan's ICT industry which provides the 'structural hole' to the global production chains (Burt, 1992). With this tie, Kunshan is indirectly linked to the innovation center of the world's ICT industry, namely Silicon Valley in California. In this paper, we will discuss these three advantages one by one. But before we do it, let us look at the agglomeration process of the Kunshan cluster.

8.2 THE AGGLOMERATION PROCESS

When China opened the Yangtze River Delta to foreign direct investment in January 1985, Kunshan quickly jumped onto the bandwagon. In terms of administrative jurisdiction, Kunshan was a county under the city of Suzhou, which was included in the opening list. The county government of Kunshan established an 'economic and technological development zone (ETDZ)' without the endorsement of the national government in an attempt to attract foreign direct investment, despite the fact that the county was merely a farming area with virtually no industrial base at the time. This local ETDZ was dwarfed by other national ETDZs in the country because of lack of resources. However, Kunshan was smart to target small Taiwanese investors who were overlooked by national ETDZs because of the lack of glamour. Because Kunshan was only 60 kilometers away from the Shanghai seaports, for Taiwanese exporters, locating in Kunshan makes little difference from the municipal areas of Shanghai (see Figure 8.1). In fact, if Hongqiao Airport was to be used for shipment, it was only 40 kilometers away from Kunshan. Better yet, Kunshan was under the jurisdiction of the Suzhou customs territory instead of the busy and bureaucratic Shanghai customs, thus the time it takes to clear customs procedures was much shorter. In later years, as Kunshan and the greater Suzhou area were developed into a big export cluster, customs procedures

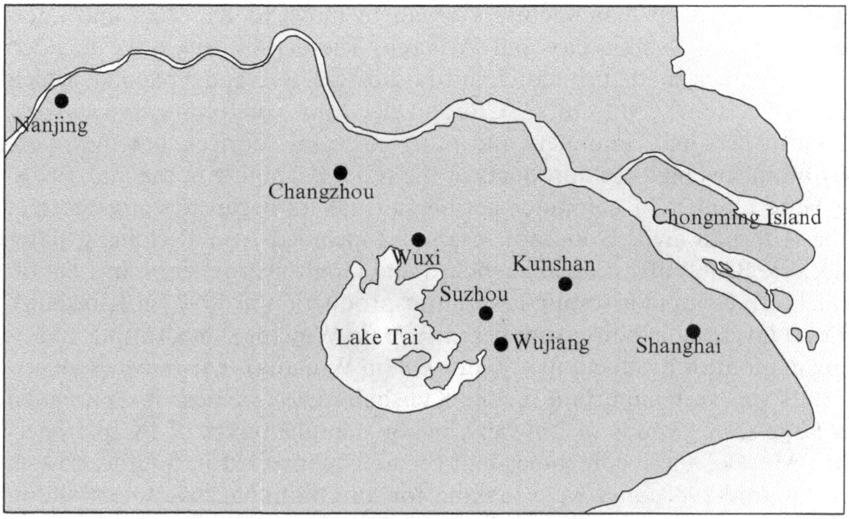

Figure 8.1 Kunshan and adjacent areas

were expedited by the creation of 'export processing zone' facilities that further smooth the flows of imports and exports.

In the early years of economic reforms in China, southern Jiangsu province was very successful in developing township and village enterprises (TVEs) that served as the locomotive of industrialization. Denoted as the 'Sunan' (southern Jiangsu) model in the literature, these local-government-controlled TVEs positioned themselves as suppliers to major state-owned enterprises located in Shanghai (Naughton, 2007, p. 282). TVEs were concentrated in the cities of Suzhou, Wuxi, and Changzhou. As a small farming town lacking capital, Kunshan was peripheral to the TVE boom of the 1980s. Instead, it turned to foreign investment for growth impetus.

In the 1980s, major foreign investments in Kunshan were in the traditional industries such as bicycles, metal fabrication, and electronics components. Because of its success in attracting foreign investments, in 1992 Kunshan was formally recognized by the central government as a national ETDZ which entitles all foreign-invested companies in the zone to a reduced tax rate of 15 percent on business income as opposed to the 24 percent rate that normally applies to foreign investors. With a national status, the administrative body of the ETDZ was also authorized to approve foreign investment projects with a capitalization below 100 million RMB. Only investment projects in excess of 100 million RMB had to be cleared by the central government. This gave local government more bargaining power vis-à-vis foreign investors. Since then, major Taiwanese computer-related manufacturers began to move to Kunshan and adjacent areas of Suzhou city and Wujiang. The earliest investors included Nantz, which made printed circuit boards (PCBs), and Foxconn, which made electronic connectors. PCBs and electronic connectors are key parts used in personal computers and other electronic devices, but they were by no means high-tech products at the time. Beginning in the mid-1990s, a large number of computer peripheral makers began to congregate in the Kunshan area. Noticeable examples included Acer Peripheral (later became BenQ) investing in keyboard and monitor production in 1994 (in Suzhou); Compal investing in monitor production in 1997 (in Kunshan); Delta investing in power supplies in 1998 (in Wujiang); and Tatung investing in monitor production, also in 1998 (in Wujiang). This wave of investments was very important for the Kunshan region because it represented a large-scale exodus of Taiwan's major manufacturers of PC peripherals. Most of these companies had previously invested in Southeast Asia in the mid-1980s and were looking for an additional investment site in China rather than a replacement. Their investments were partly driven by impending labor shortages in Southeast Asia and partly by the prospect of selling their products in China's domestic markets. As far as the domestic sales were concerned, the greater Shanghai region was obviously the top choice. This wave of investments started the agglomeration process for Kunshan. For example, when Acer Peripheral invested in Suzhou, it brought with it 14 major parts suppliers, mainly metal and plastic parts producers, which collectively located in the nearby county of Wujiang.

The agglomeration force may be originated from large-scale assemblers or from large-scale parts suppliers (Yang, 2007). In both cases, the agglomeration was essentially a backward integration process. For example, big parts suppliers such as Delta, and big assemblers such as Acer Peripheral, generated their own agglomeration effects. Those following their footsteps were mainly upstream suppliers from Taiwan. The supply chains were reconfigured and permeated when these suppliers came to locate in the same region.

In addition to tax incentives given to EDTZ, the foreign investment wave in the 1990s was aided by new tax incentives given by the Chinese government to high-tech foreign companies, which enjoy a 10 percent tax rate after 2 years of tax holiday (zero tax) plus 3 years at a 5 percent reduced tax rate. Following this incentive program, Suzhou High-Tech Park was inaugurated in November 1992 which attracted many prominent multinational firms like Phillips, Siemens, Hitachi, and Fujitsu. The congregation of large multinational firms in Suzhou, which is 30 kilometers away from Kunshan, made Kunshan even more attractive because of the benefits of horizontal integration. For example, parts suppliers to Acer

Peripheral could also sell to Phillips and Fujitsu which also produced computer monitors at the time.

However, the Kunshan area did not become an ICT powerhouse until after the second wave of investments by Taiwanese notebook computer makers beginning in 2001. The second wave erupted suddenly and proceeded very fast. By 2004, China had surpassed Taiwan to become the world's largest exporter of ICT products. Almost every major PC assembler joined the bandwagon, including Compal, Mitac, Acer (later renamed Wistron), Asustec, and Arima. Only Quanta and Inventec chose to locate in Shanghai city instead of the Kunshan cluster. This wave of investments was precipitated by the big consolidation in the world's PC industry following the bursting of the IT bubbles in 2001 whereby Compaq merged with HP, Siemens was acquired by Fujitsu, and Texas Instruments was acquired by Acer. The consolidation necessitated a larger scale of production and shorter product cycles. In addition, the diffusion of the Internet gave birth to a demand-driven production scheme, which was named 'built to order' by the industry. Each brand marketer was under pressure to produce at lower costs yet with more variety to accommodate diverse consumer tastes. China was the only answer to this mission. Mitac and Acer, both of which had formerly produced PCs in Guangdong Province in southern China, each established a new production facility for notebook PCs in Kunshan. They were convinced that it was only Kunshan that could allow them to achieve both scale and speed at the same time.

It is important to note that in the first wave of agglomeration in 1992–2000, manufacturers of PC peripherals made the investments in Kunshan spontaneously, partially responding to government incentives and rising labor costs elsewhere. In the second wave of agglomeration since 2001, it was mainly brand marketers that drove the investments, and labor cost was of a lesser concern. In other words, 'flagship' firms in the GPN orchestrated the agglomeration process, although they themselves did not engage in investments. Flagship firms were able to do so because they controlled key resources. Those who control resources in the network attain power (Pfeffer and Salancik 1978). In the GPN, this power transcends national borders.

Around the end of the millennium, HP and Dell, two leading PC brands in the world, had both adopted the 'build to order' scheme in their global operations whereby orders collected from consumer demands were to be fulfilled within a week or so by contract manufacturers. To run this scheme, proximity of suppliers is indispensable for the speedy response to different orders. Airport and customs efficiency, and air cargo capacity, are also crucial factors. South China could not compete with Shanghai in terms of air transport capacity and efficiency. In Kunshan, the congregation of parts suppliers that supported the production of computer peripherals before the year 2000 set the foundation for notebook PC relocation. Incidentally, investment of notebook PC production in China was prohibited by the Taiwan Government at the time. Brand marketers, together with their major contract manufacturers, had to lobby the Taiwan government to repeal the policy, which finally took place in November 2001. This anecdote shows the important role of flagship firms in shaping the geographical location of the global industry.

During the agglomeration process, both the number of firms and the size of firms grew in the Kunshan cluster. Supporting this process was the growing size of Taiwanese contract manufacturers who anchor the local production networks. The consolidation of the world's PC industry since 2001 resulted in market concentration of brands, which was translated into a preference for one-stop shopping. As a contract manufacturer, larger size offers the advantage of lower transaction costs in one-stop shopping (Amsden and Chu, 2003, p. 8). When contract manufacturers became larger and the contract-manufacturing market became more concentrated, their power to dictate the location of suppliers also increased. Brand marketers normally preferred their contract manufacturers, which are few in number now, to locate nearby; these contract manufacturers, in turn, also preferred their suppliers to locate in the immediate proximity. The trickle-down process drove the agglomeration. Size was all that mattered; size commanded power that prompted the co-location of related firms.

One distinctive characteristic of the Kunshan cluster from other transplant industry clusters in Southeast Asia is its extensive horizontal integration. Compared to Kunshan, industrial clusters in Southeast Asia are characterized by a higher degree of vertical integration and a lower degree of horizontal integration. This characteristic can be explained by the reconfiguration of the GPN after the 2001 IT bubbles. Along with the consolidation of the PC industry since 2001, the structure of supply chains also changed accordingly. In addition to the increase in the volume of production by each contract manufacturer (assembler), the degree of modularization accelerated. One supplier of outer cases for notebook PCs, which is a first-tier supplier to the assembler, told us that the variety of cases had been reduced from about 80 in number before 2001 to only four in recent years (interview with factory manager, April 3, 2007). This was possible because, since 2001, the variety of PCs was to be created by functional units such as memory, storage, display, and add-on devices, rather than the architecture of the PC itself. As the burden of holding inventory to support a large volume of production was shifted largely to the first-tiered suppliers, who were therefore under pressures to increase the degree of vertical integration. They had to undertake large capital investment in order to meet the increasing demand for capacity. Furthermore, they were required to locate in the neighborhood of the assemblers so that parts could be delivered in a 'just in time' fashion. A supplier of micro-motors said that it typically made two deliveries each day, and occasionally made an emergency delivery if needed, sometimes in the middle of the night (interview with factory manager, April 6, 2007).

A typical assembler under the 'built to order' scheme followed a '983' rule whereby 98 percent of parts of a computer were to be collected within 3 days of receipt of the order from the brand marketers, and the final products were to be shipped out within 6 or 7 days (Lee, 2006). Reduction of coordination costs in the network was critical to this extreme responsiveness. As the first-tiered suppliers increased the degree of vertical integration, coordination costs decreased. For example, when the supplier of outer PC cases internalized plastic and metal molding production, the transactions with vendors of metal and plastic moulds were eliminated. Reducing the number of second-tired suppliers, who were typically smaller and more vulnerable to market fluctuations, also reduced the supply chain uncertainty. Compared to the production networks which previously existed in Taiwan, the Kunshan networks are characterized by a smaller number of players, each with a larger production capacity, and thus a more stable network relationship. An example that manifests this stable relationship was that some outer case and keyboard makers organized a separate joint venture with each assembler to produce computer cases or keyboards exclusively for that assembler. Stable network relations may compensate for the weakness of local institutions.

With this unrivaled and efficient production network, aided by a massive number of low-wage workers, Taiwanese contract manufacturers quickly increased their share in the world's notebook PC market. The top five assemblers, namely Quanta, Compal, Inventec, Wistron, and Asustec, together accounted for 40 percent of notebook PC contract manufacturing in 2001. That market share quickly rose to 57 percent in 2004, after the assemblers relocated to Kunshan and Shanghai (III, 2005, p. 45). By 2008, their combined market share had exceeded 90 percent. Mainly because of their contributions, Kunshan became the top exporter among China's 54 national ETDZs, surpassing other more prestigious ETDZs such as Suzhou and Tianjin. In 2008, total exports from the Kunshan ETDZ amounted to US $33.1 billion, of which 92 percent were ICT products (Zhong, 2009, p. 195). It was estimated that half of the world's notebook PCs were made in Kunshan (www.js.xinhuanet.com, 2010/11/16).

As soon as the Kunshan cluster had become a major production base of notebook PCs, LCD panel producers quickly moved into the region around 2005. Auo of Taiwan and Hitachi of Japan both established LCD module assembly facilities in the region. These facilities not only provided flat panels to notebook PCs, but also helped transform the computer monitor industry from CRT-based to LCD-based monitors. In other words, the new LCD investment breathed new life into the old monitor industry which was the mainstay of the first-wave investments in Kunshan. In a few years, flat-screen TV production was also introduced into the region. The cluster appeared to be already in a state of self-sustained evolution.

In fact, the wholesale relocation of notebook PC production from Taiwan to China was not foreseen by anyone in the industry before 2001, not even the officials of Kunshan. The bursting of IT bubbles in 2001 was the main cause of what happened afterwards. However, it is the institutions that the local government had put in place that accounts for the success of the cluster. This set of institutions perfectly accommodates the new structures of the global IT industry where brand marketers are in urgent demand for a one-stop shopping place that offers massive quantity yet differentiated products. As Maskell (2005) explains, the emergence of a new cluster is often driven by the need for new institutions to fit the new industrial structures that arise when knowledge grows or economic activities shift. In the following two sections, we shall discuss these institutions, one set of which governs internal linkages, the other set governing external linkages.

8.3 LOCAL INSTITUTIONS

One indispensable factor for a region to succeed as a cluster is the establishment of cooperative connections to the leading centers of technology and market (Bresnahan et al., 2001). And a precondition for these connections is the functioning of relevant institutions that make the connections possible, as institutions are the foundation for trade within or between regions (North, 1990). Differences in national institutions adversely affect the performance of multinational corporations (MNCs) (Kostova and Zaheer, 1999). The issue of institutions is of particular importance to China, as it was making drastic institutional reforms to become a market economy at the time. In this section, we will discuss how Kunshan created a system of institutions that set the agglomeration process in motion by connecting with multinational enterprises, particularly those from Taiwan. In a nutshell, local institutions in Kunshan are loosely coupled with institutions in the rest of China but strongly coupled with the world economy.

As a small county with a population of roughly 400000 in 1985, the labor force in Kunshan quickly ran out of supply as foreign investment moved into the region en masse. A large number of migrant workers were imported from Northern Jiangsu Province, Hubei, and Sichuan, etc. Today, the population in Kunshan is estimated as being between 1.6 and 2 million, among which 650 000 are domicile holders, the rest being migrants without official resident status. The county government of Kunshan is one of the most liberal local governments in China in granting resident status to migrant workers. Migrant workers with a college degree are automatically granted resident status. Higher-ranked staff of local companies can obtain resident status by owning a housing property if they do not hold a college degree. They can even obtain resident status with a property purchased by the employer on their behalf without transferring the ownership. The liberal migration policy provides a stable labor supply to local companies whose operations are intrinsically labor-intensive.

Being adjacent to Shanghai is both an advantage and a threat to Kunshan. It allows Kunshan to attract skilled labor from inland provinces to migrate to Kunshan because they can take advantage of the amenities of nearby Shanghai. However, skilled labor can easily be lured away by companies in Shanghai. Kunshan's liberal migration policy toward skilled labor is a policy designed to counter the advantage of Shanghai, which runs a stringent migration policy. In the Kunshan–Suzhou region, the only prominent university is Suzhou University, which produces a limited number of engineering graduates. Attracting skilled workers from the rest of the country provides an impetus to the development of the cluster.

As more and more labor works for private as opposed to state-owned companies, the central government of China introduced several social security programs to protect private-sector workers, including health, unemployment, work injury, childbirth, retirement benefits, and housing funds. These programs and funds accumulated accordingly are to be managed by the local government. The contributions to these programs are typically shared between the employees and employers in certain proportions. Migrant workers may refuse to participate in these programs because the accumulated contributions in their personal accounts are not portable when they leave the locality. The Kunshan government stipulated low premiums for social security programs in order to encourage participation by migrant workers. In China, the uneven treatments among different groups of migrants, and between migrants and residents, create a system of differentiated citizenship (Wu, 2010). This inequality in social status is the root of social tensions in many booming industrial cities of China. By running a liberal migration policy coupled with a relatively generous offering of social services to migrant workers, such as affordable public housing and inclusive public education for the children of migrant workers (in many cities, children of migrant workers are not allowed in local public schools), Kunshan was able to maintain a good social order in a town where 'native' residents are in fact the minority of the local population.

Liberal migration policy, low social security contributions, and relatively generous social benefits suggest a loose coupling with the institutions installed by the central government. Loose coupling refers to a situation where a system contains some independent sub-systems that are not fully responsive to the core of the system (Orton and Weick, 1990). In fact, in the case of Kunshan, it chooses to be selectively responsive to the central government system. Loose coupling provides Kunshan with the needed flexibility to connect with the rest of the world. The flexibility offered by the local government is particularly important to small multinational firms which lack the bargaining power to deal with bureaucratic central government agencies. Most Taiwanese investors prefer to stay away from the central bureaucrats, and rely on local governments as their intermediaries to the system that is often predatory (Chang, 2006, pp. 119–20). The ability of local government to protect foreign investors from the risks of institutional uncertainty explains why China was able to attract sizable foreign capital despite prevalent rent-seeking activities at various levels of government (Wu, 1997). This ability is not universal, so foreign investment is unevenly distributed. The Kunshan government was liked by Taiwanese investors for its ability to solve practical problems while mediating the interventions from the central government. Taiwan Electrical and Electronic Manufacturers' Association (TEEMA) conducted an annual survey on its members about the investment climates in different regions of China since 2000. Kunshan was ranked among the top ten most competitive locations by investors in each year's survey except for the years 2000 and 2003 (TEEMA, 2010, p. 205).

In addition to being loosely coupled from the central government, Kunshan was also keen on differentiating itself from the adjacent city of Suzhou, which is much better equipped in natural, cultural, and policy resources. In addition to a national ETDZ, Suzhou also ran a 'high and new technology park,' which was eligible for a more favorable 10 percent business tax as opposed to the 15 percent tax applied to an ETDZ and could be used to attract high-flying investors. However, Kunshan positioned itself as a supplier of components and parts to the operations of larger and more prestigious MNCs located in Suzhou. Suppliers of components and parts based on conventional materials such as metals and plastics, which were not considered high-tech by Suzhou Park, were welcome to locate in Kunshan. This created a complementary relationship between Kunshan and Suzhou. The fact that Suzhou has been able to attract R&D centers of MNCs in recent years also allowed Kunshan to benefit from knowledge spillovers. Some scholars defined the boundary of a cluster by the limit of knowledge spillovers (Audretsch and Feldman, 1996; Feldman and Audretsch, 1999). In this sense, Kunshan and Suzhou, and Wujiang as well, are indeed in one cluster, with production in three regions differentiated but closely integrated.

Local institutions evolved as economic conditions changed over time. If local institutions had failed to adjust to new economic and social conditions, the cluster may have become stagnant due to 'lock-in' effects (Wei et al., 2007). The government of Kunshan was very good at making institutional adjustments that minimized the environmental impacts. The strong MNC–region bonds that guide and prompt institutional adjustments over time were considered the most valuable asset of Kunshan (Hsu, 2006). These bonds were established through long-term interactions between MNC investors and the local government, despite the fact that local officials were often promoted and left after a brief stay in Kunshan. For example, there were an estimated 50–60 000 Taiwanese expatriates working in Kunshan and there was a keen demand for education for the expatriates' children. They did not want to go to local schools where communist ideologies were taught, or to English-language schools in Shanghai which were notoriously expensive and located at least one hour away from home. The Kunshan government helped the local expatriate community obtain special permission from the central government to establish a 'Taiwan School' where Taiwanese textbooks were taught by expatriate teachers from Taiwan.

Like other local governments in China, the main enticement that Kunshan used to attract foreign investment was the provision of cheap land (Lee, 2006). As the economy grew, the value of land increased. The Kunshan government was very effective in relocating old factories from the city centers to more remote areas by expanding the city perimeters. The city centers were then refilled with new investment projects that carried higher value-added for each piece of land granted. Those who relocated away from the city centers were usually compensated with a larger size of land or by monetary rewards. This policy was nicknamed 'teng-long-huan-niau' ('emptying the bird cage for new birds'). Resale of the old factory sites to new investors would generate funds to compensate the farmers whose land was expropriated and converted into industrial estates, and to pay for infrastructure investments. Continuous restructuring of the city landscape was possible as long as foreign investment continued to flow in. When the Kunshan ETDZ was inaugurated in 1985, its size was merely 375 hectares; by 2008, the area had been expanded to 11 500 hectares (Zhong, 2009, p. 194).

The 'grant and recall' of land allowed the local government to capture most increments in land value as industry developed. The scheme worked as a surrogate for market selection mechanisms in countries where land is privately owned. Unlike a free-market economy, the Chinese system did not allow unproductive factories to 'sit on' the land for speculative purposes. The right to use industrial land can only be transferred to industrial users, subject to the approval of the local government that legally owns the land. And the local government selected lessees of land by productivity of the land, which was implicitly measured by capital investment per square meter in the early years, and in later years by output value per square meter. The switch in measurement suggested the changing policy objective from the amount of foreign capital to the value of output. The emphasis on capital intensity for each piece of land in the early years favored the investments of parts and components makers whose operations tended to be capital-intensive but the value of whose output may be low. The emphasis on output value for each piece of land in later years favored large-scale assemblers instead. The changing policy preferences were manifested in the sequence of foreign investments in the region. Recently, some low-value parts and components makers were even forced to move out of Kunshan into northern regions of Jiangsu Province where land was still inexpensive.

Sale and resale of the leasing rights was also a major source of local government revenue. For example, according to the official statistics of the Kunshan government, where data were available for 2006, the total fiscal income of Kunshan was 5.404 billion RMB, out of which only 2.164 billion RMB was budgetary income from taxes and fees, the rest being extra-budgetary income mainly generated from land sales. Continuing land sales are possible only if the 'teng-long-huan-niau' policy is sustainable. In 2006, a total of 236 400 square meters of farmland was converted into industrial and commercial usage, with 1027 households relocated. At the same time, 35 companies were relocated, with 73 000 square meters of land changing hands.

8.4 EXTERNAL LINKAGES

Whereas Kunshan was loosely coupled with domestic institutions so as to be selective in making linkages to the rest of the country, it was very active in promoting external linkages to the world markets. To make external linkages, it had to be strongly coupled with international institutions. The government of Kunshan did everything it could to make sure that multinational firms operating in the region were fully connected with the global economy. In some cases, they even directly imported Taiwanese institutions, such as the export processing zone facility, which had been proven useful in facilitating strategic linkages to global production networks (Wang and Lee, 2007).

In most cases, Taiwanese MNCs are contract manufacturers for Western brands. Their products go to Western markets which are governed by Western institutions. Their production chains, both inside and outside China, are regulated by foreign institutions. They purchase some components and parts from local suppliers, who are often subsidiaries of Taiwanese firms, and sometimes from Japanese and Korean subsidiaries in neighboring regions. They purchase from indigenous Chinese firms only materials that do not require coordination in the production process, such as packing materials and general purpose chemicals. Components and parts that need to be coordinated in the production process are normally purchased from local subsidiaries of MNCs. Standard key parts such as memories or hard disk drives are imported directly from foreign suppliers such as Samsung, Seagate, or Western Digital. These products are shipped to the designated vendor managed inventory (VMI) sites, which are often located on the assemblers' factory compounds. Contracts are typically written in English, quantity measured in thousands and millions, and prices denominated in US dollars. When there are defects in the final products, the responsibility can easily be traced back to the suppliers of those components and parts. The brand marketers assume all liabilities against the consumers and make the product recalls and compensations when defects occur. The final assemblers take the responsibility against the brand marketers, and they in turn, charge the component suppliers for the defective products. In cases where the brand marketers purchase the components on behalf of the assemblers, the brand marketers directly charge the suppliers of these components for any liabilities. The liabilities are clearly defined and everyone in the system is held accountable. There is no need to go to the local courts for dispute settlements, so local institutions are irrelevant. The terms of transactions along the supply chains also follow the international commercial norms. Trade credits are available by banking on the creditworthiness of brand marketers, and accounts receivable can be resold in the financial markets outside China because the debtors are foreign-based MNCs. The entire series of financial transactions along the supply chain are also independent of local institutions and governed by international institutions.

Financing of working capital in local production is a very important part of cross-border operations. Taking notebook computers as an example, the players along the supply chains can be separated into three layers: assemblers, first-tier components and parts suppliers, and second-tier material suppliers. Assemblers like Quanta, Compal, and Wistron are large companies undertaking labor-intensive operations in China. First-tier suppliers of components and parts like Foxconn (outer cases, connectors), Auo (LCD panels), and Yageo (passive components) are also large companies undertaking relatively capital-intensive operations. The second-tier suppliers that provide metal or plastic materials consist of many small and medium firms. With the nature of labor-intensive operations, accounts receivable from brand marketers and inventory are the major assets for the assemblers, who carry very high financial risks that have to be partially passed on to the first-tier suppliers. They do this in two ways: one way is to transfer part of the accounts receivable to the suppliers through delayed payments; the other is to shorten the lead time of delivery of components and parts so as to shed the inventory burden. The first-tier suppliers, in turn, shift some accounts receivable to the second-tier suppliers by the same method (Seki, 2005, pp. 211–22). The supply chain is therefore accompanied by a financial chain, the operation of which is based on trust that has been established through previous cooperative relationships. The chain of accounts receivable is normally refinanced by Taiwanese or multinational banks which are familiar with the international contract manufacturing operations. The financial chain allows the players on the production chain to spread the financial risks. If local companies are involved in the process, the risk-sharing scheme may be disrupted and become difficult to manage. One characteristic of the financing status of these subsidiary companies is that they are typically free of local bank debts. This makes them immune to financial turbulence or monetary policy swings in the local economy. Furthermore, because all financial transactions are denominated in US dollars, they are also immune to foreign exchange risks.

The advantage of preventing indigenous suppliers from participating in global production chains is to maintain stability of the system and to stonewall local government interventions. Although there are newcomers to the networks from time to time, all players follow the same rules of the game. In fact, all major suppliers in the networks have to be certified by brand marketers, which serve as gatekeepers of the systems. All suppliers have to conform to environmental standards, labor practices, and the like, in addition to offering a good quality of products. As brand marketers are closely scrutinized by international NGOs on human rights, working conditions within the factory compounds, and living conditions in the company dormitories, their vendors are also checked in the same way. The screening reduces the number of vendors in the supply chain, stabilizing the long-term relationships to facilitate cooperation. Indigenous firms operating under domestic institutions, which embrace separate and usually more permissive labor and environmental standards, may not wish to comply with the international institutions either.

The local production chains in Kunshan are fully self-contained under the so-called 'export processing system' whereby imported materials are allowed to enter the customs territory, with duty and VAT payable recorded in a 'duty payable account.' The liability of duty and VAT payments can be transferred to the next-stage producers who undertake processing on the imported materials until the final products are exported. The exporters can then clear the duty payable accounts by demonstrating to the customs officials that the materials embodied in the goods to be shipped out are identical to the materials that had been imported. For example, a flat panel producer can clear its duty liability on imported liquid crystal displays (LCDs) by showing that these LCDs are contained in the panels shipped to a TV assembler. In this case, the liability of duty payable is also transferred to the TV assembler who receives the panels. The relay of this duty liability continues until the final products that contain the imported LCDs leave the country. This 'duty liability chain' can be more easily managed if no local materials are mingled in the supply chains. If at a certain stage of production, some domestic-originated materials are incorporated into the chains, these materials have to be separated out when clearing the duty accounts. Domestic-originated materials are free of import duties but they are subject to locally-imposed value added tax (VAT), and part of the VAT payments can be rebated upon exporting. Because imported and domestic materials are subject to distinct tax regimes, mixing them together increases the book-keeping and compliance costs exponentially. In other words, local institutions in China discourage MNCs from seeking local linkages. Furthermore, because the 'duty payable account' system is managed and operated within a customs territory, huge administrative costs will be incurred if the processing chains transcend the customs borders. That is to say, it is difficult to write off a duty liability recorded by Customs A by exports recorded by Customs B. Therefore, it is advantageous to bring upstream suppliers and downstream processors into the same customs territory, if not the same town. For example, Kunshan, Suzhou, and Wujiang belong to the same customs territory, and therefore their 'duty payable accounts' are managed by one authority. In short, the duty rebate and administrative system in China provides a natural force for co-location of MNCs.

Because institutions are path-dependent, the fact that Kunshan is strongly coupled with international institutions makes its adjustment to changes in international environments fast and smooth. This adaptability secures its position in the global production chains. For example, beginning in 2007, the European Union started to implement a new environmental standard on ICT products, called RoHs, whereby contamination of certain toxic materials, such as lead, was restricted. The regulation affected the traditional soldering process in making electronic products where lead is used. Large contract manufacturers who work closely with European brand marketers were consulted about the availability of new technologies before the regulation was introduced. They therefore obtained first-hand information about the impending regulatory changes and already had access to modern technologies that conform to the new regulation. Indeed, the entire local production network in Kunshan benefited from the regulatory changes because competitors in other parts of the world would be likely to fall behind in adjusting to the new regulations.

8.5 TAIWANESE ALLIANCES WITH OTHER MNCs IN THE CLUSTER

In contrast to lack of linkage to indigenous firms, Taiwanese MNCs in Kunshan interact rigorously with other MNCs in the cluster, especially those based in Japan. According to official statistics (Zhong, 2009, p. 194), by the end of 2008 a total of 1564 MNC-invested projects have been approved to invest in the Kunshan ETDZ, with a total investment amount of US $13.4 billion. These projects originated from 43 different countries and regions, but the distribution of them was unknown. We do have data from the ETDZ authority which provided the country-of-origin information for investments up until 2006. Till then, accumulated FDI projects were 1357, with capital commitments amounting to US $10.881 billion. Taiwan led all countries with 302 projects, followed by the British Virgin Islands with 260 projects, Hong Kong with 204 projects, and then Japan with 122 projects (see Table 8.1). However, most projects registered in the British Virgin Islands are understood to be from Taiwanese investors. Therefore, it is actually Taiwanese, Hong Kong, and Japanese companies that accounted for the majority of FDI in Kunshan. Renowned Japanese companies in Kunshan included Shimano, Makida, Nihon Seiko, Toyota Boshoku. More Japanese companies are in Suzhou (including Matsushita, Fujitsu, Fuji Film, and Hitachi) and in Wujiang (including Mabuchi, Mitsumi, etc.).

Many Japanese companies have come to invest in this region as a joint action with their Taiwanese counterparts to establish production bases in China. For example, Shimano, the world's leading producer of bicycle gear assemblies, came to Kunshan together with Giant of Taiwan, the world's largest bicycle manufacturer. Toyota Boshoku came to Kunshan to produce textile machinery in consortium with its joint venture partner in Taiwan, Liuho Machinery Co. Mabuchi, the world's leading producer

Table 8.1 Foreign investment in Kunshan up to 2006

Country of origin	Investment projects (number)	Investment amount (US $ millions)
Taiwan	302	1001
British Virgin Islands	260	3607
Hong Kong	204	2287
Japan	122	965
USA	100	375
Singapore	66	456
Korea	40	101
Cayman Islands	29	550
Total	1357	10881

Source: Kunshan Economic and Technology Development Zone Administration.

Note: Data are based on projects approved. Countries of origin are not exhaustive.

of micro-motors also came to Wujiang with its Taiwanese partner. In fact, the Wujiang subsidiary of Mabuchi was formed as a three-way joint venture between the Japanese parent company (30 percent share), its subsidiary in Hsinchu (30 percent share) and its subsidiary in Kaohsiung (40 percent share). Mr Song, a Taiwanese national, served as the chairman of the local company in China. The company produced about 150 million units of micro-motors annually, most of which went to Taiwan-owned PC and peripheral companies (mainly producers of CD-ROMs) (Seki, 2005, pp. 292–6).

Local alliances in Kunshan were transplantations of cooperative relationships from Taiwan. Take the case of micro-motor maker Mabuchi as an example. Technologies that have originated in Japan and been modified in Taiwan were transferred to Wujiang when the joint venture was established. Taiwanese managers were valuable in maintaining or renewing the relationships with other Taiwanese subsidiaries. They were also more effective in managing local labor relations than the Japanese managers. On the other hand, the main responsibility of Japanese managers was technological development. A study by Ito (2005) showed that Taiwanese–Japanese joint ventures in China exhibited a higher survival rate than wholly-owned Japanese subsidiaries or Sino-Japanese joint ventures.

The smooth transfer of the Taiwanese–Japanese alliance to China, whether it takes the form of an equity joint venture or a purely cooperative arrangement, is rooted in the relational assets that have accumulated in the global production networks outside of China. Local institutions in Kunshan, which are strongly coupled with international institutions, make the transfer of these relational assets possible. Japan has a very different kind of business system compared to the US and to European countries, and this unique system underscores the competences of Japanese firms in the world markets (Whitley, 2007). Japanese component and material suppliers have been working closely with Taiwanese assemblers and device makers in the ICT industry for a long time. The working relationship is built mainly for the export business and is therefore tuned to international institutions. For example, Taiwanese device makers dominated the world's production of CD-ROMs, but they depended exclusively on Japan's supply of micro-motors and optical-reading heads, and sometimes high-precision metal moulds as well. Taiwanese device makers are good at reducing manufacturing costs to capture world market shares, but their competitiveness is accentuated by the strengths of key Japanese parts. Taiwanese assemblers can connect Japanese parts makers to non-Japanese brand marketers through their dominant position in the contract manufacturing business. Theoretically, western brand marketers can directly purchase from Japanese suppliers to bypass the intermediary role of Taiwanese firms, and indeed they did this in the past. However, as western brand marketers increasingly shifted product development responsibility to Taiwanese subcontractors (more on this point in the following section), they could no longer do so because these key parts had to be integrated into the products early in the design stage. In addition, Taiwanese manufacturers hold a geographical advantage in coordinating with Japanese parts suppliers, compared to, say, American brand marketers. When Japanese brands such as NEC and Toshiba were losing world market shares to American brands such as HP and Dell in the PC business, the alliances between Japanese parts suppliers and Taiwanese assemblers were further strengthened. When Japanese and Taiwanese partners co-invested in China, the advantage of proximity to other members on the global production networks could also be exploited.

For Taiwanese assemblers, the presence of Japanese parts suppliers in the cluster not only creates the benefits of geographical proximity in production coordination, but also the potential benefits of technology spillovers. Taiwanese subsidiaries invest little in R&D, except for process-related technologies. However, because mass production now took place in China with close collaboration with Japanese parts suppliers in proximity, there was a good chance for mutual learning. As the theory has suggested, the effectiveness of learning tacit knowledge is likely to improve with the reduction in distance (Audretsch, 1998). Because the protection of intellectual property rights was lax in China, restricting the flow of knowledge within the cluster where indigenous local firms were absent was also a comfort to Japanese MNCs.

8.6 SILICON VALLEY–HSINCHU–KUNSHAN NEXUS

Newsweek once ran a cover story on Taiwan's IT companies located along Sun Yat-sen Freeway stretching from Taipei to Hsinchu: 'Want to find the hidden center of the global economy? Take a drive along Taiwan's Sun Yat-sen Freeway. This stretch of road is how you reach the companies that connect the vast marketplaces and digital powerhouses of the US, with the enormous manufacturing centers of China' (Einhorn, 2005). The author considered Taiwan's IT cluster as holding a pivotal position in connecting China's manufacturing capacity to the marketplaces of the US. He argued that it would be very difficult for the world to find a replacement for the web of IT factories that Taiwanese companies have built in China to serve the entire world so effectively. The Silicon Valley–Hsinchu–Kunshan nexus is supported by common institutions that rule the exchange of goods, finance, and knowledge within and between the regions.

The rise of the Hsinchu region as a high-tech cluster is a legendary story of its own. Saxenian and Hsu (2005), for example, attribute the success of the Hsinchu cluster to a human network in the high-tech professional community which connects Hsinchu to Silicon Valley. Through this connection, cross-border flows of tacit knowledge became possible. Hsinchu was therefore able to leverage the knowledge base of Silicon Valley for independent innovations. And indeed, the innovations taking place in Hsinchu were mostly incremental and complementary to innovations that originated in Silicon Valley, and they were precipitated by proximity to large-scale yet differentiated production in the local cluster (Chen, 2008).

With the relocation of manufacturing activities to Kunshan and the adjacent regions in China, the advantage of proximity to production sites was lost. Furthermore, as personal computers became mature products, the human connections to Silicon Valley also became a less important source of knowledge. In the meantime, the knowledge nexus between Silicon Valley and Hsinchu was under risk of being bypassed by a direct link between China and Silicon Valley. Fortunately it did not happen. It did not happen because transboundary knowledge flow was not possible without MNCs to act as a medium of exchange. If Taiwan was short-circuited in knowledge flows, its position on the global production network would have been hollowed-out. Instead, Taiwan maintained its position as a connecting node between the manufacturing centers in China on the one hand, and the knowledge centers and marketplaces in the US on the other. This position was secured because Taiwan MNCs were able to bridge uncertainty and knowledge flows in the global production networks.

According to organization theory, those who bridge uncertainty in the organization gain power in the organization (Pfeffer, 1981). The major source of uncertainty in the global IT network is the volatility of market demand, which gives rise to a major risk in fixed investments whose utilization rates fluctuate with market demand. As contract manufacturers, Taiwanese firms assume most fixed investments on the supply chains and therefore bear the financial risk of swings in capacity utilization. They, however, are able to spread this risk along the supply chains, and better yet, to reduce the absolute level of risk by a flexible method of production epitomized in the 'build to order' scheme. A manager of HP said that Taiwanese contract manufacturers could take a batch order for as few as ten PCs of a specific model and deliver them in 48 hours (Einhorn, 2005). The supply chains spanning Kunshan and neighboring areas emphasize this extreme flexibility. The contract manufacturers normally receive a quarterly forecast of production orders from brand marketers 3 months ahead of actual production. However, this is only a forecast, not a formal order. The formal order typically comes only a week before the scheduled delivery date, and it is still subject to daily adjustments. Any unexpected changes to forecasts and orders are to be absorbed entirely by contract manufacturers (interview with a contractor, April 6, 2007). No other production system in the world can match this kind of flexibility to cope with demand shift.

Taiwan also bridges knowledge flows from Silicon Valley to production sites in China, acting as a translator of knowledge. As the network theory suggests, those who control structural holes in the network gain power in the network (Burt, 1992). When Taiwan's assemblers increased their market shares in the contract manufacturing business, they quickly transformed themselves from pure contract manufacturers to manufacturers-cum-designers. In other words, they began to provide product design services in addition to manufacturing services. They called themselves original design manufacturers (ODMs), as opposed to original equipment manufacturers (OEMs). Instead of manufacturing products according to the blueprints provided by brand marketers, ODMs offered product designs to brand marketers, and if accepted, they would manufacture the products accordingly. The product design services became valuable to brand marketers because they greatly reduced the costs of product design and increased the variety of product they were offering. Major brands like HP offered more than 50 models of PC each year. They could not do it all by themselves.

To collaborate with product design activities undertaken by ODMs in Taiwan, major brands like HP and Dell established their product development centers in Taiwan. These centers were staffed with local engineers with a few expatriate R&D managers dispatched from the US. The product development centers provided the basic product concepts and architectures, and worked closely with local ODMs to complete the product design. Formal collaborative relationships replaced the previous human connections as the main conduit of knowledge flows. The collaborative scheme shortened the new product development cycle from 1 year to about 3 months. Taiwanese ODMs mobilized their ample manufacturing expertise to upgrade their services and made the entire production network more competitive.

With product designs completed in Taiwan, the ODMs then took the designs to China for manufacturing. Intensive coordination took place across the Taiwan Strait in the set-up stage of production. During this stage, engineers from Taiwan flew to Kunshan and stayed at the factory sites to help set up the production lines. They carried with them important product knowledge to guide the engineering arrangements for manufacturing. The length of their stay depended on how smoothly production had gone. Local engineers in Kunshan, many of whom were expatriates from Taiwan, were responsible for solving technical problems encountered in the manufacturing processes. This time, human connections between Hsinchu and Kunshan were critical for the transboundary flows of knowledge. Kunshan accommodated the movement of Taiwanese engineers by making the living environment so amiable that the town was nicknamed 'little Taipei' by the expatriates.

The new geography of product design and production suggests that Taiwan has become the new locus of knowledge combinations in the ICT industry, while the US continues to serve as the major source of knowledge creation. The role of the US is irreplaceable because the US market remains the largest market in the world where most new product concepts are conceived and experimented upon. However, these product concepts get brought to materialization in Taiwan where knowledge from various domains are combined to produce concrete product designs. As a midway house between product concepts and product designs, Taiwan is no longer a trans-receiver of knowledge from Silicon Valley, but a translator and integrator of related knowledge. Before Kunshan emerged as the backyard factory for Hsinchu, Taiwan was able to make independent innovations because of a vertically disintegrated industry structure which allowed specialized suppliers in Taiwan to pursue localized innovations in peripheral areas (Saxenian and Hsu, 2005). With Kunshan serving as a backyard factory, Hsinchu has become a knowledge center of its own. Taiwan has been able to integrate knowledge originated from Silicon Valley and local sources to create new products. The role of local-sourced knowledge has proved to be critical as some Taiwanese ODMs have attempted to shift product design centers to China but failed (interview with a contractor, April 3, 2007).

8.7 CONCLUSION

The emergence of Kunshan as an ICT cluster resembled that of Taiwan, and can be considered as an extension of Taiwan's cluster. Taiwanese MNCs acted as a relational institution that connected the spatially-separate activities in Taiwan and China (Yeung, 2005). Through this connection, Taiwanese MNCs were able to source seemingly unlimited supplies of Chinese labor, which, in turn, allowed them to monopolize the contract manufacturing business in ICT products. By monopolizing the contract manufacturing business, Taiwanese MNCs were able to upgrade their position in the global production network by offering new services, such as product design services. The emergence of the Kunshan cluster coincided with the bursting of the ICT bubbles in 2001 when the world's ICT industry entered a consolidation stage where major brands were struggling for survival.

Kunshan offered a set of institutions that perfectly accommodated the newly emerged industrial structure after the ICT bubbles burst. The new industrial structure called for geographically-concentrated production which offered both speed and flexibility. The institutions established by Kunshan are loosely coupled with domestic institutions such that interventions from central government are minimized but they enable selective linkages to the local resources needed by foreign investors. On the other hand, the set of institutions is tightly coupled with international institutions such that the extra costs of the transborder operations of MNCs are minimized.

This institutional arrangement creates a kind of filter that only allows desirable domestic forces into the region to combine with external resources to achieve economic growth, while dispelling anti-growth factors from the region. The concept of a 'filter' differs from an export enclave which is completely isolated from the domestic economy (Dietz, 1985). In Kunshan, local linkages are selective and dynamic rather than absent. Using the concept of selective and dynamic linkages, Kunshan was able to create a locational advantage that is not available in other parts of China.

In addition to its unique institutional arrangement, the city also took advantage of its geographical proximity to Shanghai to out-compete contenders from the rest of China such as Shenzhen and Dongguan in southern China. Although Kunshan itself is a small county, the greater Shanghai area (including Suzhou) hosts a population of more than 30 million people. More importantly, Shanghai provides the amenities to attract skilled labor from inland provinces to which Kunshan offers a liberal migration policy to aid MNCs in recruiting and retention.

Although the backbone of the Kunshan cluster was Taiwanese investment, Kunshan was also successful in leveraging investments from Japan, and to a lesser extent, from Korea. Kunshan did this through its concerted efforts with Suzhou which was endowed with richer natural, cultural, and policy resources. The presence of Japanese and Korean multinationals generated synergy effects which increased the scope and depth of the ICT cluster. Japanese key component suppliers which suffered from losing the war of Japanese brands to their US counterparts in the computer industry found a sanctuary for themselves in Kunshan. The Taiwanese–Japanese alliance was an outstanding feature of Kunshan which was unparalleled in other clusters.

Despite its stunning success in devising and applying foreign investment policies, industrial policy is conspicuously missing in Kunshan. A comparison with the ICT cluster in Singapore, which is also MNC-based, will make the point clear. The Singapore government adopted a series of proactive policies to leverage MNCs present in the local economy to extend the scope of activities and upgrade the quality of services (Wong, 2008). Kunshan was equally successful in constructing a seemingly open economy like Singapore's by a special institutional arrangement, but it was unable to leverage MNCs to provide extended services to neighboring regions in China like Singapore did in Southeast Asia.

Without a workable industrial policy to enhance the value of local services by MNCs, the cluster may eventually hit a bottleneck if the main attractiveness to foreign investment declines. For example, in recent years, as labor costs rose, the local government was keen on attracting foreign investment in IC manufacturing or assembly operations. But to no avail, because MNCs in Kunshan were able to obtain IC products from imports, which are free of duty. The government recently succeeded in creating a government–private joint venture that produces LCD panels to feed the local computer monitor industry. However, whether it will succeed remains to be seen. The lack of industrial policy is, in fact, rooted in the success formula itself. The Kunshan cluster is essentially operating under the domain of international institutions instead of local institutions, and industrial policy is typically a manipulation of local institutions. Kunshan will face a daunting challenge if labor costs continue to rise: what kind of policy, if not industrial policy, can encourage local MNCs to upgrade themselves and stay rather than exit the cluster like they always did in other countries?

REFERENCES

Amsden, Alice and Wan-wen Chu, 2003, *Beyond Late Development: Taiwan's Upgrading Policies*, Cambridge, MA: MIT Press.

Audretsch, D.B., 1998, 'Agglomeration and the Location of Innovative Activity,' *Oxford Review of Economic Policy*, 14(2): 18–29.

Audretsch, D.B. and M.P. Feldman, 1996, 'R&D Spillovers and the Geography of Innovation and Production,' *American Economic Review*, 86(3): 630–40.

Borrus, Michael, 1997, 'Left for Dead: Asian Production Networks and the Revival of US Electronics,' in B. Naughton (ed.), *The China Circle: Economics and Electronics in the PRC, Taiwan and Hong Kong*, Washington, DC: Brookings, pp. 139–63.

Bresnahan, T., A. Gambardella, and A. Saxenian, 2001, 'Old Economy Inputs for New Economy Outcomes: Clusters Formation in the New Silicon Valleys,' *Industrial and Corporate Change*, 10(4), 835–60.

Burt, R., 1992, *Structural Holes: The Social Structure of Competition*, Cambridge, MA: Harvard University Press.

Chang, Chia-Min, 2006, *Taishang Zai Suzhou: Quanqiuhua Yu Zaidihua De Kaocha* (*Taiwanese Firms in Suzhou: A Study of Globalization and Localization*), Taipei: Laureate Publishing Co.

Chen, Tain-Jy, 2008, 'The Emergence of Hsinchu Science Park as an IT Cluster,' in Shahid Yusuf, Kaoru Nabeshima, and Shoichi Yamashita (eds), *Growing Industrial Clusters in Asia: Serendipity and Science*, Washington, DC: The World Bank, pp. 67–89.

Coe, Neil, Peter Dicken, and Martin Hess, 2008, 'Global Production Networks: Realizing the Potential,' *Journal of Economic Geography*, 8(3): 271–95.

Dicken, Peter, 1998, *Global Shift*, London: Paul Chapman Publishing.

Dicken, Peter, 2004, 'Geographers and "Globalization": (Yet) Another Missed Boat?', *Transactions of the Institute of British Geographers*, 29: 5–26.

Dietz, James, 1985, 'Export Enclave Economies, International Corporations, and Development,' *Journal of Economic Issues*, 19(2), 513–22.

Einhorn, Bruce, 2005, 'Why Taiwan Matters?', *Newsweek*, May 16, 2005.

Ernst, Dieter and L. Kim, 2002, 'Global Production Networks, Knowledge Diffusion and Local Capability Formation,' *Research Policy*, 31(8–9), 1417–29.

Feldman, M.P and D.B. Audretsch, 1999, 'Innovation in Cities: Science-Based Diversity, Specialization, and Localized Competition,' *European Economic Review*, 43(2): 409–29.

Gereffi, Gary, 1995, 'Global Production Systems and Third World Development,' in B. Stallings (ed.), *Global Change, Regional Response: The New International Concept of Development*, New York: Cambridge University Press, pp. 100–42.

Henderson, J., Peter Dicken, Martin Hess, Neil Coe, and Henry Yeung, 2002, 'Global Production Networks and the Analysis of Economic Development,' *Review of International Political Economy*, 9(3): 436–64.

Hsu, Jinn-Yuh, 2006, 'The Dynamic Firm-Territory Nexus of Taiwanese Informatics Industry Investments in China,' *Growth and Change*, 37(2): 230–54.

III (Institute for Information Industry), 2005, *Quanqiu Chanye Julou Weiyi Xia Woguo Xianshi Chanye Quoji Gingzhengli Zhi Yanjiu* (*Cluster Migration and Taiwanese Display Industry Competitiveness*), Taipei: III.

Ito, Shingo, 2005, 'The Surge of Japanese Investments in China Utilizing Taiwanese Managerial Resources,' Mizuho Research Paper No 4, Tokyo: Mizuho Research Institute.
Kostova, T. and S. Zaheer, 1999, 'Organizational Legitimacy under Conditions of Complexity: The Case of the Multinational Enterprise,' *Academy of Management Review*, 24, 64–81.
Lee, Chuan-Kai, 2006, *Cluster Adaptability Across Sector and Border: The Case of Taiwan's Information Technology Industry*, PhD Dissertation, City and Regional Planning, University of California, Berkeley.
Liu, Weidong and Peter Dicken, 2006, 'Transnational Corporations and "Obligated Embeddedness": Foreign Direct Investment in China's Automobile Industry,' *Environment and Planning A*, 38(7): 1229–47.
Maskell, Peter, 2005, 'Towards a Knowledge-Based Theory of the Geographical Cluster,' in Stefano Breschi and Franco Malerba (eds), *Clusters, Networks, and Innovation*, New York: Oxford University Press, pp. 411–32.
Naughton, Barry, 2007, *The Chinese Economy: Transitions and Growth*, Cambridge, MA: MIT Press.
North, D.C., 1990, *Institutions, Institutional Change and Economic Performance*, Cambridge, MA: Harvard University Press.
Orton, Douglas and Karl Weick, 1990, 'Loosely Coupled Systems: A Conceptualization,' *Academy of Management Review*, 15(2): 203–23.
Pfeffer, J., 1981, *Power in Organizations*, Boston, MA: Pitman Publishing.
Pfeffer, J. and G. Salancik, 1978, *The External Control of Organizations: A Resource Dependence Perspective*, Harper and Row: New York.
Saxenian, Anna Lee and Jinn-Yuh Hsu, 2005, 'The Silicon Valley–Hsinchu Connection: Technical Communities and Industrial Upgrading,' in Stefano Breschi and Franco Malerba (eds), *Clusters, Networks, and Innovation*, New York: Oxford University Press, pp. 235–60.
Schrage, Michael, 2007, 'The Myth of Commoditization,' *MIT Sloan Management Review*, 48(2): 10–14.
Seki, Mitsuhiro, 2005, *Taiwan IT Sangyo No Chugoku Choko Delta Shuseki* (*The Agglomeration of Taiwanese IT Industry in Yangtze Delta*), Tokyo: Shinhyoron.
TEEMA (Taiwan Electrical and Electronic Manufacturers' Association), 2010, *Liangan Heying Chuang Shangji: 2009 Nian Zhongguo Dalu Diqu Touzi Huanjing Fengxian Diaocha* (*Win–Win Business Opportunities: 2009 Survey of Investment Climates and Risks in China*), Taipei: Shangzhou Publishing Co.
Wang, Jenn-Hwan and Chuan-Kai Lee, 2007, 'Global Production Networks and Local Institution Building: The Development of the Information-Technology Industry in Suzhou, China,' *Environment and Planning A*, 39(8): 1873–88.
Wei, Yehua Dennis, Wangming Li, and Chunbin Wang, 2007, 'Restructuring Industrial Districts, Scaling Up Regional Development: A Study of the Wenzhou Model, China,' *Economic Geography*, 83(4), 421–44.
Whitley, Richard, 2007, *Business Systems and Organizational Capabilities: The Institutional Structuring of Competitive Competences*, Oxford: Oxford University Press.
Wong, Poh-Kam, 2008, 'Coping with Globalization of Production Networks and Digital Convergence: The Challenge of ICT Cluster Development in Singapore,' in Shahid Yusuf, Kaoru Nabeshima, and Shoichi Yamashita (eds), *Growing Industrial Clusters in Asia: Serendipity and Science*, Washington, DC: The World Bank, pp. 91–145.

Wu, Jieh-min, 1997, 'Strange bedfellows: Dynamics of Government–Business Relations between Chinese Local Authorities and Taiwanese Investors,' *Journal of Contemporary China*, 6: 315–46.
Wu, Jieh-min, 2010, 'Rural Migrant Workers and China's Differential Citizenship: A Comparative Institutional Analysis,' in Martin King Whyte (ed.), *One Country, Two Societies: Rural–Urban Inequality in Contemporary China*, Cambridge, MA: Harvard University Press, pp. 55–81.
Yang, Chun, 2007, 'Divergent Hybrid Capitalisms in China: Hong Kong and Taiwanese Electronics Clusters in Dongguan,' *Economic Geography*, 83(4), 395–420.
Yeung, Henry, 2005, 'Rethinking Relational Economic Geography,' *Transactions of the Institute of British Geographers*, 30: 37–51.
Zhong, Jian (ed.), 2009, *Zhongguo Jingji Tequ Fazhan Baogao* (*Annual Report on the Development of China's Special Economic Zones*), Beijing: Shehui Kexue Wenxian Chubanshe (Social Sciences Literature Publishing).

9. Semiconductor interconnectivity across the Taiwan Strait: a case study approach

Ming-chin Monique Chu

9.1 INTRODUCTION

The semiconductor industry was born in 1947, with the invention of the transistor marking the beginning of the modern information technology (IT) sector. Continuous advances in semiconductor technology in the ensuing years have revolutionized every facet of human life. Today, semiconductors are the building blocks of modern electronic systems, from personal computers (PCs) and smart phones to guided missiles. In 2009, worldwide semiconductor sales reached US $226.3 billion (Semiconductor Industry Association, 2010), and the major products included integrated circuits (ICs), optoelectronics, sensors, and discrete components. The industry is strategic not only because it contributes to national economies' high-tech development as well as defense, but also because of its links to IT, one of the defining factors in the making of power in international relations today (Chu, 2009, pp. 48–133). Because of the dual-use nature of semiconductors, the sector is vital for military establishments worldwide, and the control of (or the loss of control of) this key industry has enormous strategic implications. Hence the territorial distribution of semiconductor manufacturing activities across national borders, often as a result of pertinent sectoral globalization,[1] will change the international balance of economic and military powers. Consequently, the distribution of semiconductor industrial power has become a major issue in the study of international political economy (Gilpin, 2001, p. 80).

This chapter adopts a firm-level case study approach in order to conduct a nuanced analysis of one aspect of the sectoral globalization in the Cross-Strait context, namely the migration of Taiwanese semiconductor production activities to China. The resultant deepening semiconductor interconnectivity across the Taiwan Strait, however, has been insufficiently studied.[2] Based on a study of the migration from empirical field research, this chapter aims to fill the gap in the academic literature by presenting eight firm-level case studies in IC design and fabrication sub-sectors. In each of the studies, the following dimensions are analysed: the role of Taiwan in terms of talent, technology, and investment; the evolution of business operations; and the connections with Chinese domestic semiconductor players. It is noteworthy that the author conducted more than 160 rounds of interviews with officials and industry insiders in the United States, Taiwan, China, and England between 2004 and 2005 as well as in 2009 for the research project. In particular, senior executives at seven of the top eight chip makers in China and Taiwan were interviewed.[3] Results from these interviews are combined with findings from primary and secondary materials to form the basis of the analysis.[4]

The rest of the chapter is divided into three sections. Section 9.2 summarizes four case studies of IC design companies, while Section 9.3 examines four firms in the fabrication sub-sector. Section 9.4 sums up the two major findings of the study. First, that some Taiwanese firms and engineers have operated in China's semiconductor industry by circumventing or violating Taiwanese regulations, indicating that globalization has eroded the capacity and autonomy of the state vis-à-vis non-state actors. Second, that a gradual shift in IC design and fabrication capability across the Strait has occurred. Given the strategic nature of the industry, such a trend is expected to enhance China's comprehensive power and security, thereby potentially threatening Taiwan's long-term survival.

9.2 CASE STUDIES OF IC DESIGN SUB-SECTOR

This section summarizes four case studies in the IC design sub-sector. These companies have been chosen for the following reasons. Three of them were among Taiwan's top ten companies in 2004 in terms of sales revenue, and they are: VIA Technologies Inc. (VIA), Realtek Semiconductor Corporation, and Ali Corporation. Today, VIA's operation in China remains one of the largest among Taiwanese IC design houses. Realtek has followed a unique dual-track development strategy on the mainland which has helped Actions Semiconductor Co. Ltd. (ASC, or Actions) to emerge as China's largest fabless design firm by 2005. Ali has pioneered the migration of Taiwan's IC design activities across the Strait since the late 1990s. And the fourth company, UTC, is a small-sized firm whose expansion into China has enabled two start-ups to emerge among the mainland's top ten IC design houses by the end of 2004.

9.2.1 VIA

The first of these companies is VIA, a Taiwanese design house specializing in microprocessors, graphics ICs, and chipsets.[5] In 2001, it was Taiwan's biggest IC design company and, after Intel, the world's second-largest supplier of chipsets (*Business Week*, 2001). In 2004, it generated US $579 million in revenue, becoming Taiwan's second largest fabless design house.[6]

This company opened its first subsidiary in China in 2000.[7] 'VIA began to set up offshore operations in China when it was at its peak,' an industry player recalled in 2005.[8] With its then budding ambition to break new ground in microprocessor design, VIA began to expand its production bases on the mainland by capitalizing upon China's longstanding need for indigenously designed and manufactured state-of-the-art microprocessors. The company built its public image in China by portraying itself as a leading player capable of designing the 'China Chip' (*zhongguoxin*), and its advertisements often caught travellers' attention on their way from Beijing airport to the downtown area.[9]

Since then, VIA's operation in China has expanded. Between 2000 and 2003, Taipei approved its investments in five high-tech subsidiaries located in four Chinese cities.[10] From 2001 to 2007, the paid-in capital of its subsidiary in Beijing grew ten times, from NT $65.3 million at the end of 2001 to NT $653.6 million by the third quarter of 2007.[11] The Beijing subsidiary had about 400 employees in September 2005, with a 1:30 ratio between Taiwanese and Chinese staff.[12] While its employees in China were about 800 in 2004 (Lee, 2004), it began to hire more engineers on the mainland than in Taiwan in 2008. As of August 2009, it hired more than 2000 engineers across China.[13]

The main business scope of these subsidiaries, as disclosed in the Ministry of Economic Affairs (MOEA) data, involves sales operations and post-sales technical services to customers. These activities are permitted by Taipei, and these operations have engaged in their officially-stated businesses. As a company executive stressed in 2005, these subsidiaries provided their customers with timely technical support on the ground. He expressed it this way:

> A lot of the Taiwan customers have moved there. Most of the production is done in China . . . So you need to support your customers there. That generally means simple engineering. But the stronger the customers become there, the more R&D they start doing there, and the more R&D you need there to support them.[14]

However, these offshore hubs have also engaged in IC design work, which is still forbidden by Taipei. A company senior executive has revealed that a hierarchical division of labor has been established at the firm's operations in China, Taiwan, and the US. Design capabilities that the company has developed in its subsidiaries in China[15] have enabled these offshore hubs to engage in low-level tasks in the design flow. By contrast, operation centers in Taiwan and the US have undertaken most of the high-end design work (that is, architecture and product definition). While central processing units (CPUs) and graphics ICs are primarily designed in the US, and chipsets are designed in Taiwan, support engineering (that is, validation and software work) is completed by subsidiaries in China.[16] The subsidiary in Beijing has dealt with CPU work, whereas the subsidiary in Shanghai has focused on graphics ICs.[17]

To strengthen its ties with local semiconductor players in China, VIA established IC design R&D labs in several universities. It had one lab for CPU development at Tsinghua University and another for communications ICs at Beijing University of Posts and Telecommunications. Both programs were designed to make VIA a familiar brand name to participating students and to enable them to become familiar with the design tools VIA uses, in order to entice them to join the company in the future. However, the students in these labs were unable to deliver, forcing the company to discontinue both schemes earlier than expected. As the firm's China chief put it, 'Initially we were hoping for some substantial cooperation, but we realized that it was a difficult task for them.'[18]

Today, VIA's operation in China remains one of the largest among Taiwanese IC design houses, and is an important illustration of the migration of Taiwan's IC design sector across the Strait.

9.2.2 Realtek (and Actions)

The second case involves Realtek. Established in 1987, the company has been one of Taiwan's top ten fabless design houses specializing in communications ICs. In 2004, its sales revenue reached US $278 million; it became Taiwan's seventh-largest fabless IC supplier.

Realtek's expansion in China has involved offshore investments in fully-owned subsidiaries and informal assistance with the establishment of a start-up. On the one hand, its subsidiaries in China include Realsil Microelectronics Inc. in Suzhou, and Realtek Semiconductor (Shenzhen) Ltd. in Shenzhen. The amount of the initial investment in Realsil, which was approved by Taipei in April 2002, was US $8.8 million. It amounted to US $13.3 million by the end of 2005 (Realtek Semiconductor Corp., 2006, p. 48; Ministry of Economic Affairs, 2007). As of August 2005, Realsil employed about 100 engineers. Three to four of them were Taiwanese, while the rest were Chinese.[19] The original amount of investment in the

Shenzhen subsidiary reached US $200 000 by the end of 2005 (Realtek Semiconductor Corp., 2006, p. 48). According to Realtek's company report, the stated main business scope of these subsidiaries is as follows. The subsidiary in Shenzhen is involved in 'R&D and information service,' whereas the Suzhou hub focuses on semiconductor 'design, research, development, selling and marketing.' However, the actual business scope of these subsidiaries is hard to pin down. Several senior executives at the company headquarters were tight-lipped over the issue. A former chief of the subsidiary in Suzhou merely praised his local engineers as 'extremely outstanding.' This contrasted with what the company told the government when it sought Taipei's approval of its pertinent investments; it said its subsidiaries on the mainland would focus on IC sales 'because IC design engineering talent in China is not very good.'[20]

On the other hand, Realtek has informally shifted its resources to China to help set up a new IC design house headquartered in Zhuhai. Founded in 2001, the start-up was initially known as Cristo Capital Inc. In 2005, it was renamed as Actions, a wholly-owned subsidiary of Actions Semiconductor (Mauritius). The investment and talent flows from Realtek to Actions have been substantiated by the author's interviews with industry insiders and secondary data. As a senior Taiwanese IC design engineer observed, 'Realtek has a design house in Zhuhai. Its name is Actions. It's a product of indirect investment by Realtek.'[21] Another industry interviewee described Actions as a 'Taiwanese company.'[22] When asked to clarify the alleged linkage between Realtek and Actions, a vice president at Realtek downplayed the inter-firm tie: 'Actions has nothing to do with our company . . . It's just that Realtek's major shareholders have invested in Actions in their personal capacity.' These shareholders, he claimed, withdrew their investment in Actions for fear of government inquiry after Taiwan prosecutors launched an investigation into the investment by UMC in HeJian in early 2005. 'This is because Taipei forbids investment in IC design houses in China,' he explained.[23]

Even if Realtek's shareholders did withdraw their investments, which the author cannot verify independently, the intimate ties between the two companies have continued. In September 2005, the same vice president of Realtek whom the author interviewed travelled to China for a business trip: his first stop was the subsidiary in Suzhou, and his second was Actions in Zhuhai.[24] In early 2007, he reportedly became the president of Actions (Chen, 2007).

Furthermore, Actions' annual report (ASC, 2007, pp. 50–51) mentioned the inter-firm linkage. Five of Actions' eight board members are from Taiwan, including the CEO and the chief financial officer (CFO). Since August 2005, the company's CEO has been a co-founder and former vice president of Realtek.[25] More importantly, the report has regarded its Taiwan link as potentially detrimental to the company's operations. In view of Taiwanese regulations on IC design investments in China, the report (ibid., pp. 15–16) made the following statement:

> Certain of our employees and management, including our chief executive officer, are Taiwanese Persons. The Taiwan government may interpret its current regulations and policies . . . such that it considers one or more of our employees and management as having inappropriate control and influence. Such employees or managers, including our chief executive officer, may be required to leave the company or be subject to sanctions by the Taiwanese Government.

Despite Actions' fear that its Taiwanese connection may endanger its operations, the start-up has grown dramatically in China's IC design sector, due partly to resource transfers from one of Taiwan's most powerful fabless design houses. In 2005, its revenue reached US $155 million. It became China's first IC design firm to break the US $100 million revenue mark, and emerged as China's largest fabless design house. It was also one of the first two Chinese IC design companies to have completed successful NASDAQ Initial Public Offering (IPO). In its focused market niches, it gained a 30 percent share of the global market for non-iPod MP3 player system-on-a-chips (SOCs) (PricewaterhouseCoopers, 2007, pp. 14 and 35).

To sum up, Realtek has crossed the Strait both to set up subsidiaries that are approved by Taipei and to help establish a start-up, namely Actions, through investment and talent input which may have broken some Taiwanese regulations. Actions, in 2005, emerged as China's largest fabless design house. Given Realtek's continuous growth at home and Actions' stunning performance in China to date, Realtek's dual-track migration strategy has succeeded – at least from the company's standpoint.

9.2.3 Ali

The third case involves Ali. The company, incorporated in 1987, has been one of the world's major suppliers of ICs for the PC, peripherals, and multimedia markets. Between 1987 and 1992, it was the world's third-largest chipset supplier. With sales revenue of US $182 million in 2004, it became Taiwan's tenth-largest fabless design house. In August 2004, MediaTek, Taiwan's largest IC design house, gained 31.28 percent of ownership of Ali (Mediatek Inc., 2005, p. 25; Mediatek Inc., 2006, p. 99).

Since the late 1990s, Ali has pioneered the migration of Taiwan's IC design activities to China. 'We began to cultivate talent in China in the

1990s,' recalled a co-founder of the company. He had led Ali's ambitious expansion in China until MediaTek became the largest shareholder of the firm. Ali acquired a local IC design house in Zhuhai, subsequently set up a wholly owned subsidiary in the same city, and then merged the two companies into one.[26] Its first few investments in China may have been made without prior government approval as Taiwanese official data indicate that its first approved investment in China dated back to 2000 (Ministry of Economic Affairs, 2007). By August 2004, it had run one of the largest IC design operations in China among Taiwan's IC design firms. These bases were located in Beijing, Shanghai, Xi'an, Shenzhen, and Zhuhai, according to the co-founder.[27] Its headcounts in China at the time accounted for about 39 percent of its workforce (that is, 500 in China, 800 in Taiwan, and another 50 in the US).[28]

MediaTek's acquisition of Ali led to the downsizing of Ali's operations in China because their post-acquisition assessment concluded that the quality of the local engineers at Ali's hubs in China was unimpressive.[29] By October 2005, Ali became a company of 400 employees. Its operations in China shrank accordingly, hiring about 200 local engineers and five Taiwanese ones. By the end of 2005, only subsidiaries in Shanghai, Beijing, and Zhuhai remained (Mediatek Inc., 2006, pp. 102, 175, and 180). The co-founder viewed such a development as a blow to his vision of cultivating local engineers through the firm's extensive China hubs in order to benefit the company in the long run.

As for the main business scope of these China-based subsidiaries, there has been a gap between what has been reported to the Taiwanese authorities and what has happened on the ground. According to the Ministry of Economic Affairs (2007), these subsidiaries engage in 'sales of IC products and post-sale services.' However, the co-founder admitted that these operations, prior to MediaTek's downsizing endeavors, had also engaged in IC design. 'When we applied [for offshore investments in China], we stated that the subsidiaries in question would offer our customers "technical support." But once one arrived there, one did whatever one thought appropriate. We did some IC design projects there,' he admitted. Since 2005, major R&D work has been primarily carried out by subsidiaries in Shanghai and Zhuhai, involving mostly software-related tasks. As a senior executive at the company revealed, 'Our major investment in China is in software. The country's human capital in software engineering is good, but not in hardware engineering.'[30]

Ali's groundbreaking move to shift Taiwanese IC design production activities to China has been controversial. Some industry interviewees have regarded Ali's move to China in the late 1990s as premature because of poor intellectual property (IP) protection, the lack of loyalty to a single firm among local engineers, and the lack of a sufficient number of experienced local engineers.[31] Others have justified the production shift as a rational move to cultivate local talent ahead of its competitors in order to benefit the company in the long run. One thing nonetheless is certain about Ali's Chinese operations: their business scope has included IC design production activities, in defiance of Taiwanese regulations.

9.2.4 UTC (Hangzhou Youwang, and Hangzhou Silan)

The fourth case involves UTC, a small-scale company established by K.H. Kao in Taipei in 1990. The most important outcome of the company's expansion into China involves the rise of two start-ups, Hangzhou Youwang Electronics Co. Ltd. and Hangzhou Silan Microelectronics Co. Ltd., which were among China's top ten IC design houses by the end of 2004.

In 1994, Kao set up Hangzhou Youwang as a wholly owned subsidiary of UTC. To absorb local talent, Kao promised a seven-member Chinese team, led by Chen Xiangdong, and that he would transfer 40 percent interest in the company to them in the future. Almost all of Kao's local partners had worked at state-run semiconductor operations including State 871st Plant, a Qualified Product List (QPL) supplier to the Chinese military,[32] and Hua Yue Microelectronics Co., Ltd. In 1997, they founded Hangzhou Silan Electronics Co., and Kao initiated a 20-year equity interest transfer agreement between Hangzhou Youwang and the Chinese start-up. The deal transformed Hangzhou Youwang into a joint venture by entitling the start-up to a 40 percent interest in the company.

More importantly, the agreement supplied the start-up, which was subsequently renamed Hangzhou Silan Microelectronics Co. Ltd., with much-needed capital. According to its prospectus in 2003 (Shanghai Stock Exchange Newspaper, 2003), 'the equity interest transfer agreement increased company assets, and the subsequent investment income out of Hangzhou Youwang Electronics Co., Ltd. had a positive impact on company profits.'[33]

By 2004, Hangzhou Youwang generated annual sales revenue of 247 million Renminbi (RMB); it became China's seventh-largest IC design house and the country's sixteenth-largest semiconductor company. Hangzhou Silan did even better. In 2004, it generated 509 million RMB in sales revenue, emerging as China's second-largest IC design house and the third-largest Chinese chip firm (PricewaterhouseCoopers, 2006, pp. 12 and 18).[34]

Although UTC has never been a top-notch performer in Taiwan's chip sector, it has fostered the rise of two Chinese start-ups over the course of its investment shift across the Strait, and these were among China's top ten fabless design houses by 2004.

9.2.5 Summary

In sum, we should first note that the four cases presented above indicate the various degrees in which the migration of Taiwan's IC design sector to China has taken place. The case of UTC shows that the migration began as early as 1994, and has expanded steadily.

Second, that some Taiwanese IC design houses and engineers have operated in China by circumventing Taiwanese regulations. Although Taipei has attempted to control investments by Taiwanese persons or entities established under the laws of Taiwan in People's Republic of China (PRC) entities in the IC design sub-sector, most of the cases above indicate that these regulations have been violated or circumvented in four major ways, as follows. (1) Senior Taiwanese executives have invested in China's IC design houses in their personal capacity, without prior government approval. A key example is the investment in Actions by Realtek's main shareholders.[35] (2) For Taiwanese firms to set up subsidiaries in China without prior approval from Taipei, as evidenced in the cases of UTC and Ali. (3) For a Taiwanese firm to help set up a Chinese start-up through tortuous investment and low-key talent support, even though the two companies were seemingly unrelated. The linkage between Realtek and Actions is a case in point. (4) To engage in IC design production activities at China-based subsidiaries, as evidenced in the cases of VIA and Ali.

Third, several China-based IC design start-ups (for example, Hangzhou Youwang, Silan, and Actions) have benefited from the sub-sector migration, thereby entering China's top ten list by 2004 or 2005.[36] Hence Taiwan's IC design capability, which is second only to that of the US, has been gradually shifting to China primarily at the infra-firm level and secondarily at the inter-firm level, despite Taipei's efforts to prevent this from happening.

9.3 CASE STUDIES OF THE IC FABRICATION SUB-SECTOR

What follows is an analysis of four case studies involving IC fabrication, the segment of China's semiconductor supply chain in which Taiwanese input has exerted its strongest impact over the course of the migration. They include SMIC, GSMC, HeJian and TSMC Shanghai Co. Ltd. They have been chosen for the following reasons. SMIC has emerged as the most successful foundry company in China, housed with the largest number of Taiwanese semiconductor professionals because of the migration. GSMC is known for its high-profile connections in Taiwan, China, and the US. HeJian is one of the most controversial foundry companies spearheading the shifts of chip production activities across the Strait. TSMC Shanghai is the first Taiwanese chip maker which has invested in 8-inch wafer fabrication activities on the mainland with prior approval from Taipei.

9.3.1 SMIC

Incorporated in April 2000 in the Cayman Islands, SMIC is headquartered in Shanghai, China. It was established by Richard Chang with the backing of a multinational array of managers and engineers, capital, and technologies, including those from Taiwan. Unlike state-owned enterprises or the 50–50 Sino-foreign joint ventures established in the 1990s, SMIC represents a new business model which has emerged in China's IC manufacturing landscape since 2000. Its emergence as China's flagship chip maker cannot be separated from the role of Taiwan. In 2005, it became the third-largest pure-play foundry in the world, and its China foundry market-share was over 50 percent (SMIC, 2006b, p. 13). With a total of 10 048 employees by the end of 2006, it has remained one of the largest and most advanced foundry players in China today (ibid., p. 43; SMIC, 2007a, p. 57).

To begin with, the nature of SMIC as a multinational corporation (MNC) is evident in the multinational nature of its talent, technology, and investment. Its employees have been multinational. In December 2001, its headcount reached 1300, including 400 engineers from the US, Taiwan, Singapore, Japan, and South Korea (SMIC, 2001a; SMIC, 2001b). Soon after the firm was established, George Scalise, President of Semiconductor Industry Association (SIA), was told by the company that 25 to 30 percent of its workforce was expatriates. 'This is unheard of in my experience,' he recalled.[37] By December 2004, more than 1000 foreigners worked at SMIC.[38] In September 2005, 1100 out of its 8400 employees were expatriates; they came from 26 countries, including the US, Taiwan, Singapore, Japan, South Korea, and Italy.[39]

Since 2001, SMIC has relied on several semiconductor giants for the transfer of manufacturing technologies in exchange for either equity stakes or access to production capacity at SMIC. These MNCs include mainly Germany's Infineon (SMIC, 2002; SMIC, 2003b; SMIC, 2006a) and Qimonda (SMIC, 2007b), Japan's Toshiba (SMIC, 2001c; SMIC, 2003a), Singapore's Chartered Semiconductor, and the USA's Texas Instruments (TI), International Business Machines Corporation (IBM), and Spansion.

For instance, in December 2001, Chartered decided to transfer its 0.18-micron baseline logic process technology and to grant patent license rights to SMIC in exchange for an equity stake and access to capacity at SMIC (SMIC, 2001d). In December 2007, IBM decided to license its 45nm bulk complementary metal oxide semiconductor (CMOS) technology to SMIC in exchange for 12-inch wafer foundry service (SMIC, 2007d; Lapedus, 2008).

SMIC has also relied on multinational sources of capital for its development. Its first-phase investment amounted to US $1.48 billion by November 2001, which included about US $1 billion in equity financing and US $480 million in loans from four Chinese government banks (SMIC, 2001a; SMIC, 2004a). Related equity investors included Taiwanese and American private investors and Chinese and Singaporean quasi-public investment organizations (Howell et al., 2003, p. 93). In September 2003, SMIC raised an additional US $630 million in private placement of shares (SMIC, 2003c). In January 2004, several Chinese banks financed SMIC for the second time, which involved a US $285 million loan agreement with the company (SMIC, 2004a). In May 2005, a group of Chinese banks agreed to sign a US $600 million loan pact with SMIC's subsidiary in Beijing to help expand the capacity at the company's three 12-inch wafer fabs in the city (Clendenin, 2005; Engardio and Einhorn, 2005; SMIC, 2005c). In March 2004, SMIC went public in Hong Kong and New York, raising more than US $1.7 billion (SMIC, 2004b). Since then, the performance of its shares has disappointed investors. By March 2006, its shares had lost 58 percent of their value since it went to IPO (Brooker, 2006). By the end of 2006, Shanghai Industrial Holdings Ltd. remained the single largest shareholder of SMIC. The shareholder is believed to be the 'investment arm' and commercial arm of the Shanghai municipal government (Shanghai Industrial Holdings Limited, 2005, p. 18; SMIC, 2005b, p. 31; SMIC, 2006b, p. 37; SMIC, 2007a, p. 51).[40] In November 2008, Datang Telecom Technology & Industry Holdings Co. Ltd., which is closely linked to Beijing, agreed to invest US $172 million for a 16.6 percent stake in SMIC thereby becoming its largest shareholder (*Electronic Engineering Times Asia*, 2008).[41]

Based on the above analysis, SMIC is an MNC. Rejecting any attempt to label itself as a Taiwanese firm, SMIC has been eager to categorize itself as an MNC by highlighting the multinational sources of its capital and technologies. Despite this, a majority of industry interviewees and secondary sources have either described SMIC as a Taiwanese firm or at least cited it as a primary example of the contribution that Taiwan has made to help China catch up in the semiconductor race.[42] This prevailing view has emphasized the large proportion of Taiwanese in the company, its acquisition of proprietary technologies from Taiwan's TSMC, and its absorption of Taiwanese investment (Howell et al., 2003, pp. 93–5; Jones, 2005).[43]

The human resource flow from Taiwan to SMIC has been obvious from the outset. Over a 2-year period starting from mid-2001, TSMC alone lost more than 100 employees to SMIC, and many of them were senior engineers and managers (TSMC, 2003; Jones, 2005; ASC, 2007, p. 50).[44] By September 2005, about 650 Taiwanese worked in SMIC, accounting for 59 percent of the company's expatriate workforce.[45] As of 2005, a majority of the vice presidents and fab directors at SMIC were either Taiwanese or American.[46]

Richard Chang is the single most important figure from Taiwan who epitomizes the talent exodus to SMIC. Born in China, Chang completed university in Taiwan before heading to the US for postgraduate studies. Over the course of 20 years at TI, he helped build and manage about ten semiconductor fabs in the US, Asia, and Europe. In 1997, he returned to Taiwan to join Worldwide Semiconductor Manufacturing Corporation (WSMC), and led the company in his capacity as president from 1998 to 1999 (Einhorn, 2002; SMIC, 2007a, p. 36). Following TSMC's acquisition of WSMC in 1999, Chang and his potential venture-capital partners were in Hong Kong for talks on launching a Silicon Harbor project there, but to no avail.[47] In 2000, he landed in Shanghai to launch SMIC.

Since then, Chang has led SMIC to become China's leading foundry, amid controversy. On the one hand, his contribution to China's chip sector has been widely recognized. As a mainland Chinese engineer with more than 37 years' experience in the industry put it, 'He is very important. The world microelectronics industry might have looked at China in a different light but for Chang's 12-inch wafer fab.'[48] In the eyes of the president of an IC design start-up in Beijing, 'Chang came to China in an attempt to help the IC industry in China, and he was assisted by Taiwanese power, meaning people and dollars . . . SMIC is changing the face of China's IC industry. He takes the lead and he is the seed.'[49] Chang has been crowned with numerous awards in recognition of his contribution to China's semiconductor industry.

On the other hand, the way in which Chang has spearheaded the migration has been controversial. Taiwan's MOEA has viewed his involvement in SMIC as illegal. Despite Chang's emphasis on his US citizenship, the MOEA argued in 2005 that he had household registration in Taiwan as a Taiwanese citizen when he, without prior approval from Taipei, founded SMIC. Viewing Chang as having made an illegal indirect investment in China's semiconductor industry, the MOEA fined him NT $5 million (US $156000) in March 2005, and gave him 6 months to withdraw his investment in SMIC or face further penalties (Nystedt, 2005; Investment Commission, 2005).

To refute Taipei's accusation, Chang has taken several measures. Despite his dual US–Taiwanese citizenship, he has repeatedly stressed that he is a US citizen. He has also appealed to the Taiwanese Administrative High Court in order to overturn the MOEA's decision. In July 2005, he applied to give up his Taiwanese citizenship, which was rejected by a court ruling in February 2007. Concurrently, the MOEA reportedly said it would impose further penalties on Chang if he remained the president of SMIC Shanghai and if the company was to migrate to 65nm process technology as reported by the press.[50] In the first half of 2007, the Taiwanese Administrative High Court cancelled the fine imposed by the MOEA on Chang, on the grounds that there was insufficient evidence to prove that Chang had actual control over SMIC. A senior MOEA official admitted that if Chang's application to relinquish his Taiwanese citizenship succeeds, his involvement in SMIC would not be subject to Taiwanese regulations (Wang, 2005; Hsiang, 2007; *Tsar & Tsai Lex News*, 2007).[51] In response to the charges against him and his company, in 2005 Chang said that 'SMIC does not belong to Taiwan, and yet the Taiwanese government has made noises about SMIC's operations.' He described Taipei's handling of the case as '*shu quan fei ri*,' a Chinese idiom used to describe uncalled-for fuss out of sheer ignorance.[52]

Several industry interviewees have nonetheless raised their eyebrows at Chang. The President of a fabless design start-up in Beijing highlighted Chang's awkward position: 'He is brave enough to take the leadership, to be called a traitor in Taiwan, to come to China to develop China's IC industry.' The President of a Taiwanese subsidiary in China criticized Chang's understatement of the importance of Taiwan to SMIC:

> Chang is a dual US–Taiwanese national . . . A majority of the vice presidents and fab directors at SMIC are either Taiwanese or American. Yet he has often described his company as an MNC externally, and stressed the Chineseness of his company internally, in China, in order to downplay the company's link with Taiwan.[53]

Despite the controversy, Chang has been an icon in China's semiconductor industry. With support from more than 650 Taiwanese employees, he, until his resignation in 2009, had led the development of SMIC, which houses the largest number of Taiwanese semiconductor talents in China. As Victoria D. Hadfield, President of Semiconductor Equipment and Materials International (SEMI) North America, observed in 2005, 'Expertise and know-how about how to run a business and how to make it profitable has really helped with SMIC, which is a major player; this expertise has come from Taiwan.'[54]

The second key indication of the importance of Taiwan in SMIC's operations involves their acquisition of trade secrets from TSMC. According to a senior executive at a fabless design firm that has used foundry services at SMIC and TSMC, 'SMIC's 0.18-micron process technology was copied from TSMC.'[55] Moreover, a former SMIC engineer, as cited by TSMC's lawsuit against SMIC in the US federal court in 2004, said that 90 percent of the process SMIC had used to make 0.18-micron chips was copied from TSMC. TSMC also examined a SMIC manufactured chip, bought in the open market, to verify SMIC's use of proprietary technologies; it concluded that the device contained features similar to those in TSMC fabricated components. Furthermore, these features differed from those in Chartered-made chips, even though Chartered was SMIC's only legitimate licensor of the 0.18-micron process.

In various court filings in the US and Taiwan, TSMC identified detailed methods that SMIC had allegedly used to purloin its trade secrets and to infringe on its IPs. A primary method was to lure TSMC employees to join SMIC by stressing that those who came with TSMC's trade secrets would be offered SMIC shares and stock options. Such a tactic seemed to have worked. In an email from a SMIC executive to a then TSMC manager, instructions were given to the manager for obtaining six TSMC process flows, process targets, and equipment types. It ended with the following remark: 'Sorry for the long list, but we need a lot of material to set up the new operation' (TSMC, 2004; Jones, 2005). According to a TSMC senior director, who was formerly the said manager's superior, 'She followed the instructions and sent out the stuff . . . Then she left TSMC and joined SMIC . . . Several other people were like her. They were all spies.'[56] Siding with TSMC's accusations of SMIC, a senior executive at a Taiwanese IC design house described the CEO of SMIC as 'a criminal': 'He stole the IPs from TSMC.'[57]

However, SMIC stressed that it had received technological assistance legitimately by signing technology transfer agreements with major industry players and that it had 'a strong and experienced technical team in house that contributed to SMIC's success' (SMIC, 2004c). Despite its defense, SMIC agreed to resolve all pending patent and trade secret litigations with TSMC in January 2005 by paying TSMC US $175 million over 6 years. Both parties also agreed to cross license to each other's patent portfolio through to December 2010. The agreement did not grant SMIC a license to use any of TSMC's trade secrets, and it could be terminated upon any breach by SMIC (SMIC, 2005a; TSMC, 2005b; SMIC, 2007a, pp. 16–17).

Nevertheless, the dispute has continued. In July 2006, TSMC accused SMIC of having used and retained TSMC's proprietary information on its 0.13-micron and smaller technologies which should have been returned to TSMC under the agreement. It also argued that it would be harmed if SMIC were to disclose or transfer the above information to SMIC's third-party partners before the resolution of the case. In September 2006, SMIC filed a cross-complaint against TSMC describing TSMC's accusations as 'unfair and misleading.' In September 2007, the US court asked SMIC to provide advance notice and an opportunity for TSMC to object to any such disclosure or transfer (SMIC, 2006c; TSMC, 2007b).

The weight of evidence presented above indicates that some of TSMC's technologies migrated to SMIC without any preceding agreement. This has underscored the importance of TSMC in fostering, albeit unwillingly, the emergence of SMIC as China's top-notch foundry.

The third indication of the key role Taiwan has played in SMIC's operations concerns Taiwanese investment in the start-up (Howell et al., 2003, pp. 93–5).[58] At least two Taiwanese venture capital firms attempted to invest in SMIC without prior government approval (Huang, 2002; Huang, 2003; *Asian Private Equity Review*, 2005).[59] In addition, H&Q Asia Pacific Ltd., one of SMIC's private equity investors, has been closely connected to Taiwan. Its founder and chairman, raised and educated in Taiwan, co-founded the Technology Review Board which advises Taipei on technology matters. Since 2001, he has been a director at SMIC, an appointment he received due to his company's investment in SMIC (Howell et al., 2003, p. 94; SMIC, 2007a, p. 37).[60]

The aforementioned linkage between SMIC and Taiwan in talent, technology, and investment has thus propelled numerous industry insiders to regard SMIC as a primary, albeit controversial, product of the migration.[61]

Since its establishment, SMIC has made tremendous progress in terms of technology, production capacity and market share. Within 13 months, it completed the construction of Fab 1, its first 8-inch wafer fab in Shanghai in 2001, using 0.25-micron process technology. By August 2002, the fab was the first in China to implement a 0.18-micron logic process. By March 2008, it was ready to provide IC manufacturing services at 0.35-micron to 65nm and finer line technologies (SMIC, 2008a). An analysis of its annual wafer revenue from 2003 to 2007 by technology (Figure 9.1) indicates its migration towards higher process technologies (SMIC, 2006b, p. 13; SMIC, 2007a, p. 13; SMIC, 2008a).

Based on his visits to SMIC in 2001 and 2004, Yoshio Nishi, Director of the Center for Integrated Systems at Stanford University, said it was 'rare' that a start-up like SMIC has been able to execute its technology roadmap

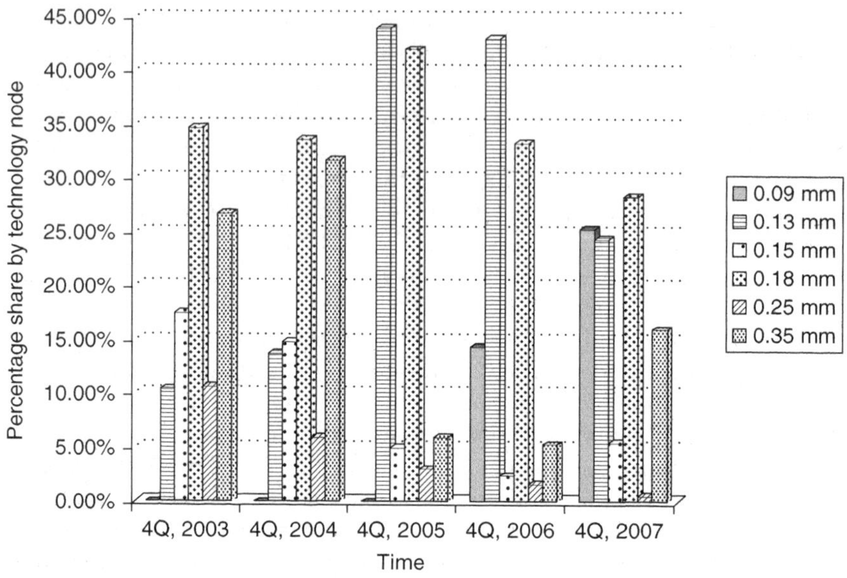

Note: Including logic, DRAM and copper interconnect only.

Sources: Company reports.

Figure 9.1 Analysis of SMIC's wafer revenue by technology, 2003–2007

as planned during the first few years of its operations. 'In May 2001, they showed me their product roadmap. In November 2001, their roadmap was executed . . . They did the same in 2002 . . . In 2004, I visited again. They are really on track. This is kind of rare,' he recalled.[62]

Industry leaders have argued that SMIC's technological progress has largely relied on foreign technology transfers from global giants and advanced semiconductor equipment suppliers.[63] As C. Mark Melliar-Smith, former President and CEO of International Semiconductor Manufacturing Technology (SEMATECH), observed in 2005, 'SMIC is dependent a lot on its equipment suppliers and a lot on transfer of technology. I don't think it's really totally indigenous.'[64] Yu Zhongyu, President of China Semiconductor Industry Association (CSIA), also admitted that SMIC's technologies and equipment had largely depended on foreign suppliers, rendering the argument that China is in control of related technologies problematic.[65]

SMIC's fab expansion has been equally impressive. By early 2008, SMIC had one 12-inch wafer fab and three 8-inch wafer fabs in its Shanghai mega-fab, two 12-inch wafer fabs in its Beijing mega-fab, one

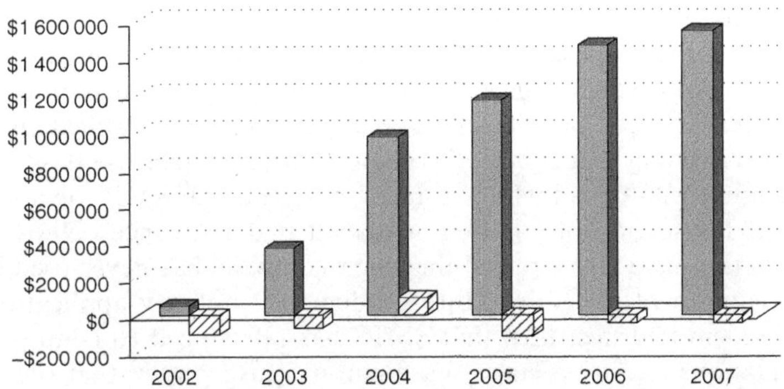

	2002	2003	2004	2005	2006	2007
Sales	$50 315	$365 824	$974 664	$1 171 319	$1 465 323	$1 549 800
Net income (loss)	–$102 603	–$66 144	$96 203	–$114 775	–$44 109	–$40 000

Sources: Company reports.

Figure 9.2 SMIC's sales and net (loss) income, 2002–2007

8-inch wafer fab in Tianjin, and an in-house joint venture specializing in assembly and testing operations in Chengdu. It also plans to start a new IC production project in Shenzhen, and to manage and operate at least two additional fabs owned or funded by local governments in Chengdu and Wuhan (Lapedus, 2008; SMIC, 2008a; SMIC, 2008b).

The number of 8-inch wafer equivalents shipped by SMIC from 2002 to 2007 increased steadily. While the company shipped 82486 wafers in 2002, it shipped more than 1.8 million in 2007 (SMIC, 2007a, pp. 20 and 23; SMIC, 2008a). At the end of 2007, its production capacity increased to 185250 8-inch-equivalent wafers per month, with a utilization rate of 94 percent.

From 2002 to 2007, SMIC's annual sales revenue grew as well. Its sales reached US $1.56 billion in 2007, an increase of 5.8 percent over 2006. With the exception of 2004, however, it had a net loss every year for the rest of the period. In 2007, its net loss reached US $40 million (Figure 9.2). Its share of the worldwide foundry market has also grown over time. In 2005, it surpassed Chartered to become the world's third-largest player with a 6.4 percent global market share, behind only TSMC and UMC (Lapedus, 2006). In the first half of 2007, SMIC remained the world's third-largest player (Lapedus, 2008).

Since its technological advances have partly relied on semiconductor equipment companies, SMIC has acquired global state-of-the-art fab tools by complying with export control regulations. A core part of their compliance has involved ensuring the US regulators that it has not fabricated chips for the Chinese military. The company's CEO said in December 2004 that the Chinese military had never contacted his company to ask for help, for which he felt 'grateful.' In the author's subsequent interview with him, he shrugged off allegations that his company supplied chips to the PLA. Claiming that only CPUs could be used as dual-use ICs for military end uses (a statement which is untrue), he said that SMIC 'is not involved in the fabrication of CPUs, nor does it make advanced chips.'[66] SMIC managers have also stressed that their company has never used imported US equipment to manufacture products for military applications. They have identified measures that SMIC has introduced to comply with US regulations and to assuage Washington's misgivings[67] that the company may have fabricated chips for the PLA.[68]

So far, SMIC's efforts have paid off. In 2003, it became a consignee to a special comprehensive license (SCL) granted to Applied Materials by Washington. Since SCL encompasses new and future follow-on orders, the US fab-tool maker with SCL does not need to file any separate licence application for each order. This shortens the lead-time needed for the delivery of Applied Materials equipment to SMIC (Lapedus, 2003). In October 2007, SMIC became one of the first five companies to be approved by the US as 'validated end-users' (VEUs) of American technology exports to China. Washington will thus remove individual export licensing requirements on shipments of controlled items to the firm. In turn, the company agrees to on-site audits by US officials and stringent record-keeping requirements. SMIC became a VEU based on, among other criteria, its previous compliance with US export controls, its non-military business operations, and its record of transparent commercial use of US-controlled technology (Leopold, 2007; Bureau of Industry and Security, 2007; Lapedus, 2007; SMIC, 2007c). Its VEU status helps to advance its technological capabilities, as it can now receive and use approved US equipment and materials without the delays and costs associated with traditional export licensing.[69]

As SMIC establishes itself as the strongest foundry player in China, it has also deepened its connections with local semiconductor players through the Multi-Project Wafer (MPW) service to China's fabless design houses and talent training schemes.

SMIC, like its competitors in China and elsewhere, has offered the MPW service to its customers on a shared-cost basis for prototyping and verification by cooperating with government-financed incubation centers in China.[70] The company subsidizes its local customers for their participation in any given MPW program by sharing the costs of the exorbitantly expensive masks used, and these subsidies are often supplemented with government ones. The impact of the program is two-fold.

First, it enables SMIC to expand its local customer base because it helps upgrade the technological capabilities of the indigenous IC design firms. It does so in a country where most local design companies are still technologically backward, trailing behind global giants in technology and market share (Brown and Linden, 2005; China Semiconductor Industry Association IC Design Branch, 2005; *Electronic Engineering Times Asia*, 2006; PricewaterhouseCoopers, 2007; *Electronic Engineering Times Asia*, 2007; PricewaterhouseCoopers, 2008). Second, it helps improve the country's IC design capabilities in due course. To cultivate local semiconductor talents, SMIC has sealed agreements with local universities to offer degrees in either microelectronics or solid-state circuitry to its technicians. In sum, both schemes have deepened the company's connections with local semiconductor players potentially fostering the long-term development of the indigenous industry.

To conclude, SMIC epitomizes the migration. It has risen in China's semiconductor industry in ways that have stunned many in the global sector, and its ascendancy cannot be separated from the role of Taiwan. Taiwan has contributed to the rise of SMIC primarily by supplying more than 650 experienced engineers and managers. Moreover, there has been a flow of process technologies and IPs from TSMC to SMIC allegedly because of economic espionage. Taiwanese investment is believed also to have fostered the establishment of the firm. None of the above cross-border flows is without controversy, as revealed by the disputes involving SMIC and its first CEO, TSMC, and the Taiwanese government. Admittedly, the company is faced with numerous challenges in its pursuit of a greater market share, technological advances, and better financial performance. These challenges include the ability to pursue endogenous technological innovation effectively, the viability of its questionable pursuit of price-cutting strategy as a way to enlarge its market share, [71] the viability of its fab expansion project, [72] and the ability to continue to ensure access to advanced fab tools. In a country long troubled with sluggish performance in what it sees as a strategic industry, SMIC has nevertheless emerged as a top-notch chip maker ready to compete with global giants, thanks to the Taiwanese migration. The semiconductor landscape in the world's fastest-growing economy has altered accordingly, alarming some in other countries who fear that they are losing their edge in an industry vital to their national economy and security.

9.3.2 GSMC

The second case study involves GSMC. GSMC was incorporated in November 2000 in the Cayman Islands. It operates a wholly owned subsidiary, the Shanghai GSMC, or Grace, in China. Grace is a pure-play foundry company with operations in Shanghai. It has high-profile connections in Taiwan, China, and the US. The co-founders of GSMC include Winston Wang, the son of Taiwan's Formosa Group Chairman Yung-ching Wang, one of the most powerful businessmen in Taiwan, and Jiang Mianheng, the son of China's former President Jiang Zemin and the Vice President of the Chinese Academy of Sciences (CAS) (Smith, 2000; Forney, 2001; Balfour et al., 2003; Howell et al., 2003, pp. 96–7). 'Jiang has aspired to foster the take-off of China's IT industry by accelerating the indigenous development of core technologies. That's why he was involved in Grace,' recalled GSMC Chairman Zou Shichang in 2005.[73] The company also had a high-profile connection with the US, namely Neil Bush, the brother of the then US President George W. Bush (Balfour et al., 2003; Carlson, 2003).[74] Like SMIC, GSMC is an MNC, and its birth cannot be separated from the critical input from Taiwan. With more than 1300 employees, Grace generated US $148 million in revenue in 2004 (Lapedus, 2005). It thus became China's fifth-largest foundry player accounting for 6 percent of the total sales revenue.[75]

To begin with, multinational sources of talent, technology, and investment have fostered the development of GSMC. In September 2005, a majority of its 1300 employees were Chinese, Taiwanese, and US nationals.[76] Out of its 150 expatriate employees, 100 were Taiwanese and 30 to 40[77] were Americans.

Grace, like SMIC, has relied on technology transfers from several foreign companies. They include Silicon Storage Technology, Inc. (SST) and Cypress Semiconductor from the US, and Sanyo Semiconductor and Oki Electric from Japan (GSMC, 2006c). For example, Sanyo started a strategic partnership with Grace in 2003. In 2008, Grace began to produce automotive chips used in car navigation systems for Sanyo, using Sanyo's 0.18-micron Not-OR (NOR) flash process technology (GSMC, 2008). In 2005, Cypress began to transfer its technologies to Grace in exchange for preferential access to Grace's foundry service. In 2006, Cypress announced that it would soon transfer to Grace its 0.13-micron C8 process technology (GSMC, 2006b).

The sources of Grace's capital have also been multinational. Its first-phase investment of US $1.63 billion included private equity financing from several countries and Chinese bank loans (Howell et al., 2003; GSMC, 2004). In 2004, Hong Kong tycoon Li Ka-shing invested US $90 million in Grace (Brooker, 2006). In 2002, Grace initially sealed a US $680 million, 5-year loan deal with seven local banks. By March 2006, Grace sought to delay payment on the loans, and the Shanghai government-controlled Shanghai Alliance Investment Ltd., chaired by

Jiang Mianheng, decided to grant Grace US $190 million in loans convertible into shares (ibid). By 2007, the Shanghai Alliance Investment Ltd. was the leading shareholder of Grace (GSMC, 2007). In contrast to SMIC's successful IPO in 2004, Grace's initial plan to raise US $1.8 billion selling shares in Hong Kong and New York has been deferred more than three times (Brooker, 2006). As of early 2008, there was no sign that Grace would go to IPO in the near future. By January 2009, Grace was in the process of merging with Huahong NEC.

Taiwan has been instrumental to the initial development of the company. As of October 2002, Taiwan was the largest source of non-Chinese employees for Grace, accounting for 19 percent of the workforce, and many of these Taiwanese engineers came from TSMC, UMC, and Nanya Technology (Chase et al., 2004, pp. 132–3). In 2005, two-thirds of its expatriate employees were Taiwanese.[78] In September 2005, the firm had about 100 Taiwanese employees.[79] Winston Wang is the key Taiwanese figure who epitomizes the migration of Taiwanese talent to Grace. Wang joined Grace to expand his business in China. He recruited several seasoned Taiwanese engineers and managers to form the inaugural senior management team of Grace. They included Nasa Tsai as the president of the start-up, and Juei-chen Tsai as the first chairperson of the firm.[80] Although all the aforementioned Taiwanese subsequently left Grace, some of the company's important positions, such as chief technology officers (CTOs) and chief operating officers (COOs), have been held by other Taiwanese.[81]

When Grace was inaugurated, optimists viewed its debut as a symbol of China's likely emergence as a dynamic hub of semiconductor manufacturing. Since then, however, numerous hurdles have obstructed the company's performance in terms of technology, production capacity and market share.

In terms of technology, Grace began to construct two fabs based on 12-inch specifications in November 2000. In September 2003, its commercial production began at its first 8-inch fab using 0.25-micron process. In September 2005, it was able to manufacture 8-inch wafers using technologies ranging from 0.25- to 0.13-micron processes, according to the company's chairman Zou. By early 2008, its technologies for production ranged from 0.25- to 0.15-micron processes. However, Grace, like SMIC, has relied on foreign technology transfers rather than in-house R&D efforts for its technological advances.

In terms of production capacity, Grace has one 8-inch fab in full production as of early 2008. In September 2005, it fabricated 25 000 wafers per month, which rose to 27 000 in 2006. In 2005, it shipped about 300 000 wafers to its customers. Its wafer shipments grew 108 percent for 2006;

it churned out about 324000 wafers for its customers (Sung and Chan, 2007).[82]

As Grace's revenue reached US $148 million in 2004, it ranked fifth amongst China's foundry firms, trailing behind SMIC, Shanghai Huahong NEC, HeJian and Advanced Semiconductor Manufacturing Corporation (ASMC). Concurrently, Grace accounted for 6 percent of the Chinese foundry sales revenue, whereas SMIC had a 42 percent share (Lapedus, 2005). Its revenue for 2006 grew 127 percent compared to 2005 (Sung and Chan, 2007). With a revenue of 1.22 billion RMB in 2006, it ranked sixth amongst China's foundry companies (Xinhua-PRNewswire, 2007).

Despite its growths in revenue and wafer shipments, Grace has remained loss-ridden (Brooker, 2006). Although it has shown signs of progress in its market performance since former Infineon CEO Ulrich Schumacher became its CEO and President in 2007 (GSMC, 2007; Tu, 2008), it was in the process of merging with Huahong NEC by early 2009.

As for Grace's cooperation with China's domestic semiconductor actors, the company's chairman Zou has initiated an important program to deepen the links between the firm and local research institutes in order to cultivate local talent. Zou has been in a position to initiate the scheme because of his capacity as the company's chairman and as a senior semiconductor scientist at the Shanghai Institute of Metallurgy (SIM) of CAS. Zou brought his students from the CAS institute to Grace after they completed a 1-year postgraduate training program. Zou explained his rationale as follows,

> Grace should work jointly with research institutes in Shanghai including SIM. Such an initiative has to center around the enterprise, as research institutes do not have advanced semiconductor equipment . . . A dozen of my research students are being cultivated in Grace. I bring them to Grace to encourage a marriage between research and production.[83]

Such an initiative, if continued, has important implications for China's IC industry and China's national security. The program helps to accelerate the transfer of technological know-how from the company's seasoned engineers, some of whom are from Taiwan, to up-and-coming local engineers at the research institute. These local engineers thereby become major assets for the long-term development of China's strategic industry. More importantly, given the institute's history as a supplier of semiconductors for military end uses, including atomic bombs, these trained local engineers at the institute may use their enhanced know-how, which is refined at Grace, as a commercial fab, to contribute to Chinese defense microelectronics undertakings. The case of Grace and its talent initiative therefore showcases the intricate ties between Taiwanese and Chinese chip actors over the course of the migration, which may have significant long-term security ramifications.

In a nutshell, Taiwan has contributed to the development of Grace, although the initial Taiwanese input far from guarantees the company's success. The firm has been faced with numerous challenges, including an unusually frequent changing of the guard in the firm's senior management team,[84] its problematic in-house technological capability[85] and its poor financial performance. In spite of this, the company's initiative to train local graduate students from the CAS research institute in Shanghai, which has a historical linkage to China's defense chip industrial base, may have an enduring impact on China's security.

9.3.3 HeJian

The third case involves HeJian. HeJian was incorporated in November 2001 in the British Virgin Islands. It then set up a wholly owned subsidiary in Suzhou, China, through Invest League Holdings Ltd., a vehicle registered in the British territory (Dean, 2002; Howell et al., 2003, p. 98; Hille, 2005).[86] Headquartered in China, HeJian runs fab operations in Suzhou. It was established by two retired senior executives from UMC with what the UMC Chairman Robert Tsao subsequently described as 'assistance' from his company. With its sales revenue of US $239 million in 2004, it ranked third amongst China's foundry companies accounting for 10 percent of the Chinese foundry sales revenue (Lapedus, 2005). With its sales of US $310 million in 2006, the company with about 1600 employees remained China's third-largest and the world's ninth-largest foundry firm (IC Insights, 2006).

Like SMIC and Grace, HeJian has positioned itself as an MNC with 'abundant foreign capital and state-of-the-art IC technologies.' First, its employee force is multinational. About 80 percent of its 1600 headcount were locals, and the remaining 20 percent were expatriates, with a majority being Taiwanese.[87] The number of Taiwanese employees doubled from about 100 in 2001 to about 200 in early 2005.[88] As for its technologies, HeJian has not established strategic partnerships with foreign chip companies on a scale comparable to that of SMIC and Grace. Instead, it has primarily depended on UMC for technology transfers, as will be discussed later. The company's capital is also multinational. By the end of June 2005, the holding company of HeJian had issued a total of 700 million shares, with the subscription price per share in the last offering being US $1.1. The value of the company was estimated over US $700 million (UMC, 2005, p. 40). By early 2008, HeJian's investment was over US $1.6 billion. Although its registered capital was US $400 million, it had invested, as of

September 2005, more than US $800 million in its operations.[89] Its capital relies on multinational equity investment and bank loans. In February 2005, the UMC Chairman identified seven companies and institutions from the US, Japan, and Singapore as initial investors in HeJian in order to deny charges that UMC had invested in HeJian. Among these investors, ICS is a Taiwanese-owned, US-based chip company, and Xilinx, one of the world's leading suppliers of field programmable gate arrays (FPGAs), is UMC's longstanding customer (Xilinx, 2004).

However, HeJian's operation as an MNC has relied heavily on Taiwan, primarily through UMC's contribution to the start-up. HeJian's local employees describe HeJian as a Taiwanese company instead of an MNC.[90] The most revealing remark regarding HeJian's Taiwanese linkage came from the president of HeJian. He admitted in 2005 that UMC 'made use of the grey areas' in existing Taiwanese regulations in order to establish HeJian. Other industry interviewees have argued that HeJian would not have come into existence without UMC. As a manager of HeJian admitted, 'HeJian is just another fab run by UMC.'[91] A senior executive at UMC's chief rival put it directly: 'HeJian is equal to UMC.'[92]

Industry insiders identify the apparent flows of UMC talent and technology to HeJian, while admitting that it is hard to pin down the inter-firm flow of capital even if it does exist.[93] As of March 2005, HeJian was staffed by about 200 Taiwanese engineers and managers, which accounted for nearly 20 percent of its employees.[94] Numerous former UMC employees have joined HeJian's senior management and R&D teams. The company's president, for one, was formerly a fab director at UMC. As a UMC customer recalled, 'Once I was at UMC, the President of HeJian was there. My UMC partner jokingly introduced the HeJian chap to me as "UMC's traitor".'[95]

Industry insiders revealed in 2005 that for a long time, UMC had knowingly transferred its proprietary technologies to HeJian in a low-key fashion in order to escape government scrutiny, while denying such linkages in public. In February 2005, Taiwan prosecutors raided UMC headquarters in order to investigate the inter-firm tie. One month later, the UMC Chairman said his company would receive a 15 percent stake in HeJian, worth more than US $110 million. This reward was to compensate for the 'past assistance' UMC had offered to HeJian, and was for its future cooperation with HeJian as long as the deal is permitted by Taipei (Tang, 2005; UMC, 2005, pp. 40–41; Wang, 2005; Dean, 2006). Subsequently, a HeJian manager expressed a sigh of relief over what by then had been a secretive inter-firm technology transfer: 'Now we can change dark into light: UMC can transfer technologies to us guilelessly in the future so long as we pay for the technologies.'[96] In public, however, UMC has reiterated that it has never transferred any technologies to HeJian.

More importantly, the disputes between the Taiwanese authorities and UMC have highlighted the controversy over the HeJian–UMC case. The UMC Chairman was subject to official penalties due to UMC's involvement in HeJian. In April 2005, Taiwan's Financial Supervisory Commission fined him US $95 600 for breaching securities laws with late disclosure of information relating to what the commission saw as UMC's illegal engagement in HeJian's operations. UMC denied the charge. Robert Tsao and John Hsuan then resigned from their positions as Chairman and Vice Chairman, respectively, of UMC. In January 2006, both were indicted for their allegedly illegal assistance with HeJian's operations without getting anything in return. Prosecutors stated that both were convicted of 'breach of trust' under Taiwan's criminal law by assisting HeJian, a move which was against the interests of UMC and its shareholders (Dean, 2006).

In 2007, the dispute saw a U-turn as two court rulings were in favor of UMC. According to the first ruling, UMC's investment in HeJian could not be classified as an investment because UMC only provided technical assistance to HeJian. The ruling added that the Taiwanese government had failed to prove otherwise, thereby invalidating the fine imposed on UMC. According to the second ruling, former UMC executives were found not to be breaking any laws by helping to set up HeJian. Subsequently, they were acquitted. Related prosecutors, however, would appeal the verdict (Solid State Technology, 2007).

In reviewing this case, Maw-Kuen Wu, Minister of Taiwan's National Science Council, argued in 2005 that UMC should not have done what it did to help establish HeJian. Nevertheless, the official had a resigned attitude towards Taiwanese chip actors which had used illicit measures to shift their production bases to China. As he put it, 'The question is whether we can find a better way to punish or regulate rule breakers.'[97]

Despite its disputed ties with UMC, HeJian, since its inception, has performed well in its technology, production capacity, and market share. It began to build fabs in Suzhou in November 2001, and its pilot run and capacity ramp-up commenced in March 2003. In June 2003, it began 8-inch wafer production using 0.5-micron process technology. In September 2003, it completed the setup of 0.3-, 0.25- and 0.18-micron logic processes and a 0.35-micron high-voltage process. In November 2003, it finished a 0.35-micron flash memory process setup. Such swift progress in technological terms is believed to have resulted from UMC's technology transfers. In February 2004, it accomplished a 0.25-micron mixed-mode process setup. In September 2005, its fab was able to mass-produce chips

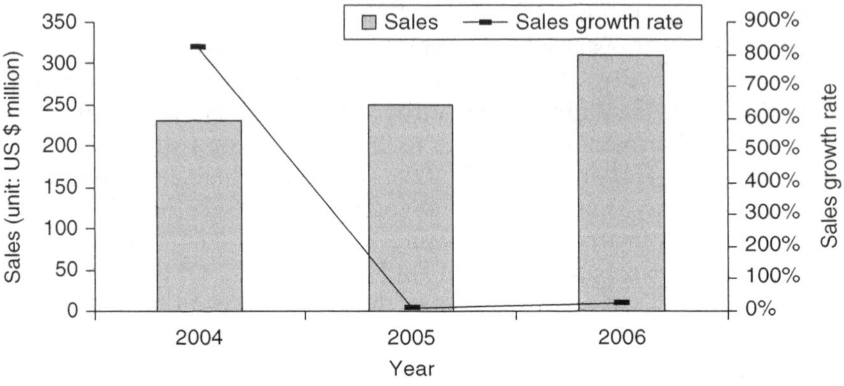

Source: IC Insights (2006).

Figure 9.3 HeJian Technology's sales and growth rate in sales, 2004–2006

using a 0.18-micron process, and to fabricate small-volume semiconductors using a 0.15-micron process.[98] In May 2006, it fabricated multi-media player chips using a 0.18-micron process for its customer, Actions. In March 2008, it announced that it would begin 12-inch wafer fabrication activities by joining Elpida to build a US $2 billion 12-inch memory fab in Suzhou with help from the local government (Sung and Chan, 2008; Reuters, 2008).

HeJian's production capacity has also grown steadily. In December 2003, it produced 14 000 8-inch wafers per month. In March 2004, it fabricated 16 000 8-inch wafers per month. By September 2005, it churned out 35 000 wafers per month.[99] The number reached 41 000 by late April 2009 (UMC, 2009). Between 2004 and 2006, its sales increased (Figure 9.3), and its market share grew accordingly. In 2004, it had 10 percent of the Chinese market share, and 1 percent of the global market share (Lapedus, 2005; IC Insights, 2006). In 2006, its worldwide market share reached 2 percent. More importantly, its increasing market share has generated profits thereby outperforming SMIC and Grace financially.

Meanwhile, the company has also cooperated with domestic chip players through MPW services and talent training programs. 'To attract potential local customers unfamiliar with our processes, we offer the MPW service to allow them to conduct either process verification or new product verification. HeJian pays for the masks used; after all, masks are very costly,' said the company's president.[100] Key participants in the given MPW program have included not only indigenous IC design houses, but also the Electronic Design Automation (EDA) Center under CAS. As the MPW program expands the company's local customer base, it may help to upgrade China's indigenous IC design capabilities.

In addition, the company has offered its inexperienced local engineers much-needed training programs because of the lack of experienced process engineers in China and the high cost of employing seasoned engineers from abroad. Ultimately, these schemes may help to cultivate local engineers thereby enlarging the indigenous talent pool. As the company's president predicted in 2005, 'We will see the emergence of a group of experienced local engineers in 2 to 3 years, and they will be viewed as treasures in China's semiconductor manufacturing industry.'

In sum, the emergence of HeJian has been one of the most controversial cases in the migration. At the height of the UMC's fight with the Taiwanese authorities over HeJian, some of HeJian's Taiwanese engineers were requested by their families in Taiwan to give up their careers in China to return home.[101] Despite the controversy, HeJian has grown steadily in China, advancing in its technological development, production capability, market share, and financial performance. Its rise cannot be separated from UMC's contributions, particularly in terms of talent and technologies, although the concrete ways in which inter-firm ties have been forged are not entirely clear to outsiders. The HeJian–UMC case has nonetheless demonstrated the inability of the Taiwanese state to control the migration. It also shows that HeJian, like SMIC, has deepened its local ties by offering MPW services to its customers and by training its locally hired engineers, thereby contributing to the development of China's strategic sector.

9.3.4 TSMC Shanghai

The fourth case involves TSMC Shanghai, a wholly owned subsidiary of TSMC. It was incorporated in August 2003 with prior approval from Taipei. Its 8-inch fab is located on the outskirts of Shanghai. In 2006, it became China's fifth-largest foundry company in terms of revenue (Xinhua-PRNewswire, 2007).

TSMC was the first Taiwanese chip maker approved by Taipei to invest in an 8-inch wafer fab in China. Its subsidiary in Shanghai has absorbed the transfers of talent, technology and investment from its parent company. Before its China-bound investment was approved by Taipei, TSMC had dispatched a team to Shanghai to initiate its China project,[102] and its fab construction had preceded Taipei's approval.[103] In June 2005, the subsidiary had more than 900 employees, including 800 Chinese and 100 Taiwanese.[104] By September 2005, its headcount reached 1000, one-tenth of whom were Taiwanese.[105]

In terms of technology, TSMC Shanghai began to mass-produce 8-inch wafers using 0.35- and 0.25-micron processes in 2004. In late 2006, Taipei lifted the ban on the transfer of 0.18-micron process to China. Thereafter, TSMC started to transfer its 0.18-micron process to its subsidiary in Shanghai, with approval from Taipei (TSMC, 2006b). Its direct investment in the subsidiary totalled US $276 million by the end of 2004. As of 28 February 2007, TSMC Shanghai had a capital stock of US $371 million (TSMC, 2005a: 140; TSMC, 2007a, p. 62).

As of 2008, TSMC Shanghai still trailed behind its competitors in China in terms of process technologies, production capacity and market share. Although TSMC remains the world's leading foundry player, Taipei's restrictions have prevented TSMC from equipping its fab in China with its latest technology. As of early 2008, its Shanghai subsidiary still used process technologies (that is, 0.35–0.18-micron) which lagged behind those available at SMIC, HeJian and Grace.

In terms of production capacity, TSMC Shanghai manufactured 5000 8-inch wafers in March 2005 and 6000–7000 in June 2005.[106] In October 2005, it produced 12 000 wafers.[107] In early 2007, TSMC hoped that its China fab would triple its output for the coming year after it began to use its 0.18-micron process (EMSNow, 2007). The performance of the subsidiary trailed behind this objective: it manufactured 31 000 wafers in December 2007, and 42 500 in December 2008; its whole year capacity reached 375 000 in 2007 and 543 000 in 2008.[108]

TSMC Shanghai's use of relatively low technologies compared to those available at China's leading foundries has undermined its market performance. According to the president of a subsidiary of a Taiwanese integrated device manufacturer (IDM) in Shanghai in 2005, 'TSMC Shanghai has followed the rules and has not used the 0.18-micron process in its fab here. Its market share has thus been taken away by others.'[109]

The financial performance of TSMC Shanghai has been mixed. While its net loss narrowed by 73.65 percent in 2006 compared to 2005, its net sales decreased by 45 percent during the same period. Its loss-ridden performance is in sharp contrast to its parent company's outstanding financial record (TSMC, 2006a, p. 52; TSMC, 2007a, pp. 65 and 68).

Meanwhile, TSMC Shanghai has cooperated with local chip players in China through three major programs. First, it has worked with Tsinghua University to cultivate local talent. Second, it has offered MPW services to potential customers in order to enlarge its local customer base. Third, it has trained its newly-hired local engineers. As of September 2005, about 150 of its Chinese engineers had been in Taiwan for related training programs.[110]

In short, the China subsidiary of the world's strongest foundry player has received resources from its parent company in terms of talent, technology, and investment. Although it uses technologies to the level permitted by Taipei and, therefore, has underperformed in the market so far, its presence in China is a long-term asset to the Chinese IC sector. TSMC's leading performance in the global foundry sector, its niche in global state-of-the-art process technology and managerial expertise, and its outstanding corporate governance record may help upgrade China's chip capability through MPW services, talent training schemes, and foundry services available at its Shanghai subsidiary.

9.3.5 Summary

The author summarizes this section with the following observations. First, among the four foundries examined, SMIC and Grace pioneered the migration in the sub-sector. Since then, the migration has continued steadily, as revealed in these cases and beyond.

Second, some of the players involved in SMIC, HeJian and Grace have led the geographical shift by circumventing or violating Taiwanese regulations. These instances in the sub-sector and beyond are summarized in Table 9.1.

Third, these firms have benefited from varying degrees of input from Taiwan in terms of talent, technology, and investment. So far, their performance has been impressive in China. In 2006, all were among China's top eight foundry firms. As they emerge as China's major foundries, their ability to contribute to Chinese foundry sales revenue and to supply chips to China's market is expected to increase accordingly. In 2004, the sales revenue of SMIC, HeJian, and Grace accounted for 58 percent of the total. If second-tier player CSMC is included, these four Taiwan-related foundries generated 61 percent of Chinese foundry sales revenue in the same year (Lapedus, 2005). More importantly, their rise has also indicated a gradual shift in IC fabrication capability from Taiwan, which houses the world's strongest foundries, to China.

Fourth, if the migration of Taiwan's sub-sector to China continues, it will assist further in upgrading China's IC fabrication capabilities through the offer of MPW services to local IC design houses and the cultivation of local talents.

9.4 CONCLUSION

In sum, the semiconductor interconnectivity across the Strait as analysed so far has two important implications. First, some Taiwanese firms

Table 9.1 Six means against Taiwanese state control by Taiwanese non-state actors spearheading the semiconductor industry migration to China

Patterns	Comments	Cases
In the name of private investment	Investments in China's chip sector by Taiwanese persons without prior approval from Taipei	• Chairman of an IC design house vs an IC design firm in Shanghai • CEO of a PC company vs a packaging and testing start-up in Shanghai • Shareholders of an IC design house vs a start-up in Zhuhai
In the name of 'technical support'	China-based Taiwanese subsidiaries engage in design tasks beyond the business scope permitted by Taipei	• A design house in Shanghai • A design house in Suzhou • A design house in Beijing
Secretive ownership change	Take-over of China-based firms without Taipei's approval to run operations banned by Taipei	Take-over of a Shanghai-based firm by a Taiwanese packaging and testing company in 2004, which applied for Taipei's approval in 2006
'I am a US Citizen'	Emphasis on US instead of Taiwanese citizenship by dual US–Taiwanese nationals who are leaders in China's chip sector	• CEO of a foundry applied to give up his Taiwanese citizenship while keeping his US one • Chairman and president of a foundry put their nationality down as 'US' in company prospectus
High-end production without Taipei's approval	Taiwanese subsidiaries engage in production activities forbidden by Taipei	• A packaging and testing firm in Shanghai • A packaging and testing firm in Suzhou
Pursuit of global state-of-the-art by firms whose inception circumvented Taipei's regulations	Taiwan-related fabs in China whose incorporation was deemed illegal by Taipei pursue technologies beyond the ceilings set by Taipei	• A foundry in Suzhou • A foundry in Shanghai Both have used process technologies for feature sizes smaller than 0.18-micron and have invested in 12-inch wafer fabrication activities in China

Source: Interviews and secondary data: Chu (2008).

and individuals have circumvented or violated Taiwanese regulations to operate in China's semiconductor industry, leaving the Taiwanese state in tatters. This finding indicates that globalization has eroded the capacity and autonomy of the state vis-à-vis non-state actors. Second, cases analysed indicate a gradual shift in semiconductor capability from Taiwan to the mainland, contributing to the take-off of China's strategic sector, which had been troubled with sluggish performance irrespective of government-led efforts. According to Klaus Wiemer, former President of TSMC and former CEO of Chartered Semiconductor, 'I don't think there would be much of a semiconductor industry in China today had it not been for Taiwan . . . Taiwan went across the Strait and started to participate in the Chinese semiconductor industry. They took money over there. They took people and management skills.'[111] Thus the Taiwanese migration has altered the semiconductor landscape in China. Given the strategic nature of the sector, pertinent Taiwanese non-state actors have helped increase China's power and security, perhaps to the detriment of Taiwan's long-term survival.

NOTES

1. For the academic literature on the production globalization of the semiconductor industry, see Flamm (1985); Henderson (1989); Brown and Linden (2005); Ernst (2005); Macher et al. (2007).
2. For earlier studies of the economic phenomena, see Howell et al. (2003, pp. 67–76); Chase et al. (2004); Cheng (2005); and Fuller (2008).
3. This is based on a 2004 *IC Insights* revenue ranking – see Jones (2005). Senior executives include the chairman, vice chairman, chief executive officer (CEO), or president of the firms in question. These firms included: Taiwan Semiconductor Manufacturing Corporation (TSMC); United Microelectronics Corporation (UMC); Semiconductor Manufacturing International Corporation (SMIC); HeJian Technology (Suzhou) Co., Ltd.; Huahong NEC; Central Semiconductor Manufacturing Corporation (CSMC); and Grace Semiconductor Manufacturing Corporation (GSMC, or Grace). Because of the sensitivity of the research topic, the author has developed a thoroughly planned strategy as far as methodology is concerned. For detailed discussions of access, interview, data reliability and constraints, see ch. 2 in Chu (2009).
4. For a summary of the migration in terms of technology, talent, and investment flows in aggregate terms and its economic security implications, see Chu (2012). For a detailed account of the migration (such as motivations) and its defense and technological security repercussions, see Chu (2009; 2013). In the author's original research project, security is defined broadly as encompassing aspects of economic, technological, and defense security, and the scope and agency of security threats is extended beyond the traditionalist military-centrism and state-centrism.
5. VIA's microprocessors accounted for 1 percent of the worldwide market. See interview with a senior executive at the company, July 15, 2005, Taipei, Taiwan; interview with the former president of a Taiwanese IC design house, July 5, 2005, Taipei, Taiwan. *Note:* Because of the large bulk of interview data in this chapter, I have not included the original materials. Readers should contact the author for related data.

6. The *IC Insights* Strategic Reviews Database provided by the CEO of UMC.
7. Interview with the head of VIA Technologies (China) Ltd., September 9, 2005, Beijing, China.
8. Interview with the president of a Taiwanese IC design house, August 12, 2005, Hsinchu, Taiwan.
9. Interview with Qinsheng Wang, Chair of Huada Electronic Design (HED) and Chair of China Integrated Circuit Design Center (CIDC), 30 August 2005, Beijing, China.
10. They include Beijing, Hangzhou, Shanghai, and Shenzhen.
11. Company data on the Taiwan Stock Exchange website.
12. Interviews with staff at the subsidiary, September 5, 2005, Beijing, China. For a different estimate, see interview with a vice president of a Taiwanese IC design house, August 10, 2005, Hsinchu, Taiwan.
13. Interviews with senior executives of the IC design house, August 4, 2009, Taipei, Taiwan.
14. Interview, July 12, 2005, Taipei, Taiwan.
15. These include subsidiaries in Beijing, Shanghai, and Hangzhou.
16. Interview with a senior executive at the company, July 12, 2005, Taipei, Taiwan. The subsidiary in Beijing had engaged in 'some projects' concerning IC design, most of which were software related. See interview with the head of the subsidiary, September 5, 2005, Beijing, China.
17. Interview with a vice president of a Taiwanese IC design house with experiences running the firm's operations in China, August 19, 2005, Hsinchu, Taiwan. VIA's operation center in Shanghai was a result of its acquisition of S3 Graphics, a specialist in graphics ICs.
18. Interview, September 5, 2005, Beijing, China.
19. Interview with the executive vice president of Realtek, August 19, 2005, Hsinchu, Taiwan.
20. Interview with Chin Tan Huang, Executive Secretary of MOEA's Investment Commission, August 18, 2005, Taipei, Taiwan.
21. Interview with the president of a Taiwanese IC design house, August 12, 2005, Hsinchu, Taiwan.
22. Interview with the president of Ningbo Sinomos Semiconductor Incorporation (NSSI), September 14, 2005, Ningbo, China. Also see interview with the spokesman of another Taiwanese IC design house, October 25, 2005, Hsinchu, Taiwan.
23. Interview, August 19, 2005, Hsinchu, Taiwan.
24. Phone interview, September 20, 2005, Suzhou, China.
25. In January 2008, another former executive at Realtek joined Actions as the vice president of marketing. See ASC (2008).
26. Interview with a co-founder and former president of Ali who had run the firm's operations in China, July 20, 2005, Taipei, Taiwan.
27. The MOEA data show that between 2000 and 2004, Taipei approved the company's investment plans in five subsidiaries located in four Chinese cities (namely Suzhou, Zhuhai, Shanghai, and Beijing). Neither interview data nor MediaTek's 2005 annual report mentioned the actual operation of the subsidiary in Suzhou. The co-founder identified one operation center in Xi'an, which was not mentioned in the MOEA data. See Mediatek Inc. (2006, p. 175); Ministry of Economic Affairs (2007); interview with a co-founder of Ali, July 20, 2005, Taipei, Taiwan; interview with a senior executive at Ali., October 27, 2005, Taipei, Taiwan.
28. Interview, July 20, 2005, Taipei, Taiwan.
29. Telephone interview with a spokesman at MediaTek, October 25, 2005, Hsinchu, Taiwan.
30. Interview, October 27, 2005, Taipei, Taiwan.
31. Interview with the president of Faraday Technology, October 20, 2005, Hsinchu, Taiwan; interview with a senior executive of Ali, October 27, 2005, Taipei, Taiwan.
32. QPL identifies the types of military electronic parts and components produced by

qualified onshore manufacturers for end-users by the People's Liberation Army (PLA).

33. A senior industry player regarded Kao as a partner of Silan. See interview, September 14, 2005, Ningbo, China.
34. Also see interview with a senior executive of a Taiwanese subsidiary, September 27, 2005, Shanghai, China.
35. In another instance not covered in the case studies presented, the chairman of a leading Taiwanese IC design house has invested, in his personal capacity, in Spreadtrum Communications Inc., which runs a subsidiary in Shanghai, namely Spreadtrum Communications (Shanghai) Co., Ltd. See interview with the CEO of Spreadtrum, December 6, 2005, Cambridge, UK. With sales of 1.1 billion RMB in 2007, it became China's third-largest IC design powerhouse. See Spreadtrum Communications Inc. (2008).
36. The emergence of Spreadtrum as one of China's top ten IC design houses in 2006 and beyond has also benefited from Taiwanese investment.
37. Interview, December 8, 2004, San Jose, CA, USA.
38. Speech by Chang at a conference in San Jose on December 7, 2004.
39. Interviews with a public relations manager and the CEO office chief at SMIC, September 30, 2005, Shanghai, China.
40. For the linkage between Shanghai municipal government and Shanghai Industrial Holdings Ltd., see Howell et al. (2003, p. 93); phone interview with a manager at HeJian, March 21, 2005, Shanghai, China.
41. On Datang's success in developing China's first indigenous core network router in 2001 and its military utility, see Cheung (2009, p. 200–21).
42. Interview with the chairman of GSMC, September 27, 2005, Shanghai, China; interview with Qinsheng Wang, Chair of HED and Chair of CIDC, August 30, 2005, Beijing, China; interview with the president of SIA, December 8, 2004, San Jose, CA, USA.
43. Also see interview with a senior director at TSMC, December 18, 2004, San Jose, CA, USA; interview with the CEO of a fabless design house, September 7, 2005, Beijing, China.
44. Also see interview with the vice chairman of TSMC and the chairman of TSMC Shanghai, June 29, 2005, Hsinchu, Taiwan; interview with the president of a Taiwanese IC design house, October 20, 2005, Hsinchu, Taiwan.
45. Interview with a manager at SMIC, September 30, 2005, Shanghai, China.
46. Interview with the president of one of SMIC's major competitors, September 26, 2005, Shanghai, China.
47. Interview with an involved venture capitalist, August 31, 2005, Beijing, China.
48. Interview, September 17, 2005, Shanghai, China.
49. Interview, September 9, 2005, Beijing, China.
50. As of that time, Taipei had banned the transfer of process technologies more advanced than those of 0.25 microns to China.
51. Also see interview with a senior trade official, July 8, 2005, Taipei, Taiwan.
52. Interview, September 30, 2005, Shanghai, China.
53. Interview, September 26, 2005, Shanghai, China.
54. Interview, February 4, 2005, Washington, DC, USA.
55. Interview with the vice president of a Taiwanese IC design house that has used foundry services at TSMC and SMIC, August 19, 2005, Hsinchu, Taiwan.
56. Interview, December 8, 2004, San Jose, CA, USA.
57. Interview, July 12, 2005, Taipei, Taiwan.
58. Also see interview with the CEO of a design house, September 7, 2005, Beijing, China; interview with the chairman of GSMC, September 27, 2005, Shanghai, China.
59. They were the Global Strategic Investment Fund and Prudence Capital Co. Both cancelled their funding commitments to SMIC due to pressure from Taipei. They were fined NT $1 million each for their illegal involvement in SMIC.

60. Also see interview with the CEO of an IC design house, September 7, 2005, Beijing, China.
61. In addition, Taiwan was the largest market for the company in 2002 in terms of sales revenue, which contributed to 47.7 percent of the company's revenue. See SMIC (2005b, p.99; 2006b).
62. Interview, December 6, 2004, Palo Alto, CA, USA. Nishi was instrumental in facilitating TI-SMIC technological cooperation in his former capacity as a senior executive at TI.
63. Interview with the CEO of UMC, July 11, 2005, Hsinchu, Taiwan; interview with a vice president of a Taiwanese IC design house which has used foundry services at TSMC and SMIC, August 19, 2005, Hsinchu, Taiwan; interview with C. Mark Melliar-Smith, former President and CEO of International SEMATECH, January 4, 2005, Austin, TX, USA.
64. Interview, January 4, 2005, Austin, TX, USA.
65. Interview, September 2, 2005, Beijing, China.
66. Interview, December 7, 2004, San Jose, CA, USA.
67. For Washington's misgivings, see interviews with Defense Technology Security Administration (DTSA) officials, February 2, 2005, Alexandria, VA, USA; interview with a US delegation, which comprised Pentagon officials and members of government-related defense microelectronics agencies, during its inspection of semiconductor facilities in China, March 16, 2005, Shanghai, China.
68. Interview with a public relations manager at SMIC, September 30, 2005, Shanghai, China; presentation of a SMIC manager at SEMI China 2005, March 16, 2005, Shanghai, China.
69. For a typical complaint about the US export control regulations, see interview with Walden C. Rhine, the CEO of Mentor Graphics Inc., December 7, 2004, San Jose, CA, USA.
70. Interview with a manager at SMIC, September 30, 2005, Shanghai, China.
71. Interview with the CEO of a leading foundry, July 11, 2005, Hsinchu, Taiwan; interview with a vice president of a Taiwanese IC design house which uses foundry services at TSMC and SMIC, August 19, 2005, Hsinchu, Taiwan; phone interview with a deputy director of the electronic industry intelligence division of the Industrial Economics & Knowledge Center (IEK), Industrial Technology Research Institute (ITRI), Taiwan, November 2, 2005, Hsinchu, Taiwan; interview with a senior director at TSMC, August 27, 2005, Beijing, China.
72. Interview with the CEO of a leading foundry, July 11, 2005, Hsinchu, Taiwan; interview with the president of Taiwan Mask Corp., November 3, 2005, Hsinchu, Taiwan.
73. Interview, September 27, 2005, Shanghai, China.
74. He was given a US $2 million, 5-year contract as a director and adviser of Grace.
75. The number of employees was provided by the company's chairman.
76. Interview with the chairman of GSMC, September 27, 2005, Shanghai, China.
77. These include Chinese returnees.
78. Interview, September 27, 2005, Shanghai, China.
79. Interview with the chairman of GSMC, September 27, 2005, Shanghai, China.
80. Interview with Nasa Tsai, September 14, 2005, Ningbo, China.
81. In August 2005, Grace appointed Shi-chung Sun as its new CTO. In January 2006, Kuan-yang Liao was recruited as its COO. Both were senior Taiwanese engineers. See GSMC (2005; 2006a).
82. Also see interview with the chairman of GSMC, September 27, 2005, Shanghai, China.
83. Interview, September 27, 2005, Shanghai, China.
84. Phone interview with a senior industry player, March 21, 2005, Shanghai, China; interview with a senior director at TSMC, December 8, 2004, San Jose, CA, USA; interview with a company insider, September 27, 2005, Shanghai, China.
85. Interview with a senior industry player, March 20, 2005, Shanghai, China; interview

with the chairman of a Taiwanese IC design house, September 21, 2005, Suzhou, China.

86. Also see phone interview with a manager at HeJian, March 21, 2005, Shanghai, China.
87. Interview with the president of HeJian, September 21, 2005, Suzhou, China.
88. Interview with a manager at HeJian, September 21, 2005, Suzhou, China.
89. Interview with the president of HeJian, September 21, 2005, Suzhou, China.
90. Interviews, September 21, 2005, Suzhou, China.
91. Phone interview, March 21, 2005, Shanghai, China.
92. Interview, December 4, 2004, San Jose, CA, USA.
93. Over 80–90 percent of the company's customers are headquartered in Taiwan. Phone interview with a sales manager at HeJian, March 21, 2005, Shanghai, China.
94. Interview, September 21, 2005, Suzhou, China.
95. Interview, July 5, 2005, Taipei, Taiwan.
96. Phone interview, March 21, 2005, Shanghai, China.
97. Interview, June 24, 2005, Taipei, Taiwan.
98. Interview with the president of HeJian, September 21, 2005, Suzhou, China.
99. Interview with the president of HeJian, September 21, 2005, Suzhou, China.
100. Interview, September 21, 2005, Suzhou, China.
101. Interviews with Taiwanese employees at HeJian, September 21, 2005, Suzhou, China.
102. Interview with pertinent TSMC staff, June 2003, Hsinchu, Taiwan.
103. Interview with a senior executive at one of TSMC's major rivals, September 21, 2005, Suzhou, China.
104. Interview with the chairman of TSMC Shanghai, June 29, 2005, Hsinchu, Taiwan.
105. Interview with the president of TSMC Shanghai, September 26, 2005, Shanghai, China.
106. Interview with the chairman of TSMC Shanghai, June 29, 2005, Hsinchu, Taiwan.
107. Interview with the president of TSMC Shanghai, September 26, 2005, Shanghai, China.
108. Email communication with a senior director at the company, March 29, 2009.
109. Interview, March 24, 2005, Shanghai, China.
110. Interview with the president of TSMC Shanghai, September 26, 2005, Shanghai, China.
111. Interview, January 12, 2005, Dallas, TX, USA.

REFERENCES

ASC (2007), *Annual Report 2006*, December 31, online, available at: <http://www.wikinvest.com/stock/Actions_Semiconductor_(ACTS)/Filing/20-F/2007/F1996831> (accessed June 17, 2008).

ASC (2008), 'Actions Appoints Vincent Lin as Vice President of Marketing,' January 29, online, available at: <http://www.actions.com.cn/en/viewNews.aspx?type=1&id=200> (accessed March 15, 2008).

Asian Private Equity Review (2005), 'When the Chips Are Down,' June 22, Hong Kong: Centre for Asia Private Equity Research, online, available at: <http://www.altassets.com/casefor/countries/2005/nz6972.php> (accessed March 5, 2006).

Balfour, Frederik et al. (2003), 'A Bush in Hand Is Worth . . .A Lot,' *Business Week*, 3862 (December 15), 56.

Brooker, Matthew (2006), 'China's Grace Seeks Debt Repayment Delay on Loss,' *Bloomberg*, March 17.

Brown, Clair and Linden, Greg (2005), 'Offshoring in the Semiconductor Industry: A Historical Perspective,' *Brookings Trade Forum*, 2005, 279–322.

Bureau of Industry and Security (2007), 'Revisions and Clarifications of Export and Reexport Controls for the People's Republic of China (PRC); New Authorization Validated End-User; Revision of Import Certificate and PRC End-User Statement Requirements,' *Federal Register*, 72 (117), 33646–62.

Business Week (2001), 'The Stars of Asia – Entrepreneurs: Wen-Chi Chen, Chief Executive, Via Technologies,' 3739, July 2.

Carlson, Peter (2003), 'The Relatively Charmed Life of Neil Bush,' *Washington Post*, D01, December 28.

Chase, Michael S., Pollpeter, Kevin L., and Mulvenon, James C. (2004), *Shanghaied? The Economic and Political Implications of the Flow of Information Technology and Investment across the Taiwan Strait*, Santa Monica, CA: RAND.

Chen, Liang-Jung (2007), 'Actions Semiconductor, a Taiwan–China Hybrid IC Design House Emerges as the World No. 1 in its Niche Market,' *Commonwealth*, 374, June 22.

Cheng, T.J. (2005), 'China–Taiwan Economic Linkage: Between Insulation and Superconductivity,' in Tucker, N.B. (ed.), *Dangerous Strait: The U.S.–Taiwan–China Crisis*. New York: Columbia University Press, pp. 93–130.

Cheung, Tai Ming (2009), *Fortifying China: The Struggle to Build a Modern Defense Economy*. Ithaca, NY: Cornell University Press.

China Semiconductor Industry Association IC Design Branch (2005), *Zhongguo Jicheng Dianlu Sheji Chanye Shinian Licheng* (*A Ten-Year Progress Report on China's IC Design Industry*), Beijing: China Semiconductor Industry Association IC Design Branch.

Chu, Ming-Chin Monique (2008), 'Controlling the Uncontrollable: The Migration of the Taiwanese Semiconductor Industry to China and Its Security Ramifications,' *China Perspectives*, 1, 54–68.

Chu, Ming-Chin Monique (2009), 'Globalisation and Security: The Migration of the Taiwanese Semiconductor Industry to China and its Implications for the US–China–Taiwan Security Relations,' PhD dissertation, University of Cambridge.

Chu, Ming-Chin Monique (2012), 'Globalisation and Economic Security: The Case of Taiwan's Semiconductor Industry,' in Blundell, D. (ed.), *Taiwan Experience since Martial Law: Economics, Politics, Society*. Berkeley/Taipei: University of California and National Taiwan University Press, pp. 549–96.

Chu, Ming-Chin Monique (2013), *The East Asian Computer Chip War*, London and New York: Routledge.

Clendenin, Mike (2005), 'Chinese Banks Agree to Loan SMIC $600 Million,' *Electronic Engineering Times*, May 26.

Dean, Jason (2002), 'Taiwan Government Investigates Investments in China Chip Firms,' *Asian Wall Street Journal*, July 25.

Dean, Jason (2006), 'Taiwan Indicts Two Ex-Officials at Big Chip Firm: Move Highlights Tensions as Many Executives Seek to Do Business in China,' *The Wall Street Journal*, January 10.

Einhorn, Bruce (2002), 'Taiwan's Silicon Invasion,' *Business Week*, 3811 (December 9), 54–5.

Electronic Engineering Times Asia (2006), 'IC Design House Survey 2006: China,' May 23.

Electronic Engineering Times Asia (2007), 'IC Design House Survey 2007: China,' May 3.
Electronic Engineering Times Asia (2008), 'Datang Holdings to Invest in SMIC,' November 12.
EMSNow (2007), 'TSMC Shanghai Plans to Triple Output,' February 28.
Engardio, Pete and Einhorn, Bruce (2005), 'No, You Can't Buy that Chip Gear,' *Business Week*, 3934 (23 May), 54–5.
Ernst, Dieter (2005), 'Complexity and Internationalisation of Innovation – Why Is Chip Design Moving to Asia,' *International Journal of Innovation Management*, 9, 1, 47–73.
Flamm, Kenneth (1985), 'Internationalization in the Semiconductor Industry,' in Grunwald, J. and Flamm, K. (eds), *The Global Factory: Foreign Assembly in International Trade*. Washington, DC: The Brookings Institution, pp. 38–136.
Forney, Matthew (2001), 'Taipei's Tech-Talent Exodus,' *Time Asia*, 157 (20), May 21.
Fuller, Douglas B. (2008), 'The Cross-Strait Economic Relationship's Impact on Development in Taiwan and China,' *Asian Survey,* 48 (2), 239–64.
Gilpin, Robert (2001), *Global Political Economy: Understanding the International Economic Order*, Princeton, NJ: Princeton University Press.
GSMC (2004), 'Cheung Kong and Hutchison Whampoa Invest US$90 Million in Grace Semiconductor,' November 23, online, available at: <http://www.gracesemi.de/enhtml/press_news_detail.jsp?newsid=100000039&id=25> (accessed March 2, 2007).
GSMC (2005), 'Grace Appoints Dr. Shi Chung Sun as CTO and Executive Vice President of Technology Development,' August 23, online, available at: <http://www.gracesemi.com/enhtml/press_news_detail.jsp?newsid=100000045&id=25> (accessed April 6, 2006).
GSMC (2006a), 'Grace Appoints Dr. Kuan Yang Liao as Executive Vice President & Chief Operations Officer,' January 19, online, available at: <http://www.gracesemi.com/enhtml/press_news_detail.jsp?newsid=100000069&id=29> (accessed March 23, 2007).
GSMC (2006b), 'Cypress Ships First Devices Made by China Foundry Partner, Grace Semiconductor, Several Months Ahead of Plan; Cypress Will Begin Transferring 0.13-Micron Process Technology to Grace in Q3,' July 20, online, available at: <http://www.gracesemi.de/enhtml/press_news_detail.jsp?newsid=100000081&id=25> (accessed March 30, 2007).
GSMC (2006c), 'Grace Semiconductor Extends Partnership in Advanced Technologies and Products with Oki,' September 11, online, available at: <http://www.gracesemi.com/enhtml/press_news_detail.jsp?newsid=100000084&id=29> (accessed March 30, 2007).
GSMC (2007), 'Dr. Ulrich Schumacher, New President and CEO of Grace Semiconductor,' September 20, online, available at: <http://www.gracesemi.de/enhtml/press_news_detail.jsp?newsid=100000125&id=25> (accessed October 19, 2007).
GSMC (2008), 'Grace Semiconductor Extends Partnership in Advanced Technologies and Products with Sanyo Semiconductor,' February 5, online, available at: <http://www.gracesemi.com/enhtml/press_news_detail.jsp?newsid=100000135&id=29> (accessed April 28, 2008).
Henderson, Jeffrey (1989), *The Globalisation of High Technology Production:*

Society, Space and Semiconductors in the Restructuring of the Modern World, London and New York: Routledge.

Hille, Kathrin (2005), 'UMC Names Hejian Investors,' *Financial Times*, February 18.

Howell, Thomas R., Bartlett, Brent L., Noellert, William A., and Howe, Rachel (2003), *China's Emerging Semiconductor Industry: The Impact of China's Preferential Value-Added Tax on Current Investment Trends*, San Jose, CA: Semiconductor Industry Association and Dewey Ballantine.

Hsiang, Cheng-Chen (2007), 'Richard Chang Defeated in his Attempt to Relinquish Taiwan Citizenship,' *Liberty Times*, February 16.

Huang, Joyce (2002), 'Venture Capitalists Question Plan,' *Taipei Times*, September 5.

Huang, Joyce (2003), 'MOEA Levies Fines on 4 Companies for Investing in China,' *Taipei Times*, January 19.

IC Insights (2006), 'Top 10 Pure-Play Foundries Forecast for 2006: IC Insights Expects a Slowing of Chinese IC Foundries' Marketshare Gains,' August 3, online, available at: <http://www.icinsights.com/news/releases/press20060803.html> (accessed December 14, 2007).

Investment Commission (2005), 'MOEA Fined Richard Chang NT$5 Million for his Investment in SMIC,' March 31, Taipei: Ministry of Economic Affairs, Republic of China.

Jones, Terril Yue (2005), 'Spying Case Underscores Rivalry of Asian Chip Firms,' *Los Angeles Times*, January 3.

Lapedus, Mark (2003), 'U.S. Tool Makers at a Disadvantage in China, Says SEMI,' *Silicon Strategies*, July 18.

Lapedus, Mark (2005), 'Updated: China's Foundry Industry to Slow in 2005,' *Electronic Engineering Times*, June 14.

Lapedus, Mark (2006), 'SMIC Tops Chartered in '05 Foundry Rankings,' *Electronic Engineering Times*, March 25.

Lapedus, Mark (2007), 'U.S. Reduces Export Controls for SMIC,' *Electronic Engineering Times*, October 19.

Lapedus, Mark (2008), 'Red Alert: China Churns out Chip Fabs,' *Electronic Engineering Times*, February 1.

Lee, Dao-Cheng (2004), 'Mainland China's IC Design Sector Still Small in Scale,' *Commercial Times*, June 3.

Leopold, George (2007), 'Updated Four Chip Makers in China Added to US Export List,' *Electronic Engineering Times*, October 19.

Macher, Jeffrey T., Mowery, David C., and Minin, Alberto Di (2007), 'The "Non-Globalization" of Innovation in the Semiconductor Industry," *California Management Review*, 50, 1, 1–26.

Mediatek Inc. (2005), *Annual Report 2004*, April 30, online, available at: <http://www.mediatek.com/upload/files/1584745e3ec079c0ea1322da00c02359.pdf> (accessed August 8, 2006).

Mediatek Inc. (2006), *Annual Report 2005*, April 30, online, available at: <http://} www.mediatek.com/upload/files/52bf32b125ea3c7546fac14e9fe40e6e.pdf> (accessed April 4, 2007).

Ministry of Economic Affairs (2007), *Taiwan's Listed Companies with Approved Investment in Mainland China*, Taipei: Ministry of Economic Affairs, Republic of China.

Nystedt, Dan (2005), 'CEO of Chip Maker SMIC Giving up Taiwan Citizenship,' *IDG News Service*, August 23.

PricewaterhouseCoopers (2006), *China's Impacts on the Semiconductor Industry 2005/Update,* New York: PricewaterhouseCoopers.
PricewaterhouseCoopers (2007), *China's Impacts on the Semiconductor Industry 2006/Update,* New York: PricewaterhouseCoopers.
PricewaterhouseCoopers (2008), *China's Impact on the Semiconductor Industry: 2008 Update,* New York: PricewaterhouseCoopers.
Realtek Semiconductor Corp. (2006), *Annual Report 2005*, online, available at: <http://www.realtek.com/investor/annualView.aspx?Langid=1&PNid=1&PFid=4&Level=1> (accessed April 6, 2007).
Reuters (2008), 'China's Hejian, Elpida Mull Chip Plant – Paper,' March 18, online, available at: <http://in.reuters.com/article/asiaCompanyAndMarkets/idINTP23202420080318> (accessed May 8, 2008).
Semiconductor Industry Association (2010) 'Global Chip Sales Decline in 2009,' Online, Available <http://www.sia-online.org/cs/papers_publications/press_release_detail?pressrelease.id=1707> (accessed 15 March 2010).
Shanghai Industrial Holdings Limited (2005), *Annual Report 2004*, online, available at: <http://www.sihl.com.hk/sihl/eng/jsp/show_doc.action?doc_type=0> (accessed March 1, 2006).
Shanghai Stock Exchange Newspaper (2003), 'Hangzhou Silan Microelectronics Co. Ltd. Prospectus – Part III,' February 19, online, available at: <http://memo.stock888.net/030219/102, 1310, 156226, 00.shtml> (accessed June 6, 2007).
SMIC (2001a), 'SMIC Raises More Than $1 Billion in Series A Round Financing,' November 10, online, available at: <http://www.smics.com/eng/press/media_press_details.php?id=51407> (accessed July 8, 2004).
SMIC (2001b), 'SMIC Grand Opening,' November 22, online, available at: <http://news.smics.com/website/enVersion/Press_Center/popupDetailNews.action?newsId=163> (accessed March 3, 2004).
SMIC (2001c), 'SMIC to Receive SRAM Process Technology Transfer from Toshiba,' December 20, online, available at: <http://www.smics.com/eng/press/media_press_details.php?id=51396> (accessed July 5, 2004).
SMIC (2001d), 'SMIC and Chartered Announce Alliance on 0.18-Micron Technology and Capacity,' December 21, online, available at: <http://www.smics.com/eng/press/media_press_details.php?id=51390> (accessed July 8, 2004).
SMIC (2002), 'Infineon Signs Major Foundry Agreement with SMIC in China,' December 9, online, available at: <http://www.smics.com/eng/press/media_press_details.php?id=51379> (accessed August 24, 2004).
SMIC (2003a), 'Toshiba to Transfer SRAM Process Technology to SMIC,' January 9, online, available at: <http://news.smics.com/website/enVersion/Press_Center/popupDetailNews.action?newsId=228> (accessed April 5, 2005).
SMIC (2003b), 'Infineon Expands Foundry Agreement with SMIC,' March 27, online, available at: <http://news.smics.com/website/enVersion/Press_Center/popupDetailNews.action?newsId=246> (accessed April 8, 2004).
SMIC (2003c), 'SMIC Raises US$630 Million in Private Placement,' September 15, online, available at: <http://www.smics.com/eng/press/media_press_details.php?id=51364> (accessed July 9, 2004).
SMIC (2004a), 'SMIC Entered into a US$285 Million Loan Agreement with Four Chinese Banks,' January 18, online, available at: <http://www.smics.com/eng/press/media_press_details.php?id=51347> (accessed December 5, 2005).
SMIC (2004b), 'Semiconductor Manufacturing International Corporation

Announces Proposed Dual Listing on SEHK and NYSE,' March 7, online, available at: <http://www.smics.com/eng/press/media_press_details.php?id=51343> (accessed March 1, 2006).
SMIC (2004c), 'SMIC will Vigorously Defend against the Trade Secret Case Filed by TSMC in State Court,' June 4, online, available at: <http://www.smics.com/website/enVersion/Press_Center/popupDetailNews.action?newsId=605> (accessed July 1, 2005).
SMIC (2005a), 'SMIC Reaches Settlement with TSMC,' January 30, online, available at: <http://www.smics.com/website/enVersion/Press_Center/popupDetailNews.action?newsId=1105> (accessed July 1, 2005).
SMIC (2005b), *2004 Annual Report*, April 7, online, available at: <http://www.smics.com/attachment/2011012018070017_en.pdf> (accessed May 5, 2006).
SMIC (2005c), 'SMIC Beijing Secures Financing for Expansion,' May 26, online, available at: <http://www.smics.com/attachment/2011012016454117_en.pdf> (accessed March 5, 2006).
SMIC (2006a), 'Infineon and SMIC Extend Agreement into 90nm Manufacturing,' January 6, online, available at: <http://news.smics.com/website/enVersion/Press_Center/popupDetailNews.action?newsId=1867> (accessed April 6, 2007).
SMIC (2006b), *Annual Report 2005*, May 2, online, available at: <http://www.smics.com/attachment/2011012015151217_en.pdf> (accessed January 18, 2007).
SMIC (2006c), 'SMIC Denies Allegations and Files Cross-Complaint against TSMC,' September 13, online, available at: <http://www.smics.com/eng/press/media_press_details.php?id=51198> (accessed June 24, 2007).
SMIC (2007a), *Annual Report 2006*, April 30, online, available at: <http://www.smics.com/attachment/2011011916123817_en.pdf> (accessed May 23, 2008).
SMIC (2007b), 'Qimonda Expands Foundry Agreement with SMIC,' August 21, online, available at: <http://news.smics.com/website/enVersion/Press_Center/popupDetailNews.action?newsId=2606> (accessed March 1, 2008).
SMIC (2007c), 'SMIC Attains Validated End-User Status from U.S. Government,' October 19, online, available at: <http://news.smics.com/website/enVersion/Press_Center/popupDetailNews.action?newsId=2726> (accessed December 27, 2007).
SMIC (2007d), 'SMIC and IBM Sign Licensing Agreement,' December 26, online, available at: <http://www.smics.com/eng/press/media_press_details.php?id=51162> (accessed June 5, 2008).
SMIC (2008a), 'SMIC Reports 2007 Fourth Quarter Results,' January 29, online, available at: <http://news.smics.com/website/enVersion/Press_Center/popupDetailNews.action?newsId=2865> (accessed May 6, 2008).
SMIC (2008b), 'SMIC Honored with SEMI China Corporate Social Contribution Award; Dr. Richard Chang Receives Industry Excellence and Contribution Award,' March 18, online, available at: <http://www.smics.com/website/enVersion/Press_Center/popupDetailNews.action?newsId=2948> (accessed August 30, 2008).
Smith, Craig S. (2000), 'A Chip Plant That Is Full of Symbolism,' *New York Times*, November 24.
Solid State Technology (2007), 'UMC Execs Acquitted in He Jian Case,' October 29.
Spreadtrum Communications Inc. (2008), 'Spreadtrum Wins Recognition as 2007 China's Top 10 IC Design Companies,' March 26, online, available at: <http://

www.spreadtrum.com/en/shown.asp?id=128&category=1> (accessed September 7, 2008).

Sung, Claire and Chan, Rodney (2007), 'Well-Driven "Small Car": Q&A with GSMC Executive VP Arthur Kuo,' *DigiTimes*, February 16.

Sung, Claire and Chan, Rodney (2008), 'Hejian and Elpida to Jointly Build 12-Inch Fab in China,' *DigiTimes*, March 18.

Tang, Theresa (2005), 'UMC Lays Down Challenge over He Jian,' *International Herald Tribune*, June 22.

Tsar & Tsai Lex News (2007), 'Different Views between the Administrative Law Court and the Ministry of Economic Affairs on SMIC's Investment,' online, available at: <http://www.tsartsai.com.tw/TTnews/Tsar%20&%20Tsai%20Lex%20News%20(English)%202007-05.htm#Different_Views> (accessed July 6, 2007).

TSMC (2003), 'TSMC Files Law Suit against SMIC for Patent Infringement and Trade Secret Misappropriation,' December 22, online, available at: <http://www.tsmc.com/tsmcdotcom/PRListingNewsArchivesAction.do?action=detail&newsid=1483&language=E> (accessed August 1, 2004).

TSMC (2004), 'TSMC Response Identifies More SMIC Espionage: More Wrong Doing Documented,' March 24, online, available at: <http://www.tsmc.com/tsmcdotcom/PRListingNewsAction.do?action=detail&LANG=E&newsid=1498&newsdate=2004/03/24> (accessed May 5, 2004).

TSMC (2005a), 'A Banner Year: TSMC Annual Report 2004,' online, available at: <http://www.tsmc.com/download/ir/annual_report/pdf/e_all.pdf> (accessed November 1, 2006).

TSMC (2005b), 'TSMC Reaches Settlement with SMIC,' January 30, online, available at: <http://www.tsmc.com/tsmcdotcom/PRListingNewsArchivesAction.do?action=detail&newsid=1593&language=E> (accessed February 2, 2005).

TSMC (2006a) *Annual Report 2005*, online, available at: <http://www.tsmc.com/download/ir/2005_annual_report/pic/E-TSMC-all.pdf> (accessed March 2, 2007).

TSMC (2006b), 'TSMC Welcomes Government Approval for 0.18 Micron Generation Technology Transfer to China,' December 29, online, available at: <http://www.tsmc.com/tsmcdotcom/PRListingNewsArchivesAction.do?action=detail&newsid=2019&language=E> (accessed December 31, 2006).

TSMC (2007a), *Annual Report 2006*, online, available at: <http://www.tsmc.com/english/e_investor/e02_annual/2006_annual_report/pdf/tsmc_e_h.pdf> (accessed June 15, 2008).

TSMC (2007b), 'California Court Issues Order on TSMC Motion for Preliminary Injunction against SMIC,' September 14, online, available at: <http://www.tsmc.com/tsmcdotcom/PRListingNewsArchivesAction.do?action=detail&newsid=2301&language=E> (accessed September 30, 2007).

Tu, Chih-Hao (2008), 'Schumacher Took Helm at Grace Semiconductor Reviving the Company,' *Commercial Times*, February 22.

UMC (2005), 'United Microelectronics Corporation and Subsidiaries Unaudited Consolidated Financial Statements with Review Report of Independent Accountants for the Six-Month Period Ended June 30, 2005,' July 19, online, available at: <http://www.umc.com/english/pdf/05_1H_consolidated-e.pdf> (accessed September 6, 2006).

UMC (2009), 'UMC Board of Directors Important Announcement,' April 29, online, available at: <http://www.umc.com/english/news/2009/20090429-2.asp> (accessed May 5, 2009).

Wang, Lisa (2005), 'UMC May Get Stake in He Jian to Placate Prosecutors,' *Taipei Times*, March 22.
Wang, Mo-Yun (2005), 'Further Penalties Awaiting Should SMIC Move to 65nm Process Technology,' *Commercial Times*, August 25.
Xilinx, Inc. (2004), 'Xilinx Announces Investment in He Jian Technology Co.,' July 27, online, available at: <http://www.xilinx.com/prs_rls/xil_corp/0490hejian.htm> (accessed June 6, 2006).
Xinhua-PRNewswire (2007), 'CCID Consulting Analyzes and Forecasts the Global and Chinese Foundry Market,' September 14, online, available at: <http://www.prnewswire.com/cgi-bin/stories.pl?ACCT=104&STORY=/www/story/09-14-2007/0004662758&EDATE=> (accessed October 14, 2007).

10. The emerging trade bloc across the Taiwan Strait in regional and global perspective

Peter C.Y. Chow

10.1 INTRODUCTION

During the first three decades after the establishment of the People's Republic of China (PRC) in 1949, economic interaction across the Taiwan Strait was prohibited and occurred illegally on a very limited scale.[1] But the situation has changed dramatically since the 1980s. First, China's economic reforms and opening of 1978–79 shifted its central command economy and autarkic trade regime toward a more market-oriented economy, still with Chinese characteristics but with increasing trade dependence on the world market.[2] Next, Taipei lifted its ban preventing citizens who had emigrated from China after communists took it over from visiting their relatives on the mainland in 1987. Trade across the Taiwan Strait was gradually liberalized, progressing from indirect trade via a third place eventually to direct trade as foreign direct investment (FDI) flowing from Taiwan to China.[3]

After decades of development, Taiwan's economy was undergoing its structural transformations soon after the worldwide energy crisis of the early 1970s. The changes were accelerated in the second half of the 1980s by the currency appreciation caused by the Plaza Accord of 1985. Upon losing its comparative advantage in the traditional labor-intensive, light manufacturing exports in the world market, Taiwan, along with other newly industrialized countries (NICs), most notably Korea, had to engage in a 'comparative advantages-augmented type of foreign direct investment' (Ozawa, 1992) to enhance its export competitiveness in the world market. Financially, Taiwan passed through the 'two-gap' trap,[4] a common phenomenon in many less developed countries (LDCs), and transformed itself from a capital recipient to a capital provider in the world economy. Therefore, outward FDI increased steadily after Taiwan undertook its structural transformation in the early 1980s and accelerated in the 1990s. The flows of outward FDI as a percentage of total gross fixed capital formation increased from less than 5 percent in the early 1990s to nearly 15 percent in the first decade of the twenty-first century. Similarly, the percentage of the stock of FDI in total GDP increased from 15 percent to more than 45 percent in the same period.[5]

Taiwan's FDI was first engaged in the Southeast Asian countries to take the cost advantages of labor and land in host countries in the 1980s. After China's paramount leader, Deng Xiao-ping, reaffirmed the reforms and openness of his country in 1992, more and more Taiwanese outward FDI was destined for China. This tendency was further entrenched after the 1997–98 Asian financial crisis. At the beginning of the twenty-first century, more than half of Taiwanese outward FDI was destined for China, with the total FDI stock accounting for more than US $100 billion.[6]

In spite of political tensions between China and Taiwan,[7] an economic incentive for Taiwanese entrepreneurs was not checked by various government regulatory policies under different administrations since the 1990s.[8] After China and Taiwan were admitted to the World Trade Organization (WTO) in 2001 and 2002 respectively, trade liberalization across the Taiwan Strait accelerated and Taiwanese FDI in China gradually dominated its overall outward investments.

Upon taking power in May 2008, President Ma Ying-jeou implemented a China-leaning policy that facilitated trade, led to the operation of direct flights across the Taiwan Strait, opened Taiwan to Chinese tourists, and concluded 15 trade pacts with China such as the Economic Cooperation Framework Agreement (ECFA) of June 2010. As reflected in its title, the ECFA is a framework preceding the Free Trade Agreement (FTA) for further economic integration between the two economies across the Taiwan Strait.

This chapter analyses the prospects of an emerging trade bloc across the Taiwan Strait in the aftermath of the ECFA, the sustainability of the probable 'Great Chinese Economic Zone,' the various 'hub–spoke' models and scenarios in East Asian economic integration, and Taiwan's options and futures under multiple equilibria of economic integration. It is organized in the following order. Section 10.2 addresses the path from economic interactions to economic integration and analyses the prospect of development from a functional trading bloc to an institutionalized economic integration. Section 10.3 analyses the trade structures between China and Taiwan and the emerging trade bloc in regional and global perspectives. It focuses on the vulnerability and sustainability of dependence on external market demand, especially in view of global imbalances and the US role in East Asian economic integration as a potential centric hub in East Asian economic integration. Section 10.4 addresses Taiwan's trade strategy to cope with a rising China and the regionalism in East Asia. It examines the three potential centric hubs in East Asian economic integration and the prospects for Taiwan to be included in those trade blocs. A TradeSim simulation based on a gravity model is conducted to exploit Taiwan's untapped trade potentials by sector/country-specific analysis for export promotion which could let Taiwan break through its cumulated isolation in commerce diplomacy and tendency of being marginalized in regional economic integration. Section 10.5 provides different scenarios of multiple equilibria to assess Taiwan's options and future from regional and global perspectives.

10.2 FROM ECONOMIC INTERACTIONS TO ECONOMIC INTEGRATION

10.2.1 The Trade-Investment Nexus and the Emerging Trade Bloc Across the Taiwan Strait

The increasing economic interactions across the Taiwan Strait since the beginning of the 1980s have resulted in a trade-investment nexus, which simultaneously arose between the other NICs and developing Asian countries (Bende-Nabende, 2003). This development was driven by the engine of globalization, which was fueled by Taiwanese multinational corporations (MNCs). These firms sought to distribute the manufacturing process at each stage of production across national boundaries in accordance with the comparative advantages in various host countries. The new international division of labor resulted in a shift from inter-industry to intra-industry trade. The latter used to dominate the trade patterns between developed countries only but has become the major trade flow between the home and host countries in developing Asian countries including Taiwan and China.

Taiwan's exports to China were induced mainly by Taiwan's outward FDI in China. By using two-stage least-squares and two-step system GMM methodologies, Chow (2012a) empirically proves that Taiwan's outward FDI has a significant positive effect on its exports to host countries as a group, with the most considerable being on its exports to China. Hence, the trade-investment nexus has emerged a 'functional trade bloc' across the Taiwan Strait.[9]

The composition of trading commodities of Taiwan's exports to China is predominated by intermediate goods, parts, and components which have accounted for more than three-quarters of its total exports in the two decades since the 1990s.[10] Most Taiwanese exports to China were induced by Taiwanese FDI in China and were further processed

Table 10.1 Directions of China's exports

Destination countries	1990–94	1995–99	2000–2004	2005–2009	2010
Japan	15.515%	17.946%	14.887%	9.029%	7.610%
United States	12.671%	18.884%	21.008%	19.532%	17.950%
European Union	11.635%	14.921%	17.163%	19.798%	19.709%
ASEAN-5	5.438%	5.692%	6.116%	6.613%	6.925%
Others (rest of the world)	54.741%	42.557%	40.827%	45.028%	47.807%

Note: ASEAN-5 includes Indonesia, Malaysia, Philippines, Singapore, and Thailand.

Data source: *Directions of Trade*, International Monetary Fund.

and assembled for re-export to industrial markets, primarily to the US and European countries.[11] Hence, there is an emerging triangular trade relationship between Taiwan, China, and the industrialized markets, especially the US.

The FDI-trade nexus across the Taiwan Strait also substantially shifted the direction of trade flows in Taiwan. Taiwan's exports to the US, which accounted for more than 30 percent of its total exports in the 1980s, have gradually declined, whereas its exports to China have been steadily increasing. In 2002, China replaced the US as Taiwan's largest export market. Hence, Taiwan's dependence on China's market for trade has deepened over recent decades. On the other hand, Taiwanese as well as other MNCs in China process, assemble, and re-export those finished goods to a third market, which consists mainly of OECD countries. Hence, the shares of US and European Union (EU) markets in China's exports have been steadily increasing since the 1990s. As reported in Table 10.1, China's exports to the US and EU markets increased from an annual average of 24.31 percent of its total exports in the 1990–94 period to nearly 40 percent in the 2005–2009 period. China's increasing dependence on the external market will be reinforced when the trade bloc across the Taiwan Strait is formally institutionalized in the aftermath of the ECFA. It will create problematic policy issues to be further elaborated in Sections 10.3 and 10.4.

Looking at the import shares of Asian countries in the US market since the beginning of the 1990s, one can find that US imports from China, Japan, South Korea, Taiwan, and the ASEAN countries persistently accounted for 35 percent of its total imports. Nevertheless, China's market shares in the US have been steadily increasing, despite the fact that those of Japan, Korea, and Taiwan have been continually decreasing, as Figure 10.1 illustrates.

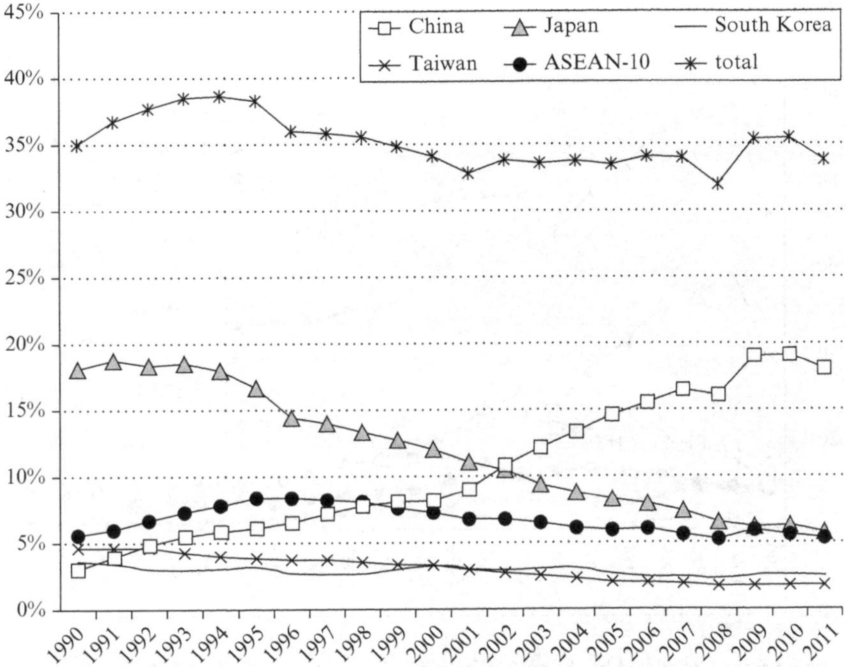

Data source: Calculated by the author from the International Trade Administration, US Department of Commerce.

Figure 10.1 Market shares of Asian countries in total US imports, 1990–2011

One can find that China's market shares in total US imports increased from 3.7 percent in 1990 to 18.10 percent in 2011 whereas those of Japan decreased steadily from 18.10 percent to 5.84 percent in the same period. To a lesser extent, Korea's market shares in the US decreased from 3.73 percent to 2.57 percent, whereas those of Taiwan decreased from 4.58 percent to 1.87 percent in the same period. The market shares of ASEAN countries increased from 5.50 percent in 1990 to a peak of 8.36 percent in 1995–96, declined after the Asian financial crisis, and remained at 5.36 percent in 2011. In other words, for those major foreign investors in China, such as Japan, South Korea, and Taiwan, market shares in the US were partly taken over by China due to their outward FDI and outsourcing in China.

The changing sources of suppliers in US imports is especially salient if one looks at the electric and electronic products; while US imports of

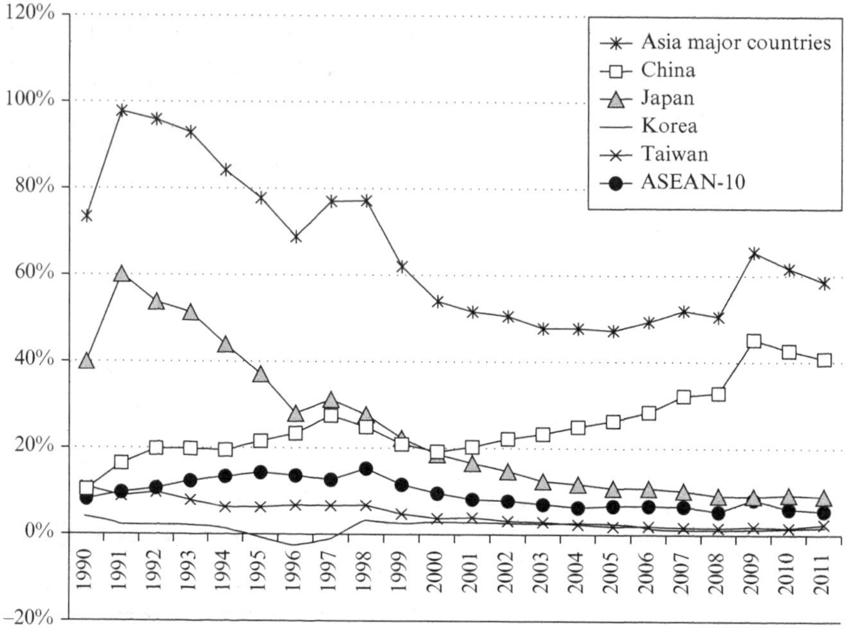

Data source: Calculated by the author from The International Trade Administration.

Figure 10.2 Trade deficits with Asian countries as a percentage of total US trade deficits

these product groups from East Asian countries increased from 48.42 percent in 1990 to 52.53 percent in 2011,[12] there is a dramatic shift among the sources of import suppliers from Japan and Taiwan to China. The market shares of electric and electronic products of Japan decreased steadily from 21.01 percent in 1990 to 6.41 percent in 2011 whereas those of China increased from 6.63 percent to 35.96 percent in the same period.[13] Meanwhile, Taiwan's market shares of electric and electronic products in the US decreased from 11.30 percent to 1.71 percent, whereas those of Korea rose modestly from 4.62 percent to 4.88 percent, and ASEAN countries declined modestly from 4.86 percent to 3.57 percent in the same period.

Consequently, the composition of the chronic US trade deficits with East Asian countries shifted among those trade-dependent economies; while the US trade deficits with Japan, Taiwan, Korea, and the ASEAN countries began decreasing in the second half of the 1990s, those with China have steadily increased. Figure 10.2 shows the trend of the changing percentage shares of these East Asian countries in total US trade deficits since 1990. Among them, China surpassed Japan as the largest source of US trade deficit in 2000, and the trend has continued since that date. The US trade deficit with China reached 45.05 percent of its total trade deficits with the rest of the world in 2009 and maintained 43.01 percent in 2010 (40.68 percent in 2011). This development not only supports the perception that China is a world factory, a world workshop, or an assembly in the world trade (Chow, 2010), but also portrays China as an important player in the global imbalances that will be addressed in Section 10.4.

10.2.2 From De Facto Integration to De Jure Integration?

The signing of the ECFA between China and Taiwan in June 2010 was a milestone in the development of economic integration across the Taiwan Strait. The trade-investment nexus and the cross-border production network may evolve from a pair of functional trading blocs into a formally institutionalized economic zone if the ECFA expands into an FTA and thus further economic integration. In the literature, the stages of economic integration could move forward from FTA to custom union, common market, economic community, and eventually to an economic union – a pathway previously observed in the EU. Though there are discussions on future developments from a 'de facto' trade bloc to a 'Great China Economic Zone,' 'Cross-Strait Common Market,' or 'Greater China Common Market,' many of these proposals will change the status quo across the Taiwan Strait and involve political sensitivity of mutual recognition of respective sovereignty between the signatories.[14] Whether China and Taiwan will overcome the political obstacles or bypass the issue of sovereignty in the drive toward further economic integration is beyond the scope of this chapter.

However, one can point out that whether the ECFA will be able to continue to function and whether it will evolve into an institutionalized trade bloc will depend on economic and socio-political developments across the Taiwan Strait and on the shifting power in the region in the future. For those interested in the political economy of economic integration, the book edited by Chow (2012b) provides some insightful evaluations on the development of Taiwanese national identity and economic interests in Taiwan since its democratization. The following sections analyse the economic aspects of the emerging trade bloc and the power shifts from regional and global perspectives, followed by assessments of its resultant impacts on the development of regional integration in East Asia.

10.3 THE EMERGING TRADE BLOC ACROSS THE TAIWAN STRAIT

10.3.1 The Effects of a China–Taiwan FTA on Trade Flows and Dependence on OECD Markets

This section analyses the effects of trade liberalization across the Taiwan Strait under a hypothetical, fully-fledged FTA on trade flows and destinations from regional and global perspectives. Numerous studies have adopted computable general equilibrium (CGE) model simulations to estimate the effects of trade liberalization on GDP, trade, terms of trade, and social welfare under different scenarios. Among them, Chen and Ku (2007), Chen et al. (2011), and Rosen and Wang (2011) report the trade creation versus trade diversion effect on member and non-member economies under various scenarios of economic integration in East Asia. Even though the marginal benefit of an FTA is substantially undercut by the high administrative costs due to different 'rules of origin' under various trade pacts,[15] these simulations show that Taiwan's GDP and trade will benefit if Taiwan is included in many of those emerging trade blocs. Through the simulations, Chen et al. (2011) found that an evolving FTA with China will beneficially affect Taiwan's GDP by 1.738 percent and export by 3.578 percent from the based period.

The results of another CGE model simulation described in Chow (2012b) show that under a fully-fledged Taiwan–China FTA, Taiwan's exports to China will increase by US $26.42 billion, whereas its exports to all other trading partners will decrease.[16] Hence, Taiwan's total exports will increase by only US $12.75 billion. Nevertheless, China's exports to all of its trading partners will increase under a China–Taiwan FTA by US $12.13 billion. More specifically, China's exports to the US will increase by US $1775 million and its exports to the EU will increase by US $1372 million from the base period. In other words, although Taiwan's trade dependence on China's market will increase, China's export dependence on the industrial markets will increase as well. Moreover, China's imports from the US will decrease by US $1264 million, and its imports from the EU will also fall by US $2852 million. This means that the chronic US trade deficits with China will be aggravated if a China–Taiwan FTA becomes fully effective. Similar results were found in another CGE model simulation summarized in Chow and Ciuriak (2012) under somewhat different scenarios and sectoral aggregations.

One common caveat of policy assessments based on CGE simulations is the lack of concerns about the inherent inability of the models to account for the externality of deepening economic integration from the dependence on external markets. As pointed out before, most of the trade-oriented economies in East Asia – especially China, Korea, and Taiwan – are highly dependent on OECD markets to sell their manufactured exports, especially the final consumption goods. One must thus ask how the US trade deficit would be affected if the current 'de facto' trade bloc across the Taiwan Strait evolves into an institutionalized FTA. The simulation results cited above show that China's trade surplus with the US will increase under a fully-fledged FTA with Taiwan. Similar CGE model simulations confirm these results.[17]

Given that China's trade surplus accounts for more than 40 percent of total US trade deficits with the rest of the world, as shown in Figure 10.2, any aggravation of the US trade deficit with China will increase trade frictions between Washington and Beijing. Under such circumstances, the US financial market, which is already vulnerable to China's appetite for disposing of its foreign exchange reserves to purchase US Treasury Bonds,[18] would be subject to 'systemic risk' if any mismanagement of trade tensions between Washington and Beijing occured. There are thus several questions to address. Can a trade bloc, such as the one currently operating between China and Taiwan, continue to depend on the external markets of OECD economies, especially the US, without any repercussions? To what extent will the vulnerability of dependence on the US market affect the sustainability of the emerging trade bloc across the Taiwan Strait? If the OECD markets, especially the US, cannot sustain the market demand of China's exports forever, then the emerging trade bloc across the Taiwan Strait will be fragile and subject to external shocks in the future.

10.3.2 The Emerging Trade Bloc in Regional and Global Perspective and its Role in Re-balancing the Global Economy

The global economic recession that was triggered by the 2008–2009 financial crisis revealed the vulnerabilities of reliance of the export market on OECD countries for those trade-oriented economies in East Asia.[19] If the dependence on OECD markets, especially the US, is not sustainable, then alternative markets are needed for the exports from those trade-dependent economies. Will China be able to cut its trade surplus with the US by increasing its domestic consumption or relocating its exports to alternative markets to substitute or supplement the US market?

Rebalancing China's trade surplus toward domestic demand is agreeable among most economists, if not policy practitioners, although there are many disagreements about how to pursue it through policy actions (IMF, 2010; Yueh, 2011). The policy issues involved are very complicated; realignment of the current trade destinations involves not only identifying the new markets but also adjusting the current structure of the composition of trading commodities. The critical issue to address is whether the current trade structure across the Taiwan Strait will be compatible with China's new domestic market demand, even if China really takes the policy initiative to rebalance its macro economy by cutting its exports and increasing its domestic consumption.[20] Or, in more concrete terms, can China's domestic market replace or supplement part of the US market for those final consumption goods processed from imports from Taiwan and others?

Intuitively, other than readjusting government budget balances, adjusting the trade imbalances will require the trade deficit country to cut its consumption (increase investment) and imports, and the trade surplus country to increase its consumption (decrease investment) and cut its exports. From the national income identity, one can easily derive the following equation to demonstrate that trade balance is the sum of the gaps between domestic saving/investment and government budget:

$$(S - I) + (T - G) = (X - M) \tag{10.1}$$

where S, I, G, T, X, and M stand for private saving, investment, government spending, tax revenue, exports, and imports respectively.[21]

If the American household savings rate only rises to its historical medium point, then Americans' savings rate must rise by roughly 6 percent of US GDP. The size of the US economy is about 2.5 times that of China.[22] The increase in Chinese domestic demand needed to absorb those consumption cuts in the US is equal to roughly 7.44 percent of China's GDP.[23] Given the current level of China's per capita income and its consumption accounting for about 40 percent of its total GDP, China's consumption would have to rise by more than 20 percent from its current level. This is clearly unlikely to occur in the foreseeable future.

In terms of consumption patterns between the two economies, China and the US are at very different levels of per capita income. The pattern of market demand and composition of consumption goods among households diverges widely between these two countries.[24] Furthermore, many policy measures intended to increase China's domestic consumption, such as liberalization of consumer credit and mortgage loans, as well as implementation of a social safety net for China's aging population, would restructure China's domestic demand toward non-tradable goods and services rather than switching it from export to domestically-produced goods.[25]

Can those exports from China be re-directed to other parts of the world such as Southeast Asia, which is moving toward another trade bloc under the ASEAN-FTA? Even though intra-regional trade between developing

Asian countries has been increasing since the year 2000, most East Asian countries are engaging in the trade of parts and components (Ng and Yeats, 2008). There is only some untenable evidence of increasing trade in final goods after the China–ASEAN FTA.[26] Therefore, for any trade bloc to be sustainable, one cannot merely focus on the supply-side of economic integration of the production network (trade in intermediate goods); a full examination of the demand for final consumption goods is needed. The growth of intra-regional trade in East Asian countries, as a mirror image of the global production network, may well depend on the sustainability of the market demand for final consumption goods that they produced.

Based on 3-digit Standard International Trade Classification (SITC) codes, more than 80 percent of China's trade with the OECD and the Asian NICs were dominated by intra-industry trade by 2000 (Chow, 2010), with China's imports of intermediate products, parts, and components further processed locally before re-export as final products to the industrial market economies. Among them, Taiwan's exports of intermediate goods, parts, and components accounted for more than three-quarters of its exports to China. Most of them are to be further processed in China before re-export to OECD markets, mainly the US and the EU (Chow, 2010). The triangular trade relations between Taiwan, the other emerging Asian economies, and Japan as exporters of intermediate products to China, which serves as a factory or workshop of the cross-border production network, is completed by the US as the market for final consumption goods. This structure illustrates that correcting the global trade imbalance must include sector adjustments of macro economies and not just expenditure-switching policies.

The increasing dependence of Taiwan on China's market will remain closely tied up with the market demand for final goods in the OECD countries, unless China's domestic demand can pick up in the near future. To the best knowledge of the author, existing literature of CGE model simulations on the effect of FTAs on trade flows does not distinguish trade in parts and components from those in final consumption goods, probably because 'standard gravity equation performs poorly by some measures when it is applied to bilateral flows where parts and components trade is important' (Baldwin and Taglioni, 2011). Though the short experience of Japan's FTAs with ASEAN countries showed that the FTA had not only facilitated exchange of intermediate goods between Japan and ASEAN and between ASEAN countries, but had also generated trade of final goods between Japan and the ASEAN countries, the net effect of the Japan–ASEAN FTA, which was implemented in 2008, on the US trade deficit is not clear yet.[27]

Given the different levels of income and the disparities in market demand in the region, most economists would reserve their judgment on the feasibility of having vital alternative markets to supplement the US for China's export in the foreseeable future. Hence, unless China's domestic demand could substantially absorb those final products,[28] the emerging trade bloc between China and Taiwan would probably be severely challenged if the global imbalances were further exacerbated and the trade tension between Washington and Beijing were to increase. Therefore, economic integration across the Taiwan Strait must be evaluated in the regional and global context by examining the sustainability of the triangular trade relationship between the US, China, and Taiwan as argued above.

By using a three-variable VAR model – that is, the domestic real GDP; the country's real exports to the US; and the country's real exports to China – Park and Shin (2011) found that exports from eight Asian countries to China, including Taiwan,[29] had 'a large and growing positive effect on the GDP of regional economies' (p. 161) during the global crisis. But after creating China's real exports to the US as the four-variable VAR model to incorporate its role as a 'derived demand,'[30] they found that 'much of the PRC's positive impact disappears at a longer horizon.' In other words, rather than reflect its own demand, China's imports from those eight East Asian countries really depends on demand for final goods from other countries such as the US and the EU. Hence, the argument that China is the engine of growth is misleading and not supported by the empirical study by Park and Shin (2011). After carefully examining China's trade structure with East Asian countries, one can only conclude that China's ability to sustain regional export growth with its domestic demand is highly doubtful at present, even though the myth of China's market has been and still is an irresistible attraction for many foreign investors from Taiwan and other countries.

Those who argue that the growing economy in China could serve as the engine of growth, primary or secondary, for the region, have to realize that the engine in China's economy has been and still is dependent on another big engines in the industrial markets. Hence, the enthusiasm of China's potential market has to be supported by more empirical evidence to prove that China's domestic demand for final goods will really increase in the aftermath of China's multiple FTAs with its trading partners. For those who argue for a simultaneous twin-engine theory, one has to point out that the functions of the second engine (China) are, at least partly, dependent on the first engine (the OECD).[31] Unless alternative markets can be found, which is not feasible in the foreseeable future as argued previously, the sustainability of the emerging trade bloc across the Taiwan Strait and, to a greater extent, the East Asian economic integration, cannot totally ignore the role of the US to accommodate the market demand for final goods. Therefore, one has to conclude that for China to serve as the 'engine of growth' in the region, or even as a supplementary second engine, substantial restructuring of the directions and trade structures are needed, which is a formidable task for all the nations involved to accomplish in the foreseeable future.

10.4 TAIWAN'S TRADE STRATEGIES TO COPE WITH THE RISING OF CHINA AND REGIONALISM IN EAST ASIA

10.4.1 The Hubs in East Asian Economic Integration and their Relations with Taiwan

In spite of the diversity of size and levels of development, the rising regionalism in East Asia has led to the proliferation of FTAs and emerging multiple trade blocs. To cope with this tendency, Taiwan has to weigh its potential benefits from joining each of these emerging trade blocs, if it has the options to choose from. Much of the literature on the bilateral and multilateral FTAs has addressed the cost and benefit of trade liberalization and economic integration, yet few studies have ever touched the issue of the impact of economic integration between the large and small economies, notable exceptions being those of Baldwin (2004) and Umemoto (2003).

Economic integration between small and large countries would not only lead to the growth of trade flows but also to dynamic shifts of factors of production between member states. In general, 'industrial clusters' would shift in favor of the large member countries due to their economies of scale. Krugman (1991) argues that the large economy with relatively large production bases would benefit from trade liberalization, cost reduction, and scale economies to become the hub, whereas smaller economies would suffer and become spokes. Hence, Krugman concludes that economic integration would eventually lead to a 'hub–spoke' scenario with the core, or 'hub,' country being surrounded by many peripheral, or 'spoke,' countries.

Krugman's model can be observed in the development of the EU,[32] in which all moveable factors of production such as capital, labor, and even technology have been relocated from the peripheral countries to the hub. In terms of the effect of economic integration on welfare and income distribution, Umemoto (2003) argues that a hub–spoke model would lead to convergence between the hub and the higher-income spoke countries, while it would cause a divergence between the hub and the lower-income spoke countries.

Economic integration across the Taiwan Strait involves two economies whose sizes are polar opposites. The total GDP of China was US $5.88 trillion whereas that of Taiwan was only US $430 billion in 2010.[33] The development of economic integration across the Taiwan Strait would cause Taiwan to become the spoke of the China-centric hub unless it undertakes trade diversification through multiple FTAs with such major trading partners as the US, Japan, and the EU (Chow, 2011).

Even though most countries would like to be the hub, 'for whom preferential access is highly valued by most or all nations in the region' (Baldwin, 2004, p. 27), very few in East Asia are qualified. The hub-ness of a nation is based on how other nations in the region would gain preferential access to it. This study adopts Baldwin's (2004) 'hub-ness' formula,[34] and calculates the potential hubs in East Asia based on trade data in 2004–2008, before the world-wide recession.

The calculated index of Baldwin's model of hub-ness is reported in Table 10.2. If one takes 10 percent as a benchmark for determining the hub-ness (Baldwin, 2004) for a nation, not only China, but Japan and the US are sensible hubs for the region in general and for Taiwan in particular. One can find from the first column of Table 10.2 that the US is a strong candidate to be the hub for many East Asian economies: its hub-ness is twice of that of Japan for China, Hong Kong, Korea, Singapore, and Malaysia. Much of the US's hub-ness is due to its role as the market of final consumption goods for its spoke countries.

On the other hand, China's being a strong hub for most of the four NICs – Hong Kong, Korea, Taiwan, and Singapore – is probably due to the FDI-trade nexus among those countries. In other words, for China to become the hub, it requires spokes such as Taiwan, Japan, and Korea to make foreign investments in China. But there is no such requirement for these three countries to become the spoke of the US hub. Had China's market not been generated by FDI flows (the S_{od}^{M} in the formula of measuring hub-ness induced by FDI flows), then China itself may not have been ready for the role of centric hub for those spoke countries.

Japan can be a hub for Taiwan and relatively resource-rich countries such as Australia, Indonesia, the Philippines, and Thailand. The EU also exhibits the characteristics of an important hub for all countries listed in the table, especially India. Moreover, the ASEAN as a group is a potential hub not only for its members, but also for Australia, Japan, and Taiwan. However, China, Japan, and the US have no more than 10 percent of hub-ness for Singapore. Perhaps that explains why Singapore has signed the largest number of bilateral FTAs of all countries in the world.[35] The

Table 10.2 The hub-ness of the three major markets for East Asia

Origin nation	Destination nation									
	US	China	Japan	Australia	EU	India	Korea	NZ[a]	ASEAN[b]	Taiwan
Australia	6.275[d]	12.479	19.125	–	11.244	5.294	7.611	4.447	10.075	3.612
China	16.576	–	7.500	1.268	18.718	1.550	4.003	0.154	5.781	4.320
EU[c]	5.788	1.564	1.082	0.480	24.747	0.588	0.564	0.068	1.153	0.195
Hong Kong	14.675	46.145	4.770	1.249	13.874	1.191	1.999	0.152	5.185	1.774
India	14.051	6.047	2.206	0.762	21.459	–	1.794	0.167	9.094	0.808
Indonesia	10.649	7.938	20.162	2.758	11.818	3.948	6.933	0.324	16.975	2.641
Japan	19.441	12.438	–	1.863	14.409	0.740	6.429	0.323	10.256	5.173
Korea	12.871	18.962	7.271	1.262	14.653	1.712	–	0.203	8.294	3.257
Malaysia	16.393	7.712	9.390	3.197	12.175	3.084	3.581	0.420	22.459	2.672
New Zealand	12.340	5.463	9.700	20.929	14.294	0.947	3.575	–	8.389	2.136
Philippines	17.518	9.721	16.437	1.057	17.396	0.322	3.612	0.129	15.110	2.100
Singapore	9.286	9.721	5.167	3.532	11.252	2.881	3.444	0.500	27.011	3.310
Taiwan	12.082	22.082	19.031	1.242	11.221	0.849	3.089	0.216	11.001	–
Thailand	13.557	8.681	12.125	3.375	13.659	1.536	1.990	0.394	16.277	2.178479

Notes:
a. NZ stands for New Zealand.
b. ASEAN includes Indonesia, Malaysia, Philippines, Thailand, Singapore.
c. EU includes 27 countries.
d. Units: percentage.

Source: Author calculated based on average trade flows in 2004–2008.

empirical results on hub-ness illustrate that the US is a strong potential hub for most countries in East Asia and support Chow's tri-polar model of East Asian integration with China, Japan, and the US as the three potential hubs with many overlapping spokes (Chow, 2011; 2012b).

10.4.2 Breaking the Tendency of Marginalization by Reaching 'Near Hub-ness'

The above analysis of hub-ness leads one to conclude that, from Taiwan's perspective, the candidates for its hubs are China (22.082), Japan (19.031), the US (12.082), the EU (11.221), and the ASEAN (11.001), with the understanding that China's hub-ness was induced by Taiwan's continuing FDI destined for China. Taiwan will not be a hub for any of the listed countries. Policy implications for Taiwan are twofold. First, after signing the ECFA with China, multiple bilateral and/or multilateral FTAs with Japan, the US, the EU, and the ASEAN are recommended. And, second, Taiwan should reach 'near hub-ness', similarly to Singapore, by signing multiple bilateral and multilateral FTAs with as many countries as possible (Chow and Ciuriak, 2012). The problem is not 'why,' but 'how.'

Now that China has become a formidable economic powerhouse with aggressive policies to drive towards East Asian economic integration, by consciously or unconsciously excluding the US as an outlier,[36] Washington will have to tackle it with appropriate policy actions. One study from the Congress Research Service indicates that the 'economic linkages can also reinforce strategic relationships. If the US trade ties were diminished as a result of being excluded, then its strategic interests and leverage could also suffer.'[37] Hence, US actions or inactions will significantly affect Taiwan's prospects of reaching its near hub-ness in East Asian economic integration.

Throughout recent decades, US involvement in the wars in Iraq and Afghanistan may have delayed, but not completely expunged, Washington's attention to the development of East Asian economic integration. While deepening economic integration in East Asia has been threatening to undercut the US influence in the region, Frost (2007) argues that a systematic and energetic American response can reinforce the US role as 'a balancing and stabilizing presence that expands opportunities for China and for its Asian neighbors.' The probable solution from Washington will require realistic and substantial commercial diplomacy to generate a concrete trade policy which could lead to a more balanced two-way trade and capital flow across the Pacific Ocean. Active policy actions from Washington would reverse the current situation, which is labeled as the 'Lucas Paradox' of having 'uphill' capital flows from low to high income countries. Hence, the US involvement with East Asian economic integration includes not only conventional trade liberalization, but also its strategic consideration to reinforce its influence in the Asia-Pacific by integrating its economy with those in the Asia-Pacific through bilateral and multilateral regional trading arrangements. The US participation in the Trans-Pacific Partnership Agreement (TPP) is the first step in the right direction for the US to come back to the region as an important player in East Asian economic integration.

The TPP was designed to be a much more liberal and comprehensive trade pact than any existing bilateral and multilateral FTAs in the region. The TPP, which includes Australia, Brunei, Chile, Malaysia, New Zealand, Peru, Singapore, and Vietnam at present, is the first trade pact undertaken by the Obama Administration. During the APEC Summit in Hawaii in November 2011, Japan expressed its interest to join, as did Taiwan. Essentially, the agreement ensures free trade in goods and services (zero tariffs between Chile, Singapore, and New Zealand) and eliminates non-tariff trade barriers, protection of intellectual property rights, quarantining of agricultural products, and government procurement. Moreover, the TPP will not override existing FTAs, thereby avoiding the 'spaghetti bowl' phenomenon that resulted from different rules of origin.

There is an 'open accession' clause within the original TPP4 (Brunei, Chile, Singapore, and New Zealand) to accept other APEC members with like-minded economies. The TPP may provide a clue towards reaching the 'open regionalism' necessary to do away with the 'spaghetti bowl' and allow marginalized economies such as Taiwan to join it. At present, a pending bill on the 'Taiwan Policy Act' in the US House of Representatives specifically recommends that the US government includes Taiwan as a member of the TPP.[38] Further efforts from Taiwan are needed to push the US government and other member states to formally accept Taiwan's application to join the TPP.[39] Moreover, if Taiwan were to actively engage in pursuing the TPP, its government would need to overcome not only political hurdles but also domestic trade politics in sectoral re-adjustments, especially in agricultural sector.[40]

On the other hand, there are several expansions of ASEAN-FTA – that is, the ASEAN + Australia and New Zealand, the ASEAN + China, the ASEAN + Japan, the ASEAN plus India, and the ASEAN + Korea. Each of these trade pacts has various coverage-of-product groups under different rules of origin. The proposal of the ASEAN + China, Korea, and Japan was under negotiation but is currently obstructed by political factors; other than Japan's attitude toward it, the ASEAN countries may have adopted a 'divide and rule' strategy to protect their own interests (Chow, 2012c, ch. 9). Aside from the 'China factor,' the complications involving Taiwan's incorporation in an FTA with the ASEAN may be easier to resolve with its member states individually rather than with the ASEAN as a group. The proposed Taiwan–Singapore FTA may be a good first step in that direction.

Comparing the TPP and the ASEAN + N, Taiwan may be better off initiating it through its efforts to join the TPP first, which China hasn't indicated its intention to join yet. China's hesitation to join the TPP is not only political; the high criteria of labor and environment standards and the protection of intellectual property rights under the TPP are probably not what China wants at present. Moreover, the US–Taiwan relationship is an important signpost for many ASEAN countries. Taiwan has a stronger comparative advantage in linking with the world's top three economies than any other countries in the region. First of all, the colonial legacy of Japan and the post-war developments in Taiwan have generated a strong technological linkage between Japan and Taiwan. Some Taiwanese firms have strategic alliances with Japanese counterparts, as Chapter 7 analysed. Second, Taiwan has cultural and language assimilates with China and heavy trade and investment flows with China. Aside from political disputes on sovereignty, the economic linkage between Taiwan and China is over and above what other countries have had. Third, the US and Taiwan have strong traditional allied relations in terms of security and economic interests. Many power and intellectual elites, as well as business entrepreneurs, were educated in the US. Therefore, if Taiwan could expand its multilateral trade and investment flows with all three of these large economies in the world, it would reach a 'near hub-ness' status in East Asian economic integration.

10.4.3 Exploiting Taiwan's Untapped Export Potential

Given Taiwan's cumulating international isolation and its political difficulties in pursuing multiple bilateral and multilateral FTAs, are there any other appropriate trade strategies to further its export growth? Chow and Ciuriak (2007) used a TradeSim gravity model of international trade to examine Taiwan's actual trade and trade potential by trade partner and by commodity to identify export markets that appeared to be under-utilized by Taiwanese exporters.[41]

In their model, the parameters of a gravity model are estimated and the resulting equation is used to calculate the expected level of particular trade flows. These expected levels of trade flows are compared to the actual level to assess the unexploited trade potential. If actual flows are substantially smaller than the expected ones, there is at least a prima facie case that the trade flow is below its potential. This is defined as 'untapped export potential' to be exploited without further tariff concessions and abolition of non-trade barriers from bilateral/multilateral FTAs. Export potentials for Taiwan were estimated for 15 sectors and 30 major trading partners in the world.[42] The results showed that Taiwan could still further exploit its export potential by penetrating those niche markets with its niche products, even without FTAs with those trading partners.[43] This is another venue that Taiwan could unilaterally pursue to further its export growth.

10.5 TAIWAN'S OPTIONS AND FUTURE

10.5.1 Scenarios of Multiple Equilibria in Economic Integration

With the ECFA signed, President Ma has been hoping China will be more tolerant of Taiwan's aspirations of joining other bilateral and multilateral FTAs with its major trading partners. But Beijing has successfully used its economic leverage to satisfy its insatiable political objectives and infiltrate Taiwan's electoral politics (Friedman, 2007), rather than allow Taiwan more participation in the international economic community. Moreover, Beijing has successfully blocked Taiwan from signing an FTA with any of those countries with which Taiwan has no diplomatic ties, even though Taiwan is legitimately entitled to sign FTAs with any WTO members. Therefore, whether signing the ECFA will save Taiwan from marginalization and confinement to China's economic orbit is yet to be determined by future developments.

There are several scenarios of multiple equilibria of economic integration for Taiwan. Each of these scenarios will have strong political consequences. Those who use the European model of economic integration and even cite the case of the closer economic partnership between Australia and New Zealand to argue that economic integration would not affect political sovereignty have completely missed the crucial point that mutual recognition was the basis for each signatory in both models whereas the ECFA has no such clause.[44] Without mutual recognition of political sovereignty, the signing of the ECFA could lead to diversified political developments between the two signatories in the future.

Even though the surveys from Wu (2012) showed that 'the rising Taiwanese identity was not impeded by the close economic relationship with China' since the early 1990s (p. 200), it is understandable that, in the face of China's unquenchable political ambition of annexing Taiwan, the rising Taiwanese identity alone will not be able to maintain the general consensus on Taiwan's independence and autonomy. Without political sovereignty, the Taiwanese identity may well be transformed into what

Cantonese or Hunanese is in China. In fact, the people of Hong Kong under the 'one country, two systems' have a rising identity as Hong Kongese as well. These issues are too complicated to be analysed within the scope of this chapter and it is extremely risky to make any projection of the uncertain political future of Taiwan merely from economic perspectives. But the development of economic integration will have a strong impact on political relations in the future. In what follows, we will simply point out the most likely scenarios on Cross-Strait relations resulting from economic integration.

In the first scenario, Taiwan will be blocked by Beijing from signing any FTAs with other countries. It will thus become a spoke in the China-centric hub only, without any trade pact with its major trading partners such as the US, the EU, and Japan. Without an institutionalized trading framework, Taiwan has already had an asymmetric trade dependence on the Chinese market, with 40 percent or more of its total exports destined for China and Hong Kong. Other than economic vulnerability, over-dependency on China's market will have political risks, as Ian Bremmer, president of the Eurasia Group, alerted President Ma in February 2012.[45] With the ECFA, Taiwan's trade with and investment in China would further rise, to the extent that Taiwan would join China's orbit economically in the short term and even politically in the long term. China's economic leverage would further infiltrate Taiwan's electoral politics and jeopardize Taiwan's 'de facto' independent sovereignty. This tendency may well fulfill Beijing's political objective of unifying Taiwan peacefully under 'one country, two systems.' Under such circumstances, the vulnerability of China's dependence on the US market may lead to the worst-case scenario of a trade war between Washington and Beijing, once mismanagement of the increasingly deteriorating relations occurs. Taiwan would then be victimized because of its economic integration with China.

A more moderate scenario is that Taiwan has no FTAs with its major trading partners such as the US, the EU, and Japan but signs a few trade pacts with tiny states of little economic significance. Such FTAs would be basically symbolic to show Beijing's benevolence but would not allow Taiwan to diversify its trade flows or reduce its dependence on China's market. The vulnerability of the trade bloc across the Taiwan Strait remains more or less the same as in the first scenario. Politically, if Taiwan could only sign the FTAs with those countries that Beijing permitted or tolerated, then Taiwan would already be under the sphere of China's influence. China's economic leverage would further infiltrate Taiwan's democracy, jeopardize its status quo of 'de facto' autonomy, and narrow the range of Taiwan's ultimate political choices. Moreover, Taiwan may have to collide with China on many of its commercial policies in dealing with the US.[46] One has to ask to what extent would this scenario – that is, a rising China to annex Taiwan economically – affect the US economic and strategic interests in East Asia ?

In a third scenario, Taiwan would break through the 'China knot' and sign the TPP with strong support from the US. Taiwan would benefit from diversified trade flows with many Pacific Basin countries, including the US and possibly Japan. Hence Taiwan would have 'freer' trade flows with multiple centric-hubs and even reach the status of 'near hub-ness' within the region. This development would lead to harmonious, multipolar, trilateral centric-hubs in China, the US, and Japan, with Taiwan to become one of the most important members within the region. If Taiwan were integrated with the three largest economies in the world, instead of just China, then Taiwan would be at an equivalent trading status to South Korea, which has signed multiple FTAs with its trading partners to cover more than 60 percent of its exports to the world. The competitive trade liberalization under multipolar centric hubs would not only benefit Taiwan, but would also balance the economic power and further contribute to regional stability. Until a region-wide free trade regime such the APEC-FTA becomes a reality, this would be a Pareto-improvement in the development of regional trading arrangements under strong US leadership. Many of these developments depend on international relations, especially policies that the US implements in order to emphasize its economic and strategic interests in East Asia.

10.5.2 Taiwan's Options and Choices, and their Significant Impacts on its Future

The emergence of the trade bloc across the Taiwan Strait and the China-centric hub in East Asian economic integration has strong repercussions on the shift of power in East Asia. The global response to this development involves not just the economic integration in the region but also power shifts in international politics. Since Japan's lost decade amid the Heisei Recession, its debilitating combination of economic malaise and political paralysis has coincided with US negligence in the region and has thus enabled China to drive toward a sole China-centric hub in East Asia. Will China restrain its influence derived from its size and economic achievements without inflicting unacceptable damage to its Asian neighbors, including Taiwan, and to the US economic and strategic interests in the region? Will the US and other Asian countries recognize Taiwan's contributions to the region's growth and overcome Beijing's pressure so as to include Taiwan in regional trading arrangements such as the TPP?

Will Taiwan be able to maintain its 'de facto' independent sovereignty in coping with China through further economic integration? Those critical questions will become important factors in determining the peace, prosperity, and stability in the region.

Taiwan's limited options to break through its marginalization may well depend on Beijing's policies as well as the responses of the US and other Asian countries, especially Japan. After all, Taiwan is a democratic country with a free enterprise market economy, whereas China has been and still is an authoritarian regime without any significant tendency toward democracy.[47] Hence, China's rise will not only affect US economic and strategic interests in East Asia, but will also challenge the core values of American socio-political system. If democracy works, the US policy-makers will have to evaluate American core values and its overall national interests in managing the Cross-Strait relations. Should the economic integration between China and Taiwan prove to be incompatible with American economic and strategic interests in East Asia, an elected government in the US may well turn its back to seek its best alternatives. Admitting Taiwan to join the TPP would be a significant political asset for the US, which has strong leverage in expanding the TPP membership to cover like-minded countries such as Taiwan. Abandoning a democratic Taiwan to be annexed with an authoritarian China certainly is not an option for the US.

The development of the emerging trade bloc and the resultant effect on the shifts of economic power in favor of China will significantly challenge the US leadership in the Asia-Pacific. Knorr argues that 'power arises from an asymmetrical interdependence. It does not matter whether the coercing actor uses the carrot or the stick' (Knorr, 1997, p. 102). Before the integration process between China and Taiwan goes too far, and before the US leadership in the Asia-Pacific slips towards China, the US has to use its economic, investment, and technological leverages, in addition to its military deterrence, to maintain its leadership as a Pacific power. Including Taiwan in the TPP will add to its strategic significance for the US because Taiwan has been its traditional ally. Moreover, Taiwan is the ninth-largest trading partner for the US, with a total of US $61.83 billion in two-way trade in 2010,[48] which is far above US trade with most of the TPP members.[49]

It would be an oversimplification to anticipate that the emerging trade bloc across the Taiwan Strait will have no political connotations in the changing international politics at all. While the US has expressed its welcome to the rapprochement between China and Taiwan to reduce the tension across the Taiwan Strait in the short term, Washington certainly will have to keep monitoring its future developments and their resultant effects on US economic and strategic interests in the Asia-Pacific in the long term. Should economic integration change the status quo on the Taiwan Strait, Japan's security would be undermined, and other US allies would be threatened as well. Therefore, Washington has to take preventive action well before the situation deteriorates.

The global economic trading system established after World War II, commencing with the General Agreement on Tariffs and Trade (GATT) and transforming into the WTO, has been weakened by its admission of China, which acquired substantial power through its economic leverages. Many WTO members may soon have to confront the stress of the proliferation of regional trading arrangements in East Asia. The deadlock of the Doha Round of trade liberalization and the lethargic pace of the APEC-FTA may lead to the realization of the 'hub–spoke' models of economic integration in East Asia. Taiwan may not have the full leverage to freely choose its best alternative in joining any of those three potential hubs, or even to reach 'near hub-ness' in the region by itself. Nevertheless, its ultimate choice of joining in any of those hubs could have substantial impacts on the shift of economic power in the region. If multilateral trade liberalization cannot be accomplished in the near future, an 'open regionalism' to include like-minded countries to join regional trade blocs is much better than excluding some qualified countries such as Taiwan for political factors motivated by big powers.

Therefore, the changing relations across the Taiwan Strait will not only affect China–Taiwan relations but also other countries such as the US and Japan. The emerging trade bloc across the Taiwan Strait involves not just how Taiwan is coping with China but also global adjustments to China's increasing prominence on the playing field of international economy. To avoid the worst-case scenario, the US has to take strong policy action by including Taiwan in the TPP.

NOTES

1. Beijing has been claiming sovereignty over Taiwan even though Taiwan has been a 'de facto' independent country since the very beginning of the PRC. The overlapping claim of Taiwan's sovereignty has generated political tensions between China and Taiwan.
2. The sum of export and import in total GDP reached 50.62 percent in 2010. Calculated from country profile of the WTO website at www.wto.org.
3. FDI from Taiwan to China was liberalized through an evolutionary process from totally prohibited, to being allowed through a third place and eventually liberalized, restricted only by a nominal cap. After both China and Taiwan were admitted to the WTO, trade was operated at a WTO-minus basis. By March 13, 2009, 2198 import commodities under 8-digit product classification of the Harmonized System (HS) code are still banned from China. Among them, 1364 are industrial products and 834 are

agricultural products. Meanwhile, there are 400 products under 'conditional import' or 'prohibited' categories. From the website of the Bureau of International Trade at http://www.trade.gov.tw.

4. The two-gap trap for LDCs occurs when saving is below investment and export is less than import at their early stages of development.
5. From *World Investment Report*, published by UNDP at http://www.unctad.org/Templates/Page.asp?intItemID=1485&lang=1.
6. The statistics are rough estimates because outward FDI in China was under-reported in the early years. Moreover, much of Taiwanese capital was detoured to some 'safe havens' such as the US Virgin Islands and the Cayman Islands, which accounted for top foreign investors in China. Tung and Huang (2012) estimated that the cumulated Taiwanese direct investment in China between 1988 and 2008 was about US $166.5 billion, which accounted for about 20 percent of China's total inward FDI.
7. China has deployed more than 1400 missiles on its coast aimed directly at Taiwan across the Strait.
8. Taiwan's government engaged in a 'southern strategy' to diversify its outward FDI toward Southeast Asia without much success. Other policies to slow down foreign investments in China went from the 'go slow, be patient' idea of former president Lee Teng-hui in the mid-1990s, to the 'active openness and effective management' policy implemented during the first term of former president Chen Shui-bian, and finally to 'active management and effective openness' in his second term without checking the ever-growing capital outflows to China.
9. A functional trade bloc is 'de facto' economic integration without institutionalized preferential trading arrangement.
10. Lin (2005) found that the percentage of intermediate products in Taiwan's total export to China increased from 70.53 percent in 1990 to 76.87 percent in 2003. Among them, the high-end intermediates increased from 2.04 percent to 26.6 percent, whereas ordinary intermediates decreased from 68.49 percent to 50.27 percent in the same period. Nevertheless, surveys from the government think tank, Chung Hwa Institution for Economic Research, showed that there is an increasing tendency for Taiwanese subsidiaries in China to become more and more 'localized' by purchasing those intermediate products locally.
11. Chow (2012a) showed that, by using the time lags of FDI as independent variables to regress the export commodities, the statistical significance of FDI on exports disappeared after 2 to 3 years.
12. Statistics of market shares by product groups was derived from North American Product Classification System (NAPCS) at the website http://www.census.gov/eos/www/napcs/napcsstable.html.
13. It was reported that 40 percent or more of China's exports of information and communication technology (ICT) products were produced by Taiwanese subsidiaries in China. See the website of Market Intelligence Center, Institute for Information Industries at www.mic.III.org.tw.
14. Wallace (1982) argued that 'any economic integration is basically a political establishment' because mutual recognition of the signatories is a pre-requisite for existence.
15. Kawai and Wignaraja (2009, p. 11) showed that the administrative cost of complying with the local contents' requirement under various 'rules of origin' of different FTAs is higher than the tariff concession. Therefore, the percentage of utilizing FTAs in East Asia is less than 30 percent. Preliminary statistics of the utilization rate of the ECFA on the 'early harvest' product list was 20.76 percent and 20.57 percent for China in 2011, and the Taiwanese government expected to reach 50 percent in 2012 when tariff rates reduced to 'zero.' See *Commerce News*, February 12, 2012.
16. Different from all other CGE simulation models, the simulation results reported here assume that all trading commodities, with the only exception of trade on 'processed rice sector,' are liberalized between China and Taiwan. See ch. 4 in Chow (2012b).
17. Of course, the causes of US trade deficits are multifaceted. I am indebted to Chen-

Yuan Tung for pointing out that 'US trade imbalance is still driven by major economic factors, such as savings, investment, consumption, and exchange rates.'

18. Though China's holdings of US securities increased 7 percent to a total of US $1.73 trillion by June 30, 2011, the percentage distribution of dollar holdings in China's foreign-exchange reserves fell to a decade low of 54 percent in the period ended on June 30, 2011, from 65 percent in 2010. See 'Beijing diversifies away from U.S. Dollar' in the *Wall Street Journal*, March 2, 2012.
19. Both China and Taiwan are trade-dependent economies with the trade sector accounting for 50.52 percent and 122.31 percent of their respective GDPs in 2010. China destined more than one-third of its total exports to the US and the EU since the mid-1990s, and its export dependency on those two economies reached nearly 40 percent of its exports in 2010.
20. Nickolas Lardy argued that the declines of China's trade surplus in total GDP, which dropped from 10.1 percent in 2007 to less than 3 percent in 2011 'are in large part the result of a weak global economy and a modest appreciation of the renminbi, not fundamental rebalancing.' See Lardy, 'China's rebalancing will not be automatic,' Asian Forum, February 22, 2012 at the website: http://www.eastasiaforum.org/2012/02/22/china-s-rebalancing-will-not-be-automatic/.
21. $GDP = C + I + G + X - M$ in national income identity. But, GDP is also equal to $C + S + T$. Therefore, one can subtract the second from the first to get the equation (10.1).
22. In 2010, the total GDP of the US was $14 582.4 billion whereas that of China was $5878.6 billion. Data from the country profiles of the World Trade Organization (WTO) at: www.wto.org.
23. If household saving in the US increases from 3 to 6 percent of total GDP, it will cut $437.47 billion of final consumption goods. If all those cuts were directly from US imports from China, it would account for 7.44 percent of China's total GDP.
24. Of course, one counterargument is to present the 30 to 50 million people in the coastal provinces of China where the per capita incomes are estimated to be three to four times the national average. Taiwanese firms may be able to take advantage of penetrating those booming markets in the coastal area.
25. Nickolas Lardy contended that it is 'to be sceptical of claims that growing levels of consumer credit will rebalance China's economy.' See Lardy, 'China's rebalancing will not be automatic,' Asian Forum, February 22, 2012 at the website: http://www.eastasiaforum.org/2012/02/22/china-s-rebalancing-will-not-be-automatic/. Meanwhile, the Chinese population will get older before they become rich. China's positive 'demographic dividends' from a young working population may well become negative as the population pyramid of its 'one child' policy develops. It is estimated that more than 30 percent of its population will be aged 60 or older by 2050. Will the demographic shift cause demand for more tradable goods or non-tradable goods? More rigorous study on the consumption pattern is necessary before reaching any conclusion.
26. I am indebted to Tain-Jy Chen for pointing out the evidence of increasing trade in final goods along with that in intermediate goods after the ASEAN-China FTA was implemented in 2010. This newly developing trade pattern, which may be mixed with the global economic recession as illustrated in Note 27, is worth further monitoring in the future.
27. US total trade deficits in 2008 dropped from US $816.2 billion in 2008, to US $503.58 billion in 2009, but rose again to US $634.58 billion in 2010 and reached US $726.38 billion in 2011. US trade deficits with major Asian countries as its total trade deficits, after the Japan–ASEAN FTA was implemented, as reported below, may well reflect the economic recession in the US rather than the shifting of trade structures.

2008	2009	2010	2011	
32.840%	45.053%	43.009%	40.68%	China
9.081%	8.870%	9.460%	8.630%	Japan

2008	2009	2010	2011	
1.642%	2.106%	1.580%	1.81%	Korea
1.397%	1.961%	1.544%	2.120%	Taiwan
5.299%	7.610%	5.877%	5.31%	ASEAN-4
50.258%	65.600%	61.470%	58.550%	Total

Source: Percentage calculated by the author from the data set from US Department of Commerce.

28. Evidence shows that Taiwanese firms benefited very little from China's 'stimulus package' during the global recession in 2008–09 due to market barriers. If Taiwanese firms could overcome the entry/market barriers in China's domestic market after a fully-fledged FTA with China, then Taiwan may be able to benefit from its trade pacts with China. The effect of the ECFA and its probably expanding product groups for trade liberalization is too early to assess at the time of writing in March 2012.
29. These eight countries are the four newly industrialized economies of Korea, Hong Kong, Singapore, and Taiwan plus the ASEAN-4 which comprises Indonesia, Malaysia, the Philippines, and Thailand.
30. The derived demand takes into account the fact that China's import demand for parts and components from East Asian countries derived from the demand for final goods from the US. Hence, China's real exports to the US are the fourth variable in their VAR model.
31. It is noted that China's exports to the US and EU accounted for nearly 40 percent of its total export whereas its export to the ASEAN-5 was less than 7 percent, as reported in Table 10.1. One can also point out that if China does not adopt fuel-efficient engines and remains dependent on oil imports, its economy will be vulnerable to external energy shocks as well.
32. In retrospect, the formation of the European Union, starting with the Treaty of Roma in the 1950s, was initiated by countries with similar sizes of economy, and then gradually enlarged through the expansion of its member states.
33. Data from country profiles of the WTO at: www.wto.org.
34. Baldwin's formula on 'hub-ness' is:

$$HM_d = s^X_{od}(1 - s^M_{od})$$

where HM_d measures the 'hub-ness' of nation d. The o stands for origin and the d for the destination. s^X_{od} is the share of original country o's export to the destination market d. s^M_{od} is the share of d's imports that come from original country o. The formula illustrates that the hub-ness depends on the importance of d's market to original nation o's exports, and on the importance of o's exports in d's imports (Baldwin, 2004, p. 29).
35. Kawai and Wignaraji (2009) had an argument on FTA hubs which was based on the numbers of trade pacts by nations. In other words, a country could plausibly become a hub if it could sign multiple bilateral and multilateral FTAs with other countries. Having examined the proliferation of FTAs in Asia, Kawai and Wignaraji argued that there are five key hubs of FTAs in East Asia, while other smaller economies have emerged as spokes. The five hubs that they chose are based on the number of FTAs concluded in those countries; Singapore had 18 trade pacts, Japan had 11, China had 10, India 9, and Korea 6.
36. Chow (2011) raised the question on whether there will be a 'Monroe Doctrine' in Asia, driven by China's rise.
37. From 'The Trans Pacific Partnership Agreement,' Congressional Research Service, 7-5700, www.crs.gov. R40502 2010.

38. The Taiwan Policy Act of 2011, H.R. 2918, was introduced by the Chair of the US House Committee on Foreign Affairs, Ileana Ros-Lethinen (R-Florida).
39. The Taiwan representative at the APEC summit expressed Taiwan's interest in joining the TPP, but no formal application was submitted. Michael Froman, Deputy National Security Adviser for International Economic Affairs commented on the TPP at the Center for Strategic and International Studies (CSIS) on January 4, 2012, saying that 'while the Obama Administration hopes to complete the negotiated text in 2012, they will not rush to meet an artificial deadline nor slow down negotiations to accommodate the accession of interested countries such as Canada, Japan, and Mexico.' Hence, the US is willing to accommodate more applicants to the TPP if it won't slow down the negotiations. Source is from the website of the CSIS at http://csis.org/event/trans-pacific-partnership-speaker-series.
40. The government think tank, the Chung Hwa Institution for Economic Research, was entrusted to conduct a feasibility study on Taiwan's participation in the TPP.
41. It examined the results from the third version of the TradeSim model developed at the International Trade Centre which is jointly sponsored by UNCTAD and the WTO (Helmers and Pasteels, 2005).
42. The top 15 sectors were ranked by current export performances in 2002–2003. The four omitted sectors were forestry and fishing products, mining and quarrying, petroleum, and recycling.
43. Detailed results of Taiwan's untapped trade potentials by countries and by sectors are available upon request.
44. President Ma argued that there was an understanding of mutual 'non-recognition' in China–Taiwan relations, yet Beijing has repeatedly claimed that there is only 'one China' and Beijing is the sole representative of China.
45. See 'Political risk guru Ian Bremmer speaks in Taiwan (2012/02/17)' from http://englishnews.ftv.com.tw/read.aspx?sno=07A7C4D36A8BB41A5A427AA27A36E118.
46. Taiwanese businessmen lobby the US congress to delink the 'most favored nation' clause with China's human rights record in the 1990s. Taiwan's foreign exchange reserve will add to that of China's to threaten the US financial market.
47. Gallagher (2002) argued that the timing and sequencing of FDI in China had legitimized the authoritarian regime of Chinese Communist Party leadership rather than promoting democracy.
48. From the website of the Bureau of Census, Department of Commerce at: http://www.census.gov/foreign-trade/top/dst/2010/12/balance.html.
49. From *Taiwan Statistical Data Book, 2011*, Council for Economic Planning and Development (CEPD).

REFERENCES

Baldwin, Richard, 2004, *The Spoke Trap: The Hub and Spoke Bilateralism in East Asia*, Seoul: Korean Institute for International Economic Policy, CNEAC Research Series, 04-02.

Baldwin, Richard and Daria Taglioni, 2011, 'Gravity Chains: Estimating Bilateral Trade flows when Parts and Components Trade is Important,' National Bureau of Economic Research, working paper 16672 at http://www.nber.org/papers/w16672.

Bende-Nabende, Anthony, 2003, 'The Trade-investment Nexus: A Literature Review, with reference to East Asia,' in Anthony Bende-Nabende (ed.), *International Trade, Capital Flows and Economic Development in East Asia: The Challenge of the 21st Century*, Burlington, VA: Ashgate Publishing Co.

Chen, Kung Ming, Ji Chou, and Chia-Ching Lin, 2011, 'The Impact of Trade Liberalization across the Taiwan Strait: Empirical Evidence and Policy Implications,' in Cal Clark (ed.), *The Changing Dynamics of the Relations Among China, Taiwan and the US*, Newcastle upon Tyne, UK: Cambridge Scholars Publisher.

Chen, Tain-Jy and Ying-Hua Ku, 2007, 'Taiwan and East Asian Integration,' in Peter C.Y. Chow (ed.), *Economic Integration, Democratization and National Security in East Asia: Shifting Paradigms in US, China and Taiwan Relations*, Cheltenham, UK and Northampton, MA: Edward Elgar Publishing, pp. 172–90.

Chow, P.C.Y., 2010, 'China as the World Market and/or as the World Factory in the Global Economy' on 'China and the World Economy – New Perspective on China's Economic Rise after Three Decades of Reform', in *Berliner China Heffte/Berlin History and Society*, 37, 39–63.

Chow, Peter C.Y., 2011, 'The Emerging Trade Bloc Across the Taiwan Strait: The Implications of ECFA and Its Aftermath for US Economic and Strategic Interests in East Asia,' in Cal Clark (ed.), *The Changing Dynamics of the Relations among China, Taiwan and the United States*, Newcastle upon Tyne, UK: Cambridge Scholars Publishing, pp. 255–76.

Chow, Peter C.Y., 2012a, 'The Effect of Outward Foreign Direct Investment on Home Country's Export, A Case Study of Taiwan, 1986–2006,' *Journal of International Trade and Economic Development*, 21 (5), 725–54.

Chow, Peter C.Y. (ed.), 2012b, *National Identity and Economic Interest: Taiwan's Competing Options and Their Impacts on Regional Stability*, New York: Palgrave Macmillan.

Chow, Peter C.Y., 2012c, *Trade and Industrial Development in East Asia: Catching Up or Falling Behind*, Cheltenham, UK and Northampton, MA: Edward Elgar Publishing, ch. 9.

Chow, Peter C.Y. and Dan Ciuriak, 2007, 'Taiwan's Untapped Trade Potentials: Risks and Opportunities in a Changing Global Trade Context,' a paper presented at the American Association for Chinese Study at the University of Richmond, October.

Chow, Peter C.Y. and Dan Ciuriak, 2012, 'The FTA Music is Playing in Asia: After ECFA, is Taiwan Joining the Dance,' *Journal of International Trade*, 26 (1), 61–75.

Friedman, Edward, 2007, 'China's Incorporation of Taiwan: The Manipulation of Community Tensions,' in Peter Chow (ed.), *Economic Integration, Democratization and National Security in East Asia*, Cheltenham, UK and Northampton, MA: Edward Elgar Publishing, pp. 29–55.

Frost, Ellen L., 2007, 'Balance of Power Politics and the Rise of China: Accommodation and Balancing in East Asia,' in William W. Keller and Carl G. Rawski (eds), *China's Rise and the Balance of Influence in Asia*, Pittsburgh, PA: University Of Pittsburgh Press, ch. 5.

Gallagher, Mary E., 2002, 'Reform and Openness: Why China's Economic Reforms Have Delayed Democracy,' *World Politics*, 338–72.

Helmers, Christian and Jean-Michel Pasteels, 2005, 'TradeSim (Third Version), A Gravity Model for the Calculation of Trade Potentials for Developing Countries and Economies in Transition,' ITC Working Paper, June, Geneva: International Trade Centre, UNCGTAD/WTO.

IMF (International Monetary Fund), 2010, *World Economic Outlook*, www.imf.org.

Kawai, Masahiro and Ganeshan Wignaraja, 2009, 'Asian FTA Trends and Challenges,' ADBI working paper no.144, available at: www.adb.org.

Knorr, Klaus, 1997, 'International Economic Leverages and its Uses,' in Klaus Knorr and Frank N. Trager (eds), *Economic Issues and National Security*, Lawrence, Kansas: Kansas University Press, pp. 99–126.

Krugman, Paul, 1991, 'Geography and Trade,' Leuven, Belgium: Leuven University Press; Cambridge, MA: MIT Press.

Lin, Yuh Jiu, 2005, 'Taiwan's Trade Imbalance with China: The Factors and the Trend,' *American Journal of Chinese Studies*, 12 (2), 139–58.

Ng, Francis and Alexander Yeats, 2008, 'Production Sharing in East Asia: Who Does What for Whom and Why?' Trade Team, Development Research Group, The World Bank, available at: http://elibrary.worldbank.org/docserver/download/2197.pdf?expires =1331478725&id=id&accname=guest&checksum=4A26F4952FF362701A9386223B56A494.

Ozawa, Terutomo, 1992, 'Foreign Direct Investment and Economic Development,' *Transnational Corporations*, 1, 27–54.

Park, Donghyun and Kwanho Shin, 2011, 'People's Republic of China as an Engine of Growth for Developing Asia?' *Asian Economic Papers*, 10 (2), 120–63.

Rosen, Daniel H. and Zhi Wang, 2011, 'The Implications of the China–Taiwan Trade Liberalization,' *Policy Analysis in International Economy*, No 93, Washington, DC: The Peterson Institute for International Economics.

Tung, Chen-Yuan and Chia-ko Huang, 2012, 'The Estimation of Aggregate Statistics of Taiwan-Invested Enterprises in China, 1988–2008,' *China: An International Journal* (forthcoming).

Umemoto, Masaru, 2003, 'Hub and Spoke Integration and Income Convergence,' The International Center for the Study of East Asian Development, Working Paper Series, Vol. 2003-01, Kitakyushuu, Japan.

Wallace, William, 1982, 'Economic Divergence in the European Community,' in John M. Letiche (ed.), *International Economic Policies and their Theoretical Foundations*, New York: Academic Press, pp. 183–223.

Wu, Naiteh, 2012, 'Will Economic Integration Lead to Political Assimilation?' in Peter Chow (ed.), *National Identity and Economic Interest: Taiwan's Competing Options and Their Impacts on Regional Stability*, New York: Palgrave Macmillan, pp. 187–202.

Yueh, Linda, 2011, 'Re-balancing China: Linking Internal and External Reforms,' *Asian Economic Papers,* 10 (2), 87–111.

Index